Cultural Heritage and Preservation

NATIONAL
ATLAS
OF
SWEDEN

EARLY STONE AGE

LATE STONE AGE

10000
9000
8000
7000
6000
5000
4000
3000
2000

Early Neolithic
Middle Neolithic
Late Neolithic

EARLY BRONZE AGE
LATE BRONZE AGE

1000
900
800
700
600
500
400
300
200
100
0

EARLY IRON AGE · LATE IRON AGE

Pre-Roman Period
Roman Period
Migration Period
Vendel Period
Viking Period

100
200
300
400
500
600
700
800
900
1000
1100
1200
1300
1400
1500
1600
1700
1800
1900
2000

EARLY MIDDLE AGES
LATE MIDDLE AGES

MODERN AGE

Vasa Period
Great Power Period
Period of Liberty
Gustavian Period
Modern Period

NILS FORSHED
ANNO 1993

Cultural Heritage and Preservation

SPECIAL EDITOR

Klas-Göran Selinge

THEME MANAGER

Central Board of National Antiquities

National Atlas of Sweden

SNA Publishing will publish between 1990 and 1996 a government-financed National Atlas of Sweden. The first national atlas, *Atlas över Sverige*, was published in 1953–71 by *Svenska Sällskapet för Antropologi och Geografi, SSAG* (the Swedish Society for Anthropology and Geography). The new national atlas describes Sweden in seventeen volumes, each of which deals with a separate theme. The organisations responsible for this new national atlas are *Lantmäteriverket, LMV* (the National Land Survey of Sweden), *SSAG* and *Statistiska centralbyrån, SCB* (Statistics Sweden). The whole project is under the supervision of a board consisting of the chairman, Sture Norberg and Thomas Mann (LMV), Staffan Helmfrid and Åke Sundborg (SSAG), Frithiof Billström and Gösta Guteland (SCB) and Leif Wastenson (SNA). To assist the board and the editors there is a scientific advisory group of three permanent members: Professor Staffan Helmfrid (Chairman), Professor Erik Bylund and Professor Anders Rapp. For this theme Managing Director Agne Furingsten has been coopted to the advisory group as a specialist. A theme manager is responsible for compiling the manuscript for each individual volume. The National Atlas of Sweden is to be published in book form both in Swedish and in English, and in a computer-based version for use in personal computers.

The English edition of the National Atlas of Sweden is published under the auspices of the *Royal Swedish Academy of Sciences* by the National Committee of Geography with financial support from *Knut och Alice Wallenbergs Stiftelse* and *Marcus och Amalia Wallenbergs Stiftelse*.

The whole work comprises the following volumes (in order of publication):

MAPS AND MAPPING

THE FORESTS

THE POPULATION

THE ENVIRONMENT

AGRICULTURE

THE INFRASTRUCTURE

SEA AND COAST

CULTURAL LIFE, RECREATION AND TOURISM

SWEDEN IN THE WORLD

WORK AND LEISURE

CULTURAL HERITAGE AND PRESERVATION

GEOLOGY

LANDSCAPE AND SETTLEMENTS

CLIMATE, LAKES AND RIVERS

MANUFACTURING, SERVICES AND TRADE

GEOGRAPHY OF PLANTS AND ANIMALS

THE GEOGRAPHY OF SWEDEN

CHIEF EDITOR	Leif Wastenson
EDITORS	Staffan Helmfrid, Scientific Editor
	Margareta Elg, Editor of *Cultural Heritage and Preservation*
	Ulla Arnberg, Editor
	Märta Syrén, Editor
PRODUCTION	LM Maps, Kiruna
SPECIAL EDITORS	Klas-Göran Selinge, Marit Åhlén
	Nils Blomkvist, Elisabeth Nyström Kronberg
	Lars Redin, Ingrid Sjöström
TRANSLATOR	Michael Knight
GRAPHIC DESIGN	Håkan Lindström
LAYOUT	Typoform/Gunnel Eriksson, Stockholm
REPRODUCTION	LM Repro, Luleå
COMPOSITION	Bokstaven Text & Bild AB, Göteborg
DISTRIBUTION	Almqvist & Wiksell International, Stockholm
COVER ILLUSTRATION	Jan-Peter Lahall/GreatShots

First edition
© SNA
Printed in Italy 1994

ISBN 91–87760–04–5 (All volumes)

ISBN 91–87760–26–6 (Cultural Heritage and Preservation)

Contents

History in the Age of the Mass Media

In this age of non-stop news flows we are drowned in cascades of information, but this does not necessarily mean that we also raise our level of understanding. The constant flow of news items may instead confuse our picture, the overall view and context of historical processes of which current events are a part. What is long-term and significant may easily be lost in the latest but short-term sensation.

These floods of information, news and advertising may lead us to believe that life moves more rapidly today than it used to, that history has accelerated. Of course this idea is false. The days and the years are not only just as long for us as for previous generations, but we also live longer now; more and more people live to be so old that they even have a historical perspective of their own lives. This ought to help to create a clarity and balance of vision in our perception of the information flow and a wish to pass on this critical attitude to the younger generation.

But when present-day history is dramatised in news broadcasts, it is often the sensational and violent events that are emphasised. This affects our picture of reality; we feel more and more alienated in a world which is depicted as dangerous and evil.

Similarly, popular history writers may also try to suggest that history is dominated by dramatic events and power-crazy men. But in our own time the science of history has more and more come to concentrate on showing how the lives of ordinary people were led in bygone days. The people who built up our society and created history, thereby handing down to us our cultural heritage, were, just like most of us, people leading a humdrum and hard-working life. It is *their* history we need to know about and bring to life if we are to understand our own cultural environment.

Our lack of historical knowledge became obvious on a broader scale during the period of unrest which heralded the 1990s. The dissolution of the Soviet Union released latent nationalistic forces in Eastern and Central Europe, just at a time when Western Europe was working for

Artefact
Something made by man

political and economic integration. It should have been possible to predict, with the benefit of historical insight, that these events would lead to instability, yet people were surprised and bewildered by the way things developed. Economists and politicians in the West were unable to understand or evaluate the nationalistic movements and their deep historical roots. They could not imagine that half-forgotten peoples could go to war in defence of their national, cultural and religious identity. Their points of view were limited to the European nation states and had never included the underlying regional and multicultural structure of Europe.

Even when discussing the history of Sweden we often use our own present-day maps. But when studying any historical period one should always use the economic and political geography of that time. Both successful popular historians and historical exhibitions tend to present the history of Sweden as if it had always taken place within our present frontiers. Using that kind of unhistorical perspective makes it difficult to explain Swedish activities on the far side of the Baltic Sea. The whole length of present-day Sweden did not exist in prehistoric times, nor in the Middle Ages. Mälardalen and the east coast were part of a unified area which also included the coasts of the Gulf of Finland. The southern part of Sweden was linked to the countries of the south Baltic, which were populated by Danes, Germans and Slavs, while the island of Gotland was for centuries the place where the spheres of interest of the Danes and the Swedes met. West Sweden turned towards Norway and the North Sea countries, and in the far north the coasts within the Arctic Circle were united by the ice-free ocean currents.

This picture of the historical geography of Sweden was valid right up to the time of the Vasa kings in the 16th century. As late as the Thirty Years War (1618–48) Sweden was an east-west rather than a north-south country. The royal highway ran from Älvsborg and Lödöse in the west via Örebro, Stockholm and Åbo through Finland to Viborg in the east.

Thus anyone who wants to depict

the history of Sweden has to rid himself of the 20th-century picture of Sweden. The decisive factors are not the prehistoric or medieval periods that have left their traces in modern Sweden. What is vital for an understanding of history is to present a picture of Swedish history within the Nordic horizon, seen against the background of Europe.

It must also be emphasised that Sweden has never been a uniform Swedish nation. Even today Sweden is a country with a Swedish, a Finnish and a Saami population, and many living Swedes have Danish or Norwegian roots. Nor would Sweden's industry, administration and education system have developed so fast without help from foreign expertise and immigrant labour. Thus Sweden's cultural heritage is not just the heritage of the Swedes. The geographical variety and large regional differences of the country have also given the economic and social history of its people a more complex course than is shown in the political-historical picture of the destiny of the nation state. So the cultural heritage has to a large extent special regional features.

The history researcher's perspective varies according to his source material. Those who dig deep into written documents meet individuals, either as private persons or as members of a collective. If one uses demographic data bases, one's perspective widens: individuals disappear into social classes and groups during the period for which we have population and vital statistics, that is, for the last three hundred years or so.

The perspective for ethnologists, archeologists and ecologists is even wider. They are rarely able to study individual life stories. Instead they reveal the slow changes in a continuous process. In museum collections, in reports and records and not least in field work they study the form and distribution of *artefacts*, the plans and functions of buildings, the character and expansion of settlements, and changes in life styles and cultural traditions. All this is related to conditions and changes in the environment: rocks, soil and water, climatic changes, land elevation and land subsidence, flora and fauna, the growth of

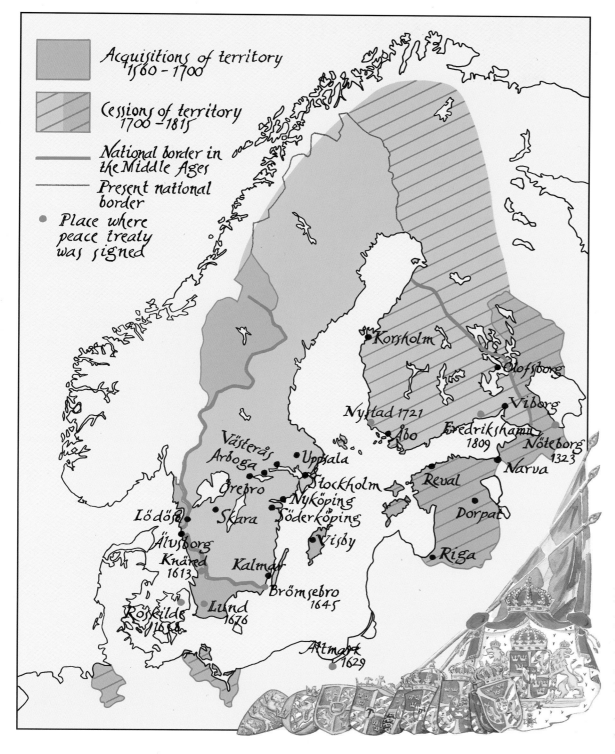

Acquisitions of territory
1560-1700

Cessions of territory
1700-1815

National border in
the Middle Ages

Present national
border

Place where
peace treaty
was signed

Korsholm

Olofsborg

Viborg

Nystad 1721

Åbo

Fredrikshamn
1809

Nöteborg
1323

Västerås

Arboga

Uppsala

Narva

Örebro

Stockholm

Reval

Lödöse

Nyköping

Söderköping

Dorpat

Älvsborg

Skara

Knäred
1613

Kalmar

Visby

Riga

Roskilde
1658

Lund
1676

Brömsebro
1645

Altmark
1629

The map shows the most important features of Sweden's historical geography: its original territory in the Middle Ages, subsequent expansion and cessions, and some historically important places and dates in this period of development. (L1)

forests or clearing and ditching.

But the major lines of development have seldom been noticeable to the individual. Deeper insight comes only when researchers from different fields summarise their results and their knowledge, as they are doing in the National Atlas of Sweden. Maps can reveal changes in the landscape, the distribution of settlement at different times and the changing patterns of economic, social and cultural life. Illustrations and diagrams can give examples of public life and places of work, family homes and the standard of living, tools and weapons that individuals have used, their everyday life and their festivals, their graves and their visions of death. And all this is seen in culture's "rear mirror", our

preserved cultural heritage.

For more than three hundred years Sweden has had a law that urges Swedes to protect and conserve the country's ancient monuments. It is not possible even to estimate the number of days' work behind the field work of archeologists and art historians, but the actual statistics that appear in their texts and maps are impressive enough. Thus almost 12,000 rock carvings have been recorded, showing in all more than 90,000 figures! And there are more than 2,500 runic inscriptions, almost all of them from the Viking Age. There are some 15,000 Bronze Age cairns scattered over Sweden and more than 9,300 barrow cemeteries from the Viking Age, to which may

be added quite a few which have disappeared as a result of centuries of cultivation.

Our churches and museums contain some 3,000 altar screens and wooden sculptures from the Middle Ages, and on Gotland alone there are 92 well-preserved medieval churches. All this puts Sweden in the front rank of research into medieval art history. In 1776 a law was passed forbidding the building of wooden churches, but during the following hundred years about 800 new stone churches were built—often to replace old medieval churches. This is an amazing number of sacred buildings, from our secularised generation's point of view.

As early as the Middle Ages there were a thousand mines in Bergslagen, and iron was smelted in about 200 blast furnaces. When Sweden was a major European power in the 17th century, about 300 ironworks were in use. Berslagen was wreathed in smoke and fumes from charcoal kilns, blast furnaces and smithies. There was a roaring and a clanging and a rushing of steam from all these workplaces, which were the foundation of the Swedish export industry and thereby the Swedish welfare state. Today it is quiet in the forests of Bergslagen; the blast furnaces are picturesque ruins framed in groves of birch trees, and the waterwheels no longer turn in the streams. The abandoned concrete factory blocks which until only a few years ago housed quite modern industries do not seem half so picturesque.

Regimental barracks in garrison towns, station buildings at minor railway junctions, water towers, town hotels, manor houses which are far too large for modern use and timbered barns—what are we to do with all these buildings which no longer have any function but which stand as monuments to the last few centuries of Swedish civilisation? Is it reasonable to preserve, restore and re-use the settings and buildings of bygone times? Yes—of that there is no doubt; their work is our heritage.

The preservation of our cultural heritage is a way of expressing respect for the continuity of our civilisation, a balanced reaction to mankind's confrontation with history; a quietly flowing spring of knowledge in the midst of our noisy rush of information in the age of the mass media—maybe a health spa?

The History of the Settlement of Sweden

All culture develops as a result of the interaction between environmental conditions and mankind's social systems and their evolution. Sweden's resources vary greatly from region to region and have been exploited in different ways at different times.

EARLY STONE AGE FROM 9000 B.C.

The history of settlement in Sweden covers more than 10,000 years. During the period following the melting of the glacial ice cap, when there was a favourable climate and leafy forests, the whole of the country's accessible area was utilised. People may have come to the northern parts from both the east and the south. Traces of these phases, which extended over more than 5,000 years, and lasted considerably longer in the north, are to be found in several tens of thousands of more or less frequently in-

habited dwelling sites, where it is possible to study technical skills in making tools from various types of rock that are quite remarkable. The basis of this civilisation was the surrounding resources, which were exploited by hunting, trapping, fishing and collecting.

LATE STONE AGE FROM 4000 B.C.

In the Late Stone Age settlement and use of resources began to be differentiated. The southern parts, which were rich in deciduous forests, were first used for extensive or small-scale farming and then for expanding cattle farming as well. The landscape gradually became more open and social groups arose. This was apparent in the building of monumental graves, mainly megalithic tombs, which occur in southern and western Sweden.

BRONZE AGE FROM 1800 B.C.

More and more of the country was exploited for cattle farming and agriculture. Belts of burial mounds in the open landscapes of Skåne and Halland and of cairns in inner Götaland, in Central Sweden and along the coasts reveal the expansion of the farming culture. In coastal environments, however, the sea's resources were of great importance. Extensive clearings, mainly in the inner parts of southern Sweden, bear witness to substantial new cultivation, probably for extensive farming with long fallow periods.

IRON AGE, 300 B.C.–1100 A.D.

More intensive farming developed, with stabled cattle, winter fodder collecting and manuring, and settlements became more permanent. Hedges and walls were built to protect fields and

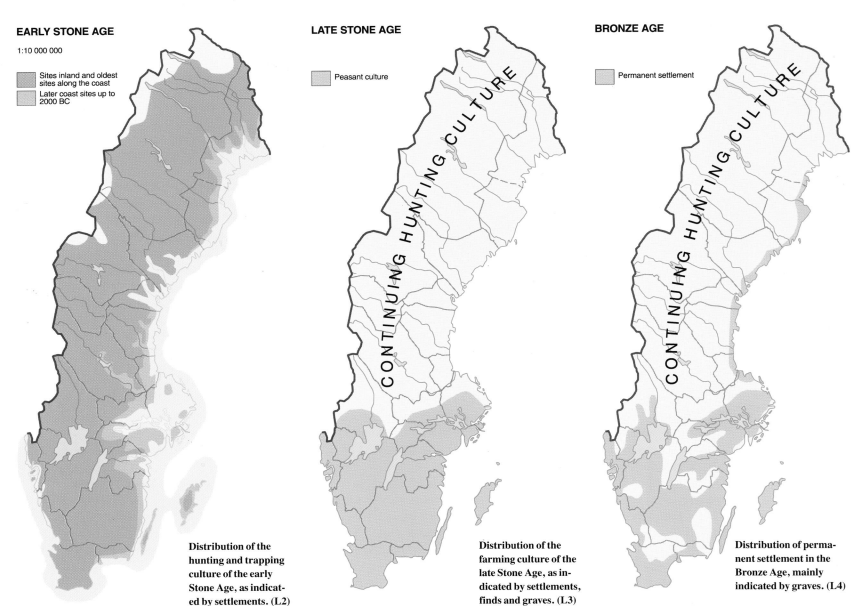

EARLY STONE AGE

1:10 000 000

Sites inland and oldest sites along the coast
Later coast sites up to 2000 BC

Distribution of the hunting and trapping culture of the early Stone Age, as indicated by settlements. (L2)

LATE STONE AGE

Peasant culture

CONTINUING HUNTING CULTURE

Distribution of the farming culture of the late Stone Age, as indicated by settlements, finds and graves. (L3)

BRONZE AGE

Permanent settlement

CONTINUING HUNTING CULTURE

Distribution of permanent settlement in the Bronze Age, mainly indicated by graves. (L4)

meadows from the grazing cattle. These have been preserved mainly on Öland and Gotland and in Östergötland. Groups of people started making and distributing iron, often in outlying districts.

An administrative organisation of the country came into being, first in the form of chiefdoms and then as hundreds and "folklands". In Mälardalen the population and number of settlements grew in the Early Iron Age. Farming increased in importance. The way in which settlements were organised was affected and villages began to arise.

Trade flourished in places that were particularly favourably located. Other places had legal or cult functions. Towards the end of this phase there were a few town-like settlements.

MIDDLE AGES – 1750

Towns now developed in earnest. Churches were built in the countryside and new parishes were founded.

Mining and the iron industry were organised during the early part of the period, and the mining districts of Bergslagen were colonised.

An agrarian colonisation of previously marginal areas was followed by a decline. In some places agricultural estates were formed, later with farming on a large scale. In peasant farming organised land division involving many parties took place. Villages had a centre (plot), infields (cultivated fields, usually in the form of mixed strips, and meadows) and outfields. Cultivated fields and meadows were owned individually but farmed collectively. Other land was in joint ownership.

Trade in iron and agricultural produce gave a financial surplus. Agricultural yields also increased, so that in the first place corn from the plains could be sold.

18TH CENTURY — MODERN TIMES, 1750 – 1950

Agriculture was modernised through land reforms and village society broke up. Both the cultural landscape and settlements were strongly affected by new cultivation and moving out from villages respectively. Increased pro-duction was necessary due to the growth in the population. Several early industries met the needs of agriculture. Ditching projects and lowering the level of lakes changed the landscape. Agriculture got a proletariat of propertyless labourers.

Towns began to grow as a result of the first stages of industrialisation. Ironworks expanded and mill towns grew up. The shortage of forests was a problem for iron production, but in the forest regions forestry flourished.

From the mid–19th century onwards there was a surplus of labour in agriculture. Many workers could not find a job in industry either, and chose to emigrate. Around 1930 half of the population was employed in agriculture, which reached its maximum area of cultivation at this time. In the middle of the 20th century only one fifth of the population of Sweden lived in the countryside. The varied cultural landscape which was created by subsistence farming has in part disappeared, being replaced by monoculture and large-scale farming.

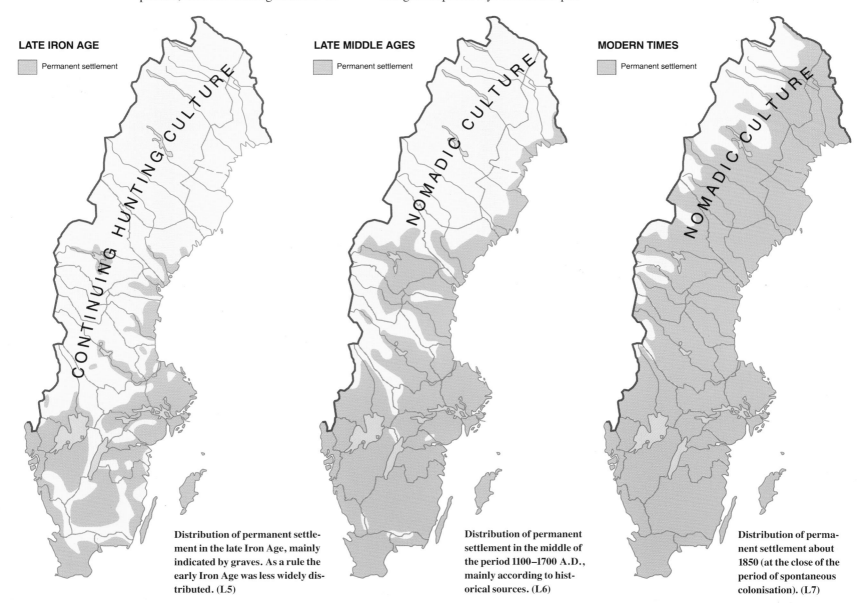

LATE IRON AGE

Permanent settlement

CONTINUING HUNTING CULTURE

Distribution of permanent settlement in the late Iron Age, mainly indicated by graves. As a rule the early Iron Age was less widely distributed. (L5)

LATE MIDDLE AGES

Permanent settlement

NOMADIC CULTURE

Distribution of permanent settlement in the middle of the period 1100–1700 A.D., mainly according to historical sources. (L6)

MODERN TIMES

Permanent settlement

NOMADIC CULTURE

Distribution of permanent settlement about 1850 (at the close of the period of spontaneous colonisation). (L7)

Early Hunting Cultures

Mankind's Immigration after the Ice Age

Rather more than 20,000 years ago a large ice sheet spread out over northern Europe. If human beings lived in Sweden before this date, any traces of them were obliterated by the ice. Some 13,000 years ago the southern part of Sweden was freed from ice, which made it possible for fauna and flora to spread northward again.

The communities which had been established south of the ice sheet in what today is northern Germany moved north in search of reindeer, which were their most important game. The oldest known remains of human beings in present-day Sweden are about 11,500 years old. They were found at Lake Finjasjön in northern Skåne, and their implements are similar to those found in Germany. As a great deal of water was still locked up in ice, the level of the sea was much lower and there were land bridges between Sweden, Denmark and England. Implements were similar throughout continental Northern Europe.

Gradually larger areas of land were freed from ice, but the climate varied during the appproximately 3,000 year long period when the ice was melting. 11,000 years ago there was a rich fauna of moose, red deer and giant deer as well as predators such as wolves and wolverines. Large areas of grassland were scattered with groves of birch and willow. Traces of human habitation have been found right up to the southern edge of the south Swedish highlands and along the west coast. The settlements were camps of tents in which small family groups spent short periods of time. Where rivers flowed in and out of lakes it was possible to fish salmon and catch reindeer by battue in the water. As the shoreline in southern Sweden was lower than today, we do not know of any coastal settlements there, but a rich supply of sea fauna may have been of great importance.

After a dramatic fall in temperature, a little less than 1,000 years later there was an equally dramatic rise in temperature. The grasslands were replaced by sparse pine and birch forests. This process was not completed in Sweden until the land ice had retreated from northern Sweden about 9,000 years ago.

During this period additions to the fauna were the European bison (wisent), the aurochs, the wild horse, the wild boar and the beaver. Traces of human beings were still few and far between, however. Most dwelling sites are to be found on the west coast. What today is high land in the terrain were at that time small islands or tongues of land on which coastal settlements were established.

Land, Sea and Man

Most of the dwelling sites we know of from the Early Stone Age are situated on dry, well-drained land. Not much more than stone tools and the debris from their manufacture have been preserved there. A small number of sites near marshy land, however, give us a better insight into hunting cultures.

BOG SETTLEMENT

Shallow lakes rich in nutrients were attractive places. The banks of reeds along the shores grew broader and broader. To be able to get access to open water it was necessary to move the camps out into the reed beds.

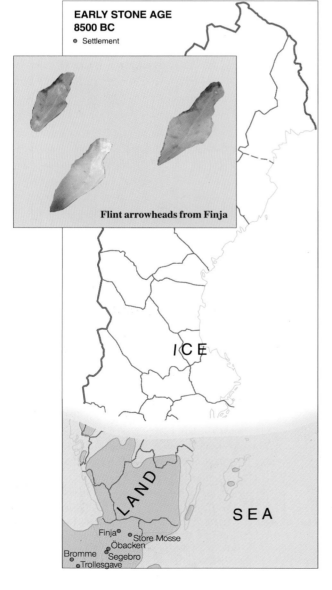

EARLY STONE AGE 8500 BC
• Settlement

Flint arrowheads from Finja

ICE

SEA

LAND

Finja
Store Mosse
Öbacken
Bromme
Segebro
Trollesgave

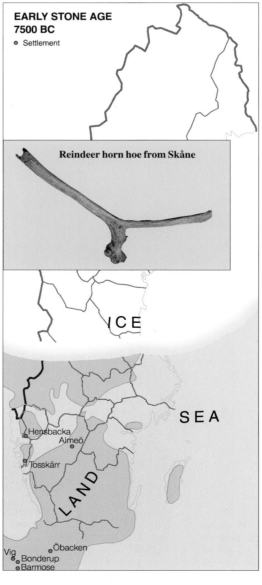

EARLY STONE AGE 7500 BC
• Settlement

Reindeer horn hoe from Skåne

ICE

SEA

LAND

Hensbacka
Almeö
Tosskärr

Vig
Bonderup
Barmose
Öbacken

The melting zone of the land ice lay in the central Swedish depression. The Baltic Ice Lake was dammed and the west and east coasts lay under water. Parts of the southern Baltic were land and a bridge of land stretched across the North Sea to England. Few reindeer-hunting dwelling sites are known in Skåne. (L8)

The land ice remained in Norrland. The Baltic was a bay called the Yoldia Sea. The bridge of land between southern Sweden and the continent still existed. Few dwelling sites are known, most of them on the west coast high above the present shoreline. (L9)

Layers of mud and peat later covered the settlements, thus preserving them. Such dwelling sites have been discovered when cutting peat, for example at Ageröd and other peat bogs in Skåne.

A firm surface was created with the help of branches and bark on which a small square or oval hut was built. One family lived here for a month or

Micro blades struck from a block of dark quartzite from a dwelling site at Varris in Vilhelmina, Lappland. An example of early Stone Age technology.

so at the most during the summer. Deposits of rubbish on the lake bed show that gathering nuts was important and that the sites were used during the autumn. Remains of meals and implements of bone and wood have been preserved, and sometimes vegetable matter as well. Time was given to gathering food so as to have an easily accessible supply of food in the winter.

The surroundings offered a variety of fishing. Fish traps made of osier and bast rope have been found. Swimming and wading birds were hunted, as were beavers. In the woods round the lake red deer, roe deer and wild boar were the game. As shading trees like lime and elm were established, the undergrowth decreased, reducing the supply of food for large forest animals like the aurochs and the moose.

SHORE SETTLEMENT

A large number of dwelling sites from the Early Stone Age have been found along the lake shores. They are not so

well preserved but, in the same way as the bog sites, were used for short periods of time by small groups of people. In the winter they moved away from the marshy areas to live with other families at the "base" camps both inland and along the coast. Large parts of the present sea bed off southern Sweden were dry land at that time. Marine archeological investigations have shown that there were dwelling sites along the former coastline, but little is known about their extent. Further north there has been considerable land elevation, and there we find today coastal sites inside the present coastline.

Approximately 9,000 years ago the level of the sea in southernmost Sweden was more than 10 metres lower than today. A rise in temperature resulted in parts of the polar ice cap melting, thus raising the sea level. Approximately 8,000 years ago the sea had reached a level corresponding to today's, but then it rose even further. As a result of land elevation these shorelines now lie several metres above the present sea level. This means that these coastal sites are accessible for investigation, though sometimes covered by shorelines.

THE SKATEHOLM SITE

Settlement during the latter part of the Early Stone Age is represented by the results of excavations round what once was a sea bay at Skateholm near Trelleborg. The favourable environment at Skateholm has made it possible to carry out intensive studies of this coastal settlement.

Around 5500 B.C. a small, sheltered bay was formed where the Skateholm river now runs out into the sea. In the middle of it there were small islands that stood a few metres above the water, and here people settled. The sites were in use for several centuries. Water with varying degrees of salinity and a good supply of nutri-

Elevation of the land led to the isolation of the Baltic, now called the Ancylus Lake, which rose and flooded the land to the south. Dwelling sites along the coast at that time, sites in bogs inland and the earliest sites in Norrland belong to this period. (L10)

Several rises in sea level led to the formation of sounds in the south, creating the Littorina Sea. In southern Sweden, too, the sea rose above today's level. Numerous dwelling sites are found along the coasts and inland in most parts of the country. (L11)

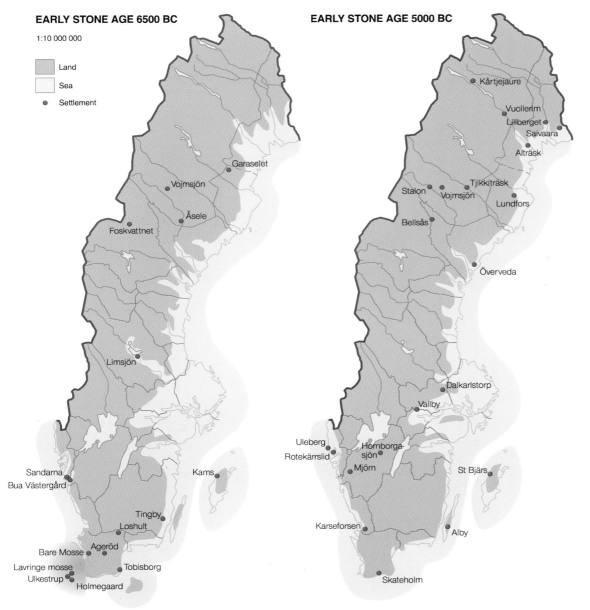

EARLY STONE AGE 6500 BC

1:10 000 000

Land
Sea
Settlement

Garaselet
Vojmsjön
Åsele
Foskvattnet
Limsjön
Sandarna
Bua Västergård
Kams
Tingby
Loshult
Bare Mosse
Ageröd
Lavringe mosse
Ulkestrup
Tobisborg
Holmegaard

EARLY STONE AGE 5000 BC

Kårtjejaure
Vuollerim
Lillberget
Saivaara
Alträsk
Tjikkiträsk
Stalon
Vojmsjön
Lundfors
Bellsås
Överveda
Dalkarlstorp
Vallby
Uleberg
Hornborga-sjön
Rotekärrslid
Mjörn
St Bjärs
Karseforsen
Alby
Skateholm

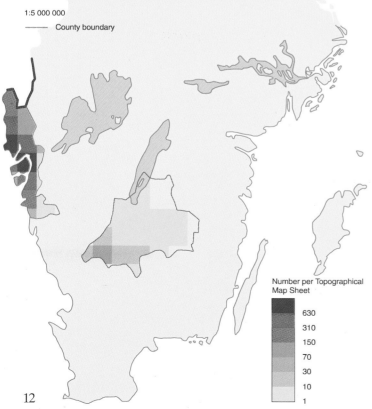

DISTRIBUTION OF STONE AGE SITES IN THE COUNTIES OF JÖNKÖPING AND GÖTEBORGS OCH BOHUS

1:5 000 000

——— County boundary

Number per Topographical Map Sheet

630
310
150
70
30
10
1

When the shallow lakes began to fill up with decayed vegetation, the settlers were forced to live in a marsh-like environment to be able to establish camps by the water. This bog site was used for a month or so in the autumn for fishing and gathering nuts.

ents attracted plenty of cod, herring and flat fish. The shoreline banks were a resting place for seals.

The landscape north of the lagoon was dominated by shady trees such as elms and limes, offering shelter to a rich fauna. Forest glades created by beaver dams were covered in rich vegetation which was grazed by the big forest animals.

This environment provided a surplus big enough to support a fairly large group of people for generations within a limited area. It was difficult to move about in the forest landscape, so the sea and rivers made natural transport routes.

A rise in the level of the sea increased the size of the lagoon and land was flooded, forcing people to move to higher ground. Several sites record movements of this kind over about one thousand years. The area within which settlement occurred comprises all in all some thousand square metres.

Excavations revealed marks left by posts and pits of various sizes, as well as piles of charcoal and soot. There were food remains and flint debris in the layers of rubbish. Some pits filled with rubbish had once been used for cooking and fermenting. Some were the sunken floors of huts, the largest being 11 by 6 metres in size.

More than 60 graves were found at Skateholm very close to the dwelling site. The dead had been buried in the ground lying on their backs but also crouched or sitting. They had been buried with their personal implements

and ornaments. Dogs had also been buried in the same way.

The combination of cultural layers, houses, pits and graves makes Skateholm unique as an excavations site but certainly not as a prehistoric form of settlement. Occasional discoveries of this kind have been made at several other sites.

COASTAL SITES IN THE WEST AND THE EAST

On the west coast there were sites with a great deal of rubbish in the form of mussel and mollusc shells, called in Danish "kökkenmöddingar" (kitchen middens). In the middle of the coastal stretch it is usual, because of changes in the land elevation, to find Early Stone Age sites, mainly with the technology typical of the site at Sandarna, covered with later shore deposits. On the east coast coastal settlements have to be sought several kilometres inland from the present shoreline.

The fact that the number of known sites is greater on the west than on the east coast is because more extensive investigations and recordings have been made there. The higher to-

More than 60 graves were found at one of the sites at Skateholm. One of them contained two men, one lying, the other sitting up. Burial offerings included a stone axe, which was placed at the left extremity of the lying man.

pography also means that the sites lie within a narrower shore zone than on the low-lying east coast. The many dwelling sites on the west coast reflect, however, the fact that the rich, varied marine environment provided a basis for stable settlement. From the base camps in the inner skerries it was possible to fish among the islands and hunt wild animals inland, as is shown by the bones found at sites in the Göteborg district. Very many inland lake sites are also known, for example at Hästefjorden, Mjörn and Hornborgasjön.

Our knowledge of the Stone Age on the east coast is mainly based on investigations near Kalmar and on the Baltic islands. The south Småland coast has many sites, and foundations of buildings have been excavated at Tingby. The lime-rich soils of Gotland and Öland have preserved bones well. Large sites rich in finds such as Alby on the east side of Öland or cemeteries like the one at Lummelunda on the west side of Gotland give us some idea of settlement during the Early Stone Age.

Central Sweden

Our knowledge of the early hunting culture in eastern Central Sweden was previously based on isolated finds, mainly in the form of picked rounded axes and chipped axes. The height above sea level at which the rounded axes have been found indicates that most of them are from 5000–4000 B.C.

EARLY DWELLING SITES

A small number of Early Stone Age sites have been investigated since the 1970s. A characteristic feature is the dominance of local quartz as the raw material for tools. Together with cooking pits and brittle-burnt stones this is reminiscent of Norrland sites of the same period. There are traces of small, narrow flake tools and chipped stone axes, which are also found both in the north and in the south.

At sites in Dalarna and northern Värmland surface finds have been made of handle cores and keel scrapers made of porphyry and other local rocks by the same technique. One site at Lake Limsjön in Dalarna has been

dated to about 6500 B.C. Here the remains of two huts were found in the form of stick and post holes. Other finds consist of cores and scrapers of the types described above. The site had three huts round a "yard". It lay on a bay at that time, and the bones are from animals that suggest both summer and winter settlement. The site was probably a base camp.

Thus from about 6500 B.C. there were hunting settlements in the area, characterised by microlith technology and mostly using local flint-like stones and some quartz. About 4000 B.C. quartz became the wholly dominant material. Thus concentrations of picked axes and quartz sites reflect later activities related to the coast and adapted to a long process of change in the shoreline and settlement.

PITTED-WARE CULTURE

About 3000 B.C. there appears in the coastal areas of central and southern Scandinavia a mixed economy primarily based on seal-hunting and pig-rearing, which had a characteristic style of pottery. It developed in marginal areas of the first Scandinavian peasant farming culture, called the funnel-beaker culture. It is possible to see how the seasonal hunting stations of the funnel beaker peasants became more and more specialised. This mixed economy is called the pitted-ware culture.

There are many graves in these coastal settlements. The dead have

A 20-year-old woman dressed in a skirt with a fringe of seal's teeth lay in the Pitted-Ware cemetery at Ajvide on Gotland. She had with her pottery, beads, bone needles and fishing hooks, and an amulet bag containing five hedgehogs' jaws.

LIHULT-TYPE AXES

1:10 000 000

Number of axes per parish

● 6-

● 1-5

Picked axes (map on right) are among the most frequent finds from the early Stone Age. They are found in the coastal areas settled at that time, in concentrations that indicate the extent of the settlement. Chipped axes of the Lihult type (named after a site in Bohuslän) are more or less contemporary. They seem to have spread from a westerly production centre. Both types are made from local types of stone. (L13, L14)

A Lihult axe from Herrestad in Bohuslän

PICKED AXES

A picked axe from Floda in Södermanland

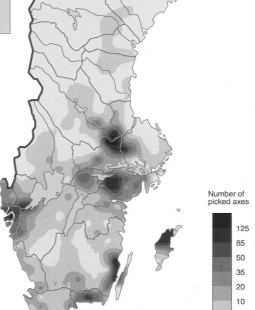

Number of picked axes

125
85
50
35
20
10
1
0

The banks of fire-cracked stones are the remains of huts with surrounding banks of rubbish at dwelling sites which, about 3000 B.C., were the centre for a group of people. They were probably inhabited for most of the year and often stood at the outlets of lakes, surrounded by high land.

been laid on their backs or in sleeping position in flat ground, often with ornaments and bone and horn objects attached to their clothing. These graves lie within the sites, and on Gotland there are also flat-ground cemeteries.

The pitted-ware tradition exhibits great differences from one area to the other, which has led people to question the existence of a uniform culture. Instead it has been suggested that the tradition grew up as a result of the local hunting and farming cultures. This culture form ceased to exist about 2000 B.C. when farming expanded.

The dwelling sites of the Pitted-Ware culture are with few exceptions spread round the coasts of southern and central Sweden. The map shows a sample of some of the most important ones. (L15)

SELECTED SITES FROM THE PITTED WARE CULTURE

1:5 000 000

Orsand
Mårtsbo
Torslunda
Persbo
Åloppe
Mjölkbo
Körartorp
Korsnäs
Brunn
Åda
Fagervik
Rörvik
St Ek
Säter
Fiskevik
Frugårdssund
Alvastra
Bokö
Ire
Bua
Gisebo
Visby
Väster-
Hallehög
Fridtorp
bjers
Ajvide
Humlekärrshult
Stora
Förvar
Gullrum
Köpingsvik
Jonstorp
Möllehusen
Siretorp
Ringsjön
Limhamn
Sibbarp
Skillinge
Hagestad

14

Hunting Culture in Norrland

THE EARLY STONE AGE

The oldest dwelling sites in Norrland are in Jämtland and Västerbotten and date from about 7000 B.C., when the inland ice sheet still covered parts of the interior. The earliest colonisation was from the west (Tröndelag in Norway). Later there was colonisation from both the south (Central Sweden) and the east (northern Finland).

The landscape that met the immigrants was covered with bushes and plants. This vegetation was not like that of the present-day tundra and was not ideal for reindeer grazing. On the other hand both moose and beaver probably felt at home.

Conditions close to the melting ice were special, leading to natural disasters such as overflowing ice lakes and rivers that changed their courses. The rapid elevation of the land caused earth tremors. The earliest people lived in a less secure environment than succeeding generations.

Gradually pine, birch and aspen invaded the landscape, forming the first forest. The climate was similar to our own, but 8,000 years ago it became warmer and more humid. Light, deciduous woods grew up in Norrland on damp ground and pine forests on infertile till. The tree line crept up 200 metres higher than today, and the mountain areas were smaller.

Finds from the early sites consist mainly of handle cores and keel scrapers. Small, narrow, thin flakes, micro blades, were struck from the cores and used as cutting edges for tools such as spear and arrow heads. This technology appears in many parts of Sweden between 7000 and 5000 B.C. Flint was used in the south, and local raw materials such as dense quartzite, intermediate rocks, porphyry, jasper and tuff in the north.

Quartz was used more and more, worked with a new technique, since it was widely available in many parts of Central Sweden and Norrland. Most sites with quartz technology date from about 4700 B.C. onwards.

The sites are less than 100 m^2 in size. Often a few stone tools and debris are found round the traces of a hearth or a cooking pit. These sites were used temporarily by a small group of people. The early sites are on ridges close to bogs, on headlands or on small islands, often high above the water level. Their position may mainly be dependent on the availability of food for the game. The risk of natural disasters may also have been a factor.

The considerably fewer medium-sized sites are on low shore plateaus by bays, often where a stream ran in. They may have been small base camps and yield more finds.

THE LATE STONE AGE

From the river Ljungan up to the Vindelälven, before 4000 B.C., huts were built that were later surrounded by rubbish: brittle-burnt stones, debris of stone-tool making, worn-out tools, remains of food and slaughtered animals. The tools are mostly made of quartz. These banks of fire-cracked stones often lie in groups at sites that were base camps for a group of people. They utilised an area round the base camp for hunting and fishing. The bone remains are predominantly from moose, but beaver and fish bones, mainly from pike, show that their diet was complemented with other animal food. These banks lie at the mouths of streams by lakes, some way from the shore and sometimes on islets. The sites were inhabited for most of the year. Where the lakes were well stocked with fish, there were shore sites which also yield plenty of fire-cracked stones. These may have been summer fishing sites. Settlement was fairly permanent.

Along the coast there are sites which indicate intensive seal hunting. One of these, at Överveda in Ångermanland, was in use between 3500 and 2500 B.C. The finds are predominantly slate tools. Net sinkers show that fishing was of great importance, too. This is also true of the quartz sites at Lundfors in Västerbotten, which were in use about 4000 B.C. There are similar summer and winter

The first dwelling sites in Norrland appear to have been short-term camps for moose and beaver hunting. During the end of the early Stone Age and most of the late Stone Age permanent dwelling territories are predominant in the forestland. About 1000 B.C. a more mobile pattern emerges, when people move between the forests and the lower parts of the mountains.

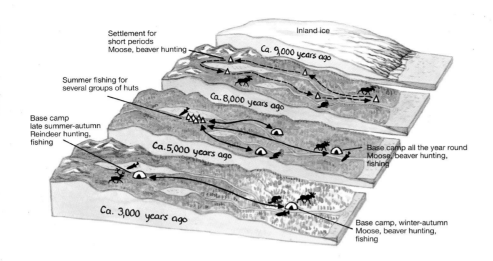

Inland ice

Settlement for
short periods
Moose, beaver hunting

Ca. 9,000 years ago

Summer fishing for
several groups of huts

Ca. 8,000 years ago

Base camp
late summer-autumn
Reindeer hunting,
fishing

Ca. 5,000 years ago

Base camp all the year round
Moose, beaver hunting,
fishing

Ca. 3,000 years ago

Base camp, winter-autumn
Moose, beaver hunting,
fishing

Stone-Age sites in the interior of Norrland from different times have been visited repeatedly. Most date from 1500 B.C.–500 A.D., that is, the Bronze Age and the early Iron Age. The map shows 2,600 or more sites within the river systems of the Ljungan, Indalsälven and Ångermanälven. Many sites were discovered when surveying for hydro-electric power stations. The survey of prehistoric monuments, which covered large areas, gives a fairly good picture. In the mountain districts, however, as in eastern Jämtland and the coastal district, there are gaps due to incomplete surveying. More sites have now been registered along the middle reaches of the Ljungan and the Gimån. (L16)

STONE AGE SITES IN CENTRAL NORRLAND

1:2 500 000

Number per Economic Map Sheet

- 31-62
- 15-30
- 7-14
- 3-6
- 1-2

sites along the coast of central Norrland. Groups of people utilised a relatively small area close to the coast for hunting and fishing.

At Vuollerim on the river Luleälven there are some unusually well-preserved remains of huts beside a prehistoric river bed. They are 11 by 5 metres in size and were surrounded by low banks of earth, rubbish and fire-cracked stones. Hearths, storage and cooking pits have also been found there. The implements are mostly made of quartz. Most of the animal remains were of moose, but beaver, forest birds and fish were also used. The place was a permanent base camp for most of the year. Shore sites may have been connected to the base camp.

The Stone Age in Tornedalen was previously known by what are called Northern Bothnian tools. Several dwelling sites were discovered here in the 1980s, with comb-decorated pottery of an eastern type. One of these, at Lillberget near Överkalix has been partially excavated. Large sites with many hut foundations have also been discovered at, for example, Saivaara near Haparanda, which do not have comb pottery but debris and quartz tools, and which were situated close to the contemporary coast.

LATE HUNTING SITES

At the beginning of the Bronze Age, about 2000 to 1500 B.C., the pattern of inland dwelling sites and their economy changed. In contrast to the rest of Sweden there were genuine hunting communities here as late as the Iron Age, at least until 500 A.D. and later in the north than in the south. There were large, mobile hunting groups in this period whose economy and life style, at least in upper Norrland, was largely based on reindeer hunting, but moose hunting and fishing were still important. These people now lived in larger units along rivers, and moved between forest districts and the lower mountain areas.

Finds from these sites include implements and debris of quartzite and pottery, mixed with asbestos. Metal objects of an eastern type and moulds show that metalwork was practised in these hunting communities.

A large number of the hunting sites in inner Norrland date from this late period. Hunting cultures gradually ceased to exist, the hunters adapting to other social systems, such as farming in central Norrland and reindeer husbandry in upper Norrland.

Stone Age Peasants

Fundamental changes in man's living conditions mark the transition from the Early to the Late Stone Age. After having been hunters and food gatherers, people now made their living mainly by being farmers. A common name for the Late Stone Age is the Neolithic period.

The Early Farming Stone Age

The distribution of thin-butted flint axes gives an overall picture of the settlement areas that were established in the early Neolithic period around 4000 to 3000 B.C. Farming settlements existed at that time in many parts of southern and central Sweden. They were common in the fertile farming areas of Skåne, Halland, Västergötland, Östergötland, Södermanland, Närke and Uppland. Early

farming settlements have also been found on Öland and Gotland and in parts of Småland. Finds of early Neolithic axes have also been made in other areas, such as Bohuslän and Dalsland. The distribution of axes indicates in general the limits of early farming culture, which in archeological contexts is called the funnel-beaker culture.

The early Neolithic sites are located in areas with light soils. In eastern Central Sweden the sites were closely connected with the shoreline at that time, which was 35–40 metres higher than today.

Studies from various parts of Sweden show that these early farmers cultivated simple varieties of wheat like emmer and einkorn, and barley. The domesticated animals were cattle, swine and sheep or goats. Dogs had been kept since early times. The economic importance of cultivation compared to hunting and fishing at this time has been much discussed. There were various types of sites: temporary fishing places on the coast or by lakes, places where quartz or flint-stone was quarried and base sites where crops were cultivated and cattle reared.

These dwelling sites were relatively small. Investigations in Skåne indicate a size of 600–800 m^2. In the 1980s and

1990s whole foundations were uncovered at digs in both Sweden and Denmark. These buildings are small, about 12–15 m long and 4–5 m broad. A characteristic feature is their slightly elliptical shape and that they were divided into two aisles by a central row of posts. Buildings like this have been investigated at Mossby in southernmost Skåne and at Brunneby in Östergötland.

The early farmers' communities consisted of small, single-family settlements which were moved at regular intervals within a limited area. Previously it was presumed that their farming methods were based on extensive slash and burn. This kind of system meant burning parts of a forest perhaps every thirtieth year, with a fallow period in between. This system required large areas of land. Today archeologists and Quaternary geologists propose instead—or as well— a system of smaller, well-cultivated fields, which might well be called "garden farming". In its earliest form it was based on a kind of hoe cultivation, but around 3600 B.C. a simple form of plough was introduced to southern Scandinavia. This did not turn the earth but only cut the sward.

The distribution of a culture over a certain period may be illustrated by various cultural evidence. The best form is a widespread distribution of settlements. If there is a general burial custom, preferably with visible monuments, graves are also reliable. Finds of a certain, dated type of general artefact may also be used, if other evidence is not available. Our knowledge of Neolithic settlement is very uneven; it is best though not complete in the totally-cultivated districts. There are graves only in certain areas. All known settlements and graves lie within the area which has yielded finds of thin-butted flint axes—carefully shaped and polished, thus easily discovered. They give us the best overall picture of the frequency and distribution of early farming culture, even though there is some over-representation in the flint districts. (L17)

The ground plan on the right is of the foundation of a two-aisled house with three roof-supporting posts from Mossby in Skåne. The illustration shows what a house of this type and the surrounding landscape might have looked like about 3500 B.C. Small enclosed fields were worked with hoes, and the cattle grazed freely in the forest glades.

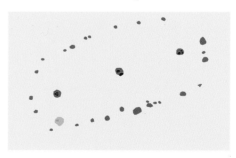

THIN-BUTTED FLINT AXES

1:10 000 000

Number of axes per grid square

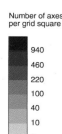

940
460
220
100
40
10
1

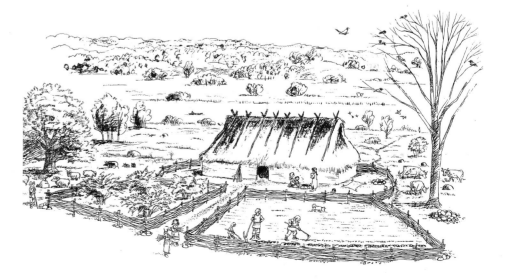

Five large passage graves stand on a ridge in the table-land at Karleby in Västergötland, parallel with the village from historic times. It is possible that there has been continuity of settlement since Neolithic times.

The Age of the Stone-Chamber Graves

The most obvious Stone Age monuments that we see in the landscape today are the great stone-chamber graves: dolmens and passage graves from the earlier periods and gallery graves from the final period.

DOLMENS

Dolmens are the smaller of the two older types, with a horizontal stone slab or a boulder roofing a rectangular or polygonal chamber. In some cases the dolmen chamber may be placed in an oblong earth mound, and is then called a long dolmen. The dolmens of Bohuslän differ from those in Skåne in being constructed with flat granite slabs and not with glacial boulders.

Dolmens were first built about 3500 B.C. A relatively small number of them have survived to the present

day; there are about 40 both in Skåne and in Bohuslän and about 95 in the whole country. This is presumed to be a very small part of the original number. Investigations in Denmark indicate that perhaps only ten per cent have been preserved. Studies of ancient cadastral records carried out when the latest inventory of ancient monuments in Malmöhus county was made suggest a similar situation. Approximately 80 stone-chamber graves that had disappeared were recorded in this survey.

PASSAGE GRAVES

In contrast to the oldest dolmens, passage graves were originally intended for several burials—as many as a hundred or so in one grave are known—in a rectangular or oval chamber which has a passage leading roughly to the south-east and is usually placed in a barrow. Their distribution is in part similar to that of the dolmens, with the addition of Västergötland and Öland. In particular Falbygden in Västergötland emerges as a real stone-chamber district with more than 250 known passage graves within an area measuring 40 by 25 km. The largest passage grave in Scandinavia is to be found here, situated in a row of five large passage graves near the village of Karleby. The chamber is 17 m long and the passage 11 m long. Passage chambers were first built about 3200 B.C. They are all later than the dolmens, but may have been used for later burials.

There are also a few atypical stone-chamber graves on Gotland (Tofta) and in Östergötland (Alvastra).

GRAVES OF THE BATTLE AXE CULTURE

1:10 000 000

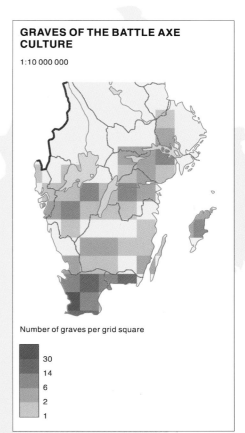

Number of graves per grid square

	30
	14
	6
	2
	1

The Battle-Axe culture graves under flat ground are spread over the whole area of farming culture; the fact that many graves have also escaped detection is proved by the numerous finds of battle axes. (L20)

BATTLE-AXE CULTURE

One of the most discussed cultures in southern Scandinavia is what is known as the battle-axe culture or single-grave culture, as it is called in Denmark. The burning question was whether this culture was brought to Sweden or not. Because of the shape of the battle-axes it was long called the boat-axe culture.

In 1962 Mats P Malmer was able to

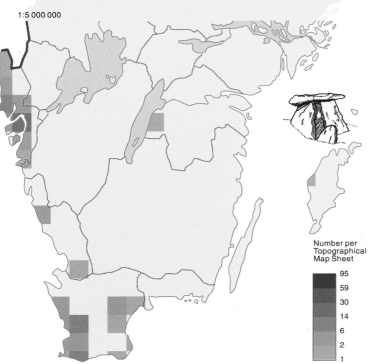

DOLMENS

1:5 000 000

PASSAGE GRAVES

Number per Topographical Map Sheet

	95
	59
	30
	14
	6
	2
	1

Early stone chamber tombs, dolmens and passage graves are found within the same areas, with one important exception: the numerous passage graves in Västergötland. In these areas the early farming culture was probably the most socially developed one. (L18, L19)

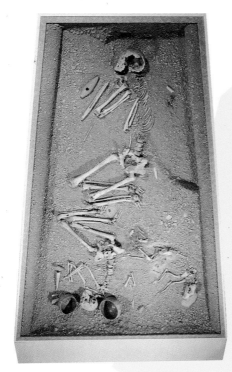

Reconstruction of a double grave for a man and a woman from the Battle-Axe culture at Bergsvägen in Linköping. Burial offerings include a battle axe, three other axes, pottery and a dog.

One of two large gallery graves at Brande-rud in Holm, Dalsland is built of heavy stone slabs.

prove that the battle-axe culture had not been brought to Sweden but had developed from the funnel-beaker culture. Among other evidence the distribution of various types of implements shows that the same sorts of soils had been tilled in Skåne, which also suggests that cultivation and not merely cattle rearing was important.

The battle-axe culture is primarily known through grave finds, as very few dwelling sites have been investigated. The dead were buried in flat ground in oval pits and were placed in wooden coffins which were packed into stone structures. The placing of the bodies and the accompanying grave objects followed a strict ritual. The body was usually placed on its side in a sleeping position with the legs bent and facing east. The grave objects also have their fixed places. In the male graves the battle axe was placed at the head, a clear indication of its importance as a status symbol. A few graves are in the earlier stone-chamber graves.

The Late Neolithic Age

Towards the end of the Stone Age several important changes took place; the farming culture spread over wider areas and there was a more dense settlement of the land.

GALLERY GRAVES

This type of stone-chamber grave consists of a rectangular chamber, usually 3–8 m long, built of and covered by flat slabs of rock. This type often, as for example in the Göta älv area, also has an outer construction of vertical slabs. There are primarily two types of cists: large galleries with several chambers and an opening in the dividing slabs, and cists with a single chamber.

The gallery graves lie scattered in the terrain, not infrequently far from other prehistoric monuments. According to the Ancient Monument Register there are some 1,500 gallery graves in Sweden, spread over a considerably larger area than the earlier stone-chamber graves. Kronoberg county has most cists, followed by the western Swedish counties. Gallery graves were the dominant type of grave in the late Neolithic period, that is, the latest period in the Stone Age, but there are stone cists from the early part of the Bronze Age as well. This type of grave may be dated to between 2300 and 1800 B.C.

During this period there was also another type of grave on flat ground without any visible signs above ground—especially in Skåne.

SETTLEMENT

It was not until the 1960s that Late Neolithic settlements were first found, often small ones with rather few objects. Pit houses, that is, underground house constructions, were investigated in Skåne in the 1960s. During extensive excavations at Fosie near Malmö it was possible to identify

GALLERY GRAVES

1:5 000 000

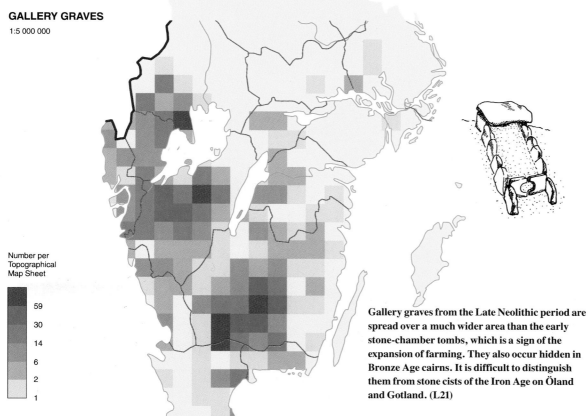

Number per Topographical Map Sheet

59
30
14
6
2
1

Gallery graves from the Late Neolithic period are spread over a much wider area than the early stone-chamber tombs, which is a sign of the expansion of farming. They also occur hidden in Bronze Age cairns. It is difficult to distinguish them from stone cists of the Iron Age on Öland and Gotland. (L21)

The floors of large Late Neolithic longhouses, with heavy centre posts and side posts at the large site at Fosie near Malmö.

18

Alvastra

Ystad

post-supported long houses from this period. These houses were of varying sizes, 9–18 m long and 5–6 m wide. They were spread among a number of settlements on elevated land.

At Piledal east of Ystad a 33-metre long and about 5-metre wide house was found which bore a close resemblance to houses which were discovered on Bornholm. Excavations at Linköping revealed a long house some 20 m long and 6 m wide which can be compared to the Fosie houses.

Late Neolithic settlement gives the impression that there were both isolated farmsteads and almost hamlet-like groups of houses as at Fosie. Finds from this period such as flint daggers and flint sickles and simple shaft-hole axes are much more widespread and frequent than older types, which is an indication of the spread of agriculture.

Two Important Investigations

THE YSTAD AREA

A project in the Kabusa area east of Ystad led to the discovery and excavation of a considerable number of sites. These may be dated to the introduction of agriculture, about 4000 B.C. to about 3200 B.C. The sites are all small, about 600–1,200 m². Continuous settlement throughout most of the Late Stone Age may be presumed. We can see how the sites move within the area, often only a few dozen metres. The population at a site consisted of a family group of 8–10 persons. Farming was based on permanent fields.

We can follow the development of the settlement over almost 800 years. There is a change in settlement towards the end of the funnel-beaker culture period. New ideas from the pitted-ware culture are evident, mixed with characteristic features of the funnel-beaker culture.

The battle-axe culture expanded over a larger area, and large quantities of accidental finds have been made in the interior of this area, both from this culture and from the Late Neolithic period. Few dwelling sites are known from these periods. They are small and yield insignificant finds in contrast to the funnel-beaker sites, where larger numbers of finds are often made.

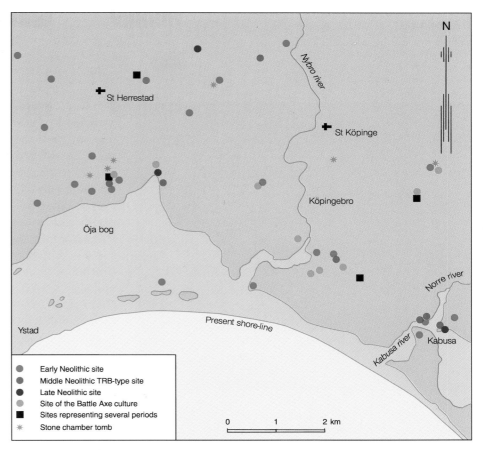

Early Neolithic site
Middle Neolithic TRB-type site
Late Neolithic site
Site of the Battle Axe culture
Sites representing several periods
Stone chamber tomb

0   1   2 km

Stone Age farmers in the well-investigated Ystad area have left sites from all the Neolithic periods. Their locations match the local geographical conditions well.

ALVASTRA PILE DWELLING

One of the most remarkable remains of the Stone Age in northern Europe is the pile dwelling at Alvastra, situated in a bog at the foot of Omberg, near the south-west shore of Lake Tåkern. Wood and other organic material has been preserved well in the marshy land, which means that we know a great deal about life in this pile dwelling. It reveals traces of both the funnel-beaker culture and the pitted ware culture.

Dendrochronological studies have made it uniquely possible for archeologists to study the early stages of the site, its expansion and period of use. We know exactly how long the pile dwelling was in use — 42 years, though not exactly when, but probably about 3400 B.C. This pile dwelling is now thought to have been a ceremonial centre at which people gathered for various communal purposes.

A row of vertical poles of oak and alder at the Alvastra pile dwelling is visible where the covering culture layer of peat has been removed. This is a major construction from the first year of the site; in the background, smaller posts for huts.

Bronze Age Settlement

The distribution of graves gives a broad overview of Bronze Age settlement, while remains of dwelling sites give us a more detailed picture. Our knowledge of the location of graves and dwellings and of their design and finds gives us some idea of the society of that time; to this we can add the information provided by rock carvings, cup marks and traces of cultivation. Graves and rock carvings are made with respect to social and ideological factors. Dwelling sites are the result of daily life and everyday needs, of economics and ecology.

A group of Bronze Age barrows at Glumslöv and Härslöv in Skåne are spread out in typical fashion on the high parts of the cultivated landscape.

Totally-cultivated districts

In parts of southern Sweden, principally in Skåne and southern Halland but also in Västergötland and Östergötland, large areas of land are totally cultivated. Intensive cultivation in an area may mean that prehistoric remains have been removed or covered up.

BARROWS

During the Early Bronze Age (particularly between 1500–1300 B.C.) people were commonly buried in a coffin made from an oak trunk or stone slabs, which was covered by a large, monumental barrow of earth or turf. The height varies between two and six metres and these mounds may be from 10–15 m up to 40 m in diameter. Simpler graves in flat ground also occur. The burial custom may indicate social and economic class differences, with chieftains in the monumental barrows and "ordinary" people buried under flat ground. Large mounds full of grave gifts are known in many parts of Europe and are connected with the existence of chiefdoms.

There are today in Denmark about 20,000 large barrows from the Early Bronze Age, but there were probably twice as many originally. In Sweden the large Bronze Age barrows are mainly in Skåne and southern Halland, standing like monuments on the higher parts of the cultivated landscape. Here lie between three and four thousand graves of this type. The large barrows are not evenly distributed but occur in scattered groups. These concentrations tell us which areas were most attractive for settlement. The fertile clayey till of Skåne was the economic basis of those people who were buried in the great Bronze Age barrows.

Large mounds from this period are also known to exist in Småland, Västergötland, Östergötland and Bohuslän. The Håga barrow near Uppsala contained a unique ceremonial grave and is the northernmost known example of this burial custom. In these areas, too, the connection with fertile soils is evident, for example on the fertile plain in western Östergötland round Lake Tåkern.

BRONZE AGE BARROWS

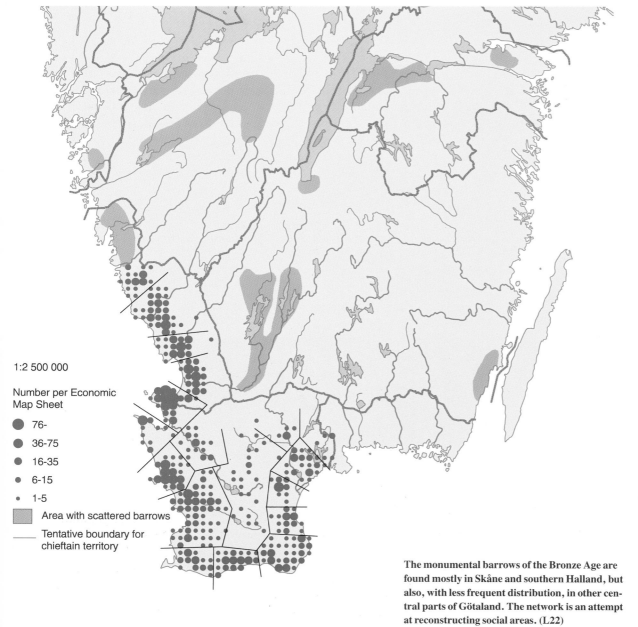

1:2 500 000

Number per Economic
Map Sheet

- 76-
- 36-75
- 16-35
- 6-15
- 1-5

Area with scattered barrows

Tentative boundary for
chieftain territory

The monumental barrows of the Bronze Age are found mostly in Skåne and southern Halland, but also, with less frequent distribution, in other central parts of Götaland. The network is an attempt at reconstructing social areas. (L22)

BRONZE AGE CAIRNS

1:5 000 000

Number per Topographical Map Sheet

	310
	150
	70
	30
	10
	1

A monumental ship-formed flat cairn at Snäckedal, Misterhult, Småland.

On Gotland the cairns are often spread out on meadows by the coast. The large cairn in the background lit up by the rays of the sun is Uggårda Roir in Rone, the largest on the island and one of the largest in Sweden.

DWELLING SITES AND FLAT-GROUND GRAVES

Although settlement during the Early Bronze Age in southern Sweden can be identified by the distribution of large mounds, there have been few discoveries of house foundations or other remains of dwelling sites from this period. Those positively identified building foundations from the Early Bronze Age which have been found are three-aisled long houses with indoor roof posts and wattle-and-clay walls. Foundations of this type have certainly been ploughed away to a large extent in totally-cultivated districts.

During the Late Bronze Age cremation graves under flat ground are predominant in totally-cultivated districts and the monumental forms disappeared. Urn graves were also placed in the outer layers of the older mounds. The absence of visible graves above the ground makes a general survey impossible.

Flat-ground graves are found as a result of working the land. Their distribution is therefore not representative of the prehistoric situation, but instead shows the areas where land exploitation and archeological excavations have been most intensive. This

is also true of the distribution of known dwelling sites and remains of buildings from the Late Bronze Age, which are considerably more numerous than from the earlier phase.

Remains of a large number of buildings from the Late Bronze Age have been found in the fields of the totally-cultivated districts when the surface soil has been removed. The buildings are revealed by regularly occurring dark patches—the remains of the posts that held up the roof. The most common type is the three-aisled long house, 15–22 m long and 5–8 m wide, constructed with two rows of roof posts.

Cairn graves and settlement

Outside the totally-cultivated districts cairn-type graves give the best indication of settlement during the Bronze Age. Flat cairn-like structures without earth are also found in the same areas as these cairns. Occasional stone ships are found, on Gotland for example. There are large flat cairns and barrows with raised centres and edges in Halland and Västergötland, which sometimes contain finds from the Bronze Age. The size of the cairns decreases towards the end of the Bronze Age and, instead, cemeteries become more common, in Mälardalen in the form of flat cairns round a boulder.

Bronze Age vaulted cairns are the prehistoric type of grave that is most widespread in Sweden. The map records more than 15,000 cairns, all situated outside cemeteries. In the same areas there are also numerous small and flat cairns of bare stone. (L23)

THE GRAVE-TYPE CAIRN

Cairns without earth are often a monumental type of grave, also accentuated by their location. Most of them stand in isolation or in small groups. Approximately 15,000 such cairns are known to exist in Sweden. There are, in addition, many cairns from the Bronze and Iron Ages which are located in cemeteries.

These cairns are vaulted like a cupola, and most of them are round. Oval and square cairns are also found, as well as long cairns, built up gradually in a long, narrow form. Round cairns may have a diameter of a few metres up to 35–40 m; a few are even larger. The largest cairn in Sweden is the Kivik grave in Skåne, which is 75 m in diameter and contains a large stone coffin carved with figures. The longest typical long cairns are about 80 m long.

Cairns are built entirely of stones, often of the same size. Their volume and visible constructional details such as edge chains of selected stones,

There are several heaps of fire-cracked stones with their typical slanted profile at a settlement site at Ovangärstad in Vikbolandet, Östergötland. In one of them you can see plenty of brittle-burnt stones on the surface.

a dry-wall edge and a flat surrounding brim suggest a conscious architectonic design.

There are often concealed constructions within such as concentric chains of stones, inner dry-walls, stone chambers or cists. Variations in richness of design are particularly noticeable in coastal districts.

During the Early Bronze Age the burial of unburnt bodies in stone coffins was common. This burial custom was gradually abandoned in favour of cremation. Cremation graves in cairns and flat cairns are sometimes in urns or small coffins, but the burnt bones are often scattered inside the structures.

DISTRIBUTION OF CAIRNS

Most cairns date from the Bronze Age. Apart from the southern Scandinavian barrow districts they are absent only from the hunting areas of the northern Swedish interior. Cairns are found both in characteristic coastal districts and in inland districts. The coastal cairns should be seen in relation to corresponding cairns on the Norwegian, Finnish and Baltic coasts.

A remarkable belt of cairns exists along the *West Coast*, with their densest concentration from the Onsala peninsula up to the Norwegian border. They are richly varied in shape and construction. Most of them have monumental locations on the crowns and ledges of hills within the rugged and bleak coastal area. The coastal environment was of decisive importance for the livelihood of the cairn builders.

In *inner Southern Sweden* there is a central area in Kind round the upper reaches of the Ätran and its tributaries and another in Värend round Lake Helgasjön. There are many great cairns in the latter district. One of the mightiest of Sweden's cairns, 60 m in diameter, is at Tun in Västergötland. On Lake Vänern and along the Värmland water courses some of the cairns are placed on the shoreline. The cairns stand on forest-clad moraines along rivers and valleys, within the Västergötland Silurian area on ridges in the field landscape of the high plateau. Some cairns, mainly in Småland, contain a stone cist, which suggests continuity between the Late Neolithic period and the Early Bronze Age. These belts of cairns usually stand above the highest shoreline on sandy soil suitable for extensive agriculture.

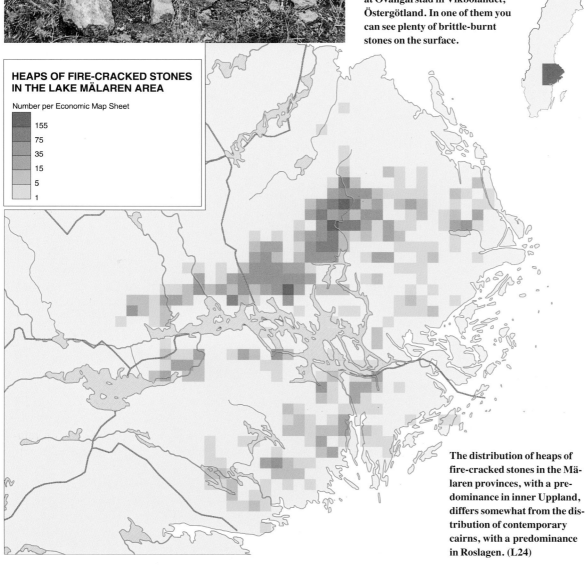

HEAPS OF FIRE-CRACKED STONES IN THE LAKE MÄLAREN AREA

Number per Economic Map Sheet

	155
	75
	35
	15
	5
	1

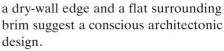

The distribution of heaps of fire-cracked stones in the Mälaren provinces, with a predominance in inner Uppland, differs somewhat from the distribution of contemporary cairns, with a predominance in Roslagen. (L24)

A reconstruction of life at a Bronze Age settlement, situated as on the map below, illustrates how the rich environment by the shore was used for diversified means of livelihood, such as farming, cattle rearing, hunting and fishing.

A BRONZE AGE SETTLEMENT AT RASBO, UPPLAND

Metres above sea level

- 25
- 20
- 15
- ⬭ Cairn
- ● Flat cairn
- ▲ Heap of fire-cracked stones
- — Contour line

Map of a Bronze Age settlement at Rasbo, Uppland, showing how the settlement follows the contemporary shoreline with its graves close by.

A group of cairns at Ölmevalla, Halland, stands in a bare coastal landscape, which because of little elevation of the land still gives a good picture of the original relationship of the graves to the sea.

In *Eastern Sweden* a belt of cairns runs from Blekinge along the coasts of Småland and Östergötland up to Mälardalen. In this latter area the cairns are spread out over a wider area inland, yet they are connected with the Bronze Age coast although land elevation has drained bays and fairways.

Many cairns are found along the north-east coast of Småland. Here the cairns and small flat cairns—sometimes forming cemeteries—stand in a broken moraine and rocky landscape, generally without any connection with better soil but close to contemporary bays and shores. Further south in Möre there are large cairns on low ridges on today's agricultural plains. Many concentrations of cairns are found in inner Roslagen and inner Södermanland.

Most cairns on Gotland and Öland stand within a narrow zone just back from the coast. Many of them are large. Some form the core of later cemeteries.

Along the *Norrland coast* from Gästrikland to southern Norrbotten there is a narrow belt of cairns and flat cairns close to the coast. The graves are placed by the shoreline of their period and are connected with coastal means of livelihood. Most of them lie 25 to 40 m above sea level and are from the early and middle parts of the Bronze Age, while a few of them placed lower down are from the Early Iron Age. The earlier group is more varied and is in a clear majority in the north; from Medelpad southwards the later group is well represented.

Sites with Heaps of Fire-cracked Stones

The relationship between graves and dwelling sites poses a general problem of interpretation. Our knowledge of graves has for a long time been relatively good compared to our knowledge of dwelling sites. Many sites in farming districts have been damaged or destroyed. On the West Coast sites with stone implements may also be from the Bronze Age, while the relationship between dwellings and graves

Bronze objects from the Bronze Age of both native and foreign origin have been found in Sweden. These include weapons such as axes, swords and spearheads, dress pins and neck and arm rings of bronze. All native objects are made of imported bronze.

Imported bronze objects have been found mainly in Skåne and on Gotland, but also in Västergötland, Östergötland, Värmland and Mälardalen. In most cases they have been deliberately deposited—"sacrificed". Bronze objects are also found in graves.

There is evidence of a barter system for "luxury" or "prestige" goods in most parts of Europe during the Early Bronze Age, which indicates a stratified society.

Among the more remarkable bronze finds are a scimitar from Heda, Östergötland, an example of an early import from a far-off land. The Pile find from Tygelsjö in Skåne is one of the oldest metal hoards in Sweden, containing a mixture of west and central European objects.

The unique find of 13 ceremonial shields at Fröslunda on Kålland, Västergötland, is from the Late Bronze Age. They are presumed to have come from northern central Europe, and only some 20 in all were known previously.

Another deposit from the Late Bronze Age, which also indicates central European contacts, is the bronze armour for a horseman found at Eskelhem on Gotland. Yet another important find is the Hassle find from Glanshammar in Närke. A bronze cauldron, two bronze pails, two swords and 12 bronze plates were found when digging a ditch. The swords are of the central European Early Iron Age type, and the two pails are probably of northern Italian origin (photo p. 68).

along the Norrland coast is less well-known and may vary considerably.

In Mälardalen and Östergötland there are, apart from graves and rock carvings, many dwelling sites with characteristic heaps of fire-cracked stones. These are rubbish heaps made up of brittle-burnt stones from hearths and cooking pits mixed up with ashes and charcoal. They also contain pottery sherds, animal bones, grinding stones, chipping stones, crucibles for melting metal and so on. For this reason they are an important source of information about living and work patterns. Recent investigations have also revealed remains of post-built long houses of the southern Scandinavian type.

In Uppland, Västmanland and Södermanland there are some 5,200 known heaps of fire-cracked stones and in Östergötland another 500. Such heaps are also found on Gotland, along the Småland coast, on the Kålland peninsula in Lake Vänern, and a few in Bohuslän and at other places. Most of them are from the Bronze Age, but they may also date from the earliest Iron Age. The greatest concentrations in Sweden are north of Enköping, and around the flat Uppsala plain.

If we are to understand the location and background of prehistoric remains in the coastal landscapes, we need to know how the shoreline has changed. These changes were caused partly by elevation of the land and partly when the level of the sea rose. This was a vital factor in the emergence of settlement in Mälardalen during the Bronze Age, which stabilised and became more densely settled in the Iron Age.

Dwelling sites with heaps of fire-cracked stones are usually located in transitional areas between till and sedimentary soils. In the densely-settled areas in Uppland they lie close to the calcareous and fertile clayey tills. The graves are placed somewhat higher up and farther from the shore, indicating the areas of settlement in general, whereas the heaps of stones mark the actual dwelling sites. Rock carvings and cup mark sites are located close to dwelling sites and graves, and often close to the fields. Plough marks under dwelling remains and graves show how the fields were cultivated. Pollen analysis provides information about land use and the development of the cultural landscape in general.

Farming and above all cattle rearing were predominant in areas like Skåne, Halland, Möre, Gotland, Falbygden, Östergötland and Mälardalen and were also extensive in the southern Swedish highlands. Hunting, fishing and gathering food were probably important activities, to varying extents. Farming was less important along parts of the West Coast, in Värmland, and along the Småland coast and the Norrland coast, where hunting and fishing dominated.

This object to fire one's imagination was found in a bog at Balkåkra near Ystad. It was probably used in a cult ceremony, perhaps to carry sacrificial offerings. It has been dated to the earliest Bronze Age.

One of the best-preserved of the ceremonial shields from Fröslunda in Västergötland, with a decor typical of Sweden's very late Bronze Age, that is, the earliest Iron Age and the Hallstatt culture in Central Europe. Fröslunda is now the most important find place in Europe for such shields.

Rock Art

On a rock carving at Hede in Kville, Bohuslän a warrior is wearing a helmet and carrying a sword with a winged chape and a shield decorated with bosses, objects which may be dated by finds to the late Bronze Age.

Sweden has a considerable number of rock carvings and paintings. For a long time the dating and cultural background of rock carvings remained unclear. As late as the mid–19th century it was suggested, because of the many ship figures, that the carvings depicted Viking adventures. But it was established that they belonged to the Nordic Bronze Age culture in 1869, when B E Hildebrand identified swords in the Ekenberg carving near Norrköping as being typical of the Early Bronze Age. Dating Bronze Age carvings has become more accurate since then. Carvings in Norrland, as well as rock paintings throughout the country, are earlier, some from the end of the Early Stone Age.

DISTRIBUTION OF ROCK ART

Rock carvings and paintings are unevenly distributed in Sweden. Northern Bohuslän, the Norrköping district and south-west Uppland are the richest areas, but south-east Skåne and Tjust also have quite a few. In Norrland Jämtland has most sites, but the greatest number of figures are at the Nämforsen rapids in Ångermanland, where some 2,000 are carved in the rocky banks of the river. There are about 2,500 rock carvings in Bohuslän, Uppland has almost 1,200 and Östergötland some 800. These carvings comprise altogether more than 90,000 figures, 50,000 of which are in Bohuslän. They represent ships, people, animals and other things or consist of symbols or cup marks. Cup marks are the commonest type: in Bohuslän they comprise 65 per cent of the figures, in Östergötland 80 per cent and in Uppland 90 per cent. The greatest variety of figures is in Bohuslän, with a large proportion of ships, people and animals. Ships are also common in Uppland and in Östergötland, where animals are also frequent. Scenes are commonest in Bohuslän, often showing warriors, ploughmen, dancers and other human figures. In Östergötland hunting scenes are most frequent.

Rock carvings in Norrland are completely dominated by the hunting culture. Moose in their natural size are carved on rocks at the water's edge at Gärde and Lake Ånn in Jämtland. These carvings are probably the oldest in Sweden.

SETTINGS OF THE ROCK CARVING

The landscape in Bohuslän is characterised by small, open settlement areas on clayey plains and fracture valleys surrounded by steep mountain ridges. Rock carvings are found on rocks which have been polished by ice and are often washed by water, at the foot of the mountains along the cultivated clayey soils. The Bronze Age graves, large cairns and small flat cairns lie on hilltops and ledges facing the open country. The known dwelling sites are not so numerous, but they often lie close to carvings. In Uppland and Östergötland there are graves and dwelling sites with heaps of fire-cracked stones in the rock carving districts, but also outside them. In Södermanland, Västmanland and Tjust, too, there are similar Bronze Age remains close to rock carvings.

The reason why such large numbers of rock carvings occur in certain Bronze Age settlement areas but not in others is difficult to understand; there may be religious or social factors involved. It has been suggested, for example, that they might be substitutes for real votive objects. The location of rock carvings in relation to other prehistoric remains enriches our understanding of the cultural landscape of the Bronze Age.

Some of the most frequent types of figures in rock carvings are shown here from genuine prototypes with their archeological terms and the most general interpretations of their content and meaning.

Figure	Term	Interpretation
	Ship	Boat: battle ship, trading ship; usually, however, a symbol: sun ship, death ship, fertility, votive offering
	Crew mark	Crew on a ship, sometimes with heads and arms, sometimes with paddles
	Human figure	As a rule males; often phallic, armed, sometimes posing (worship, lure-blowing, procession); tall men: gods, warriors; females in coitus, procession
	Foot-sole	Bare or shod feet, often in pairs: footprints of an invisible god, territory marking by men
	Animal figure	Wild (deer, boars, moose): hunting game, totems. Domestic animals: cattle, pigs, dogs; horses: draught-animals, status symbols
	Circle figure	General sun symbol; crossed circles also stylized wagons (sun wagons, chariots); shields, torques
	Weapon	Axes and swords most frequent, spear heads; depicting real artifacts: status symbol or votive offering
	Frame or net figure	Non-uniform and difficult to interpret: trapping nets, standards or symbolic maps are some interpretations
	Cup mark	Universal symbol of life, fertility and possibly the female sex; also occurring outside the rock carving areas and older and younger than the rock carving tradition
	Scene	Figures engaged in one activity, certainly produced at the same time

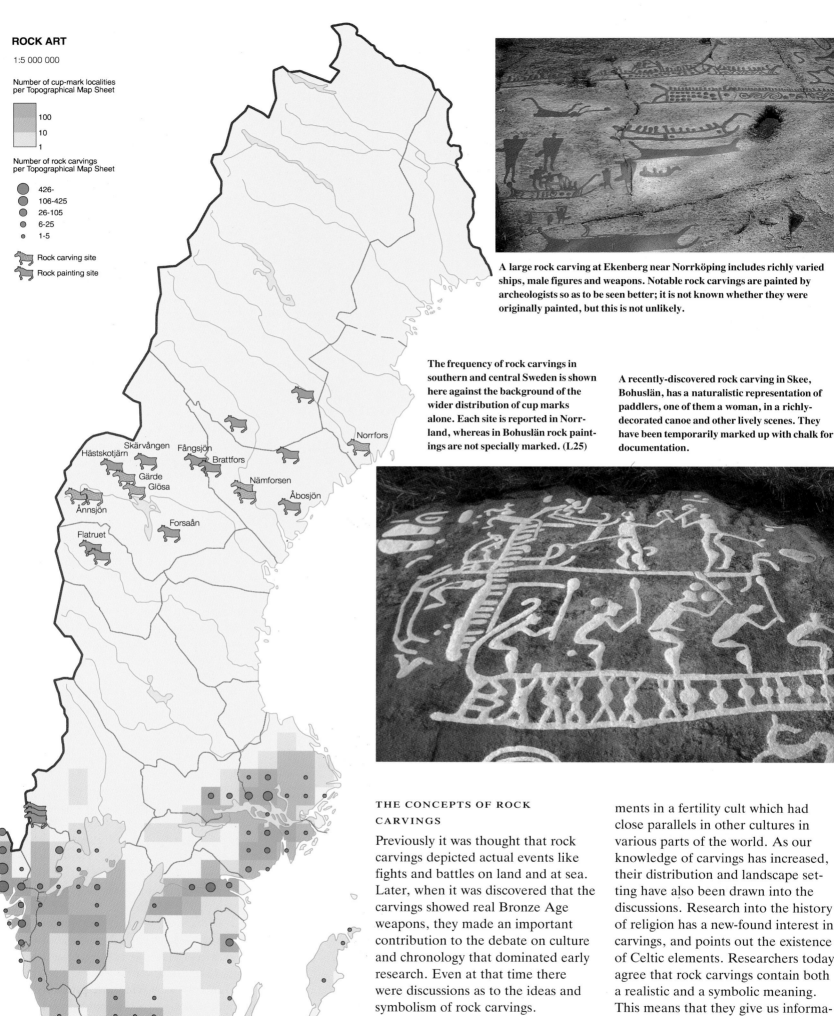

ROCK ART

1:5 000 000

Number of cup-mark localities
per Topographical Map Sheet

100
10
1

Number of rock carvings
per Topographical Map Sheet

426-
106-425
26-105
6-25
1-5

Rock carving site

Rock painting site

Norrfors

Skärvången   Fångsjön
Hästskotjärn   Brattfors
Gärde
Glösa   Nämforsen
Åbosjön
Ännsjön
Forsaån
Flatruet

A large rock carving at Ekenberg near Norrköping includes richly varied
ships, male figures and weapons. Notable rock carvings are painted by
archeologists so as to be seen better; it is not known whether they were
originally painted, but this is not unlikely.

The frequency of rock carvings in
southern and central Sweden is shown
here against the background of the
wider distribution of cup marks
alone. Each site is reported in Norrland, whereas in Bohuslän rock paintings are not specially marked. (L25)

A recently-discovered rock carving in Skee,
Bohuslän, has a naturalistic representation of
paddlers, one of them a woman, in a richly-
decorated canoe and other lively scenes. They
have been temporarily marked up with chalk for
documentation.

THE CONCEPTS OF ROCK CARVINGS

Previously it was thought that rock
carvings depicted actual events like
fights and battles on land and at sea.
Later, when it was discovered that the
carvings showed real Bronze Age
weapons, they made an important
contribution to the debate on culture
and chronology that dominated early
research. Even at that time there
were discussions as to the ideas and
symbolism of rock carvings.

Emil Eckhoff realised that the location of carvings close to grave cairns
was significant. Until the Second
World War the debate was dominated
by Oscar Almgren's theory that the
carvings were religious and ritual ele-

ments in a fertility cult which had
close parallels in other cultures in
various parts of the world. As our
knowledge of carvings has increased,
their distribution and landscape setting have also been drawn into the
discussions. Research into the history
of religion has a new-found interest in
carvings, and points out the existence
of Celtic elements. Researchers today
agree that rock carvings contain both
a realistic and a symbolic meaning.
This means that they give us information about religious concepts and
social conditions during the Bronze
Age, for example about fertility cults
and the emergence of a warrior class
in many parts of Europe.

The most important rock carving area in Sweden, and one of the most important in Europe, is on the hill slopes surrounding the Tanum plain in northern Bohuslän. The graves are on the hills above, and the plain was of great importance for the Bronze Age cattle farmers.

The two largest and perhaps oldest rock carving figures in Sweden are on the rock at the top of the falls in the river at Gärde in Offerdal, Jämtland: two life-size moose. Alongside, there are tracks of moose. There are also Stone Age dwelling sites nearby.

A rock painting with 8–9 animal figures, mainly moose, and two man figures, is on the vertical face of a precipice at Lake Hästskotjärn in Kall, Jämtland.

SETTINGS OF THE NORTHERN ROCK FIGURES

The settings of rock paintings and of the northernmost rock carvings are totally dominated by the hunting and fishing culture. In Jämtland, Härjedalen, Ångermanland, southern Lappland and Västerbotten they occur close to shore dwelling sites and trapping pits, in groups or large systems. There are notable prehistoric remains of this type at, for example, Lake Fångsjön in Ströms Vattudal, one of Sweden's richest prehistoric hunting areas and at Nämforsen and Lake Ånn. The sites in Norrland and Värmland give a good picture of a prehistoric hunting environment since the contact with water still exists.

The paintings in southern Sweden also often lie in areas rich in dwelling sites, for example in Tumledalen near Göteborg, where the paintings lie within a very compact set of dwelling sites from the end of the Early Stone Age. The paintings in Bohuslän have lost contact with the shore on account of land elevation; several of them now lie in uncultivated country at high elevations which in Mesolithic times were central coastal sites for hunting, fishing and settlement. A few paintings in Norrland, however, including those at Flatruet in Härjedalen, lie high up in the hunting area without any original contact with the shore.

THE CONCEPTS OF THE NORTHERN ROCK PICTURES

The rock pictures of the hunting and fishing culture were created, like the rock carvings, to send messages to the world around them, both the physical and the spiritual world. The subjects are stereotyped, but in many cases produced with great artistic skill. All known paintings have a strong ochre-red tone which comes from a pigment based on iron oxide. In many cases this mineral is to be found close to the paintings, often oozing from fissures in the rock. The lines are usually about a finger's breadth wide, which suggests that they were painted without brushes.

The paintings are without exception placed on almost vertical rock walls which slope slightly inwards. Both paintings and carvings reflect their surroundings closely, as the animal figures are from the local fauna. Moose are the dominant animals in the north; there are also reindeer and bear. In Värmland, too, moose are dominant, and they also occur in Bohuslän. The painting at Tumlehed is dominated by a red stag, which also occurs in one of the paintings in Värmland. These animals were important game, so the rock figures must have had a primary function in widespread magic hunting rites. This is also true of carvings of wild boars and red deer at Norrköping. The figures may also have served as totem symbols, that is, tribe emblems, but this interpretation lacks credence since the same animals are frequent not only in Sweden but also in Norway, Finland and the whole of northern Russia. On the other hand it is evident that the moose held a significant position in hunting culture cosmology in the whole of this area. The theory has also been advanced that these figures belonged to the proto-Saami cultural sphere preceding the domestication of reindeer.

The oldest carvings are probably about 6,000 years old, but it is more difficult to establish their latest date. One painting in Bohuslän seems to date from the Bronze Age, that is, about 3,000 years later. So far it has not been possible to date these paintings by scientific methods.

27

Graves and Iron Age Settlement

The largest cemetery in western Sweden at Dimbo in Västergötland is a good example of the relationship between cemeteries and settlements. The cemetery contains some 300 graves, and by the 16th century the village had more than 20 homesteads.

The illustration shows normal types of Iron Age graves and their terms and forms. The four at the top are the most common, especially in the round form, and may have different centre and edge constructions. All except the Iron Age dolmens may be found in each variant form.

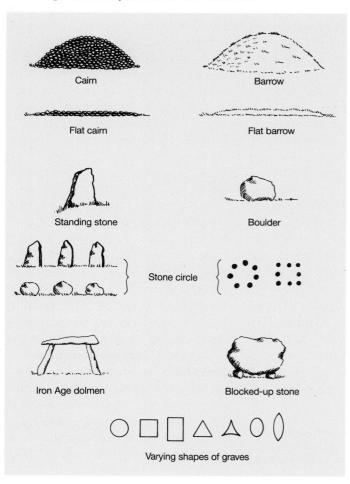

What is a grave?

In our time and culture a grave is a private place for memories, reflection and regret; it has a function more for those still alive than for those who no longer have any needs. But graves also have ideological overtones, and a graveyard need not be old for status symbols and other indications of social prestige to be evident.

The function of the grave as a *monument*—a memorial for the family or the clan—was essential for prehistoric man as well, since he had the same psychosocial background as we. Symbols of a society's *ideology* were also important; burial rituals and funeral customs depended on people's concepts of life after death and of the supernatural in general. These included the choice of funeral—cremation or inhumation. But the grave as a *symbol* was of greater and more practical significance in those days than now. In this sense graves bear witness more to the living than to the dead.

The grave's role as a *social* symbol is reflected in its external features: the type of monument, its size and architecture. High status is also indicated by internal features; above all the objects buried with the dead reflected their economic status. But these objects were not visible to the outside world after the funeral rituals—even though these were important—and they were primarily of religious significance. Low status may have been expressed by the absence of a grave monument above the ground—or of any sort of grave at all.

Graves have often functioned as *territorial* indications of claims of heirs or the clan to the land where their ancestors lived. Both the centre of the territory and its boundaries may have been marked by graves. Sometimes the grave of the first ancestor on a farm has had special symbolic significance, and the medieval provincial laws reflected the view that Iron Age cemeteries were proof of the villagers' claim to their land.

The *location* of graves was chosen with regard to the possibility of the landscape to create monumentality, to preserve the graves and to mark the connection with the dwelling site. In contrast to buildings, graves were

built to be seen by future generations for all time. During prehistoric times graves were plundered and covered with other graves, and in later times they were damaged by cultivation, but in many parts of Sweden the conditions are favourable for the preservation of prehistoric graves.

From an archeological point of view these hundreds of thousands of graves may therefore be seen as *documents* of colonisation and settlement. Detailed knowledge of prehistoric local communities may be obtained by investigating graves and dwelling sites. By these means it has also been possible to deduce the chronology of grave types, without which this general picture of the development of colonisation and settlement in the Iron Age would be impossible.

Graves and Cemeteries

The graves of the Stone and Bronze Ages are solitary monuments that dominate the whole landscape and lie scattered in sparse groupings. As a rule the graves of the Iron Age occur in cemeteries, lying close together, side by side, in an area set aside for burial. One definition is that a cemetery contains at least five graves at a maximum distance of 20 m from each other, but many cemeteries consist of several dozen or hundreds of graves. The distinction between individual graves and cemeteries is not, however, a matter of chronology alone. It is also dependent on social factors.

Cemeteries with cinerary urns beneath the ground were used in the Late Bronze Age in southern Sweden. It also happens that cairns and flat cairns of the Bronze Age type lie so close together that they are recorded as cemeteries. Solitary graves of Iron Age types also occur. Apart from the remains of damaged cemeteries these occur mainly in two archeological areas. In Götaland, mainly in the highlands, there are solitary flat cairns or barrows and stone circles or groups of such types. These date from the early Iron Age and are also found in cemeteries of the same period. In Bohuslän and Dalsland and in the Iron Age districts of Norr-

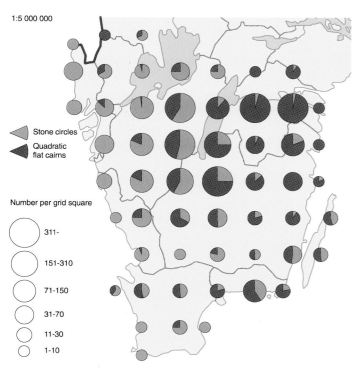

1:5 000 000

◁ Stone circles

◀ Quadratic flat cairns

Number per grid square

○ 311-

○ 151-310

○ 71-150

○ 31-70

○ 11-30

○ 1-10

About 1,550 stone circles and 2,400 square flat cairns, located either isolated or in small groups, are registered in Götaland. (L26)

Four urns of well-made pottery, used as containers for bones at the pre-Roman cemetery of Ekehögen in Onsala, Halland, resemble contemporary pottery from Jutland.

A cemetery at Amundtorp in Norra Lundby, Västergötland, contains among other types three monuments of standing stones: a stone circle (this side of the fence), a stone ship and a stone square.

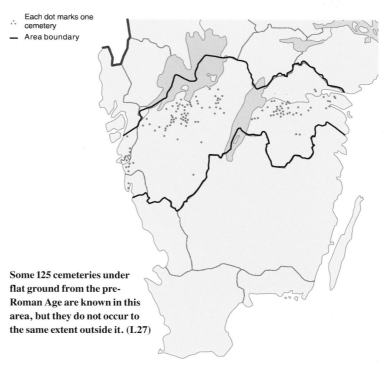

∴ Each dot marks one cemetery

— Area boundary

Some 125 cemeteries under flat ground from the pre-Roman Age are known in this area, but they do not occur to the same extent outside it. (L27)

land there are similarly scattered graves of the barrow type, also mostly from the Early Iron Age, but also in cemeteries of the whole period. In eastern Central Sweden there are mainly cemeteries, most of which have been well preserved, which has made the analysis of Iron Age districts most reliable here.

It is not clear why land was set aside for cemeteries. An important factor ought to have been that the settlements were stable ones. The use of the land may also have been regulated, that is, the result of cooperation between part-owners in an enclosure or a village.

STONE CIRCLES AND SQUARE FLAT CAIRNS

These two characteristic types occur in Götaland, often singly or in small groups, whereas they are more uncommon in Svealand, where they usu-

ally stand in cemeteries. Their distribution shows great variations. Stone circles are predominant in western Sweden and squares in Östergötland. The ideology behind these types of graves is unknown; both contain simple burials of cremated bodies from the Early Iron Age. Squares often stand outside the present-day settlement, while circles are both within it and outside. In the latter case there is probably a connection with a mobile culture and extensive farming, mainly on high land where they occur together with large areas of clearing-cairns.

CEMETERIES FROM THE PRE-ROMAN IRON AGE

A particular kind of old cemetery is found in the two central provinces of Götaland and on the West Coast. It consists of hidden graves packed close together under the ground in sandy ridges on the clay plains. The clay was used for pasture while the sandy soil was cultivated. These cemeteries contain a complete population with regard to age and sex, which becomes unusual at a later date. They were mainly used in pre-Roman times. New graves were not placed on top of old ones, which implies that these were marked above the ground, with wooden sticks or stones, for example. Some become normal Iron Age cemeteries around the beginning of the Christian era.

Early Cemeteries in South-West Sweden

It is difficult to make an overall analysis of the cemeteries preserved in this region. There are not very many of them, but they vary greatly and their dating back to the Early Iron Age is not wholly reliable.

CEMETERIES WITH FLAT CAIRNS AND BARROWS

One type of combination is similar to the early cemeteries in eastern Sweden and is dominated by round flat structures. They may consist of bare stone or be covered with turf but are always low. A central construction may consist of selected stones and the edge may be marked by a chain of stones or a bank of earth. Variations are particularly common in Västergötland.

Cairns sometimes form part of the cemetery. These may date back to the Bronze Age but may also be contemporary with the Iron Age graves. Small cemeteries consisting of cairns and flat cairns only may belong entirely to the Bronze Age. Such cemeteries are found on the West Coast, and in Värmland, southern Västergötland and Småland. It is the *dominance* of flat structures of the early types that characterises this group.

"STONE CEMETERIES"

This combination of graves is dominated by constructions using selected stones. Solitary standing stones are common. Stone circles, squares and ovals as well as ship-formed ones are combined with standing or rounded stones. One particular type is the Iron Age dolmen, common in southwest Småland. Cairns, flat cairns and triangles of bare stone may also be included, together with a few flat barrows. Some cemeteries have many unfilled stone settings (consisting of a stone edge only), either round, oval or ship-formed.

DATING AND CULTURAL BACKGROUND

All these cemeteries were used during the Roman Iron Age and the Migration Period. Cremation graves are predominant, but rich graves containing inhumed bodies also occur. The two maps covering a total of about 1,635 cemeteries give a picture of the extent of the settlement, to which should be added scattered Iron Age graves and on the plains destroyed graves.

Number of cemeteries per Topographical Map Sheet

75
35
15
5
1
—— Limit of report

There are about 950 cemeteries in south-west Sweden dominated by flat cairns and flat barrows (left) and about 680 cemeteries dominated by monuments of selected stones (right). (L28, L29)

In the cemetery called Torsa Stones in Almesåkra, Småland, is a triangular flat cairn of bare stones and a few standing stones in a circle.

The cemetery on Hjortahammar's headland in Blekinge is of the same type as at Hjortsberga; in the foreground, quadratic unfilled stone settings.

The cemetery at Hjortsberga, Blekinge, has 120 monuments: barrows and triangular flat barrows surrounded by a gully, but a majority of low, as a rule unfilled stone settings with stone edges, most of them in ship form. Such cemeteries in Blekinge are from the late Iron Age.

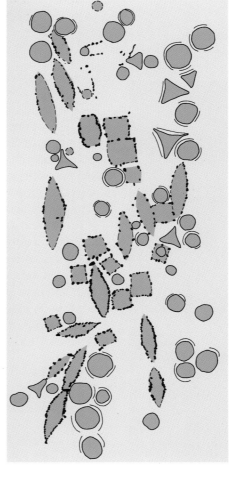

Number of cemeteries
per Topographical
Map Sheet

300
155
75
35
15
5
1

More than 4,400 early Iron Age cemeteries of the
east-Swedish type are known, most of them in the
Lake Mälaren area and in eastern Östergötland.
(L30)

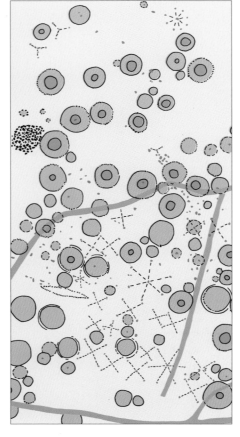

The largest cemetery in Uppland of the same type as the one at Jordbro is
near Malmby in Närtuna. It has, among other types, round, flat barrows
with stone edges and standing stones.

Cemeteries of flat cairns and barrows are most common in Västergötland and in other districts which have
been settled continuously since the
Early Iron Age. "Stone cemeteries"
often lie in forestland outside present-
day settlement districts. There is a noticeable concentration of them in
north-western Småland and southern
Västergötland, where large areas do
not have barrow cemeteries from the
Late Iron Age. Two extreme examples are the neighbouring municipalities of Vaggeryd, with 79 "stone
cemeteries" and one barrow cemetery, and Värnamo, with 11 "stone cemeteries" and 103 barrow cemeteries.
The most resonable explanation is
that parts of the early settlement area
were abandoned during the Late Iron
Age, while other areas were colonised
and flourished.

In Halland, Värend, Skåne and
Blekinge there are a number of large
cemeteries of standing stones, stone
circles and squares, stone ships and
unfilled stone settings, but also with
barrows and turfed triangular structures. They date from the Early Iron
Age onwards or only from Late Iron
Age.

A section of Sweden's largest cemetery from the
early Iron Age, at Jordbro in Österhaninge,
Södermanland. The cemetery consists of 675
visible graves, including round, flat barrows,
standing stones and stone circles and squares,
joined together here by dotted lines. The photograph to the left shows uncovered, flat barrows
with a central cairn and an outer stone edge.

The Early Iron Age in Eastern Central Sweden

It has long been known that certain
cemeteries in Central Sweden may be
dated to the Early Iron Age, mainly
Roman times and the Migration Period.
As in Western Sweden these cemeteries are dominated by round, low flat
barrows, which may also have corresponding constructions in the centre
and round the edges. In the earliest
parts there may be flat cairns which
date back to the Late Bronze Age
and pre-Roman times.

There are also small numbers of
other types with local variations. Solitary cairns are common in Roslagen.
Standing stones are found in several
areas, in Uppland often in the earliest
parts. Solitary triangular and square
structures occur frequently, turfed in
Mälardalen and often with bare
stones in Östergötland and Kalmar
county. Stone circles are most common in Kalmar county, the number
decreasing further north.

The map also shows sparse cemeteries of cairns and flat cairns in what
were originally coastal sites. They
date from the Bronze Age and are
numerous along the north coast of
Småland, where an area from Mönsterås to Gamleby contains some 250
such cemeteries, reflecting the coastal
occupations of the Bronze Age.

Most of the 4,430 recorded cemeteries are small—between 5 and 20
graves in each. The number of graves
grows with every excavation with
a factor from two to ten in comparison with the number previously recorded, partly because of graves
found under flat ground and partly
because low graves have been concealed by humus and vegetation.

Particularly in Mälardalen these
cemeteries lie on higher and lighter
soils than later cemeteries and at
some distance from settlements in historic times. There are, however, in
some large cemeteries graves of both
the early and the late type, which suggests a long, local continuity of settlement. Parts of Mälardalen and
eastern Östergötland have a much
greater density of cemeteries than
both other parts of the region and
south-west Sweden. Even though
cemeteries have been preserved better in these parts of Sweden, differences in population and/or burial
customs must be taken into account
when trying to explain this situation.

The largest cemetery on Öland, at Gettlinge, has more than 300 graves with typical monuments: standing stones, stone circles and squares and stone ships, as well as barrows and numerous flat barrows.

The cemetery called Gålrum in Alskog on Gotland shows, among others, typical flat barrows with a central cairn and an outer edge of stones.

Iron-Age Cemeteries on Gotland and Öland

Cemeteries on Gotland and Öland cannot be grouped chronologically in the same way as on the mainland, but have their own combinations. The geology and topography of the islands give the cultural landscape a homogenous character. On the other hand there are great differences in the size, shape and chronology of these cemeteries. There are about 310 cemeteries on Öland and about 980 on Gotland. It show the lowest figures in a few totally-cultivated areas and in areas with large forests.

On *Gotland* several cemeteries were established with cairns and stone ships during the Bronze Age. Some were extended and grew large during the Iron Age, while others were abandoned. Many were established during the pre-Roman Iron Age. A number of large cemeteries were in use throughout the Iron Age, while others were abandoned during the Roman Iron Age; yet others were established then or during the Late Iron Age. During the whole of the Iron Age round and very low, flat barrows are predominant.

On *Öland* cemeteries were often established during pre-Roman times. They are dominated by low, broad, flat barrows, but include standing stones, stone circles, stone squares, stone ships, square flat cairns, stone

cists on the surface and sometimes barrows. Small cemeteries may be connected with stone house foundations from the Early Stone Age, while the large ones are located on the elevated shorelines near villages from historical times and the best land for cultivation. They contain graves from both the Early and the Late Iron Age, and the settlements probably have a complex history.

The "large" cemeteries, 54 on Gotland and 15 on Öland, also have an even distribution. The largest of all are on Gotland, with one exception in coastal parishes which in many cases have known harbours from the Viking Age.

Iron-Age Graves in Northern Sweden

Iron-Age graves in Norrland and Dalarna are found in two quite different settings mostly with different types of monuments. Firstly, there is a permanent farming district along the coast and the lower river valleys and round Lake Storsjön in Jämtland. Secondly, there are scattered graves and cemeteries along the shorelines inland at the same places as the early hunting and fishing culture sites. There are also scattered barrows in the mountain valleys of upper Härjedalen.

IRON-AGE FARMING DISTRICTS

Graves in the permanent farming districts are with very few exceptions of the barrow type. With local variations some 20 to 60 per cent of graves probably belong to cemeteries, fewer in Jämtland. The map is therefore based on the total number of known graves, both preserved and lost. Just over 8,500 are known—3,200 in Hälsingland, 2,715 in Medelpad, 1,515 in Ångermanland, 670 in Jämtland and 410 in Dalarna. Of these 75 per cent are preserved on average.

The barrows lie within the infields of the present-day villages which form the central parts of the districts of historical times, thus demonstrating the continuity of the cultural setting. In Medelpad and Hälsingland the earliest ones were made during the early Roman Iron Age, and in the other provinces during the Migration Period. The graves are of the same type even during the Late Iron Age. Large barrows containing rich finds are limited to the Early Iron Age and mark chieftains' farmsteads, for

The parishes on Öland and Gotland have a comparatively even distribution of cemeteries as a result of the islands' generally similar conditions for settlement. (L31)

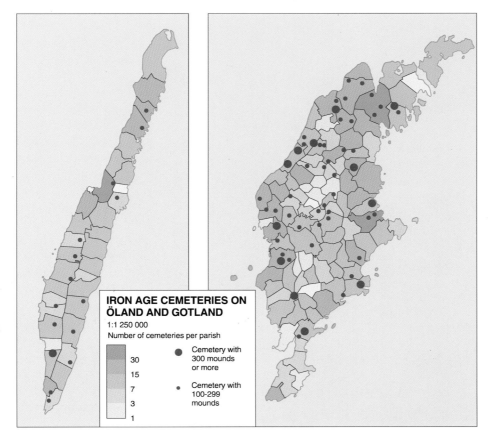

IRON AGE CEMETERIES ON ÖLAND AND GOTLAND

1:1 250 000

Number of cemeteries per parish

30	● Cemetery with 300 mounds or more
15	
7	• Cemetery with 100-299 mounds
3	
1	

IRON AGE GRAVES IN NORTHERN SWEDEN

1:5 000 000

Number of graves in agrarian areas
per Topographical Map Sheet

630
310
150
70
30
10
1

Grave sites in hunting grounds

● 10 or more graves
• 2-9 graves
— Limit of report

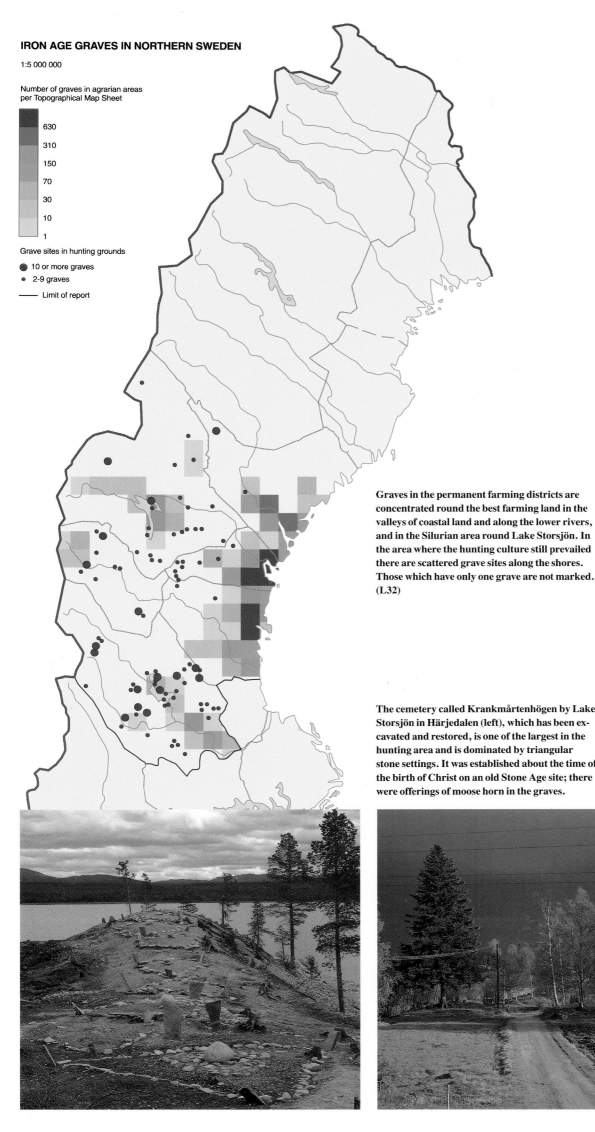

example in Högom and Njurunda in Medelpad and Hög in Hälsingland. The finds indicate a decline of settlement during the Vendel period (600–800 A.D.) and a new period of expansion during the Viking Age.

HUNTING-GROUND GRAVES

There are small cemeteries and sparsely scattered graves along the shorelines inland, usually insignificant flat cairns of bare stone but also real cairns and in the north barrow-type graves. In all some 700 are known. They have no connection with historical settlements but lie at or near Stone-Age-type dwelling sites, though no chronological connections have so far been established. The large cemeteries in Dalarna and Härjedalen are from the Early Iron Age and often contain votive offerings of moose horn. A barrow cemetery in northern Ångermanland is from the Viking Age, and the scattered graves may date from both the Early and the Late Iron Age. They are connected with the exploitation of hunting grounds, and in Dalarna with direct iron production.

Some 60 barrows from the Late Iron Age in the mountain valleys of Härjedalen are connected with both trapping pits and later shealings. They are the highest-situated prehistoric graves in Sweden (up to 900 m above sea level) and compose a unique cultural environment with parallels in Norway.

Graves in the permanent farming districts are concentrated round the best farming land in the valleys of coastal land and along the lower rivers, and in the Silurian area round Lake Storsjön. In the area where the hunting culture still prevailed there are scattered grave sites along the shores. Those which have only one grave are not marked. (L32)

The cemetery called Krankmårtenhögen by Lake Storsjön in Härjedalen (left), which has been excavated and restored, is one of the largest in the hunting area and is dominated by triangular stone settings. It was established about the time of the birth of Christ on an old Stone Age site; there were offerings of moose horn in the graves.

A typical, small barrow cemetery at Vattjom in Tuna, Medelpad, has some of the oldest grave finds from the Norrland farming community, dated to the first century A.D.

Barrow Cemeteries from the Late Iron Age

The largest group of cemeteries consists of barrow cemeteries from the Late Iron Age. Approximately 9,340 are known within the area recorded, that is, the mainland of Götaland, Svealand without Dalarna, and Gästrikland. Of these 3,525 are situated in Uppland, about 2,250 in Södermanland, just over 800 in Östergötland, about 680 in Småland, about 570 in Västmanland and 430–440 in both Västergötland and Bohuslän, while the other provinces have fewer.

COMPOSITION AND DATING

The barrow cemeteries are of uniform design. They are dominated by steeply vaulted barrows in certain areas, mainly in Finnveden, as well as in other parts of Småland and in Bohuslän and Dalsland. There are fewer real barrows in Central Sweden, and most of the graves consist of not very vaulted, flat barrows, which do not differ from the vaulted barrows with regard to their contents. In the West Coast provinces and Dalsland oval shapes are fairly common. Single large barrows may occur, especially in Västergötland and Mälardalen. A few turfed triangular and ship-formed flat barrows are found everywhere, and in Uppland a late variant consisting of

The cemetery called Kånna Barrows south of Ljungby, Småland, with some 300 graves, is completely dominated by the typical, very vaulted barrows of the Finnveden district. The oval variant is a western type.

rectangular ones is common.

As mentioned above, dating to the Early Iron Age is possible in Bohuslän and Dalsland, and some large cemeteries are continuations of earlier ones. Large cemeteries may also have been established in the Migration Period, and both large and small cemeteries were established throughout the Late Iron Age. The size of a cemetery depends both on the

length of time it was in use and on the size of the settlement and its organisation. Cremation with scattered burnt layers on the original ground surface is the dominant form of burial custom until the final phase, when inhumation was introduced under the influence of Christianity.

CEMETERIES AND SETTLEMENT

The distribution pattern of cemeteries is primarily dependent on settlements and social conditions in the Iron Age, but it is also affected by other factors. One such factor is the destruction of graves through cultivation, which may have occurred in places in every province but had its greatest effect in totally-cultivated districts, where almost all the land was cultivable. In the eastern Swedish provinces, however, both cemeteries and buildings lie on small strips of rocky and till waste land in plains and valleys.

Another factor is the influence of other burial customs, such as burial under flat ground, which was significant at least in the old Danish provinces. The spreading of Christian burial customs from the south to the north affects the number of graves in the final phase. The villages are also smaller in Mälardalen than in Skåne and Västergötland, for example, which means more cemeteries per unit area. The areas with most cemeteries were fully colonised during the Viking Age, whereas the South Swedish Highlands, for example, were sparsely settled at that time, becom-

BARROW CEMETERIES, LATE IRON AGE

1:5 000 000

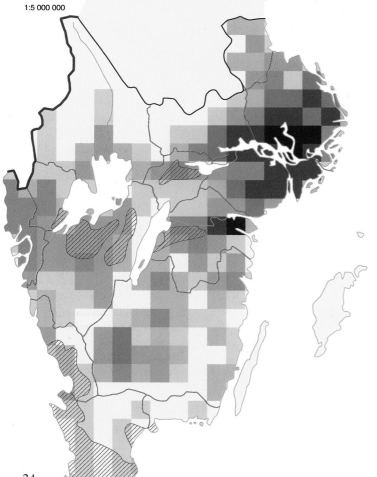

Number of cemeteries

- 300
- 155
- 75
- 35
- 15
- 5
- 1

///// Totally-cultivated district

—— Limit of report

The largest stock of prehistoric remains in Sweden from one period—perhaps around 200,000 separate graves—is to be found in the 9,300 or more cemeteries from the late Iron Age. Their distribution—apart from the totally-cultivated districts—illustrates the settlement-historical conditions from which the Sweden of historic times grew up. (L33)

ing more densely settled during the Middle Ages.

Taking these reservations into account, the map gives some idea of the extent of settlement at the end of prehistoric times. It is complemented by the map of Iron Age districts in Norrland, and in southern Sweden at least 60 cemeteries from the map of "stone cemeteries", most of them in Värend and Blekinge, should be included.

At the top of the hill at Granby in Orkesta there is a 40-metre-long house foundation terrace on which a huge hall was built, dated to the Viking Age. To the right a large runic inscription on a rock is visible, telling us that one of the owners of the farm in the 11th century was named Finnvid.

The distribution pattern contains many interesting, negative features. One of them is the empty areas along the future national border between the old Danish provinces and Småland/Västergötland. There are also empty areas along the border forests between Svealand and Götaland. Other gaps are noticeable along the western side of Lake Vättern and the boundary between Kalmar county and Kronoberg county, as well as along the central part of the coast of Småland. No permanent agrarian settlements arose in any of these three areas until the Middle Ages, and the same is true of Bergslagen, which also has no cemeteries.

It is also possible to see changes between the maps of the Early Iron Age and this one. From central Uppland, with equal figures for the Early and the Late Iron Age, colonisation is apparent towards northern Uppland/Gästrikland, the lower basin of Lake Mälaren and the archipelago. In Östergötland several areas round Linköping show higher figures for the Early Iron Age, which suggests that there was a concentration of settlements in the later period. Round Jönköping the already-mentioned lack of

The cemetery at Åsa on the island of Selaön in Södermanland has the characteristic close connection with the village toft. What is more unusual is its size, with 250 visible graves, whose variations indicate that the cemetery dates back to the early Iron Age. To the latest Viking period belong barrows, a rune stone and probably a monumental stone ship as well.

barrow cemeteries is noticeable in areas with significant settlements from the Early Iron Age. Bohuslän, Dalsland and Värmland appear to be a colonisation region during the Late Iron Age, even if certain barrow cemeteries are older.

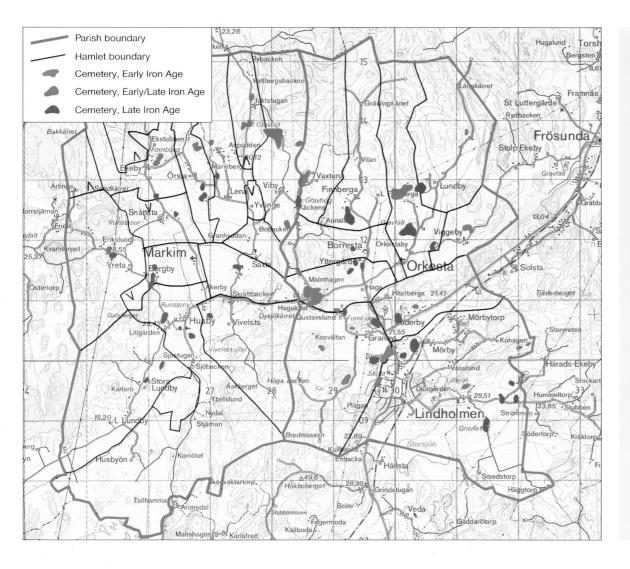

Legend:
- Parish boundary
- Hamlet boundary
- Cemetery, Early Iron Age
- Cemetery, Early/Late Iron Age
- Cemetery, Late Iron Age

MARKIM AND ORKESTA

The map presents a detailed picture of cemeteries and the development of settlement in a compact Iron Age district. Three types of cemetery are seen here: 19 Early Iron Age cemeteries, three of which are unusually large; at least two cemeteries showing continuity between the Early and Late Iron Age; and some 40 Late Iron Age cemeteries. Some of them—at Orkesta, Finnberga and Lundby—are also unusually large, while other villages have several cemeteries, for example Borresta, Bergby, Husby and Granby. The early cemeteries are on light soil in present-day forestland, the later ones near the villages, on the slopes of the hillocks down to the clay plain.

These well-preserved cemeteries allow us to estimate the size of the settlement and population during the Iron Age. Most of the early cemeteries and dwelling places were abandoned around the middle of the 10th century and a more compact settlement was gradually established closer to the clay plains, which also meant changes in farming methods.

Agriculture during the Iron Age and the Middle Ages

The cultural landscape of Sweden is characterised by long continuity. Prehistoric remains and place names demonstrate how the living countryside has its roots in prehistory. During expansive periods new settlements were established—sometimes only to be abandoned in the next period of decline. Increasingly intensive exploitation of the land also obliterated many of the traces of former eras in our old core districts.

When the totally-cultivated district of Vinberg, Halland, was the object of a test investigation, several indications of settlements were found. The upper picture shows the position of an uncovered dwelling site in the arable land and the lower picture a house foundation from 400 A.D. being excavated.

In one part of Grödinge parish in Södertörn seven villages were abandoned when three manor farms were established, of which Berga has now disappeared. Several villages lie under Snäckstavik. Six deserted villages have one or more preserved Iron Age cemeteries. Klippsta and Svalsta (the present vicarage) in the north are preserved hamlets, while Karshamra in the east still has some buildings but the fields belong to Snäckstavik.

Concealed Dwelling Sites

Prehistoric remains hidden by cultivation are to be found mainly in totally-cultivated districts, where both prehistoric settlement and later deep ploughing were extensive. Modern investigations in these districts have revealed a concealed cultural landscape, covered up by cultivation.

Many sites cannot be identified in historical sources. They appear as hearths, post holes and pits of various kinds which can sometimes be puzzled together to form clear building foundations. Furnaces for the production of iron and fragments of crucibles and moulds have also been discovered. Obvious cultural layers are usually missing because the upper layers have been removed by tillage.

Numerous hidden dwelling sites are known both in areas of heavy clay and those with sandy soils, in districts like the coastal plains of Skåne and Halland. Dwelling sites have also been discovered on the plains of Östergötland, Västergötland and Närke. They usually lack any connection with villages known in history.

Many dwelling sites consisted of isolated farmsteads with two or three buildings. Sometimes, however, up to ten buildings have been identified at one and the same site. Larger complexes are to be found at places like Snöstorp in Halland, where 50 building foundations were discovered, and at Fosie near Malmö, where almost 100 foundations, spread among six dwelling areas and covered over by cultivation, were investigated. In these cases the areas had been inhabited for a thousand years or more. Many of the hidden sites can be dated to the Late Bronze Age-Early Iron Age. The most recent ones have affinities with the well-preserved Iron-Age farmsteads, which we are in a better position to study outside the totally-cultivated districts.

Deserted Hamlet Tofts

Hamlets which are known from historical sources have also disappeared as a result of eviction, that is to say, the farms were demolished after the inhabitants had been forced to move.

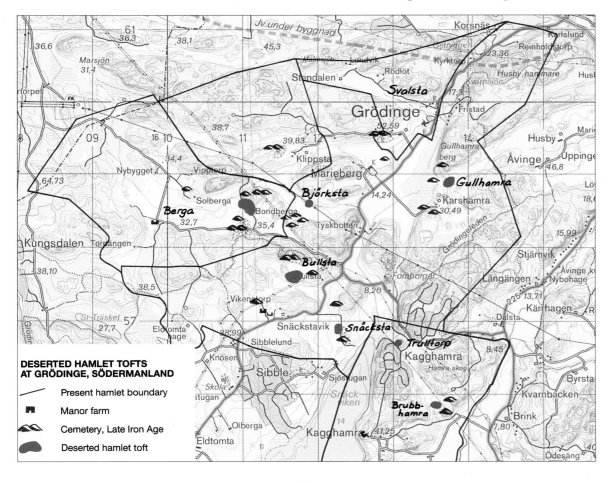

**DESERTED HAMLET TOFTS
AT GRÖDINGE, SÖDERMANLAND**

— Present hamlet boundary

■ Manor farm

Cemetery, Late Iron Age

Deserted hamlet toft

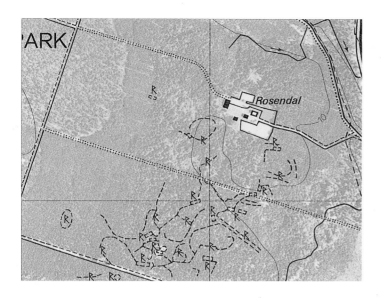

In Böda Crown park, Öland, there is a well-preserved hamlet with 12 house foundations, surrounded by a network of stone walls and cattle tracks to the outfields; to the west is a small cemetery. The croft called Rosendal was built in historic times.

During the Great Power period (17th century) officers and officials were paid by the State by being granted Crown or tax land. Thanks to this, together with buying up peasants' land, the nobility rapidly increased its land ownership two and a half times, which resulted in the formation of manor farms. Impressive manor houses were built on these estates, and the original hamlet buildings were gradually demolished. Within manor farms the division of properties and new cultivation decreased, which often resulted in the preservation of the foundations of old settlements, mainly deserted Iron-Age and medieval hamlets, often with adjacent Iron Age cemeteries. Very many manor farms were established during the 17th century in Mälardalen and Östergötland.

A later wave of establishing manor farms occurred during the 19th century, when land was redistributed and the inhabitants of many hamlets in the fertile farming districts were evicted. In these cases evictions were usually followed by cultivation, which also often meant that the old village sites were ploughed over.

Large parts of the cultivated area of the early Iron Age remain in former outfields on both sides of a parish boundary. The cemeteries are at the top of the forested moraines, and stone walls wind their way through the open pastures. The illustration gives a picture from the Iron Age looking eastward from the cemetery in the centre, with the cattle track and a dwelling site and fences round the infields (fields and meadows). Gistad, Östergötland.

Iron-Age Farms

Sweden's well-preserved remains of Iron-Age farms make it possible for archeologists to understand prehistoric environments and provide us with rich material for studying the development of settlements and living conditions.

HOUSE FOUNDATIONS

Despite their wide geographical distribution deserted farm tofts have features in common. The most characteristic ones are the foundations of buildings which lie within the central parts of the farms. They occur singly or in groups of two or more and are usually 20–30 m long and 8–10 m wide.

Particularly in central Norrland, but also on the mainland in general, houses were erected on man-made terraces which often have one to three sides lined with stone, while the upper long side is provided with a trench. On Öland and Gotland there are stone foundations with 2–4-metre-wide banks walled with stone, i.e. the walls have a drystone edge on both the inside and the outside, with the space between filled with small

Grödinge
Gistad
Böda

37

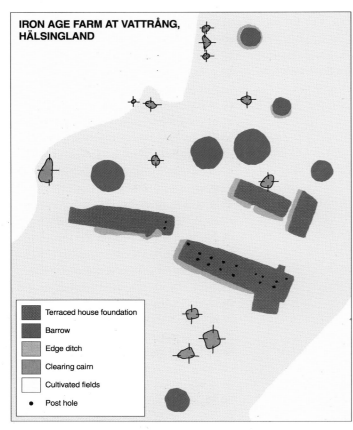

IRON AGE FARM AT VATTRÅNG, HÄLSINGLAND

Terraced house foundation

Barrow

Edge ditch

Clearing cairn

Cultivated fields

• Post hole

Some 160 deserted and never reoccupied Iron Age farms, each with one or more house foundation terraces and graves, are known in northern Hälsingland and southern Medelpad. They were abandoned around 500 A.D. The detailed map above shows a farm with four house foundation terraces, seven barrows and several clearing cairns at Vattrång in Harmånger. The largest terrace is 37×10 m. (L34)

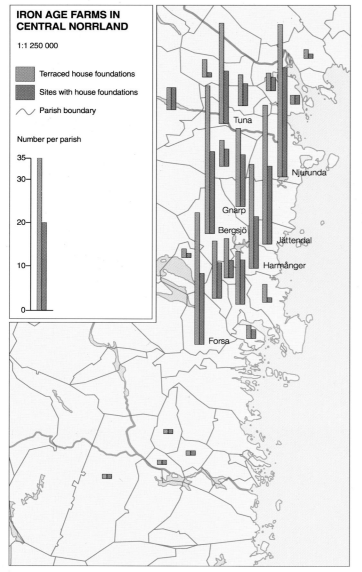

IRON AGE FARMS IN CENTRAL NORRLAND

1:1 250 000

Terraced house foundations

Sites with house foundations

Parish boundary

Number per parish

35
30
20
10
0

Tuna

Njurunda

Gnarp

Bergsjö

Jättendal

Harmånger

Forsa

stones and earth. Both terraces and foundations usually had three-aisled houses. Different parts of these houses functioned as dwelling space, stables etc. A few foundations are known from the Bronze Age, but most of them can be dated to the Roman Iron Age and the Migration Period.

Approximately 1,800 house foundations of the banked type have been recorded on Gotland. These foundations and their stone-wall systems are evenly distributed across the whole island and there are about 15 of them in each parish. Three of the largest parishes, Fårö, Lärbro and Kräklingbo, have at least 60 foundations each. On Öland there is a total of about 1,000 foundations, with an average of 25 per parish. The two parishes with most foundations are Högby with about 75 and Böda, which with its 125 or so foundations has more than any other parish.

Two hundred foundation terraces are known in Hälsingland and 85 in Medelpad, to which may be added a few in southern Ångermanland. There are also quite a few foundation terraces in the central Swedish districts.

FARM LANDS

There are graves close to the house foundations. The number varies, but both scattered groups and small cemeteries occur. In particular on the farms in Norrland the few graves lie very close to the foundations. On Öland and Gotland and in parts of the mainland farm foundations and graves are linked together by stone wall systems.

Examples from Östergötland prove that these farms comprised about three hectares of fields which were manured and cropped every year. Barley was the main crop, but rye and oats also occurred. Cattle, swine, sheep, goats and horses were common domestic animals. Each farm required about 30 hectares of meadowland and access to pasture.

There are large complexes of house foundations on Öland which lie on easily-cultivated land with good pasture, including meadows along the sea shore. These foundations often lie in village-like groups, surrounded by networks of stone walls, which indicate that several farms cooperated over enclosures. Other groups of foundations with less evident stone walls lie on the edge of or out on the heathland.

This picture of the distribution of the farms may be interpreted as showing the result of moving out from the earlier settlement areas. A large number of Early Iron-Age farms, both on Öland and elsewhere, were abandoned during the Migration Period, which mean that the foundations

The relics of Gotland's and Öland's rich, cultivated landscapes from the early Iron Age are evenly distributed over the whole of the islands, but are better preserved in some parishes than others. (L35)

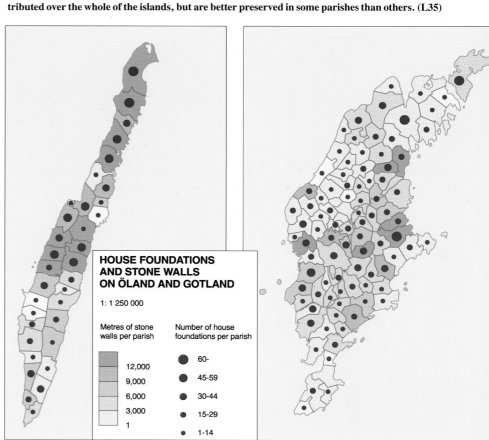

HOUSE FOUNDATIONS AND STONE WALLS ON ÖLAND AND GOTLAND

1: 1 250 000

Metres of stone walls per parish	Number of house foundations per parish
12,000	● 60-
9,000	● 45-59
6,000	● 30-44
3,000	● 15-29
1	• 1-14

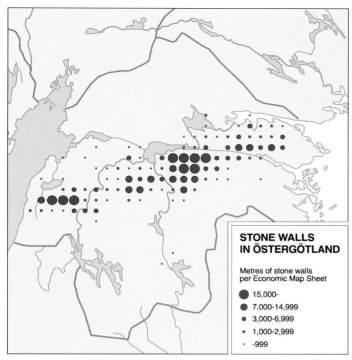

Stone walls are found in profusion on the rolling plain east of the river Stångån and in transitional areas between the western, totally-cultivated districts and the forests, as well as in Vikbolandet and just west of the Stångån. Their frequency reflects the original number but is also dependent on recent cultivation. (L36)

STONE WALLS IN ÖSTERGÖTLAND

Metres of stone walls per Economic Map Sheet

- 15,000-
- 7,000-14,999
- 3,000-6,999
- 1,000-2,999
- -999

have been preserved into our times. Plague, a less favourable climate and over-exploitation of the land may be the explanations. The villages alongside the elevated shorelines had more stable sites and are still inhabited.

ENCLOSURES

Stone wall systems are characteristic remains of Early Iron-Age farms. They consist of lines of stones one to three rows wide and sometimes stratified, which often wind their way for miles across the landscape without any straight lines or symmetry.

These stone walls are the remains of abandoned enclosures, comparable with the simple stone walls of later times. Their function was to separate infields—fields and meadows—from outlying grazing land and they enclosed cultivated fields, folds and cattle tracks.

On the mainland these stone walls are found where forestland meets the open plains; they have been best preserved where flat clayey land meets clusters of sandy and tilly hills and knolls.

The land used for crops—often in the form of enclosed fields—lay within the zone where easily-cultivated, sandy soil meets lower-lying, damper, clayey ground. The clay soils are now drained and cultivated, but used to be waterlogged meadows. The cattle grazed on the poor till areas until they could be let into the fields after the hay and corn had been harvested.

There are plenty of stone wall systems on Gotland and Öland, where 360 km and 310 km respectively have been recorded. The Gotland parishes of Boge, Buttle and Kräklingbo have more than 16 km of walls, while Böda, Långlöt and Runsten on Öland each have more than 30 km.

On the mainland Östergötland holds pride of place with a total of 450 km of stone walls—in the parish of Skärkind alone 50 km have been measured. In contrast Södermanland seems to lack them almost entirely. They do occur, however, irregularly in many parts of southern Uppland and in southern Västmanland. As for other parts of Sweden, a few isolated occurrences have been recorded in Västergötland and Småland. The stone walls on the plains may have been destroyed by cultivation, but on the other hand there may have been fences of less permanent material than stone.

A cattle track between two stone walls runs up to a settlement at Ryckelsby in Ekeby. Alongside the cattle track there are traces of cultivated old infields and several quadratic flat cairns are in the neighbourhood.

The extensive system of stone walls at Särstad in Rinna lies where the plain meets the forest. The long cattle track probably links up several settlements and runs out into grazing grounds in the forest.

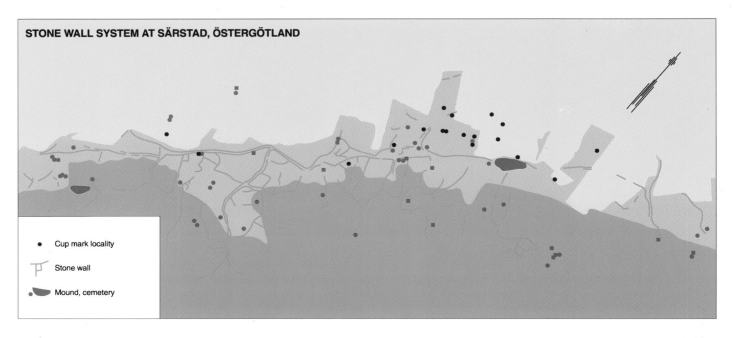

STONE WALL SYSTEM AT SÄRSTAD, ÖSTERGÖTLAND

- Cup mark locality
- Stone wall
- Mound, cemetery

Field parcel

Mound

House foundation

Stone wall

Clearing cairn

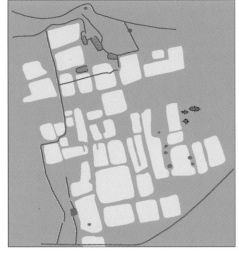

A large area at Vinarve in Rone consists of square field plots separated by banks and dated to the late Bronze-early Iron Age. Even though it has been partly cultivated since, it is clearly visible from the air. A farm, probably from the Roman Iron Age, was placed over the field plots, with house foundations and stone walls of the usual type for that period.

An area of steeply terraced fields and countless clearing cairns, created when the hillside was cultivated, can be seen at Allgustorp in Hasslöv on the northern slope of Hallandsås. Its date is unknown, but it might well be medieval.

**FOSSILIZED FIELDS
ON HALLANDSÅS**

Fossilized arable land

Field terrace

Clearing cairn

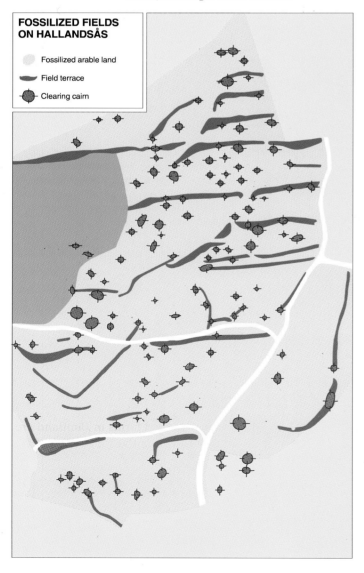

Fossilised Fields

Whether traces of ancient cultivated landscapes are preserved or not depends on the way in which the land was used at later stages. Fields, for example, may have been set aside as pasture and never ploughed up again. Deserted fields can then be left as fossilised fields. This term comprises a whole range of forms. Our knowledge of their distribution, forms and dating is as yet incomplete; only a few examples are given here.

FORMS

On Gotland there are many fossilised fields of a type similar to those on the continent and in the British Isles, where they are called Celtic fields. They consist of square or rectangular fields about 30 by 40 m square, generally bowl-shaped and surrounded by 5 to 8-metre broad banks. These fields lie on sandy soils in blocks that can comprise as much as 150–250 hectares. Approximately 150 such blocks of fields are known on Gotland, and

Medieval ploughman, portrayed in 1437 by Johannes Rosenrod at Tensta Church, Uppland.

they can in general be dated to the period 500 B.C.–200 A.D. Smaller blocks are found in Skåne and Västergötland.

These fields were cultivated by very simple ploughing, with a small part under cultivation for perhaps 2 to 3 years, while the rest was left fallow for 8 to 10-year periods. The lack of manure resulted in the cultivated part becoming impoverished, which was compensated for by moving cultivation successively round within the area. In the end the infertile subsoil was reached, and then the field had to be abandoned. It was therefore necessary to open up new fields, which meant that the acreage of arable land gradually increased.

Other types of fossilised fields occur on the mainland. One type was of long strips of parcelled land separated by banks of stone and earth. Some of them are as much as hundreds of metres long, while they vary in width from 7 to 40 m. They are usually grouped in areas of 50 hectares or more, in southern Västergötland, for example. They also often have numerous heaps of cleared stones.

Fossilised fields may also consist of terraces following the contours of the land, which were formed at the lower edge of fields by ploughing. This type may sometimes occur together with the previously-mentioned type of field, but they may also form larger areas consisting only of terraced fields. The terraces may be dated from prehistoric times up to the Middle Ages.

Other types of fossilised fields are mainly from the Middle Ages, including convex strips interspersed with hollows, called ridged fields. They usually lie on light soils, preferably on a slight slope. In general they are 4 to 10 m broad and almost one metre high. Their length may be up to 50 m or more. This type occurs in Bohuslän and Västergötland, but one fine specimen is at Hästhagen in Närke, near Örebro.

AREAS WITH CLEARING-CAIRNS

Numerous cairns of stones cleared from fields may also occur in areas with no other evident traces of cultivation. These cairns are low and round, usually 2 to 6 m in diameter and 2 to 4 dm high. In general they lie relatively close together, varying in number from fifty or so to over one thousand. The area covered is sometimes as much as 150 hectares.

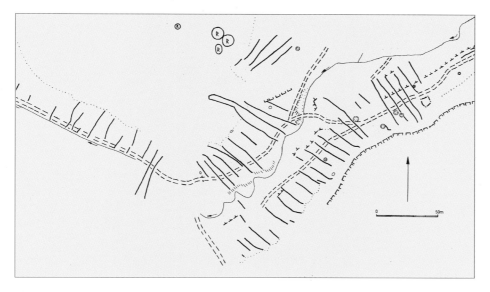

Area of ridged and furrowed fields in forestland on both sides of a stream at Kampetorp in Skee, Bohuslän. We know from historical sources that there was a farm here, Soltvet, which was deserted by the Middle Ages. Three Iron Age graves indicate that the place was also probably inhabited at the end of the early Iron Age.

These areas are situated on well-drained till or sandy soil above the highest coastline, so they contain plenty of unsorted stones and boulders. It is common for isolated graves of the Bronze Age or Early Iron Age types to lie among these relics of cultivation. Judging by the graves, cultivation may be dated to the Late Bronze Age up to the Roman Iron Age, that is, to about the same period as the large areas of fields on Gotland.

Traces of cultivation are scattered throughout many parts of southern and central Sweden. Several areas of fossilised fields of prehistoric types have been recorded in the forest districts of Halland and Västergötland. There are many important occurrences in Småland, mainly areas with clearing-cairns. Considerable fossilised field areas are also found on Hallandsås and Linderödsåsen, for example.

Deserted Medieval Farms

During the early Middle Ages there was extensive colonisation outside the old Iron Age districts. New farms were established in the outfields and what had previously been uninhabited land received its first permanent settlements. In the middle of the 14th century this trend was broken, turning into what is usually termed the late medieval agricultural crisis. There are several reasons for this cri-

The deserted farm of Svedäng, north of Lake Alsensjön, has now been cleared and is preserved.

sis, but the decline in population caused by the Black Death is one reason why many farms were abandoned at this time.

We only partly know the extent of this disaster, but it varied greatly. Historical investigations show that up to 40 per cent of farms in some areas were devastated. When settlement and cultivation ceased on some farms, their fields were used as meadows and pastures by neighbouring farms. Tenant farmers were able to choose to live on the more centrally placed farms. Those smaller, more isolated farms which had been colonised at later dates, often on poor soil, were then abandoned.

Remains of deserted farms have only sporadically been preserved, since these farms were to a large extent recolonised from the 16th century onwards. Traces of the medieval colonisation period consist mainly of a number of fossil fields, of either the terraced or the ridged type.

"ÖDESBÖLEN" IN JÄMTLAND

The best examples of the remains of complete medieval farms are to be found in Jämtland. Some 300 deserted farms are mentioned in historical sources, about 240 of which have been identified. Approximately 70 of these are so well preserved that it is possible to determine their original area and boundaries. They have remained completely untouched since their devastation, but were often used as hayfields.

These deserted farms mostly lie high up and isolated, some way outside the older farm districts. They lie on slopes with their fields arranged in terraces that follow the contours. The number of fields varies from one or two large fields to several small ones. The terraces are usually 0.2 to 1.5 m high, but in extreme cases may be 2.5 m high. Cairns of cleared stones also occur in large numbers, and in some cases cattle tracks, house foundations and cellars have been identified. The terraces suggest a field acreage of 3 to 6 hectares; a few, however, are considerably larger.

The deserted farms in Jämtland are mostly found on the fringe of the basin of Lake Storsjön. Only three have burial mounds from the Iron Age. Isolated deserted medieval farms are also found in northern Dalarna, Härjedalen and Ångermanland.

The spit of land between the lakes gives an interesting picture of deserted farms; as a rule there is one for every present-day hamlet—Kösta, whose village site lies north of the lake, has two. All the farms were established in the early Middle Ages, but half of them were abandoned in the late Middle Ages, evidently as a result of amalgamation.

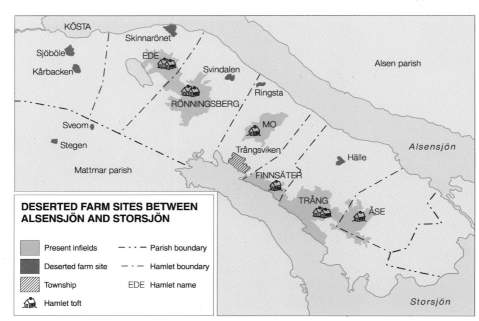

Strongholds and Power

Hill Forts

The term hill fort is an old name for fortified places from the Iron Age. Their form and location in the countryside varies from one part of the country to another. Most of them make use of the terrain's natural features for defence, usually by being located on hill tops.

The constructed parts of hill forts, together with precipices, cliffs, marshes and water, formed a strategic system. The more accessible sides of the hill tops are fortified with stone banks, and there are often outworks in the form of low ramparts on the slopes of the hill. The extent of the ramparts varies but can be as much as hundreds of metres long, a few metres high and, after having collapsed, ten metres or more broad. There are often dry-stone walls in the best preserved parts of the banks. When in use they were probably reinforced with timber coffers and wooden palisades. They often have clearly marked entrances, through which paths lead up to the hill top. Originally the entrances were probably provided with gates. Circular enclosed ring forts also occur on flat ground.

They may either have massive stone walls with many remains of constructions or consist of turfed ramparts.

Many hill forts—usually with massive ramparts—stand along old navigable channels, which means that they have been classified as offensive fortifications. They may have been the strategic forts of that time. Other hill forts, usually less strongly fortified, lie hidden away from settlements and are presumed to have served as places of refuge for people and cattle in times of danger.

Some hill forts contain cultural layers and have visible house foundation terraces inside or outside the ramparts. The finds are seldom of a military kind, but suggest a normal life of farming, cattle rearing and craft work. These forts are situated in the settled area of that time and can be called fortified farms. The contemporary term for them was *sten* (stone)—a word which often appears in the name of the nearest village or the name of the hill fort. Many of the ring forts on Öland have numerous house foundations laid out according to a plan.

Excavations have mainly been carried out in the provinces round Lake Mälaren, in Östergötland and on Öland and Gotland. Several hill forts have been dated to the period 200 to 600 A.D. The ring forts on Öland were fortified settlements in the Early

HILL FORTS

1:5 000 000

Number of hill forts per
Topographical Map Sheet

31
16
8
4
2
1

1,140 hill forts are known in Sweden, between Stenshuvud in Skåne and Frösön in Jämtland. There are 345 in Södermanland, 156 in Uppland, and 133 in Östergötland; Bohuslän has 111, Gotland 76 and Småland 68, while the other provinces have fewer. Their distribution is dependent on topographical conditions as well as the extent of Iron Age settlement. (L37)

A hill fort on Tarsta Hill in Sköllersta, Närke. It is typical of the larger hill forts in central Sweden, with more than 400 m long banks, double in places, and with partly preserved dry-stone walls up to 2 m high. There is a house foundation terrace inside.

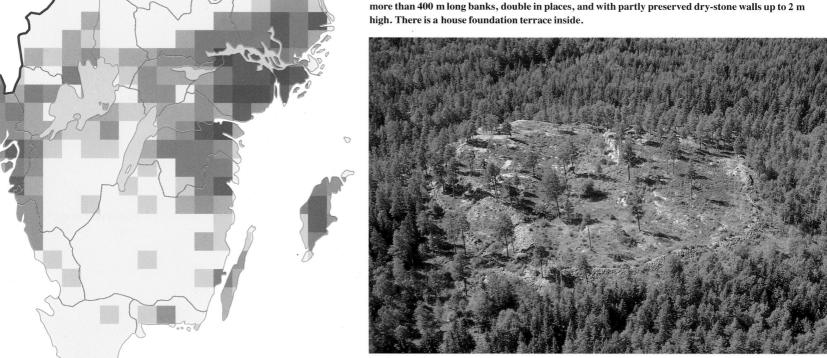

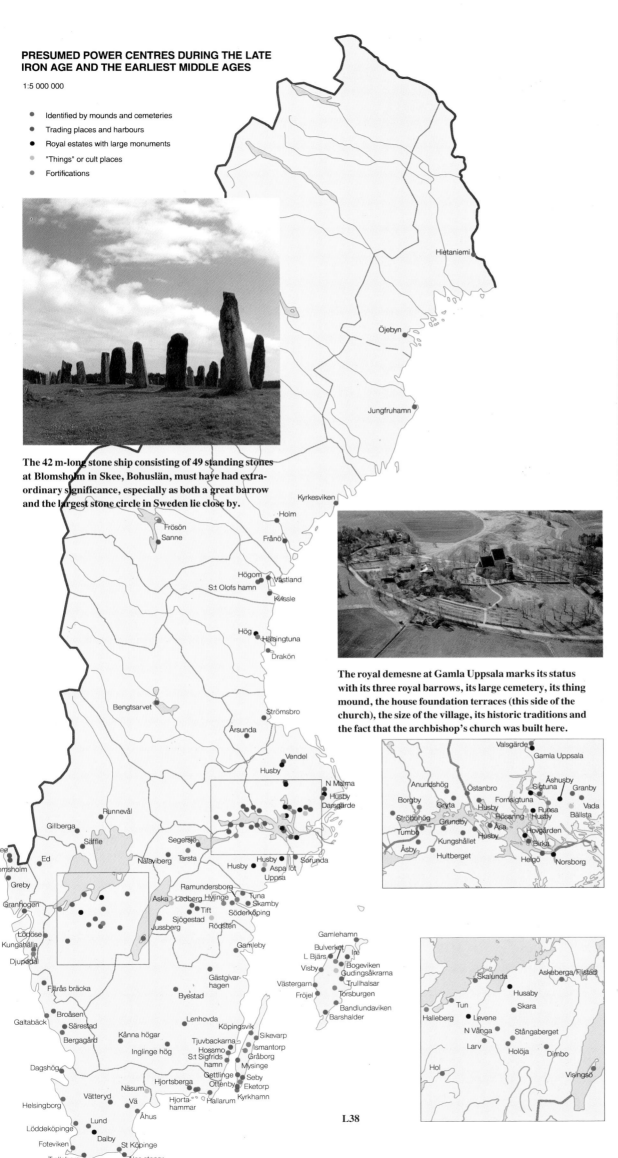

- Identified by mounds and cemeteries
- Trading places and harbours
- Royal estates with large monuments
- "Things" or cult places
- Fortifications

The 42 m-long stone ship consisting of 49 standing stones at Blomsholm in Skee, Bohuslän, must have had extraordinary significance, especially as both a great barrow and the largest stone circle in Sweden lie close by.

The royal demesne at Gamla Uppsala marks its status with its three royal barrows, its large cemetery, its thing mound, the house foundation terraces (this side of the church), the size of the village, its historic traditions and the fact that the archbishop's church was built here.

Iron Age, but were also used during the Viking Age and the early Middle Ages.

The largest hill fort in Sweden is Halleberg in Västergötland with an area of 20 km². The vast Torsburgen on Gotland has the longest ramparts. Other large forts, such as Ramundersborg near Söderköping, Träleborg on Mösseberg and Mjälleborgen on the island of Frösön, like the ring forts on Öland, also had other functions than pure defence.

CENTRES OF POWER IN THE LATE IRON AGE AND THE EARLY MIDDLE AGES

As early as the Iron Age certain settlements developed into centres for larger areas or for special functions, often in connection with the exercise of power. Different sources indicate these sites with different reliability. Finds from various excavations may reveal widespread trading at a settlement, high social status of those buried in specially constructed graves or extensive cult activities. Uninvestigated prehistoric sites can also provide at least indications of more than local importance. These include graves of monumental dimensions which are centrally located in a district. From experience we know that they contain the remains of chieftains. This may also be true of cemeteries unusually large compared to those in the neighbourhood, which may indicate that the place had a larger than usual population. Trading places may be indicated by their location. Royal demesnes, especially in the provinces of Svealand, are often mentioned in the oldest historical sources or known by the name *husaby*, which means that the farm was part of the early medieval Crown estate Uppsala öd. Constructed thing places are known in a very few cases, while cult places are more common from the early Iron Age. Some hill forts or other fortresses suggest, through their location, finds or construction, that they had more than local importance. Many places reveal several of these clues. Royal demesnes which are only known through history are not included. Rune stones also occur, but the fact that they are noteworthy has not alone been considered sufficient qualification. There is often local continuity to early medieval finds, structures or historic sources.

L38

Runic Inscriptions

The Runic Alphabet

The oldest runic alphabet of 24 staves was created around the time of the birth of Christ. The Latin alphabet and other sources were its models. In the 6th century it was in use in practically the whole of northern Europe; the majority of inscriptions using the oldest alphabet have been found in southern Scandinavia.

This oldest alphabet is called the primitive Norse runic series. Inscriptions using these staves are found on portable objects such as weapons and ornaments, but seldom on standing stones. The texts are brief and often difficult to interpret.

The primitive Norse series was used until the 8th century A.D., when it was superseded by the Viking series, which has 16 staves. This exists in two main versions, standard runes and short twig runes. The Viking runic series was used only by Scandinavians.

HISTORY OF RUNIC RESEARCH

The first runic researcher was *Johannes Bureus* (1568–1652). In 1594 he and a few draughtsmen began to record runic inscriptions in Sweden.

Many inscriptions which no longer exist today are in these early records, giving us good insight into the contents of the lost texts.

Since then men like *Olof Celsius* (18th century) and *Richard Dybeck* (19th century) have followed Bureus' lead.

In the early 20th century publication was started of all the runic inscriptions in Sweden in the series "Sweden's Runic Inscriptions".

Viking Runic Inscriptions

More than 2,500 Viking runic inscriptions have been recorded on Swedish territory, most of them incised on memorials during the last few decades of the 10th century and the 11th century. The majority of rune stones are found in the densely-populated, prosperous areas, but with a clear predominance round Lake Mälaren and particularly in Uppland. It was usually chieftains that had rune stones raised in their memory. Some 500 other runic inscriptions in stone have been recorded in the rest of Scandinavia and in other parts of the Viking world.

The texts are built up according to a formula. The names of those who had the monument raised and the name of the dead person and their family relationships form the main part.

Runic texts have regional variations in the choice of words and spelling. Inscriptions from Mälardalen, for example, often state that the stones were raised "in memory of his good son" etc. But above all in inscriptions in Västergötland they read in memory of "his son, a very capable young man" etc.

ORNAMENTATION

Rune stones are mainly considered to be memorial stones containing written text, but they are also superb works of art.

Rune stone styles are divided into a central Scandinavian and a southern Scandinavian type. The characteristics of the central Scandinavian type are animal figures in gentle, flowing lines with a flexible rhythm, whereas the southern Scandinavian style is characterised by abrupt lines that are not joined in gentle transitions but collide with each other.

CHRISTIAN ELEMENTS

The main period in which rune stones were raised coincided with the Christian mission. This is evident from the inscription on the northernmost rune stone, on Frösön in Jämtland: "Östman, son of Gudfast, had this stone raised and this bridge built, and he let Jämtland be Christian. . . " The significance of Christianity and its expansion is also evident from the crosses that often decorate rune stone inscriptions and that many inscriptions end with a prayer. This can be simple: "May God help his soul", or a little longer: "May God and God's mother help his spirit and soul, grant him light and paradise." Sometimes the person was baptised on his death bed.

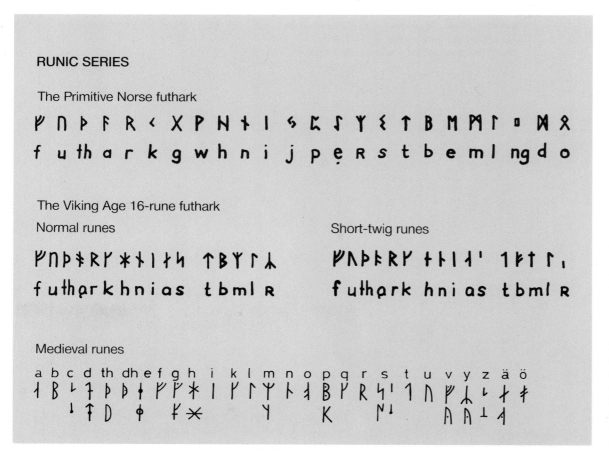

RUNIC SERIES

The Primitive Norse futhark

f u th a r k g w h n i j p ẹ R s t b e m l ng d o

The Viking Age 16-rune futhark

Normal runes

f u th a r k h n i a s t b m l R

Short-twig runes

f u th a r k h n i a s t b m l R

Medieval runes

a b c d th dh e f g h i k l m n o p q r s t u v y z ä ö

Runic signs are made up of vertical main staves and slanting staves. Runes were primarily intended to be carved in wood. The lines cut straight across or at an angle across the grain. In the Viking runic series most of the runes were used for several sounds. No distinction was made between voiced and unvoiced consonants, for example: t and d were both written with the t rune.

RUNE STONES

1:5 000 000

Number of Viking Age rune stones/10 km² per municipality

- 10-
- 5-9
- 1-4
- -1
- No rune stones
- • Stone inscription using the Primitive Norse runic series
- • Rune stone mentioned in the text

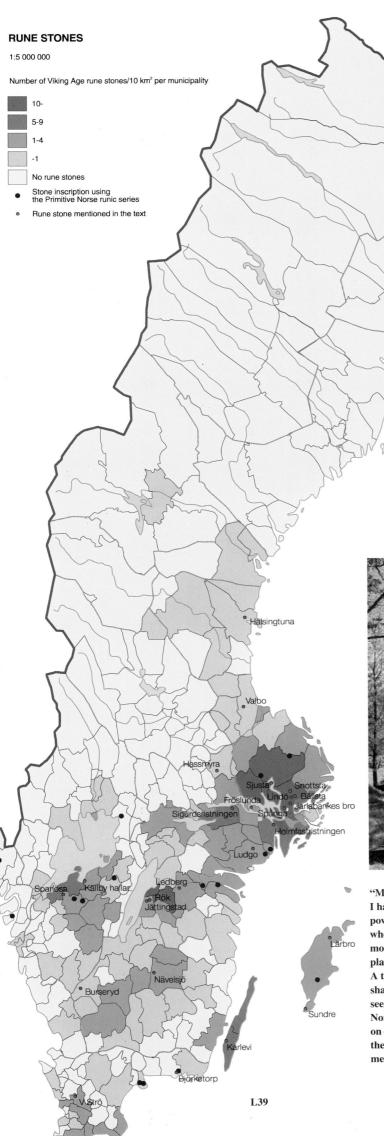

Hälsingtuna

Valbo

Hassmyra

Sjusta
Fröslunda Lindö Snottsta
Sigurdsristningen Spånga Bälsta
Jarlabankes bro
Holmfastristningen

Ludgo

Sparlösa Källby hallar Ledberg
Rök
Jättingstad

Lärbro

Sundre

Nävelsjö

Burseryd

Karlevi

Björketorp

V.Strö

L39

A stone at Hög's Church in Hälsingland is carved with the staveless runic series. The inscription begins at the bottom left and reads: "Gudnjut Truson had this stone raised and made the bridge for his brothers Åsbjörn and for Gudlev".

The rune stone at Högby, Östergötland, has inscriptions on two sides:"Torgärd raised this stone for Assur, her uncle. He ended his life eastward in Greece". The back (below) bears a verse in an Old Nordic metre.

"Good man Gulle
sired five sons.
Fell on Föret
fierce fighter Åsmund,
ended Assur
eastward in Greece
was on Bornholm
Halvdan killed
Kåre was *atuti*.
Dead too is Boe.
Torkel carved the runes."

The rune stone in Altuna churchyard in Uppland was raised to the memory of a father and his son, who according to the text were burned to death in a house. The most interesting feature of this carving is the images on one narrow side which depict the Aesir god Thor fishing. Thor is catching the Midgård snake on a hook baited with an oxhead.

"Mighty rune secrets I have hidden here, powerful runes. He who breaks this memorial shall ever be plagued with fury. A treacherous death shall be his fate. I foresee ruin." Primitive Norse runes inscribed on one of the stones of the Björketorp Monument, Blekinge.

Runes and ornamentation are filled in with red paint. When the inscriptions were new, they were painted in bright colours. The majority of inscriptions are found on standing stones. Mainly in Mälardalen they are also found on flat rocks. The inscription on the rock at Spånga reads: "Andvätt and Gärdar had these runes carved for Sven, their father, and Kättilvi, for her husband."

INSCRIPTIONS OF VIKING EXPEDITIONS

1:5 000 000

▨ Ornaments of South Scandinavian style	● On the eastern route
▨ Mixed area ornaments	■ On the route of Ingvar the Far-travelled
▢ Ornaments of Mid-Scandinavian style	● On the western route
	● Unspecified destinations

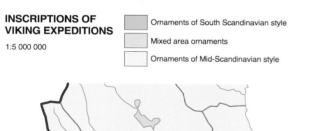

Expeditions to far-off countries were an important part of Viking life, which is why foreign journeys are often mentioned in runic inscriptions. Many stones were raised in memory of men who died in distant lands. But Vikings also returned home as rich men. A well-known expedition to the east was led by Ingvar the Traveller. Almost all the participants died in the Middle East. Many Ingvar stones were erected in their memory. (L40)

RUNIC INSCRIPTIONS REFLECT SOCIETY

Even though the inscriptions on rune stones are often short and stereotyped, they tell us a good deal about Viking society, about road and bridge construction, about the creation of "thing" meeting places, about pilgrim journeys and Viking expeditions.

Complex inheritances may be followed in various inscriptions, carved to the memory of persons belonging to the same family. Sometimes a chieftain's family can be traced for several generations. In Täby, north of Stockholm, there lived a man called Jarlabanke who had several stones raised in his own memory. Thanks to other inscriptions we also know about his grandmother and grandfather, mother and father, uncles, brother and sons.

Other inscriptions tell of journeys to distant lands, of men who took part in Viking expeditions to the east or to the west. Some returned home rich, others died far from home and were buried in foreign soil. Some 30 stones were raised to the memory of men who took part in the well-known Ingvar expedition to Särkland (probably in the Caucasus) and died in the east. Place names such as Gårdarike, Greece, England, Miklagård, Jerusalem and Bath are mentioned.

PLACE NAMES

The earliest evidence of many village and farm names is to be found in Viking runic inscriptions. Mention may be made of Lindö and Borresta in Uppland, Hassmyra in Västmanland, Fröslunda in Södermanland, Högby and Jättingstad in Östergötland and Sundre on Gotland. There are examples of place names from almost every province on rune stones.

The earliest evidence of the name Sweden is inscribed on a rune stone at Ludgo in Södermanland. The inscription relates that Anund and Ragnvald were "strongest in Suiðiuðu". The name Svitjod means "the land of the Svea people". The Swedish name for Sweden, Sverige, means the realm of the Sveas (Swedes).

PERSONAL NAMES

Runic inscriptions give us good insight into the system of Viking personal names. Many names, like Torsten, Björn and Ingrid are still used today, while others, like Grimulf, Orm and Vigärd have fallen into abeyance. The names usually contained two elements.

RUNIC VERSE

Some runic inscriptions are in verse, often using the ancient Nordic metre of eight short alliterated lines. One verse inscribed on a boulder in Södermanland reads: "I know Håsten/and Holmsten, brothers/ our greatest runemasters/ in Midgård./ They raised the stone/ and many staves (wooden monument)/ for their father/ Frösten." The earliest example of rhyming verse is on a stone at Vallentuna church north of Stockholm in a free translation: "In Holm Sea he drowned/ his boat went round/ only three safe and sound."

CONSERVATION OF RUNE STONES

Responsibility for conserving rune stones lies with a section of the Central Board of National Antiquities called The Rune Unit. Conservation and care are vital operations, not least now that we know that polluted air hastens the decomposition of stone surfaces. Geologists, chemists and stone conservationists are working to find methods to make surfaces more resistant to pollution.

Another threat is the growth of scrub in the cultural landscape. Runic inscriptions which are not preserved are soon overgrown by scrub if no one clears it. They become hard to reach, but above all the environment becomes less favourable for them. Algae, moss and the like grow well in damp and darkness, concealing the lines of the inscriptions. An overgrown inscription is cleaned with great care by specially trained stone conservationists, after which they are painted by a runologist.

Several medieval fonts were given runic inscriptions. It was common at that time for the object itself to speak through a runic text. The font at Burseryd Church in Småland is inscribed: "Arinbjörn made me. Vidkunn priest wrote me. And here I shall stand a while."

RUNIC INSCRIPTIONS IN THE CULTURAL LANDSCAPE

Most runic inscriptions are found at or near their original sites, albeit with regional variations. Rune stones are not grave stones but memorial. They were usually placed along roads, often at a crossroads, a ford, or a bridge, but sometimes in an Iron-Age cemetery. Sometimes they state that those who had the stone raised also "made the bridge for his soul". On a rock near Södertälje there is the inscription "Holmfast had this road laid and this bridge built in memory of Gammal, his father, who lived at Näsby." The inscription on a rune stone east of Uppsala tells that those who had the stone raised also built a ford.

In many places where today the land is drained and water is a long way away there was a great need for bridges and fords in the Viking Age. The sea level in Uppland is about five metres lower today than it was in the 11th century.

Relatively many rune stones are found close to or in churches, where they were usually taken to be built into a wall or act as a threshold stone and the like. Most of them probably stood close by, perhaps sometimes at a district meeting place which existed before the church was built. This is probably the case with the Rök stone in Östergötland, which has the longest of all the runic inscriptions and has given its name to the church.

Many rune stones act as boundary

Runic inscriptions were integrated in the cultural landscape. They were placed where many people would see them, at roadsides, by bridges, at mooring places and at cemeteries.

markers, either for hundreds, parishes or villages, and usually where a road crosses the boundary. There is a rune stone on the boundary between two Viking villages: "Here shall the stone stand between the villages".

RUNE WRITERS

Quite a few people knew how to read and write runes, but it was easier to carve a message on a piece of wood than to master hard stone. There were skilful rune masters who carved inscriptions to order, one of whom was Åsmund Kåresson. He established and developed the Uppland style of runic inscriptions and was followed by Fot, Balle, Livsten, Visäte and Öpir.

Medieval Runes

The custom of raising memorial stones with runic inscriptions ended about 1100, but runic staves continued to be used for a long time after. The number of staves was increased so that each one corresponded to a letter in the Roman alphabet. Most inscriptions were on wood, but many medieval grave monuments were decorated with runic inscriptions. Most of them are on Gotland.

There is a stone slab in the church at Lärbro with the inscription: "May God have mercy on Hegvar's soul, who lies here . . . five thousand years and one year less than two hundred years were from Adam to the birth of Christ. One thousand years and three hundred years and fifty years from the birth of Christ to the Black Death." It was laid in 1350 on the grave of one of the victims of the Black Death.

RUNES IN DALARNA

Runes were used in Ovansiljan up to modern times and the staves have been developed as Dalarna runes. An interesting feature is the message stick. A village meeting in Älvdalen in 1818 was summoned by means of a message stick inscribed: "This evening there will be a village meeting at the usual place."

CALENDAR STICKS

Prime sticks were a kind of perpetual calendar inscribed with runes that were connected with the church. They were used in a number of places as late as the 19th century.

Routes and Fairways

Part of a sunken road system with many tracks along the medieval Erik Tour in Sandhem, Västergötland.

Roads were originally links between farms and districts, but in time they attract settlements. This road through a valley in Gnarp, Hälsingland, provides a good example.

Ancient Routes and Roads

Throughout almost the whole of prehistoric time and in many parts of Sweden until a later date roads consisted of simple tracks that followed the terrain and could be changed according to needs. This type of track is still found today, mainly in the form of *sunken paths*. These tracks or furrows are the result of erosion where the ground slopes in the same direction as the track and consists of soil. When it rains it is difficult to walk along a sunken path, so people chose to walk or ride along the edge. This led to the creation of new, parallel sunken paths, in extreme cases dozens of them.

In order to avoid damp, loose or uneven ground people prefered to travel on gravel soils, rocky ground or ridges. The latter in particular provided good *ridgeways*. When bogs had to be crossed, *corduroy roads* could be laid, consisting of a bed of logs and branches. Corduroy roads were probably used even before the Iron Age. At least from the Late Iron Age onwards *embankments* of sand and gravel were built. In a few cases *paved roads* were laid, in the first place near settlements or grave monuments. *Bridges* of wood over open water have been built at least since the Late Iron Age. Especially on rocky ground or in the mountains tracks would be marked by *signs* like standing stones or cairns.

Routes whose existence cannot be proved by preserved remains in the landscape may be substantiated by tradition, as with the Lapp *migratory tracks* between the mountains and the forests, or *pilgrim ways* from various parts of Sweden to St Olav's grave in Trondheim. According to medieval laws newly-crowned kings had to travel round the country on the *Erik Tour*, which included specified crossings of province boundaries, where the people would meet the king.

An old road, known as "King's Route", across rocky land between Ronneby and Bräkne-Hoby in Blekinge. This place is also called "Runamo" after a supposed runic inscription—a natural phenomenon which was wrongly interpreted in the Middle Ages.

OLDER ROAD ENVIRONMENTS

1 Draget, Håtuna, sunken road systems
2 Dalkarlsbacken, Kungsängen, early state road construction
3 Rösaring, Viking "ceremonial way", maze
4 Göta country highway, Brännkyrka
5 St Söderby, Ängby, ford, rune stone, cemetery
6 Skålhamravägen, Vallentuna/Täby, rune-stone road and bridges
7 Benhamra, Vada, and Ekskogen, Kårsta, rune-stone bridges
8 Kungshamn, Flottsund, sunken road system
9 Jarlabankes bro, Täby, embankment, rune stones
10 Lingsberg, sunken road, embankment, rune stone
11 Lundås-Gråska, Edebo
12 Vik-Balingsta, prehistoric road, rune stones
13 Gryta-Salnecke, Erik Tour, bridge, rune stone
14 Östanbro, river crossing, Erik Tour, great barrows
15 Björklinge, ford, sunken roads
16 Högsta and Lövsta, two sunken road systems
17 Tumbo, rune stones by ancient road
18 Överselö-Tynnelsö, rune stones by ancient road
19 Blacksta, rune stones by ancient road
20 Önnersta-Penningby, Erik Tour
21 Aspa löt, Ludgo, thing site, rune stones
22 Stavsjö-Krokek, Erik Tour, monastery ruin
23 Släbro, sunken roads, embankment, rune stone
24 Border Sjögestad/Viby, sunken roads, rune stones, cemetery
25 Askeby, rune stone, sunken road, ford
26 Holavedsleden, Mjölby, sunken roads
27 Trehörna, sunken road, road embankment
28 Uppåkra, Vallsjö, rune stone, sunken roads, ford, cemetery
29 Flisby, rune stone, cemetery
30 Byestad, prehistoric road, large cemetery
31 Sillastigen, Angerdshestra
32 Nissastigen, Sandseryd, sunken roads
33 Munkabro, Nydala/Hagshult, corduroy road
34 Gunnarshylte bro, Hagshulta spänger, Hagshult, two corduroy roads
35 Ingemarsbo, Fryele, stones for road maintenance
36 Upplöv-Ed, sunken roads, rune stone
37 "Getaryggarna", Råshult, ridgeway
38 Sävsjö, Lenhovda, hamlet toft, cemetery
39 Heda-Värnhem
40 Vimmerby, medieval highway
41 Dalsebo-Krokarp, two embankments
42 Hjärpestad-Långöre
43 Rönnerum, Iron Age village
44 Lärbro, corduroy roads and names
45 Vatlings, Fole, paved road and picture stone
46 Gervide, Sjonhem, road embankment, Iron Age house foundations
47 Sälle, Fröjel, sunken road, cemetery
48 Ronnarve, Öja, sunken road through fossil field
49 Änge, Buttle, picture stones by ancient road
50 Hall, ancient monuments by ancient road
51 Stavers väg, Burs, road with traditions
52 Annelund, Visby, sunken road through cemetery
53 Roma stormyr, corduroy road
54 Runamo, Bräkne-Hoby, road crossing flat rock
55 Brömsebro, bridge, memorial stone
56 Kärreberga, sunken road system, fossil field
57 Vendike, Hjärnarp, sunken road
58 Högeväg, Maltesholm, embankment to castle
59 Grydebjär, Hörja, sunken road, ancient monuments
60 Pinedalen, Gudmundtorp, embankment
61 Rommelåsen, sunken road system
62 Kungsmarken, Södra Sandby, sunken roads, prehistoric fields
63 Fjärås bräcka, ridgeway with barrows
64 Hallandsås, Hasslöv, sunken roads
65 Fotstad, Övraby, sunken road system
66 Ljungby, cemetery, sunken road

The map shows a limited sample of preserved ancient road environments, the approximate routes of old Pilgrims Ways, which can only in a few cases be discerned in the landscape, and the medieval Erik Tour (royal route), which largely coincides with old and present-day country roads. (L41)

Growth of the Road System

The growth of systematically built roads was primarily the result of the expansion of central power and town culture.

The type of road varied according to the need. Country roads on bare ground were usually so bad that people avoided them for long and heavy transport, using wherever possible water transport instead. Where it was not possible to transport goods by boat, winter roads and sledges were preferred.

Winter roads were predominant in the southern Swedish highlands and north of the line between Lake Vänern and the mouth of the river Dalälven, but also locally, for example in Roslagen. The advantages of these roads were that they allowed heavy transport, were straighter, shorter and more comfortable and that they did not require much road work. In addition it was easier for the peasants to find time for transportation in the winter. Winter roads were of decisive importance for the export of heavy goods, market trading and the mining industry.

Country roads have always been used for shorter and less organised journeys which did not involve transporting heavy or bulky goods. Many

67 Drängsered, Gamla Kyrkvägen, sunken roads
68 Gunnarsjö, sunken roads, embankment
69 Danseredsliden, Härryda
70 Järneklevsvägen, Herrestad/Högås,
71 Grössby gata, Ucklum, village street/church road
72 Dyne-Hogdal, AK road 20th century
73 Trossö-Kalvön-Lindön, AK road 20th century
74 Kobbungen, Hogdal, sunken roads
75 Råggärd, road along moraine
76 Ingared, Hemsjö, sunken road, cairns
77 Hästebräckan, Hemsjö, extremely steep road
78 Ridvägen, Timmele, sunken roads
79 Roasjö, sunken road systems
80 Viskastigen, Öxnevalla
81 Karl XII's way, Dals Ed/Töftedal
82 Brurefjället, Tisselskog, old country road
83 Korsbyn-Bolsbyn, Hemmingsbol-Slobol
84 Kroppefjäll, track marked by stones
85 Mariedal, Ova, sunken road system
86 Norra Åsarp, sunken roads
87 Kymbo Tall, 35 sunken road system
88 Eriksgatuleden, large sunken road systems
89 Hackebergsskogen, Fölenè, sunken road system
90 Risveden, Erska/Hålanda, sunken road system
91 Karleby långa, village and passage graves
92 Källby hallar, rune stones, cemetery
93 Runshall, Håkantorp, sunken road, rune stone
94 Pilgrimsleden, Millesvik
95 Ambjörby, Norra Ny, sunken road
96 Eda forts with old roads
97 Långjohanstorp, Mangskog, embankment
98 The De la Gardie and Birgitta roads, Ödeby, castle roads
99 Kungsvägen, Djupadal-Oppboga, Erik Tour
100 Skagershultsmossen, corduroy road
101 Getaryggen, Edsberg, ridgeway
102 Skävesund, Glanshammar, ridgeway, cemetery

103 Anundshög, Badelunda, rune-stone road, cemetery, sunken roads
104 Linnévägen, St Kopparberg/Bjursås
105 Hjulbacka, Hedemora, sunken roads, cemetery
106 Granmor-Nittsjö, church road
107 Östbjörksta-Västanå, village street
108 Hedbyn-Gärdsjöbo
109 Strömbacka-Älgered, old country road
110 Årsunda, ridgeway
111 Österfärnebo, ridgeway
112 Hallstaåsen, Hög/Hälsingtuna, ridgeway
113 Kristinavägen, Hamrångefjärden
114 Cycle track, Los, log-floating road with km-stones
115 Finnhuvudvägen, cemetery, St Olof's well
116 Kungsnäs, Selånger, pilgrims harbour
117 Borgsjö, pilgrims' way, St Olof's well
118 Utvik-Ry, Nora
119 Skalstuguvägen, Åre, arched bridges
120 Stenen i Grönan dal, carved stone
121 Hummeltorp, Nordmaling
122 The Judges Road, Lycksele/Arvidsjaur
123 The Norway Road, Vilhelmina
124 The Norway Road, Sorsele
125 "Svältnören", Malå, cycle tracks
126 "Svältsnören", Degerfors, cycle tracks
127 The Ore Road, Gällivare to the coast
128 The Silver Road, Arjeplog-Piteå
129 The Kristina road, Piteå
130 Sangis, the oldest coastal road, embankment, bridge, memorial stone
131 Skridevad, Lannaskede, rune stone, embankment, hundred boundary
132 Glömsjö-Nederby, rune stones, embankment, sunken roads, parish boundary
133 Ramundeboda, province boundary, monastery ruin, Erik Tour

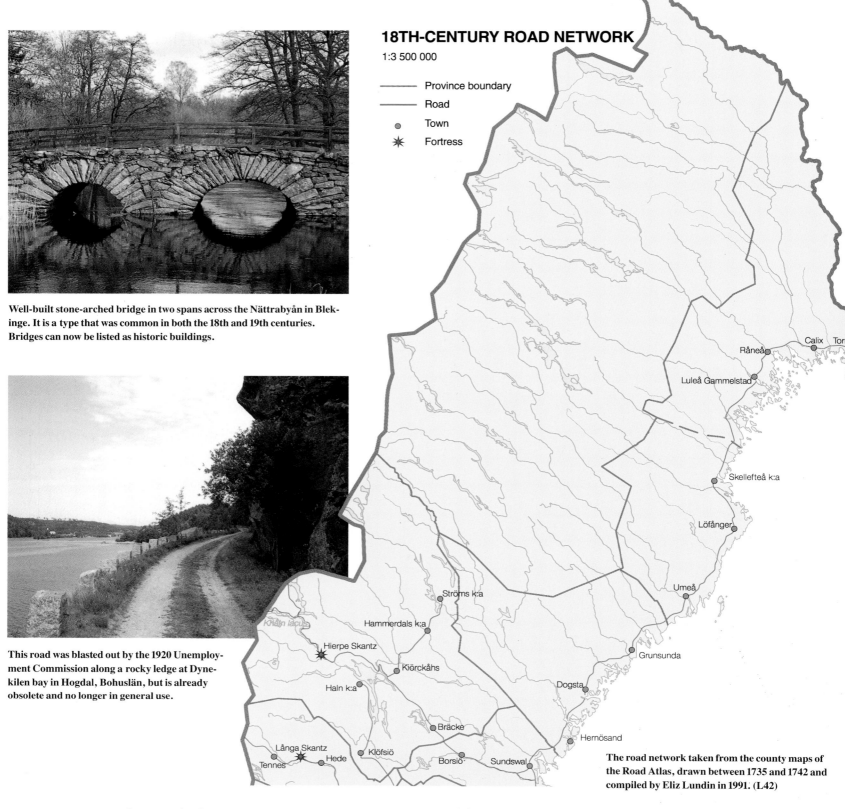

Well-built stone-arched bridge in two spans across the Nättrabyån in Blekinge. It is a type that was common in both the 18th and 19th centuries. Bridges can now be listed as historic buildings.

This road was blasted out by the 1920 Unemployment Commission along a rocky ledge at Dynekilen bay in Hogdal, Bohuslän, but is already obsolete and no longer in general use.

18TH-CENTURY ROAD NETWORK

1:3 500 000

— — — Province boundary
———— Road
● Town
✳ Fortress

Calix Tornea
Råneå
Luleå Gammelstad
Skellefteå k:a
Löfånger
Umeå
Ströms k:a
Hammerdals k:a
Grunsunda
Hierpe Skantz
Kiörckåhs
Dogsta
Haln k:a
Bräcke
Hernösand
Långa Skantz
Klöfsiö
Tennes   *Hede*   *Borsiö*   *Sundswal*

The road network taken from the county maps of the Road Atlas, drawn between 1735 and 1742 and compiled by Eliz Lundin in 1991. (L42)

journeys in the peasant community could be completed within one day, like day work and church visits or visits to mills, smithies and for tree-felling. Days or even weeks were needed for journeys to the hay mires, to burn-beaten lands, hunting grounds or shealings up to 100 km away. The town population usually travelled less than the peasants.

Walking was the commonest way of getting about until the 19th century. Walking some 20–30 kilometres a day was not uncommon. During the Middle Ages beggars, pilgrims, monks and nuns travelled far and wide. Many travellers were looking for seasonal work or peddling from

farm to farm, at least from the 16th century onwards. The Saami reindeer farmers led a nomadic existence for many generations, moving annually between forest and mountain.

Since the Middle Ages it had been forbidden in principle to travel freely; one had to carry a pass, especially on journeys outside one's home county. The need to carry a pass was not abolished until 1860.

Riding was for reasons of cost only for propertied farmers, merchants, officials and soldiers. It was possible to travel on horseback far and fast even on very primitive roads. King Karl XII is said to have ridden 300 km in one day. Travelling by coach was

difficult and time-consuming in most parts of the country right up to the 19th century.

THE POSTHORSE SYSTEM

The Alsnö ordinance of 1279 regulated travelling with an obligatory posthorse system. Travellers were to pay for this service, but carriers of royal letters had the right to demand free travel. This was a burden for peasants who lived along public highways. The national law of 1442 required the establishment of taverns at every 20 kilometres. Payment per ten kilometres was laid down as early as the 16th century, but effective travelling was not possible until the regulation

concerning inns was passed in 1649. All travellers, including the king's men, were to pay for horses and lodging according to a fixed rate. This obligation to provide horse and carriage lasted up to the next inn. The normal speed at which one travelled was 5–10 km an hour. The posthorse and inn system was still partly in use as late as 1933.

The regulation of 1649 concerning inns required all public highways to be measured and provided with *milestones*. All measurements were made from the royal palace in Stockholm; the milestones were set up to remove suspicions about the system of payments. Soon travel handbooks were published containing the names of inns, rates and maps. The first to gain wide circulation was Biurman's "Road Guide", 1743. Road signposts were regulated by law in 1734. Regular postal services were provided along certain roads in 1636.

ROAD MAINTENANCE

The national law of 1350 obliged peasants to provide and maintain a road six ells wide (about 4 m) on suitable ground. Even the most important roads were only partly usable for coaches; in 1544, for example, Gustav Vasa demanded that the road across Tiveden should be cleared for coaches. In the 1660s it was possible to travel by carriage between Stockholm and Luleå. State grants for road construction were introduced in the 17th and 18th centuries, when the most important country highways were rebuilt for coach traffic, provided with ditches and surfaced with gravel. Macadam was used on some roads from the middle of the 19th century. Large numbers of stone bridges, usually arched, were built from the 18th century onwards. Ferries were used to cross broad rivers or lakes. In the summer traffic was obstructed along most roads by cattle gates. It was not until 1927 that it was decided that cattle gates should be removed from public highways.

Sweden was divided into road maintenance districts in 1891, where road shares determined how far each landowner was responsible for maintenance. Road maintenance stones which indicated responsibility for maintenance were set up earlier. The National Road Administration was established in 1841, but road administration in general was not nationalised until 1944.

Mile posts were made of wood, stone and cast-iron. Left, one in limestone carved with Karl XI's monogram in high relief from Jönköping County, centre, a common type from the time of Karl XII in Skaraborg County, and right, an unusually ornamented cast-iron post in the mining district of Örebro County from the time of Adolf Fredrik.

Waterways

It was a long time before the road network and road transport was able to compete with water transport. Water transport could provide a faster service and carry heavy loads without demanding the large investments needed for road construction. One special kind of waterways were the canals, which at times were of great industrial and commercial importance but which today are cultural-historical tourist attractions.

COASTAL ROUTES

Trading places were established at strategic spots which had natural harbours and in time some of them were granted town status. Others served mainly as over-night harbours and stopping places for sea travellers. There are quite a few carved inscriptions in rocks at these places, and sometimes the foundations of old chapels.

SEA MARKS AND LIGHTHOUSES

Sea marks were set up to guide ships, and there are plenty of remains of

This beacon at Fituna in Södertörn, with a view across the sea approach to Södertälje, is built on a Bronze Age cairn. Perhaps there was a need, both in the Bronze Age and later—but for different reasons—to keep a lookout over the fairway.

those built of stone along the routes. During the Middle Ages and earlier it was mostly striking natural features in the landscape that were used for navigation. The most impressive sea marks are, however, the lighthouses.

Lighthouses were first built in Scandinavia as early as the 13th century. Progress was slow, however, and up to 1786 there were only eleven lighthouses in Swedish waters. The Falsterbo lighthouse was built in 1202, the lighthouses at Kullen and Nidingen a few years later. To begin with only wood fires were used as the source of light. During the 17th century coal came into use, in open fires. From the end of the 18th century

closed lanterns with glass windows were introduced. During the Middle Ages and right up to the 18th century wax or tallow candles were also used, often in large numbers grouped as beacons.

BEACONS

A different kind of communication system consisted of beacons set up in long lines for signalling with smoke or fire. This system was most common along the coast, but in several areas stretched inland. In times of danger the beacons were lighted, quickly spreading the warning. The origin of these beacons is uncertain; they were occasionally built as late as the First

Reconstruction based on an old drawing of the 16th-century Danish pivoted lighthouse.

LIGHTHOUSE STATIONS BEFORE 1786, MEDIEVAL HARBOUR SITES AND MAJOR CANALS

1:10 000 000

- ● Lighthouse station
- ● Medieval harbour
- ⌒⌒ Canal

Harbours	
1	Hamnholmen
2	Kongahälla
3	Galtabäck
4	Luntertun
5	Skanör/Falsterbo
6	Elleholm
7	Lyckå
8	Utlängan
9	S:t Sigfrids hamn
10	Pata
11	Vållö
12	Kyrkohamn
13	Kapelludden
14	Kårehamn
15	Örehamn
16	Västergarn
17	S:t Olovs holm
18	Gamla hamn
19	Barösund
20	Enskär
21	Granhamn
22	Kappalshamnen
23	S:t Olovshamn
24	S:t Olovshamn
25	Kyrkesviken
26	Jungfruhamn
27	Kyrkbyn

Canals	
28	Dalslands kanal
29	Göta kanal
30	Hjälmare kanal
31	Kinda kanal
32	Strömsholms kanal
33	Säffle kanal
34	Trollhätte kanal

Several simple medieval harbours have been preserved in an abandoned state. The oldest lighthouses are often of great cultural and architectural value. Our canals are nowadays of importance mostly for tourism: the larger ones are listed. (L43)

BEACON SITES ALONG PART OF THE EAST COAST

1:2 500 000

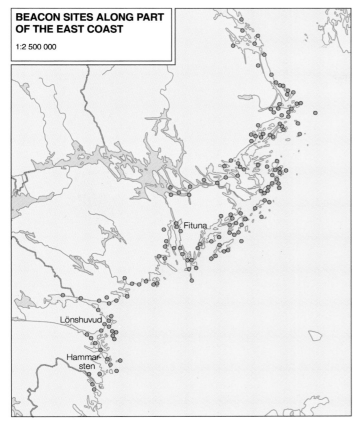

Beacon sites along the coast from northern Uppland to southern Östergötland according to historical sources and place names. Only one at Fituna in Södertörn, one at Lönshuvud in Vikbolandet and one at Hammarsten in Valdemarsviken have been preserved. (L44)

World War. A few have been preserved along the coasts of Östergötland and Södermanland and in Västernorrland. A similar but later invention was the optical telegraph system established in the Stockholm archipelago about 1800.

FISHING HUTS

There are plenty of remains of simple buildings or sheds in the outer archipelagos of Sweden. They consist of stone banks, which formed the lower sections of the walls. Most of them lie well protected in bays or sounds; they were used mainly for fishing from the Middle Ages onwards. The large numbers along the West Coast may date from the times when herring fishing flourished. Along the coast of Norrland there are many such sites in exposed positions considerably higher up in the terrain. These were used for late-winter seal-hunting during the

A large maze with a cross-shaped plan at Rödkallen in the Luleå outer archipelago in an environment typical of these late ancient monuments.

later part of the Iron Age and the early Middle Ages. Elevation of the land has moved these sites far back from the present-day shoreline, which helps us to date them.

MAZES

Mazes or labyrinths of stone are often found close to fishing villages or sheds in the archipelago. Judging by their location, but also by local tradition, it seems that they were connected with magic rites and conceptions concerning fishing. Other traditions suggest that these mazes were built for magic purposes concerning navigation, to avoid dangers, for example. Most known mazes are from relatively late historical times and lie at low levels.

SHED FOUNDATIONS AND LABYRINTHS

1:10 000 000

Number of shed foundations per Topographical Map Sheet

100
50
10
1

• 1-5 labyrinths

⬤ Some 40 labyrinths

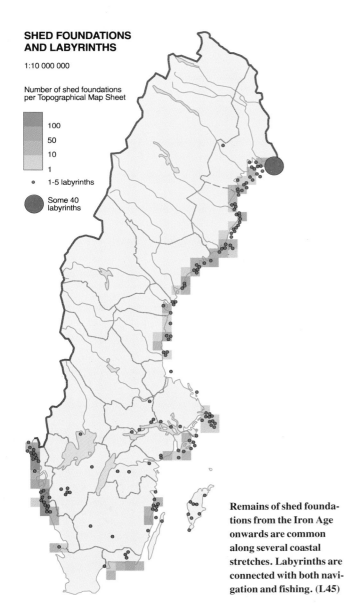

Remains of shed foundations from the Iron Age onwards are common along several coastal stretches. Labyrinths are connected with both navigation and fishing. (L45)

SHIPWRECK SITES

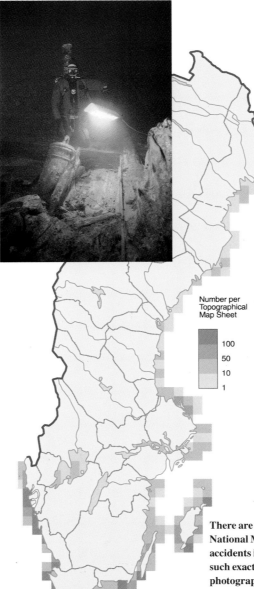

Number per Topographical Map Sheet

100
50
10
1

SHIPWRECK SITES

Shipping kept mostly to certain fairways and places, which led to a larger number of shipwrecks in those particular areas. The number of shipwrecks also tells us which coastal areas were particularly dangerous for shipping; it is here that the remains of wrecked ships are particularly common. The old wrecks of wooden ships are very well preserved in the Baltic because the stone borer or ship worm, which quickly destroys wood in saltier waters, is not found in that sea.

There are details of some 10,000 wrecks in the records of the National Maritime Museum. Most of them were caused by accidents in the 18th and 19th centuries. About half of them have such exact positions that they can be marked on a map. The photograph is from a marine archeological excavation carried out in the 1980s of the wreck of the royal warship "Kronan", which sank in a sea battle off southern Öland in 1676. (L46)

The Cultural Landscape of Iron

The history of iron manufacturing in Sweden began during the 6th and 7th centuries B.C., or possibly some centuries earlier. Since then iron has been produced in Sweden with the help of various techniques and in various areas until our own times. Not until people started to produce iron from native ores did they start to utilize metals seriously. This led to considerable changes in their life styles.

Direct and Indirect Iron Production

During prehistoric and historic times Swedes produced iron mainly according to two principles, which are usually called direct and indirect production; the former often used to be called the low-technological method. In this method malleable iron is produced directly. In the other, pig iron is first produced with a high carbon content. This pig iron is then refined to malleable iron by reducing the carbon content.

Direct iron production usually took place in bloomery furnaces, but during the 16th century it was also produced in bloomery forges. Bloomery furnaces were the only known method for producing iron in prehistoric times, and they survived among the peasants of northern Dalarna and Härjedalen until the mid–19th century.

Indirect iron production usually took place in blast furnaces, using hard rock iron ore. It has been in use in Sweden since the 12th century.

Iron Production: Bloomery Furnaces

The raw materials for the bloomery furnace process were usually various kinds of limonite ores, mainly lake and bog ores but in some parts of Sweden "red soils" as well. Bog ore was dug out of bogs in the summer, while lake ore was collected from lake beds when it was possible to work from the ice. This ore was then left to dry over the summer before it was taken to the furnace. Most furnaces were placed close to the lake or bog that provided the ore. It was relatively easy to construct a bloomery furnace and the problem of transporting heavy ore was avoided.

Before feeding the ore into the furnace it had to be roasted. This was done on an open fire to remove sulphur and water of crystallization, otherwise these impurities would have affected the process in the furnace.

Apart from ore, wood and charcoal were important resources. A shortage of forests for wood and charcoal has often been the limiting factor for iron production in the world; only exceptionally have supplies of iron run out. But Sweden scarcely had any shortage of wood to limit the use of the direct method.

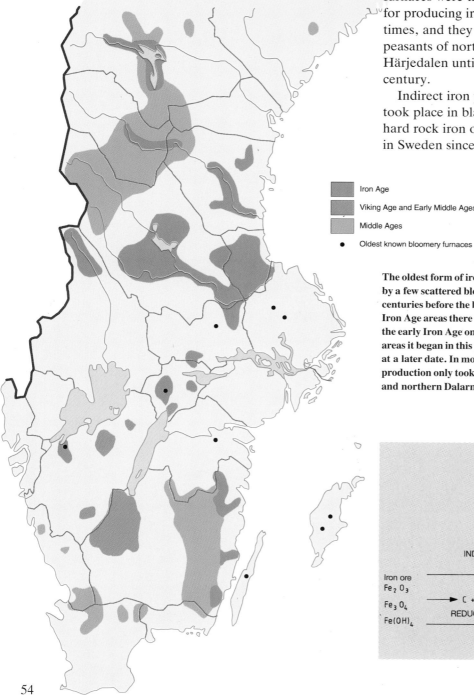

DIRECT IRON PRODUCTION

1:5 000 000

Iron Age

Viking Age and Early Middle Ages

Middle Ages

● Oldest known bloomery furnaces

The oldest form of iron production is represented by a few scattered bloomery furnaces from the centuries before the birth of Christ. Within the Iron Age areas there was iron production from the early Iron Age onwards; in the Viking Age areas it began in this period and in medieval areas at a later date. In modern times direct iron production only took place in inner Norrland and northern Dalarna. (L47)

Diagram of the difference between the chemical-technical processes in indirect and direct iron production. The difference in result is that production is much greater in blast furnaces and that the iron ore is utilised more economically.

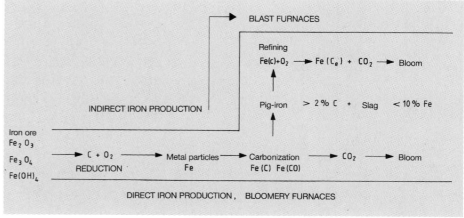

An uncovered bloomery furnace above the shoreline of Lake Storsjön at Ångron in Myssjö, Jämtland. At a site where iron was produced there is usually, apart from the bloomery furnace itself, at least one slag heap and a "fell-stone" where the bloom was worked; there are sometimes traces of roasting and of the blower as well.

The largest known find consists of 126 spade-shaped iron blanks and was made at a mire near Månsta in Näs, Jämtland.

19th century. The last evidence that we have of iron being produced by direct production is from the mid–19th century, in the parish of Storsjö in northern Härjedalen.

Småland, Halland, Västergötland, Dalarna, Härjedalen, Hälsingland and Jämtland were the principal areas for direct iron production during the Middle Ages, with a peak in the 14th and 15th centuries. Written sources usually identify iron by its place of origin: Jämtland iron, Härjedal iron, Kalmar iron and so on.

Today we know of a total of some 5,000 sites throughout the country where direct iron production occurred, most of them in Småland, Dalarna, Hälsingland and Jämtland.

OCCURRENCE AND CHRONOLOGY

The oldest evidence of iron production is spread across the southern parts of Sweden. In several cases dating is based on C^{14} tests, but these do not provide a clear-cut picture. The oldest known furnaces are to be found on Gotland and Öland and in Västergötland, Västmanland, Närke and Uppland. The designs of these furnaces indicate two different traditions of iron production.

The last written observations of direct iron production were noted in 1869 by Nils Månsson Mandelgren at Storsjö in Härjedalen.

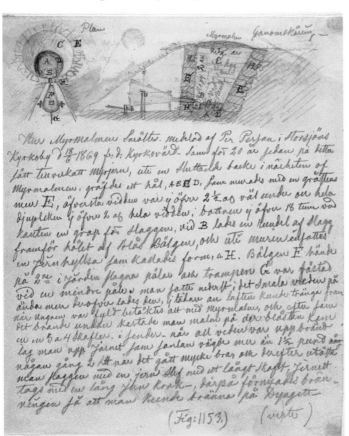

The first flourishing period of Swedish iron production was during the Roman Iron Age and the Migration Period (0–550 A.D.). During this period considerable amounts of iron were produced in Västergötland, Småland, Närke, Västmanland, Dalarna, Gästrikland, Hälsingland and Jämtland. Iron production seems to have reflected changes in economic conditions in the southern Baltic area, and evidently suffered from a decline in many parts of Scandinavia in the later half of the 6th century. In several of the areas mentioned above production did not pick up until the 9th century.

During the Viking Age large quantities of iron were produced in Dalarna, Gästrikland, Hälsingland and Västergötland, and production started in Småland. During this period iron was almost entirely produced in outlying areas. Previously uninhabited districts were gradually populated, either temporarily or permanently. This population lived to a large extent from iron production. The most typical district for this development was Dalarna.

The early Middle Ages saw the most significant innovation in the history of Swedish iron production—the introduction of the blast furnace in the late 12th century. It might be supposed that an innovation of this magnitude would have completely replaced previous methods, but this was not the case. Direct iron production continued to account for large quantities of iron. Not until the 16th century did a considerable decline occur, which continued until the early

The iron produced in bloomery furnaces in the Iron Age was distributed in the form of iron blanks. The spade-shaped type is the most common and is clearly connected with production in Norrland; the scythe-shaped type may be connected with production in Småland. Both date from the Migration Period to the Viking Age. These finds vary greatly in size, and the number of known objects is about 1,500. (L48)

DEPOSITS OF IRON BARS

1:10 000 000

- Spade-shaped type
- Rod or scythe-shaped type

Finds per parish
- ○ 4-6
- ○ 2-3
- ○ 1

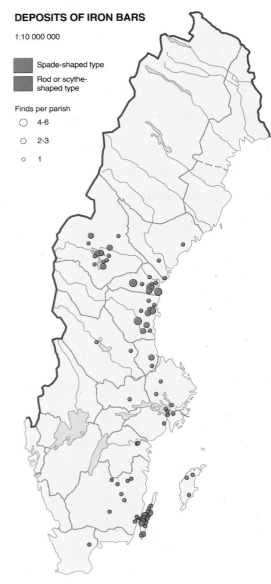

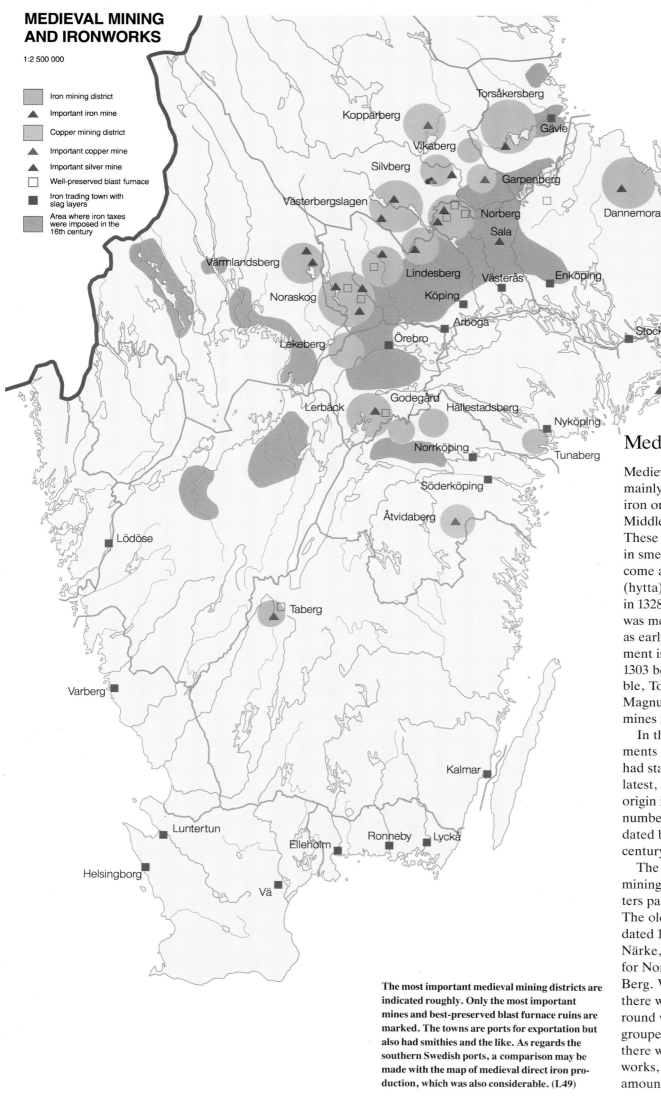

MEDIEVAL MINING AND IRONWORKS

1:2 500 000

- Iron mining district
- ▲ Important iron mine
- Copper mining district
- ▲ Important copper mine
- ▲ Important silver mine
- ☐ Well-preserved blast furnace
- Iron trading town with slag layers
- Area where iron taxes were imposed in the 16th century

Torsåkersberg
Kopparberg
Gävle
Vikaberg
Silvberg
Garpenberg
Västerbergslagen
Norberg
Dannemora
Sala
Värmlandsberg
Lindesberg
Västerås
Enköping
Noraskog
Köping
Stockholm
Lekeberg
Arboga
Örebro
Utö
Godegård
Lerbäck
Hällestadsberg
Nyköping
Norrköping
Tunaberg
Söderköping
Lödöse
Åtvidaberg
Taberg
Varberg
Kalmar
Luntertun
Ronneby
Lyckå
Elleholm
Helsingborg
Vä

The most important medieval mining districts are indicated roughly. Only the most important mines and best-preserved blast furnace ruins are marked. The towns are ports for exportation but also had smithies and the like. As regards the southern Swedish ports, a comparison may be made with the map of medieval direct iron production, which was also considerable. (L49)

Medieval Mining

Medieval metal production consisted mainly of the mining of copper and iron ores, and towards the end of the Middle Ages some silver ore as well. These ores were processed to metals in smelting works. The first time we come across the term *smelting work* (hytta) is in the will of Birger Persson in 1328, but Kopparberget in Falun was mentioned in a written document as early as 1288. Another early document is a letter of exchange dated 1303 between the Lord High Constable, Torgils Knutsson and King Birger Magnusson in which iron and steel mines in Norberg are mentioned.

In the light of these written documents it is possible to say that mining had started by the 13th century at the latest, but in all probability it had its origin in the 12th century. A large number of smelting works have been dated back to the later half of the 12th century.

The majority of our medieval mining districts were granted their letters patent in the mid–14th century. The oldest ones we know today are dated 1340 for Västra Berget in Närke, 1347 for Kopparberget, 1354 for Norberg and 1412 for Värmlands Berg. Within each mining district there was one or more mining fields round which the smelting works were grouped. During the Middle Ages there were at least 200 smelting works, and the number of mines amounted to thousands.

IRONMEN AND SMELTING WORKS

We meet in the written source material from the Middle Ages a new social group in Sweden: the ironmen. They were to carry on their work in the foundries up to the 1870s, when the last ironmen's smelting works were fired for the last time.

The ironmen's organisation was formulated in laws during the 17th century but the regulations go back to medieval traditions. Ironmen were organised in mining teams and smelting teams, in which they worked as part-owners. The work in the mines was organised by the mining teams. The actual work was carried out by employed mineworkers. The smelting teams organised the work in the foundries, which was also carried out by hired workers. The work of the ironmen themselves consisted in activities such as transportation, roasting and blowing, whereas maintenance and heating of the furnaces was done collectively.

These mining districts were great consumers of charcoal, corn and oxen, the latter for hides to be made into mine ropes, which meant that large farming districts were involved in the mining industry.

THE MINING DISTRICT OF NORBERG

Norberg in Västmanland is considered to be one of the oldest mining districts. The important mining fields at Norberg were located centrally: the Kolningsberg and Klackberg fields, which were probably referred to in the letter of 1303 about the steel mine, and the Risberg field where one mine was in use until 1981.

The smelting works lay round the mines, many of them mentioned by name in the Middle Ages, either as smelting works or as the villages they gave their name to.

There are plenty of foundry ruins in the Norberg mining district, but also a few well-preserved smelting works, including the timbered works at Landforsen and the well-preserved ironworks of Ängelsberg. Together with Lapphyttan these give a relatively complete picture of the development of industrial iron production from the Middle Ages up to our own time.

NORBERG MINING DISTRICT

— Hamlet boundary

▢ Remains of blast furnace

● Mine

▲ Remains of tilt hammer

Ingolsbenning

Rabbats-benning

Anders-benning

Håkans-benning

Fröbenning

Halvarsbenning

Nyhyttan

Olsbenning

Norberg

Malm-kärra

Karbenning

Nyhyttan

A general map of Norberg and its 17th-century village boundaries gives a picture of how the mines are situated along the ore deposit and the blast furnaces located where there was water power. Village names that refer to blast furnaces are marked. Most villages certainly grew up as a result of medieval iron production.

Stable

Iron store

Smithy

Smithy

Charcoal house

Smithy

Blast furnace

Iron ore store

Roasting pit

Slag heap

Slag heap

Slag heap

Smithy

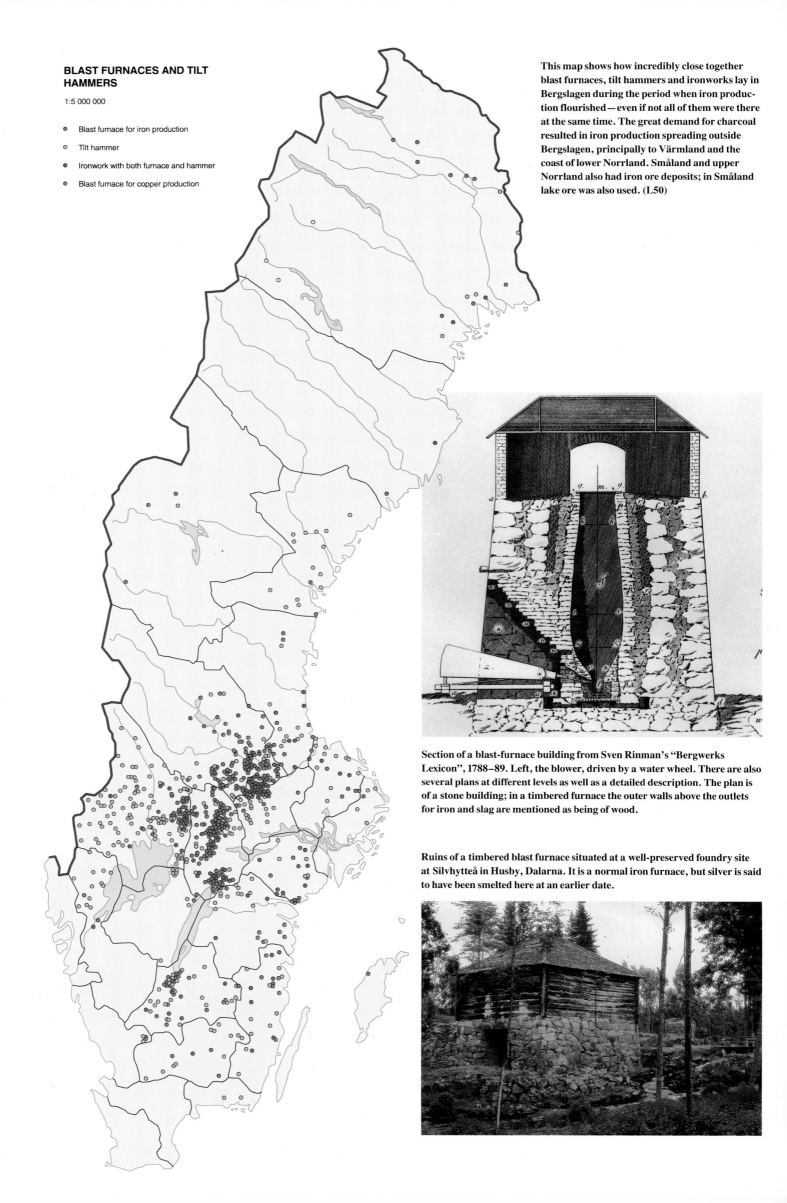

BLAST FURNACES AND TILT HAMMERS

1:5 000 000

- ● Blast furnace for iron production
- ○ Tilt hammer
- ● Ironwork with both furnace and hammer
- ● Blast furnace for copper production

This map shows how incredibly close together blast furnaces, tilt hammers and ironworks lay in Bergslagen during the period when iron production flourished — even if not all of them were there at the same time. The great demand for charcoal resulted in iron production spreading outside Bergslagen, principally to Värmland and the coast of lower Norrland. Småland and upper Norrland also had iron ore deposits; in Småland lake ore was also used. (L50)

Section of a blast-furnace building from Sven Rinman's "Bergwerks Lexicon", 1788–89. Left, the blower, driven by a water wheel. There are also several plans at different levels as well as a detailed description. The plan is of a stone building; in a timbered furnace the outer walls above the outlets for iron and slag are mentioned as being of wood.

Ruins of a timbered blast furnace situated at a well-preserved foundry site at Silvhytteå in Husby, Dalarna. It is a normal iron furnace, but silver is said to have been smelted here at an earlier date.

Swedish Ironworks, 1600–1850

The Ängelsberg Foundry in Västervåla, Västmanland, was built in its present form in the 1770s, but dates back to the medieval Englikobenning foundry. It was closed down in 1919 but is well-preserved in its entirety. In the area there is also a bar-iron smithy, several old dwelling houses and store houses as well as Ängelsberg's manor house, built about 1750. The site comprises as a whole a complete ironworks community of international interest.

Around the year 1600 German blast furnaces replaced the old Swedish blast furnaces, which can be seen at Lapphyttan, for example. A large number of Crown ironworks had been established during the time of Gustav Vasa. Swedish iron exports had at that time partly replaced osmund iron production with bar iron production. A new refining process in the form of German forging was brought into use, and these considerable changes gave Swedish iron improved production and market capacity. There was also at the same time a considerable increase in the production of copper at Kopparberget in Falun.

Ironworks policies pursued by Axel Oxenstierna and Carl Bonde led to an expansion of privately-owned works, which replaced many of the old ironmen's works. These ironworks towns gave iron production an effective form under private ownership. It was to last until the 1970s, but from the mid–19th century limited companies were the usual form of ownership for iron production.

In the 1630s French blast furnaces and the Walloon forging process started to come into use. Walloon forging was mainly used in the mining district of northern Uppland and southern Gästrikland, and in Finspång in Östergötland. During the 17th and 18th centuries the Walloon works towns became famous all over Europe, and followed a characteristic plan.

During the 1830s several of the old refining methods were replaced by the last of the great craft methods, called the Lancashire forging process. All the old methods later became obsolete when ingot steel processes were introduced after C F Göransson had successfully used Bessemer blowing at Edsken in Gästrikland in 1858.

THE IRONWORKS TOWNS OF BERGSLAGEN

During the 17th and 18th centuries Swedish iron production developed into complete industrial townships, many of which are still functioning, such as Surahammar, Hallstahammar and Långshyttan. There are hundreds of these townships all over Bergslagen.

One of the best preserved examples is Ängelsberg in the Norberg mining district. Ängelsberg Mill has a long history as a foundry village, Änglikabenning, which was taken over by Per Höök in 1681. He rebuilt the old blast furnace and developed the village into an ironworks town. During the 18th century a manor house was built, the furnace and hammer were developed, the farm section was improved with larger stables and a good many homes for both overseers and workmen were built. The industrial parts of the plant were integrated with the millowner's mansion and other houses to make a complete community.

A more impressive form is to be found in the Walloon towns of northern Uppland: Österby, Gimo, Söderfors, Leufsta, Forsmark and Harg, for example. They are in every respect larger than corresponding mill communities in inner Bergslagen. After the Russian raids in the 18th century the mills were rebuilt as architectural entities, with a stylish mansion, streets, churches, workshops and so on. What lay behind it all was the high quality of Dannemora ore. The ironworks towns of Uppland are some of the finest industrial environments in Europe.

Österby is one of the best-preserved Walloon ironworks in Uppland. This view from the east shows two streets in the foreground. Behind the pond lies the manor house, built in the 1760s according to J E Rehn's plans. To the right, at the pond's outlet, the Walloon forge from 1794 — the oldest preserved one in Sweden — and behind it an old street.

Traps and Trapping

Hunting and Trapping

Hunting, trapping and fishing are our oldest means of livelihood. After agriculture had been introduced, they continued for a long time to be important complementary parts of the economy. Today they are mostly leisure activities.

A distinction is usually made between *hunting* and *trapping*. When hunting a hunter is active in getting his prey, usually using a weapon; when trapping he is more passive, relying on permanent devices and implements which function in his absence. Sometimes the distinction is not very clear, for example when animals were driven towards traps.

Hunting has only left chance traces: spent arrowheads of stone or iron, or sometimes bones at a slaughtering place. Very few trapping devices above the ground have been preserved since they were constructed of perishable materials such as wood, branches, skins and rope. Where trapping devices were constructed below ground level they have been preserved. The largest group comprises trapping pits, which were used both to catch animals for food and to protect cattle from predators. As for fishing, almost everything used was perishable; nor can it be studied on the spot.

Trapping Pits

Trapping pits for moose and wild reindeer occur in the same area as the Stone Age northern Scandinavian hunting culture, that is, generally speaking north of the limit of the Norrland terrain. Most of them lie in the central parts of the interior, with smaller concentrations and sparse occurrences closer to the coast. Almost 30,000 trapping pits are known, a third of which are in Jämtland. The present-day picture is least representative in Lappland and Norrbotten.

Trapping pits for moose and wild reindeer are found throughout northern Scandinavia, with the majority in the forests inland, where they were for moose, while reindeer pits are found in mountain districts and in the Arctic area. Wolf pits are found sparsely scattered within the whole of the marked area. (L51)

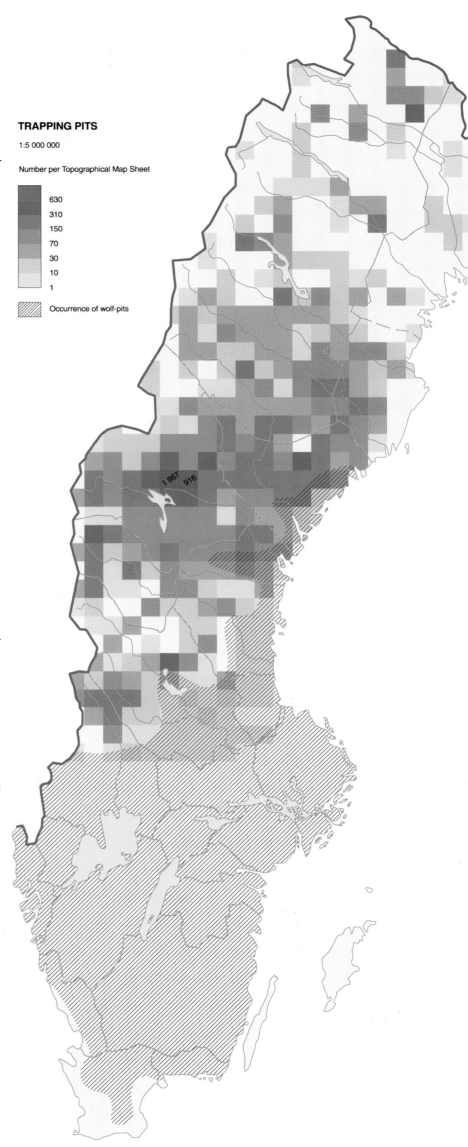

TRAPPING PITS

1:5 000 000

Number per Topographical Map Sheet

630
310
150
70
30
10
1

Occurrence of wolf-pits

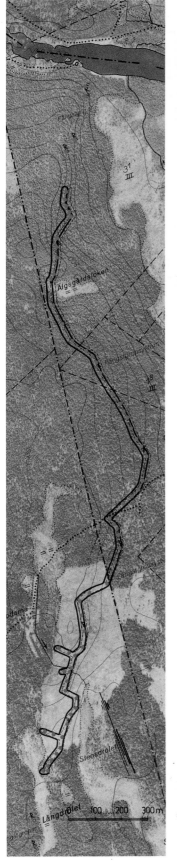

Along the Hårkan, a tributary of the Indalsälven, in Lit and Häggenås there are more than 350 trapping pits within 15 km. The picture shows part of an unusually dense system of 43 pits within 660 m, dating from the Viking Age and located on sandy pineland at Husås.

South of the Sladderforsen rapids in the river Långan (top of map) there is a trapping-pit system of 62 pits on both sides of the parish boundary between Lit and Aspås in Jämtland. It extends towards the north and south with a few more isolated pits. To the south there is a smaller system towards the Indalsälven, so that the whole of the 4.5 km broad headland between the rivers may have been blocked. There are also large systems north of the Långan.

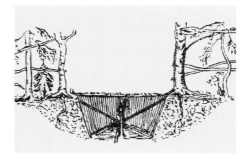

With the help of information from informants in Härjedalen Erik Modin reconstructed about 1900 a wood-lined trapping pit with a spear in the middle.

PIT CONSTRUCTION

A trapping pit today looks like a bowl-shaped or funnel-shaped, round or oval pit surrounded by a bank of earth and often with a long, narrow depression in the centre. They are usually 2.5–5 m in diameter and 0.5–2 m deep, depending on their age and the kind of soil, and entirely covered with grass. When they were in use they had sloping walls faced with wood and a rectangular wooden box at the bottom. Other pits had a round or square bottom equipped with pointed stakes or spears. The stakes and the box were to keep the animal trapped in the pit. The bank of earth increased the depth of the pit and levelled out the surrounding ground. Originally the mouth of the pit would have been masked with branches, twigs, moss and the like. Their construction is known thanks to old descriptions and excavations.

TRAPPING PIT SYSTEMS

Trapping pits lie either singly or in groups in good moose grazing ground, or arranged in long lines or systems. The former type were provided with bait, a bunch of leaves, for example, and pointed stakes in the pit are common. The pit systems had pits connected by fences of timber, fallen trees, branches and so on to guide the animals across the pits, which often had wooden boxes at the bottom. These systems were placed across the animals' paths and migratory routes, their length and the number of pits depending on the width of the track and the supply of animals. They would be put in order at the beginning of each season, usually the late autumn and early winter. They may have been renovated at irregular intervals and can be dated by the C^{14} method in the humus layer in the banks of earth.

Most of the largest systems, which comprise several hundred pits and are several kilometres long, are in the hilly, Silurian terrain of Jämtland, where there are no natural passes but good grazing ground for moose. They are placed at an angle to rivers, while others run parallel to them where there are suitable animal paths. The large systems may have been organised as part-ownership enterprises, and medieval diplomas show that they were treated as property that could be inherited or purchased, often called *moose yards* (älgsgård), a term which also occurs in place names.

This is what it may have looked like when moose passed through a prepared and barred trapping-pit system in a Norrland forest, before hunting with guns made pit-trapping uneconomical.

DATING AND CULTURAL BACKGROUND

The oldest known trapping pits in Sweden are in the interior of Väster-botten county and have been dated to a period before 4000 B.C. There are also datings from later periods of the Stone and Bronze Ages in Jämtland, Ångermanland and Dalarna. The number of datings increases during the Iron Age, reaching a peak in the Viking Age and the early Middle Ages, when several large systems were constructed in Jämtland. There are fewer datings from recent times. Repeated renovations of several pits have been identified. In Åsele, for example, there is one pit with seven layers of renovations dating from the Late Stone Age up to the Migration Period. Pit systems belong mostly to prehistoric and medieval times, whereas isolated pits are often from later periods.

The trapping pit method was prob-ably introduced with the earliest hunting culture in northern Scandina-via and was used in this culture until the Iron Age. Inside the Arctic Circle and in parts of the high mountains trapping pit systems were used to trap wild reindeer, before reindeer hus-bandry was introduced, as well as moose. Pit trapping later became part of the peasant economy and may have played an important part in integrat-ing the hunting and farming cultures. During the flourishing economy of the Viking Age and the early Middle Ages pit trapping was probably also used commercially for the trade in hides and horn.

A trapping pit for wolves at Stora Bystad in Gäll-stad, Västergötland, is 5 m in diameter and 3.5 m deep, with completely preserved dry-stone walls and flat bottom.

WOLF PITS

Before wolves were exterminated, pits were used to trap predatory animals in farming districts in most parts of Sweden. These pits were constructed singly close to settlements at places where the animals were known to go. They were round or square in shape and often walled with stone. They were baited with meat and had a lid which kept the animal in the pit. Re-mains of larger constructions, called wolf yards, have also been found.

Trapping Devices

Our knowledge of trapping devices made of perishable materials is far too imperfect to present in general maps. However, we should like to de-scribe a few devices whose remains still can be seen in the countryside. The reports are from recent times, but many methods may have had their origins much earlier. All the de-vices described here were banned long ago and as a rule only the rotted relics remain, while others like bird boxes are still to be seen, even though it is forbidden to take eggs from them. One method of trapping is still practised by a few licence holders: snaring white grouse. The following section refers to Norrland and south-ern Lappland in particular.

WEDGING DEVICES

A fox stump consists of a pole with two or three prongs. When the animal jumps up to get the bait on these prongs, its paws get stuck between them and it is left hanging. Used for foxes and wolves.

CONFINING DEVICES

Cages, cribs and boxes all look like a house with three walls and an open end fitted with a trapdoor which, when it is sprung, falls down and shuts in the animal. The cribs were made of timber and were used for the big predators and beavers, while the cages and boxes were for foxes, bea-vers, martens, badgers and birds.

A yard is an enclosed fold which an animal could jump into but not out of. Used for wolves, foxes, hares and other animals.

A bag net is a sack-like net on a long handle under which animals could be trapped. Used for forest birds, black grouse in particular, and martens and hares.

A net could be used to trap ani-mals, for example when driving them from their dens. It was used for most forest animals as well as forest birds, ducks and the like.

BATTERING DEVICES

A battering device consists of several logs which, on being released, strike an animal and pin it to the ground. It was used for bears and other preda-tory animals, hares and forest birds.

A log trap consists of two logs, one of which is set to fall against the other in the same way as a battering device. Used for most forest animals, includ-ing moose, beavers and otters.

A spring trap consists of two iron jaws and a spring which is set off by an animal treading on it or pulling the bait. The spring forces the two jaws together, trapping the animal's leg or some other part of its body. Used for most forest animals, and for cranes, swans and geese.

SNARING DEVICES

A snare is a running noose in which an animal is snared and strangled. When used for small animals it was attached to a forked stick, and for large animals it was suspended be-tween trees or bushes. A hand snare was pulled over an animal's head, a squirrel, for example. A throwing snare was thrown over larger animals like wind reindeer and moose. A flick snare was attached to a springy tree trunk which was tied down and which straightened up when it was sprung, lifting the animal up into the air. Used for moose and bears, foxes and hares. A tip snare was similar, being attached to a long pole whose weight lifted up the animal when the snare was sprung.

Reconstructions of some common types of traps. Above left, a fox stump, next to it an otter battering trap, below left, a hare log and beside it an iron spring trap. Their form certainly varied from district to district and according to the animals to be trapped.

Area with information on trapping devices. (L52)

An unusual but instructive example of a permanent fishing device is this considerable construction across the Kukkola rapids in the river Torneälv at Karl Gustav, Norrbotten. A device of this type was originally built to catch salmon, which had been a commercially-exploited fish since the Middle Ages. Nowadays it is used mostly to catch whitefish, not least for tourists.

WOUNDING DEVICES

Fixed spears were used—apart from in trapping pits—in wolverine log traps, where a spear was attached to a log, spearing the animal when the log fell.

A hook was swallowed by the animal. Baited hooks on ropes were used for catching sea birds. Sharpened sticks sprung by sinews were put in the bait for wolves. When it had digested the food it would die.

A trip gun was some kind of weapon, a gun or a spear, which was set off by a trip wire. Used for wild reindeer, moose and most predatory animals.

FENCES

In the mountains or in sparse forests long rows of poles were erected with something frightening at the top. Wild reindeer were driven between these rows of poles which converged towards an enclosure or a ravine, where the animals were killed or captured. Fences of the same kind as those used in trapping pit systems sometimes had snares instead of pits. Such devices were also used by Saami when they hunted wild reindeer. Along the coast of Norrland stone walls containing bird snares have also been found on open rocky ground.

The Role of Hunting

In Norrland and above all in Lappland hunting, trapping and fishing were of great importance until very late in history. They were primary forms of subsistence for colonisers and those with little land. The balance between hunting and trapping was changed when modern guns became available, but in many areas they only lost their importance as primary occupations when forestry work became common.

The Nordic Museum in Stockholm has drawn up trading statistics for the parish of Tärna in Lappland for two ten-year periods around the year 1900. At that time trapping was the second most important export industry, accounting for a quarter of the sales value in Mo i Rana. White grouse accounted for 90 per cent, more than 80 per cent of which had been snared. Capercaillie, black grouse and hazel grouse, and animal hides, came next in importance. Wild reindeer and beavers must also have been of great value in earlier times. Today moose are the most important game animals.

The Saami Cultural Environment

The area utilised by the Saami today covers parts of four countries. Ever since the Early Stone Age there has been a mobile hunting culture in a considerably larger area of northern Europe. A much debated question is in what way the historically known Saami culture is related to this hunting culture.

The Saami as a people were sporadically mentioned in written sources from about the time of the birth of Christ. The visible traces in the landscape today may date back to the last thousand years before Christ. Most of them, however, are from considerably later times.

Area with Saami reindeer husbandry today seen in relation to the distribution of the early Finno-Scandic hunting culture of the Stone Age type. (L53)

The simple, oval or rounded rectangular hearth of lying stones, here from Jämtland, is a "fossil clue" for Saami culture. It has been used both in tents along migratory routes and in permanent cots in the mountain residences.

Saami Cultural Remains

The Saami area is a rich cultural landscape with its own special character, but there are no complete recordings of Saami cultural remains. The following are a few examples of relatively well-known areas.

THE OVIKS-ANARIS MOUNTAIN AREA IN JÄMTLAND

When a survey was made of part of the area, some 120 Saami cot foundations, often in groups, with storage pits, reindeer enclosures with visible remains of wooden fencing and trapping pits were identified.

There were also bone hoards close to the cot sites. The bones left after meals were collected in a special place, a bone hoard, under a small cairn or in a crevice, covered over with stones. Originally this custom was of ritual significance.

THE KUTJAURE AREA IN LAPPLAND

Almost 1,500 remains of old Saami culture have been found in the Kutjaure area, which covers some 110 km². Most of them (ca. 60%) are open hearths belonging to dwellings or temporal sites. They are visible today in the form of a square or oval collection of stones which used to be in the centre of a Saami cot.

There are also trapping pits and storage pits in this area, as well as sacrifice sites and bone hoards.

Some 70 reindeer grounds indicate the importance of reindeer husbandry. A reindeer ground was an area close to a temporary camp where the reindeer where gathered to be milked. A reindeer ground can be identified by the luxuriant growth of grass caused by intensive manuring.

SAAMI TRACES IN COASTAL AREAS

Place names show that Saami stayed along the coast of the Gulf of Bothnia in early times. An example in the south is Hornslandet near Hudiksvall, which offers good coastal fishing but poor conditions for cultivation.

New surveys have identified isolated, as yet undated cot foundations in the Norrbotten archipelago. Some of the islands there were used for grazing reindeer.

Saami remains are also to be found between the rivers Piteälv and Luleälv. Colonising farmers often settled at old forest Saami dwelling sites.

In the present-day residences there are often traditional Saami cots, but also houses of varying ages and types. Their location in relation to reindeer pasture land and other natural resources is, however, usually the same as earlier. From the Saami residence of Kårtjevuolle in Tjäktjavagge, Lappland.

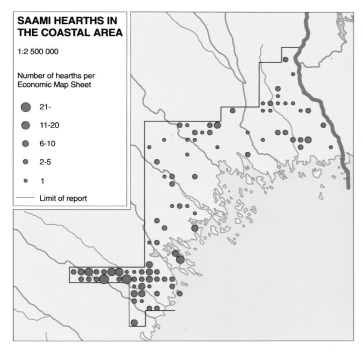

1:2 500 000

Number of hearths per
Economic Map Sheet

● 21-

● 11-20

● 6-10

● 2-5

· 1

— Limit of report

Saami relics—mainly hearths—found during new surveys in the coastal land
of Norrbotten. They are numerous in the sparsely-populated area along the
county boundary, fewer where permanent settlement is denser. (L54)

. . . AND IN THE FORESTS

Most dwelling sites from the old hunting culture are to be found in forestland, and it was here that the Saami
migratory routes passed between the
winter and summer pastures.

A large number of remains of early
Saami culture have been found in Arjeplog. Some 200 hearths and four
cooking pits were excavated at Rackträsk, and were dated from the 10th
century to the 19th century.

These Saami hearths bear witness
to thousands of years of traditions.

A special investigation
between lakes in
Arjeplog, Lappland,
gave rich rewards.

SAAMI REMAINS AT RACKTRÄSK, ARVIDSJAUR

Kakel

Dellaure

Rackträsk

● Cooking-pit

○ Hearth

● 34 hearths

／ Trapping pit system

A Saami cot foundation at Vivallen in Tännäs, Härjedalen, could be dated to about 800 A.D.,
that is the early Viking Period.

Traditional turf cot, Lappland

There are hearths of various types
from every era, for example round
hearths from Stone Age sites; but
most of the hearths are rectangular or
more or less oval. Trapping pits have
also been found. The practice of
catching large animals in trapping pit
systems was a method developed by
the old hunting culture which may
well have been used later by both
Saami and settlers.

Cot Foundations in the Mountains

A number of beliefs and rules were
connected with the various parts of
a Saami cot. In the centre lay the
hearth, *arra*. The inner part, *boassjo*,
opposite the door was the cooking
area but also a holy place. To the left
and right of the entrance lay the
working and sleeping areas.

One type of cot foundation, traditionally called *stalotomt*, is known
from the mountain region of northern
Scandinavia. A dwelling site often
consists of three to five foundations in
a row. They are slightly oval in shape,
with a broad, platform-shaped bank,
a hearth in the centre and a somewhat
sunken floor. Most of them date from
the Viking Age and the early Middle
Ages and represent a new utilisation
of the mountain area, presumably for
hunting wild reindeer or for tending
domestic reindeer in the summer.
Opinions are divided as to where
their inhabitants spent the rest of the
year.

VIVALLEN IN TÄNNÄS

One dwelling site at the mountain
shealing of Vivallen in north-west
Härjedalen has been in use for many
hundreds of years. A large, rectangular hearth containing unburnt reindeer bones from about 800 A.D. was
found in a Saami cot foundation.
There is another similar structure
from the early 13th century. A pile of
rubbish has been dated to the 11th
century. The hunting of animals for
their fur may be the explanation of
the good contacts with the surrounding world which the nearby graves
bear witness to.

BIELITE, VILHELMINA

The main camps of the mountain Saami, the autumn and spring camps
were located on the sides of the
mountains on fairly high, dry and protected plateaus. There are good examples of these sites in the birch forests
close to the mountains at Bielite.

Early Saami Graves

According to traditional Saami burial customs the dead were buried away from the camp and were not to be disturbed. The graves often lay on islands or headlands by lakes.

In forestland underground earth graves were probably the most usual type. Stone and cave graves are more common in the mountains. Cave graves are usually found in natural rock crevices, under boulders and in similar places. Stone graves or stone cists may consist of slate slabs, looking like a rectangular coffin, with the slabs standing on edge and one or more stones forming a lid or leaning against each other.

IRON-AGE GRAVES

Pre-Christian graves are known in the whole of the Saami area. Those that have been definitely identified as Saami are from the Viking Age or later. It is difficult to make a distinction between the Iron-Age graves in the hunting grounds and the Saami graves. This applies to cemeteries in Härjedalen, Dalarna and Gästrikland, where there are cinerary graves

A grave at Lake Abelvattnet in Tärna, Lappland, built of large stone slabs

under flat cairns from about the time of the birth of Christ. A great deal depends on when one chooses to apply the word Saami to descendants of the old hunting culture and how one defines the term Saami. In marginal areas features from burial customs of other cultures were adopted.

A whole cemetery of 21 graves containing inhumations under flat ground has been investigated at Vivallen in north-west Härjedalen. The corpses were wrapped in birch bark, possibly with specially sewn coverings for the hands, head and feet. This pre-Christian Saami burial custom is known from the Iron Age in Norway and from at least one 14th-century grave near Tärnaby in Sweden.

Burial objects at Vivallen are mainly from the 11th and 12th centuries. They indicate both the economy and the contacts that people had with the surrounding world. Arrowheads for hunting and small bronze pendants are of Saami style. From Finland and Russia in the east came dress ornaments of bronze, from Norway silver coins and from north-west Europe silver ornaments.

SUMMER GRAVES

Summer graves date from the time after the arrival of Christianity. They may have been used by both Saami and settlers.

If a person died in the summer a long way away from the nearest churchyard, a corpse might be interred temporarily in a summer grave and later be taken to church, in the winter over snow and ice.

BEAR GRAVES

Bears were worshipped in the whole of northern Eurasia as holy animals. Saami bear graves are only known from the western Saami area, that is, present-day Norway and Sweden.

After a bear had been carried home with various ceremonies and its meat had been eaten, all the bones had to be buried in as good order as possible—so that the bear could be resurrected, as they said. In most cases the bones were laid directly on the ground and covered with turf. Some bear graves were on islands, others in a cave, under logs and birch bark or in a cairn.

The most northerly known bear grave, at Jokkmokk, has been dated to the 10th century. Most of the other known graves seem to be from the 17th and 18th centuries.

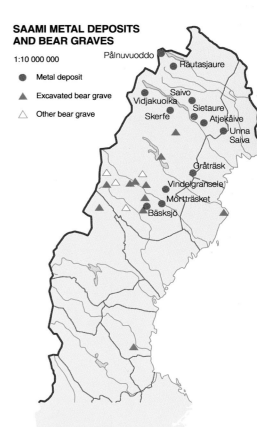

SAAMI METAL DEPOSITS AND BEAR GRAVES

1:10 000 000

- ● Metal deposit
- ▲ Excavated bear grave
- △ Other bear grave

Pålnuvuoddo
Rautasjaure
Saivo
Vidjakuoika
Sietaure
Skerfe
Atjekåive
Unna Saiva
Gråträsk
Vindelgransele
Mörtträsket
Bäcksjö

Saami metal deposits are spread throughout the whole of Lappland, while bear graves principally occur in Västerbotten county. (L55)

Saami Metal Hoards

A large number of metal objects from the period ca. 1000–1350 have been found deposited at some dozen places in northern Sweden. Some of these finds are at large sacrifice sites with deep layers of bone and horn, mainly from reindeer. Others may have been dwelling sites, hiding places and so on. The objects are from the whole of northern Europe. Many of them have the appearance of amulets.

The Annual Cycle of Reindeer Husbandry

What is said here does not refer to modern reindeer husbandry but to earlier conditions. The reindeer husbandry year is a cycle based on the reindeer's search for grazing. In the winter they graze on moss and lichens in the forests; in the spring and autumn they keep to the lower mountains and in the summer to the high mountains.

The way in which the mountain Saami tend their reindeer is characterised by long migrations. The calves are marked in the summer in the mountains. In the autumn comes the rounding up and sorting of the herds. The mixed herds are divided up among their owners according to the

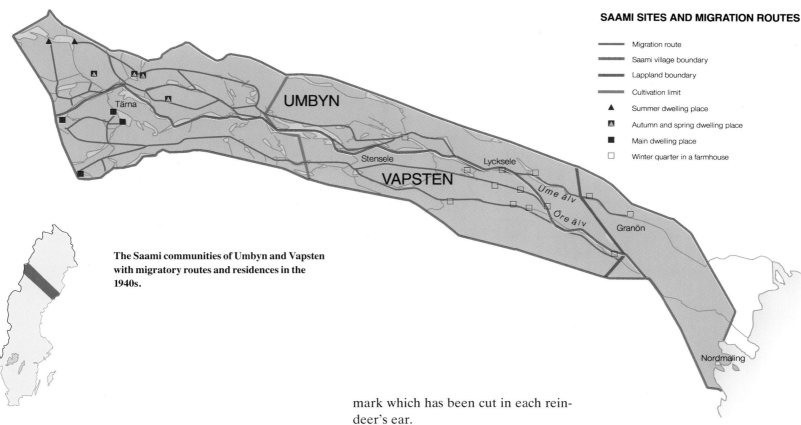

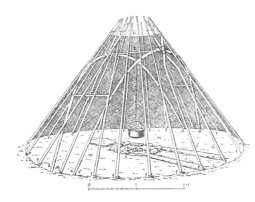

Migration route
Saami village boundary
Lappland boundary
Cultivation limit
▲ Summer dwelling place
◩ Autumn and spring dwelling place
■ Main dwelling place
☐ Winter quarter in a farmhouse

UMBYN

Tärna

Stensele

VAPSTEN

Lycksele

Ume älv

Öre älv

Granön

Nordmaling

The Saami communities of Umbyn and Vapsten with migratory routes and residences in the 1940s.

Drawings of some traditional Saami features: top, a wooden fence of the type used for reindeer enclosures; middle, a store shed, *àjtte*, built on root supports; below, a tent cot of the bow-pole type with a hearth.

mark which has been cut in each reindeer's ear.

The places where the mountain Saami spent the spring and the autumn, usually with permanent turf cots and wooden store huts, lay just below the tree line, in the birch tree belt. When they moved or were in the mountains they took poles and covering with them to built tent-like cots.

They spent long periods at the old sites, yet these sites are often difficult to detect when they have not been used for a while. The Saami did not want to disturb nature unnecessarily and often used the material available on the spot.

A reindeer fence is an enclosure often shaped like a large round yard surrounded by several smaller "chambers"; these enclosures are part of 20th-century reindeer husbandry.

FOREST SAAMI

Forest-Saami culture differs from mountain-Saami culture. Forest-Saami are in the coniferous forests all the year round. In the summer the reindeer graze on the mires, while the pine heaths with their rich supplies of reindeer lichen are their winter grazing grounds.

They made short transfers between their many permanent sites, which were not far apart. Reindeer were used as draught animals or pack animals. Fenced enclosures were common. Special smoke fires were used to protect the reindeer from mosquitoes, gnats and flies. Timber-built cots became more and more common.

Modern reindeer enclosure with side paddocks at Överuman in Tärna, Lappland

Places of Sacrifice and Popular Belief

Prehistoric Sacrificial Cults

Various rituals involving sacrifice, magic and cults were performed to bring good luck in hunting and survival in life by the immigrants of the *Hunting Stone Age*; these offerings were in the form of weapons and parts of animals.

During the *Farming Stone Age*, for example, collections of unused, thin-butted axes or sickles of flint were placed in hoards, and clay pots containing food were buried in bogs to please the gods and ensure better harvests and fertility. Large quantities of pottery shards outside passage graves in both Skåne and Västergötland suggest that ritual ceremonies were performed not only at burials but also at remembrance feasts for the dead.

During the *Bronze Age* offerings were made to the gods in bogs and overgrown water courses or in deposits under boulders on dry ground. These offerings might consist of single decorated weapons like axes, swords and spearheads or of more ceremonial objects like bronze lures, gold bowls, cult chariots and shields. Particularly towards the end of the period collections of offerings are more common, most of them found in southern Sweden. The numerous occurrences of rock carvings and cup marks carved in the rock were important cult and magic elements.

During the *Early Iron Age* weapons and horse harness were offerings deposited in rivers and bogs. Clay pots containing food and wooden objects predominate in other places such as Käringsjön in Halland. Horses and human beings were sacrificed at Skedemosse on Öland, probably as regular seasonal offerings, while weapons and gold may have been deposited on special occasions such as times of war. Most places of sacrifice during the Early and Middle Iron Ages have been found in Skåne and on Gotland. During the Viking Age weapons were sacrificed, as at Gudingsåkrarna on Gotland.

Finds of sacrificial offerings of stone axes often contain strikingly unworn axes. Find of thin-butted flint axes from Skiringe in Mellösa, Södermanland.

One of the most remarkable of the late Bronze Age sacrificial finds was discovered at Hassle in Glanshammar, Närke. It consists of a large cauldron, two Italic pails, two swords of Central-European type and 12 beaten plates.

Other Prehistoric Cult Places

There were probably many other now unknown assembly places for various ritual purposes close to prehistoric settlements. They are indicated by place names or place-name elements like *-vi, -hov* and *-lund*, and sometimes *-harg-* and *stav-*. Place names containing the names of gods like Frö, Njord, Oden, Tor and Ull may also be connected with cult places.

Probable examples of such permanent cult places are some 80 known rectangular constructions like building foundations. They have mostly been found in Mälardalen and southern Sweden and are usually in Bronze Age settings. They are normally 10–25 m long and 6–10 m wide; some, however, are up to 50 m long. They have broad stone banks with stone edging round a somewhat hollowed middle. Since they do not contain hearths, post holes, entrances or layers of domestic deposits, they have been interpreted to be the foundations of cult buildings or cult enclosures.

During the Iron Age barrows were also built over burnt-down houses, as discovered mainly in the coastal dis-

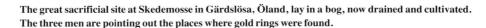

The great sacrificial site at Skedemosse in Gärdslösa, Öland, lay in a bog, now drained and cultivated. The three men are pointing out the places where gold rings were found.

IMPORTANT PREHISTORIC VOTIVE OFFERINGS

1:10 000 000

- Area with Saami votive sites
- Important Saami votive find
- Stone Age
- Bronze Age
- Iron Age

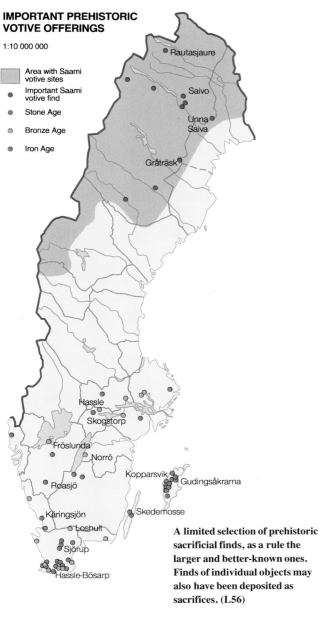

Rautasjaure
Saivo
Unna Saiva
Gråträsk
Hassle
Skogstorp
Fröslunda
Norrö
Kopparsvik
Gudingsåkrarna
Røasjö
Skedemosse
Käringsjön
Loshult
Sjörup
Hassle-Bösarp

A limited selection of prehistoric sacrificial finds, as a rule the larger and better-known ones. Finds of individual objects may also have been deposited as sacrifices. (L56)

PREHISTORIC CULT SITES

- Area with mounds with edge earthworks
- Grave mound above a burnt-down house
- More than one cult house
- One cult house

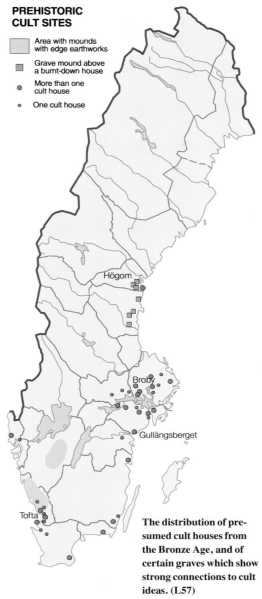

Högom
Broby
Gullängsberget
Tofta

The distribution of presumed cult houses from the Bronze Age, and of certain graves which show strong connections to cult ideas. (L57)

so be the explanation of occasional roads which lead up to or are situated in cemeteries.

The phallos-like shapes which a number of standing stones have are connected with fertility cults. Apart from an obvious image like the Rödsten in Östergötland, this may also be true of certain picture stones on Gotland as well as standing stones in some stone circles supported by a pair of cobbles. A number of names of standing stones can also be interpreted similarly.

Saami Places of Sacrifice

The Saami places of sacrifice, mostly discovered in Lappland, are a special type of cult place. They are connected with striking natural features such as boulders, precipices, islets, streams and the like. Some contain many offerings of metal objects from the Iron Age and the Middle Ages, but most of them are of reindeer horn or bone. Wooden or stone monuments were erected at many of these places, known as "sejtar". These were used as idols.

Holy Wells

It is impossible to distinguish clearly between *spas, holy wells* and *Midsummer Wells/Trinity Wells*, since the same well may have been used for different purposes over long periods of time. Holy wells are found from Skåne up to northern Ångermanland; almost every parish has had one or more. In the Christian era they were often visited by many people at special times—in the south of Sweden at Midsummer and further north at Trinity. The boundary for these customs runs through northern Östergötland, Närke and southern Värmland. These wells could also be visited by individuals for various reasons all the year round.

Usually offerings were made to the wells for health, especially in cases of paralysis, eye trouble and sores. In olden times offering a votive object and drinking the water were supposed to be done in silence. It was not until

tricts of central Norrland. The barrows have been interpreted to be places where the farm inhabitants or the family worshipped their ancestor or as an expression of respect for their forefathers.

Mainly in the west of Sweden there are also scattered occurrences of very flat barrows with a broad surrounding bank which may have been the foundation of a burial house. Sometimes other graves are surrounded by an enclosure which might have served to mark off the cemetery.

Concepts about the journey to the land of the dead may be the explanation of other grave types such as inhumation in a boat, ship-formed flat barrows and stone ships. This may al-

Below a Bronze Age barrow containing a magnificent grave at Håga near Uppsala lies a 40-metre-long stone-clad bank structure with a 5-metre-wide empty inner chamber.

At Rödsten (Redstone) farm in Grebo, Östergötland stands a stone image whose connection with a fertility cult is evident. According to tradition the stone is painted red to ward off evil from the farm, whose name goes back to the Middle Ages.

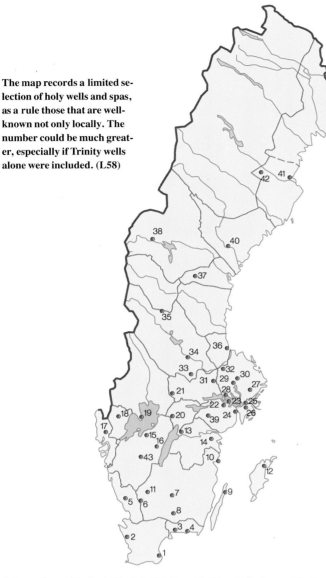

The map records a limited selection of holy wells and spas, as a rule those that are well-known not only locally. The number could be much greater, especially if Trinity wells alone were included. (L58)

IMPORTANT SACRIFICIAL WELLS AND SPAS

1 St. Olof's Well in St Olof, north-west of Simrishamn
2 Ramlösa Spa, south-east of Helsingborg
3 Sacrificial well at Asarum, north of Karlshamn
4 Ronneby Spa
5 Höstena Springs (artesian, associated with many legends), Vessigebro
6 St Sigfrid's Well at Femsjö (triangular, in a rock crevice)
7 Children's Wells at Ödetofta, Tolg, with more than 5,000 coins from 1350 onwards
8 St Sigfrid's Well at Urshult, with rock inscriptions
9 St Olof's Well at Källa Old Church
10 Spa with 30 wooden houses at Källvik in Lofthammar.
11 St Sigfrid's Well east of the site of the old church at Kållerstad (a votive church) with a memorial stone
12 Hånger Well at Gann Church ruin in Lärbro with a memorial stone.
13 Medevi Spa in Västra Ny
14 Söderköping Spa
15 Husaby Well, by tradition used for the baptism of King Olof, 11th century
16 Ingemo Well at Dala
17 King Östen's Well at Foss Church, mentioned by Snorre

18 St Ola's Well (with offerings) in Steneby
19 St Lars' Well in Millesvik
20 Porla Health Spa north-east of Laxå
21 Loka Health Spa south of Grythyttan
22 St Eskil's Well west of Strängnäs
23 Fröjdeborg's Well in Ytter-Selö
24 St Tore's Well in Södertälje
25 Ugglevik Well in Stockholm
26 St Botvid's Well in Salem
27 St Olof's Well in Fröslunda
28 Svinnegarn Well with many traditions
29 Sala Well in Uppsala
30 Sacrificial well at Old Uppsala
31 Sätra Spa in Kila
32 Östa Wells west of Tärnsjö (artesian, Trinity well)

33 Lövmarken Well in Söderbärke
34 Frostbrunnsdalen in Stora Tuna
35 "Cross Well", mentioned in 1403 as a boundary mark on the old national border between Dalarna and Härjedalen
36 Lervik Well north-east of Gävle
37 St Olof's Well at Borgsjö
38 St Olof's Well at Ristafallen rapids
39 Bie, a spa with chalybeate springs in Floda
40 Sånga Well, Sånga Church
41 Brunnsgården's Spa and Baths, Skellefteå
42 Linder's Mineral Spa with memorial stone, Norsjö
43 Sacrificial Well at Alboga Church, mentioned in 1754

A SACRIFICIAL WELL IN UPPLAND

In the report "Investigations of Antiquities" from 1673 for Seminghundra, Pastor Iöran Leijman of Frösunda writes: "8. On Thorsholma Field there is a Well, by name St Olof's Well, which is said to have been the object of much worship and where many people have offered Coins and other things.

9. A figure of St Oluf with Crown and Axe is in Frösunda Church."

In "Description of Frösunda Parish", 1852, Johan Nilsson, a surveyor, writes in his introduction: "There are no mineral or health spas. — Another well, called St Oluf's, containing good drinking water, is situated on Thorsholm's infields close to the road and noteworthy because the young people of Frösunda and neighbouring parishes gather there on the eve of Trinity Sunday to drink the health-giving waters, to take hire for the following season and not least to play, wrestle and even fight."

These reports seem clearly to show that sacrifices were the primary activity, and judging by the priest's wording, ancient, that is to say, "pagan" or perhaps "Popish". Hardly 200 years later this custom has become normal Trinity Day "taking of the waters" with entertainment. Many wells may have developed in the same way. As late as 1952 the well was described as being more or less in its original state, but it has now been replaced by two cement rings. Unfortunately this, too, is a common fate.

A few wells are illustrated in Erik Dahlbergh's "Svecia Antiqua et Hodierna". If one is to believe the illustration, Ingemo Well in Dala was in frequent use. The text reads: "Illustration of the old well called *Yngemokialla*, to which in former pagan and Catholic times small offerings were often made to gods and saints."

Effigies vetusti Fontis dicti Yngemokialla ad quem olim gentilismi et Papismi temporibus frequentes fiebant munusculorum oblationes Diis et Sanctis.

A well-known holy well is Hånger's Well near the ruins of Gann Church in Lärbro on Gotland. Traditionally, though not certainly, Israel Kolmodin composed the well-known summer hymn "The Flower Season's with us" here.

Two offerings of branches lie by the sides of an old country road at Jonsbol in Visnum, Värmland. In 1710 a farmer was attacked here by two farmhands on his way home with 500 silver coins in his purse. The two farmhands were later executed. The branches mark the scene of the crime and the place where the victim was found. The tradition lives on.

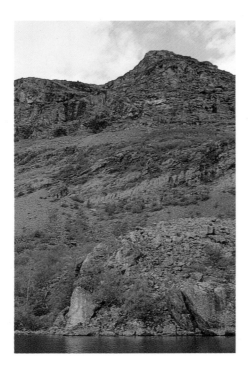

This Saami site of sacrifice by Lake Rautasjaure in Torne lappmark is in a landfall of rocks of different colours. When it was investigated in 1909 more than 500 objects of a Saami or eastern type were found, as well as more than 400 Norwegian and Western European coins and brachteates from the period 1000–1200 AD and a large number of reindeer horns and bones.

the middle of the 19th century that people began to dance and sing round the wells, which were often decorated with leaves.

A holy well or spring should preferably have water running towards the north and the water should be acid or contain iron. A well was thought to have its greatest powers at midnight or at sunrise. The votive objects were usually pieces of metal, coins or pins.

Behind this cult of wells there probably lay a popular belief in the power of water to heal, so the well water was used for both drinking and washing. In a few cases churches were built over or by holy wells. The Catholic church encouraged the cult of holy wells, as witnessed by the many wells named after saints, whereas they were usually disapproved of by the Reformation church. The fact that the custom of drinking well or spring water survived for so long was partly due to the upper class's custom of taking the water at spas which was established at the end of the 17th century and reached its peak in the 19th century at many spas and seaside resorts.

One special group comprises the *St Olof Wells*, which are found along the pilgrim routes to the grave of the Holy King at Nidaros (Trondheim), mainly along the rivers Ljungan and Indalsälven and to a lesser extent in other nearby provinces. The fact that the cult of Scandinavia's principal saint, Saint Olof, was widespread is proved by the many churches and ikons dedicated to him in the Scandinavian countries.

The few *votive churches*, most of them in Götaland, are less well known; those who wanted to be successful in business ventures or who sought a cure for their ills travelled long distances to make their votive offering.

"Giants' kettles" were used as holy wells in several cases, especially in western Sweden. Triangular hollows in the rock, with or without running water, were used for the same purpose mainly in Småland. Many wells and springs are today overgrown or have been drained.

Other Votive Customs

Votive stones are heaps of small stones and/or branches thrown down as offerings. They are usually connected with a belief in ghosts, lying mostly by roads or paths where someone had died by accident or had been murdered. Passers-by threw stones, sticks or branches on the heap to appease the ghost and persuade him not to cause trouble. Sometimes offerings were made for good luck—not to be mauled by a wild animal, for example. This phenomenon was common in many parts of Sweden, but also has regional names. "Kavel stones" on Gotland are used as road signs. Votive stones were piled up for good fishing and "shame stones" to point out undesirable persons. Sticks were also placed under overhanging rocks to which some tradition was attached, to act as props.

Many old Swedish farms had *guardian trees* to protect them. They were connected with the belief that such trees would bring good luck to the farm. Ash trees were preferred. There is often mention of offering food and drink to these trees. It would bring bad luck and danger to a farm and its inhabitants if a guardian tree was destroyed.

Hollow trees or trees with their branches or trunks grown together were used to cure diseases, especially rickets (the English disease). The sick child was pulled through the hole or under a root, which was supposed to cure it. Toothache pine trees were used to cure toothache; usually a stick or a nail covered with pus from the tooth was inserted into the tree, which would then take over the pain by magic. If someone cut down one of these trees he would get all the pain that was embedded in the tree.

Especially in Götaland there are traditions that precipices were used in ancient times as *death drops*, to kill off the old and the infirm. These stories were probably introduced by scholars from Old Icelandic literature and taken over by popular storytellers.

Simple votive offerings were also made to large rocks and boulders, especially those that had natural hollows, called "fairy mills" by the local peasantry, which could be rubbed with ointment against disease. Some lakes, rivers or streams were also the recipients of simple votive offerings.

Our Churches

DIOCESES AND CATHEDRALS

1:10 000 000

- Medieval cathedral
- Cathedral from modern times
- Previous parish church

Luleå

Härnösand

Karlstad   Västerås   Uppsala

Strängnäs   Stockholm

Skara   Linköping

Göteborg   Visby

Växjö

Lund

The division of diocese in Götaland and Svealand mostly dates back to the Middle Ages but has also been adjusted to agree with changing national borders (Göteborg) and as a result of growth in the population (Karlstad, Härnösand, Luleå, Stockholm). (L59)

Kristine Church in Falun is a striking feature of the town square, characterised by the prosperity that came from the mining industry. It was designed and built by Hans Ferster, a master builder of Stockholm, and was consecrated in 1655.

The cathedral at Lund, consecrated in 1145, has rich sculptural decoration in the Rhenish and Lombardian styles.

There are today more than 2,500 parish churches belonging to the Church of Sweden. Most of them date back to medieval times but even the later churches usually have some connection with an earlier church site. The churches which were abandoned have sometimes survived as deserted churches or ruins or only in the form of memorials in the old churchyards.

Churches are very different in different parts of the country, with regard to both age and appearance. The architecture of the church building and its surroundings reflects the changing values of its district and community, as do changes in church services. Thus every church provides information about people's changing conditions through its history, architecture, interior and furnishings and through preserved grave memorials, church accounts and records.

Church environments include not only the churchyard but often other buildings, too, such as belltowers, stables and parish cottages.

Cathedrals

Seven of today's thirteen dioceses date back to the Middle Ages and have kept their original cathedrals. Typical features of medieval cathedrals are the great transept chancels and the multi-aisled naves. The oldest cathedral is that of Lund, consecrated in 1145 for the Archbishop of Den-

mark. Only the eastern part of the first bishop's church in the archbishopric of Sweden, at Gamla Uppsala, survived a fire in the 13th century.

It often took many years to build a cathedral. Uppsala Cathedral, the largest in Sweden, was built between 1260 and 1435. The cathedral at Linköping was begun in the 1230s but was not completed until about 1500.

In Visby and Stockholm medieval parish churches have become cathedrals as a result of new dioceses being formed. Kalmar Cathedral was a diocesan church between 1678 and 1915. The youngest cathedral is at Luleå and was built in 1893.

Town Churches

There were very often many churches in the oldest medieval towns: 19 in Lund, at least 12 in Visby, and five in Sigtuna. The town plans of the 13th and 14th centuries included a centrally-located church by a market square (old Kalmar, Stockholm, Örebro) and abbeys for the mendicant orders were also often founded at that time. Medieval town churches were usually built of brick, and have in many cases grown over the centuries with the addition of chapels.

After the Reformation only one parish church was normally left in each town; sometimes it was a former abbey church (Arboga, Sigtuna, Sölvesborg). Towns in later centuries

BENEDICTINES
1 Lund
1 *Lund* •
2 *Bosjökloster* •
3 *Börringekloster*

AUGUSTINIAN CANONS
4 Dalby •
5 Kungahälla ○

CISTERCIANS
6 Alvastra ○
7 Nydala • ○
8 Herrevad •
9 Varnhem • ○
10 *Gudhem* ○
11 Julita ○
12 *Vreta* ○
13 Roma ○
14 Ås ○
15 *Askeby* •
16 *Sko* • ○
17 Riseberga ○
18 *Vårfruberga* ○
19 *Solberga* ○
20 Gudsberga ○

PREMONSTRANCIANS
1 Lund
21 Öved ○
22 Tommarp ○
23 Vä/Bäcka-
   skog • •
24 Dragsmark ○

ORDER OF ST JOHN
25 Eskilstuna
26 Kronobäck ○

DOMINICANS
1 Lund
27 Visby ○
28 Sigtuna •
29 Skänninge
30 Skara
31 Kalmar
32 Lödöse
33 Åhus ○
34 Västerås
35 Halmstad
36 Strängnäs
29 *Skänninge* ○
31 *Kalmar*
38 Stockholm

FRANCISCANS
27 Visby ○
39 Söderköping •
1 Lund
30 Skara
40 Uppsala ○
41 Enköping ○
42 Ystad • ○
43 Trelleborg ○
38 Stockholm •
5 Kungahälla
44 Nyköping ○
45 Jönköping ○
46 Arboga •
47 Linköping ○
38 *Stockholm*
48 Marstrand •
49 Malmö ○
50 Krokek ○
51 Nya Lödöse ○
52 Växjö ○
35 Halmstad
53 Torkö ○

BRIGITTINES
54 *Vadstena* • ○

CARMELITES
55 Landskrona ○
56 Örebro ○
57 Ny Varberg ○
58 Sölvesborg •

THE HOLY GHOST
49 Malmö

CARTHUSIANS
59 Mariefred ○

ANTONINES
60 Råmundeboda ○

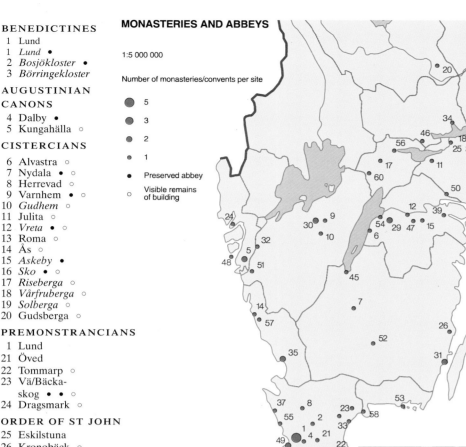

MONASTERIES AND ABBEYS

1:5 000 000

Number of monasteries/convents per site

● 5
● 3
● 2
• 1
• Preserved abbey
○ Visible remains of building

Medieval monasteries were established at 60 places in present-day Sweden. The list gives the monastic orders in the order of their establishment; within each order the oldest monastery is placed first (between the late 11th century in Lund and the 1490s for the latest ones). The names of nunneries are italicised. The extent of the preserved ones is varying: from the majority of buildings (Alvastra) to one or two walls (Åhus). (L60)

The Dominicans came to Sigtuna in the first half of the 13th century. Maria Church, which is still standing, was consecrated in 1255 and has been used since the Reformation as a parish church.

The Cistercian monks came to Varnhem in Västergötland in the mid–12th century and built their church first. South of the church lies the excavated monastery garden, surrounded by the ruins of buildings. The monastery wall is marked in the west.

were planned to have churches according to need. In Karlskrona, for example, three churches were started about 1680: Fredrik's Church for the ordinary people in the town, Trinity Church for its German inhabitants and Admiralty Church for the fleet and the naval shipyard. As Sweden has become more and more urbanised in modern times, the number of town churches has increased greatly.

Monasteries and Abbeys

Monasteries played an important part in the religious and cultural life of the Middle Ages. From the late 11th century up to the end of the Middle Ages over 70 monasteries and convents were established in what is Sweden today. Their property was confiscated by the Crown at the Reformation, and many of the buildings were torn down to provide material for the 16th-century palaces. It is nevertheless still possible to enjoy the atmosphere of a medieval monastery at Alvastra and other places where ruins are still standing.

Some dozen abbeys became ordinary parish churches at the Reformation, thus being preserved to our time, but very little of the architecture or decorations reveals their original function. The abbey churches were divided up by railings into different sections, separating monks from lay brothers and ordinary people. Nuns were usually placed in a gallery.

One of the oldest preserved abbeys was built at the beginning of the 12th century and used by the Cistercian nuns at Vreta. The church at Varnhem, which is from a slightly later date, served the monks of the same order. The remaining 13th and 14th-century churches of the mendicant orders include St Maria's at Sigtuna (Dominican), St Peter's at Ystad (Franciscan) and Riddarholmen Church in Stockholm.

The medieval monasteries also had living quarters, offices and other buildings, usually arranged round a courtyard with cloisters. In a few cases considerable remains have been preserved thanks to the buildings being used for other purposes. Unusually much remains of the 14th-century double monastery of the Holy Birgitta at Vadstena, where, apart from the church itself, the nuns' living quarters and parts of the monastery can be seen.

Västergötland

There are unusually many, almost 50, Romanesque churches preserved in Västergötland. This province also has a large number of typical 19th-century churches. At the beginning of the 13th century there were more than 500 churches here. Medieval parishes were small and many churches were probably built by individual lords. It later became necessary to amalgamate parishes and quite a number of churches were demolished.

The church at Våmb near Billingen was built in the 12th century and is one of many well-preserved examples of Romanesque churches in Västergötland.

The small Romanesque churches have a rectangular nave for the congregation and a lower, narrower chancel which has either a square end wall (Götene, Marka, Kungslena) or a semi-circular apse (Suntak, Dalum, Kinne-Vedum). The churches with towers include the resplendent one at Husaby, where the mighty west tower is flanked by two smaller stair turrets.

Västergötland is also famous for its medieval stone sculptures: decorated doorways (Södra Ving, Gösslunda) and carved facades (Forshem). Three quarters of the churches still have their medieval fonts. Many grave memorials, not least in the shape of 300 "lily stones", bear witness to a rich tradition of stone masonry. Västergötland is in a class of its own with regard to medieval bells as well, having some 250 in working order.

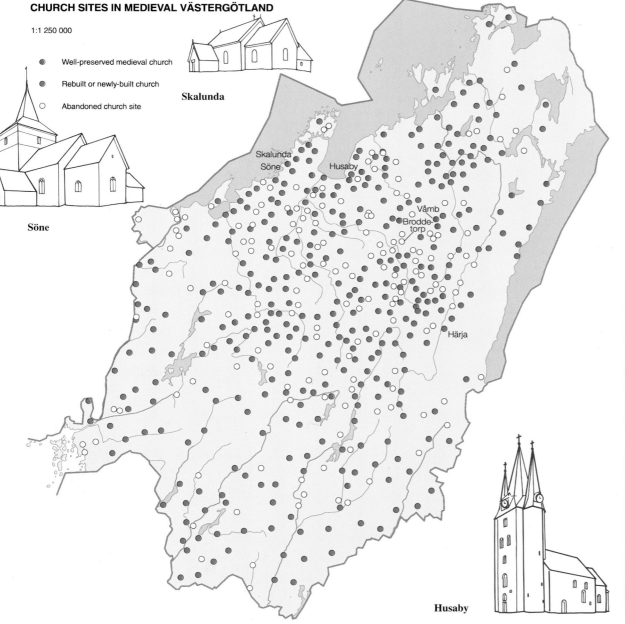

CHURCH SITES IN MEDIEVAL VÄSTERGÖTLAND

1:1 250 000

- ● Well-preserved medieval church
- ● Rebuilt or newly-built church
- ○ Abandoned church site

Skalunda

Söne

Husaby

Västergötland's medieval churches lay close together on the plains, and even the forest districts had comparatively small parishes. Since then small parishes have been amalgamated and churches demolished or rebuilt. Their ruins or foundations are often to be seen in deserted churchyards, but in some cases they have been ploughed up. A few present-day parishes are of a later date than the Middle Ages.

Härja Church, whose nave has been rebuilt, has a Romanesque south doorway with a 12th-century decorated lintel (upper picture below).

The Broddetorp Altar of gilded copper is from the Romanesque church at Broddetorp, now demolished. It is one of Sweden's very few surviving Romanesque altar decorations (lower picture).

THE MEDIEVAL CHURCHES OF GOTLAND: MURAL PAINTINGS AND STAINED GLASS WINDOWS

1:1 000 000

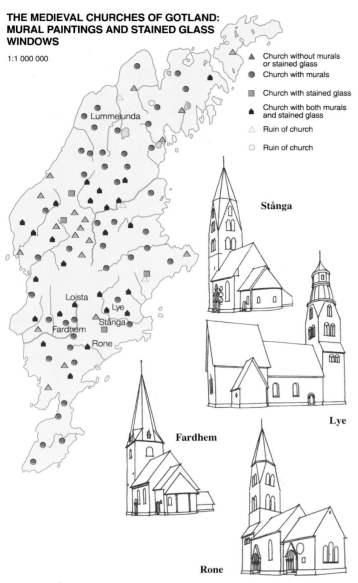

△ Church without murals or stained glass
● Church with murals
▪ Church with stained glass
▲ Church with both murals and stained glass
△ Ruin of church
○ Ruin of church

Stånga

Lye

Fardhem

Rone

The nave portal at Stånga Church from the mid–14th century is one of Gotland's most impressive monuments to the island's superb medieval stone masons.

Gotland's medieval churches with their murals and stained glass. The drawings show four typical examples of the churches' varying architecture. Fardhem is a well-preserved Romanesque church from the late 12th century, with a tower, nave, chancel and apse. At Lye a large Gothic chancel with a sacristy was added to a Romanesque tower and nave. Stånga has a well-preserved Romanesque chancel with an apse and a High Gothic nave and tower from the mid–14th century. Rone is a pure Gothic church with a square-ended chancel from the 14th century. (L62)

Scenes from the childhood of Jesus form part of the well-preserved stained-glass windows at Lojsta Church. This picture shows the birth of Jesus. The style is late Romanesque, and the stained glass has been dated to the mid–13th century.

Lummelunda Church is an example of how a large High Gothic chancel replaced an earlier Romanesque chancel. The Romanesque tower and nave have been preserved, however, as there were no further funds for rebuilding.

Gotland

The medieval churches of Gotland, well preserved and richly decorated, form a unique group among the church buildings of Scandinavia. All but three of Gotland's 95 parish churches are medieval. The churches have a special architectural history, as the oldest Romanesque ones were usually enlarged in several phases during the 13th and early 14th centuries. The Danish conquest of Gotland in 1361 marked the beginning of a long period of unrest and economic decline, which meant that there were no rebuildings or major changes of the churches. The effects of the Reformation on the churches in Visby were disastrous. Only St Maria's, the present cathedral, survived as a parish church. Of the others, ten have been partly preserved as ruins.

Gotland is rich in easily quarried and worked limestone, which is the building material for most of its churches. In the south part of the island, where there are easily accessible sandstone deposits, this material was used for building. The churches were decorated with richly ornamented doorways, and Gotland has by far the richest display of carved medieval stonework in Sweden. The skilful masons also made richly decorated fonts; both fonts and other carved stone ornaments, for doorways, for example, were also made for export and were shipped to the mainland and to other Baltic countries.

Scandinavia's richest collection of medieval stained glass is also to be found on Gotland. No fewer than 29 of its churches still have large or small displays of this rich form of decoration. Medieval mural paintings have also been widely preserved.

Enånger Old Church in Hälsingland is extensively decorated with murals. They belong to the Tierp group and date from about 1470.

The chancel ceiling in Dingtuna Church, Västmanland, depicts St Olov competing by boat with his pagan brother Harald for the crown of Norway. Monsters are trying to hold Olov back but do not succeed. This scene was painted by Albertus Pictor in the mid–1470s.

The Middle Ages

MURAL PAINTINGS

Most of the still-existing mural paintings have been damaged by being whitewashed or through later alterations to the buildings. Thus what can still be seen are often very fragmentary remains. Nevertheless these murals form a cultural heritage of great value. Most of them were uncovered and conserved during 20th-century restorations, and isolated discoveries are still being made. Respect for the original paintings, even though they may have partly disappeared, is the guiding principle for modern conservation. The original glowing colours of the paintings have usually faded and sometimes been altered, including those that were never covered with whitewash. Swedish mural paintings were usually made al secco, that is, on dried plaster, and the layers of paint are fragile. They run the risk of being damaged by an unsuitable indoor climate, dirt and bleaching by sunlight, so they require special care and attention.

Medieval murals are full of narrative scenes from the Bible and legends of the saints. These scenes are always framed by or in later medieval times entwined in richly decorated borders and wreathes. Churches were decorated to the glory of God, so the names of the artists are usually unknown. Only in a few cases do we know who they were, thanks to inscriptions.

The nave of the old church at Dädesjö in Småland is still standing. The wooden ceiling is one of the most remarkable of the medieval decorations preserved in its original form. Thirty medallions depict the Christmas Gospel and other scenes. Here we see the slaughter of the children at Bethlehem, the flight to Egypt and two scenes from the legend of Steven. The master painter's name, Sigmund, appears in a runic inscription in the triumphal arch. The paintings are Early Gothic and presumably from the end of the 13th century.

The Danish king was the patron of the church at Vä in Skåne, and the mural paintings were commissioned by him about 1130. Artistically they match the best of Europe's monumental painting at that time.

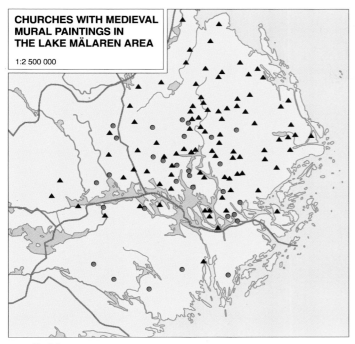

● Murals by Albertus pictor
▲ Murals by other masters

Tensta Church in Uppland was painted in 1437 by Johannes Rosenrodh. The patron was Bengt Jönsson Oxenstierna, owner of the Salsta estate, who is portrayed on the north wall of the chancel.

Uppland was the centre of late medieval Swedish church painting. Almost 60 per cent of the churches there have known paintings, while in Västmanland and Södermanland the figures are 25 per cent and 15 per cent respectively. Albertus Pictor and his school account for about 25 per cent of the decorated churches. (L63)

ALBERTUS PICTOR

The churches in Mälardalen in particular still contain many rich late medieval wall paintings from the 15th and early 16th centuries. Albert the Painter, Albertus Pictor, probably started his work as early as the 1460s. We know that he married the widow of Johan the Painter of Stockholm in 1473, taking over his workshop. He was then active both as a painter and as a pearl-embroiderer of church fabrics for more than 30 years. His name was mentioned for the last time in 1509.

Albert employed a large number of assistants. He worked mainly in Södermanland, Västmanland and western Uppland. Paintings by Albert and his workshop have been preserved in some 30 churches, and in six of them his signature has been identified. In Lid Church he even portrayed himself, kneeling; the damaged inscription in Latin reads: " . . . have mercy on me, Albert, who painted this church."

One of his finest and best-preserved works, consisting of more than 150 scenes, is at Härkeberga Church in Uppland. These rich paintings originally glowed in deep reds, greens and blues, but the centuries have faded their splendour and the red has turned to brown.

Other names in 15th-century Uppland painting are Johannes Rosenrodh and Johannes Ivan, both active before Albert. In the Tierp group we find Johannes Ivan's successors who, being outcompeted by Albert, did much of their work north of Uppland.

PAINTINGS IN SKÅNE

Although the medieval churches of Skåne have usually been heavily restored and rebuilt, the largest collection of Sweden's medieval wall paintings are to be found in this province. Paintings have been identified in almost 200 churches, 50 or so of them from the Romanesque period. Today many of them are no more than fragmentary ornaments.

Some Romanesque paintings have been preserved only above the later vaulted ceilings, but here they are fortunately quite untouched. Some of the most remarkable Romanesque decorations are to be found at Vä, Vinslöv, Finja and Lyngsjö.

The High Gothic paintings of the 14th century include the works of the Snårestad group, mainly in the churches round Ystad. A large number of murals were also painted during the 15th century, including the works of the Fjälkinge group, which are in some ten churches, and the Vittskövle group, to which the largest number of Late Gothic murals belong.

Some 120 of Skåne's approximately 240 preserved medieval churches have known wall paintings. Those in the Gothic style are in the majority, but quite a few older Romanesque works have also been preserved. (L64)

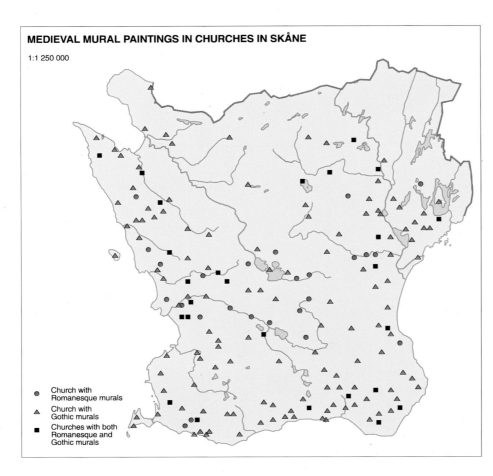

MEDIEVAL MURAL PAINTINGS IN CHURCHES IN SKÅNE

1:1 250 000

● Church with Romanesque murals
▲ Church with Gothic murals
■ Churches with both Romanesque and Gothic murals

PRESERVED MEDIEVAL WOODEN CHURCHES

1:10 000 000

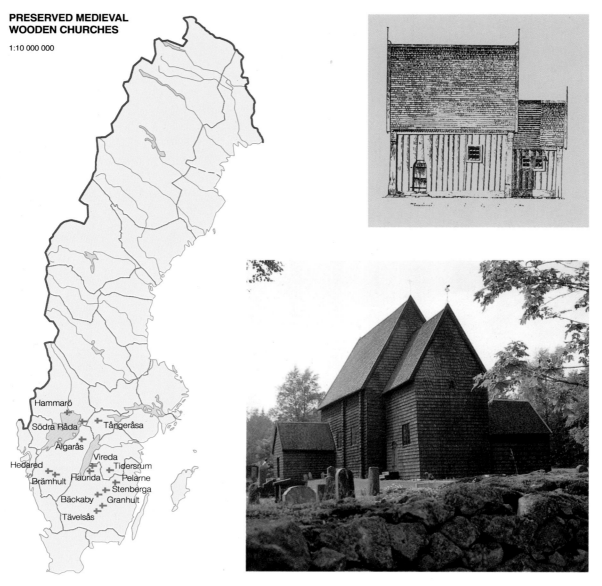

Hammarö
Södra Råda · Tångeråsa
Älgarås
Vireda
Hedared · Tidersrum
Brämhult · Flaurida · Pelarne
Stenberga
Bäckaby · Granhult
Tävelsås

Only 14 medieval wooden churches are preserved. Within the same area another 230 are known from archeological and historical sources: 110 in Småland, 72 in Västergötland, 44 in Värmland and 4 in Närke. They were replaced by 18th and 19th-century churches built of stone. (L65)

WOODEN CHURCHES

Churches built at the time of the Christian mission are generally presumed to have been constructed of wood. Even after the church had consolidated its position and stonework had become general in the 12th century, wooden churches continued to be built in the poor forest districts. In Småland, for example, a very large number of churches were built of wood, only seven of which have survived. There are another six in the rest of the country. However, a large number of medieval wooden churches are recorded either in archives or through archeological excavations. Most of them were not destroyed until the great period of church building in the 18th and 19th centuries.

The great skill of Swedish carpenters is also evident in the churches' elegant and slender roof truss constructions. These were a native contribution to the otherwise imported architecture and technology of the Romanesque stone churches. The roof trusses seem often to have been left open in the earliest phase of the churches, so they were visible from inside the buildings. Decorative profiles and bevelling ornament these wooden beams, which have mostly been preserved. There is also a reflection of the wood-carving art of the Viking Age in the wall plates and rafter foots, which were decorated with dragons, monsters and intricate ribbon patterns.

Hedared Church in Västergötland (top) is Sweden's only surviving stave church. It was first built around 1500 to replace an earlier one of the same type. It is reproduced here at 1:200.

The oldest of the preserved medieval wooden churches is Granhult Church in Småland (lower picture above), dated by dendrochronology to the 1220s. It is built of horizontal timbers; the only later alterations are the large windows and extensions for the sacristy and porch.

Södra Råda Church in Värmland was built in the early 14th century. Like Granhult it has survived as a deserted church. The ceilings are clover-shaped wooden vaults—the only surviving ones in the country. The well-preserved paintings in the chancel are from 1323, while those in the nave are signed Amund, 1494.

Decorated rafter foot from Hagebyhöga Church in Östergötland.

The altarscreen at Jäder Church in Södermanland depicts the childhood of Jesus and the Passion. It was made in Brussels about 1514 in the workshop of Jan Borman. The door paintings are by Jan van Coninxloo. Flemish mystery screens of this type and quality have been preserved mainly in Sweden. The cathedrals of Strängnäs and Västerås each own three.

CHURCHES WITH FLEMISH TRIPTYCHS AND CHURCHES WITH WOOD SCULPTURE BY HAAKEN GULLESSON

1:10 000 000

■ Church with Flemish triptych

● Church with wood sculpture by Haaken Gullesson

Some 30 preserved Flemish altar-screens were imported about 1500. Haaken Gullesson was the leader of a wood-sculpture workshop. (L66)

The Swedish Reformation was very tolerant of medieval church decoration. Altar screens, images of saints and murals were allowed, provided they did not lead to abuse, that is to say, Catholic rituals and the worship of saints. It was not until the Age of Enlightenment and the consequent wave of modernisation that medieval sculptures and fonts were moved away. They were generally speaking preserved, however, and are now once again to be found in our churches. A few form part of museum collections.

The medieval wood sculptures and altar screens preserved in Sweden are a considerable part of the common European stock. About 3,000 pieces of sculptured wood have survived, representing not only domestic production but also extensive imports from various parts of Germany such as Saxony, Westphalia, the Rhineland and in late medieval times Lübeck and other towns along the south coast of the Baltic. In the Late Middle Ages magnificent altarscreens were also imported from Flanders.

A Madonna, made at Haaken Gullesson's wood-sculpture workshop, in Attmar Church in Medelpad

Very many medieval fonts, which have many different designs, sometimes fairly simple in form, have been preserved. The more elaborate ones are richly decorated, as is this Romanesque font from Löderup Church in Skåne, sculptured about 1160 by the anonymous master mason "Magister Majestatis" (below left).

Brigittian textiles made in the nunnery at Vadstena have a special place in the history of Swedish textiles. This relic casket, covered with embroidery, was made there in the 15th century.

79

The Admiralty Church, Karlskrona, consecrated in 1685, was probably designed by Eric Dahlbergh. This large cruciform church, the largest wooden church in Sweden, is in the strict Baroque style of the period.

During the 17th century and the early 18th century most churches were still built of wood, and in the smaller ironworks and fishing chapels wood was the only material used. Some ironworks chapels later became parish churches, like those recorded here. When timber was used for large churches, the technology and design varied considerably. Below are some typical examples of plans on the same scale in chronological order from the 1620s to the 1790s. (L67)

WOODEN CHURCH BUILDINGS FROM THE 17TH AND 18TH CENTURIES

1:10 000 000

- ● Parish church
- ● Chapel
- ● Church whose ground plan is shown to the left

1. Ulvö fiskekapell
2. Amiralitetskyrkan
3. Ekshärad
4. Roslags-Kulla
5. Malingsbo
6. Habo
7. Frödinge
8. Vemdalen
9. Mossebo
10. Karl Gustav

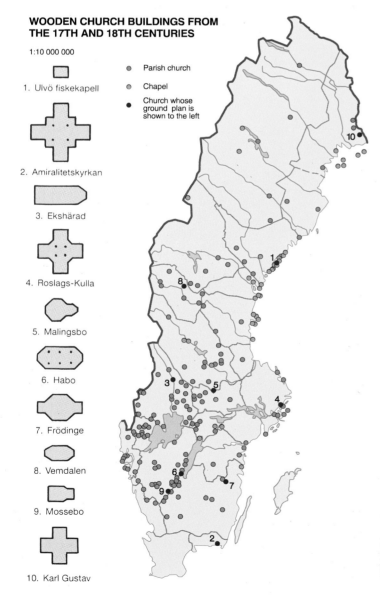

Modern Times

TIMBER CHURCHES

The Swedish tradition of timber building continued to be used after the Middle Ages in churches. From the Reformation up to the middle of the 18th century churches were built almost entirely of wood. Some replaced old wooden churches but others were completely new churches and chapels in newly-settled areas. Wooden churches are a common sight in southern Västergötland, Dalsland and Värmland, and the rapid expansion of ironworks communities led to extensive church building in Västmanland and Dalarna as well. The colonisation of the interior of Norrland also resulted in many churches and chapels being built. The many fishing chapels along the east coast are another characteristic feature.

Medieval timber churches imitated contemporary stone churches, but the new wooden churches of the 17th and 18th centuries, which usually required larger dimensions, demanded new constructions and new techniques. Builders and carpenters developed local traditions and an impressive range of skills.

The decoration and interiors of wooden churches also developed indi-

The great three-aisled, shingle-clad church at Habo, Västergötland, with a tower and triangular chancel, was rebuilt in 1723. The extensive decorations were painted between 1741 and 1743 by Johan Christian Peterson and Johan Kinnerus. The pulpit and altar piece were created by Jonas Ullberg in 1723. The interior is typical of the provincial ideal of a late Baroque church. The church is part of a church village: a vicarage, parish hall and the like.

vidual characteristics. The interiors were very suitable for paintings, and a large number of local master painters emerged during the 17th and 18th centuries, not least in western Sweden. A hundred or so master painters decorated more than 500 churches in Bohuslän, Dalsland, Halland, Småland, Västergötland and Värmland in the 18th century. Stone churches were decorated, too, with paintings on wooden ceilings and gallery fronts. A hundred or so well-preserved western-Swedish decorations may still be seen today, the most impressive of which are at Habo.

The 17th century introduced a period of change in the furnishing of church interiors, which were gradually renovated and adapted to the Protestant services of that time. Works

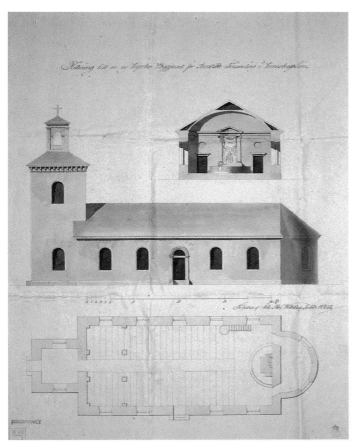

The church at Annerstad, Småland, designed in 1823, is an example of the simple late Neoclassical churches which are connected in the diocese of Växjö with Bishop Esaias Tegnér. During his period in office (1824–46) the number of churches of this type increased from 27 to 59.

ALTARPIECES BY ARTISTS FROM JÄMTLAND AND BY PEHR HÖRBERG

1:10 000 000

● Altarpiece by Johan Edler

● Altarpiece by Jonas Edler

● Altarpiece by Pehr Hörberg

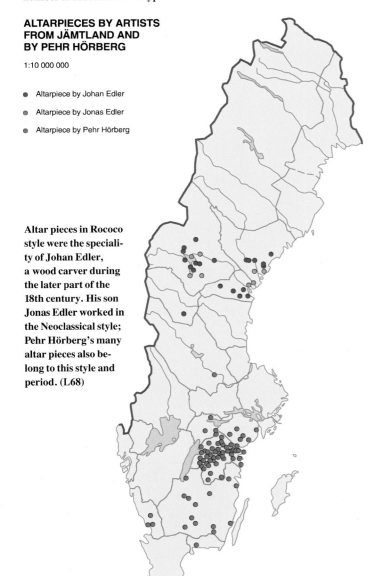

Altar pieces in Rococo style were the speciality of Johan Edler, a wood carver during the later part of the 18th century. His son Jonas Edler worked in the Neoclassical style; Pehr Hörberg's many altar pieces also belong to this style and period. (L68)

by contracted masters passed on the latest styles to native sculptors, painters and craftsmen. These baroque and rococo interiors with their magnificent altarpieces and pulpits still give old churches their special character.

NEO-CLASSICISM

Completely new ideals were introduced with the neo-classical church designs of the late 18th century. The rational approach to religion and education of the Age of Enlightenment, the gradually more rapid increase in the population and the predilection of King Gustav III and his architects for the neo-classical style created the great, white churches which are such a striking feature of the landscape in so many parts of Sweden. Almost 800 new churches, examined by the Royal Inspectorate and approved by the government, were built between 1760 and 1860 to replace the many churches, often wooden ones or medieval stone churches, which were considered too small, dilapidated and unfashionable. The map reveals that the ideals of neo-classicism were adopted to very varying degrees in different parts of the country.

Simplicity and austerity of form and a range of colours limited to grey, white and gold became the dominant features of church interiors. Altar decorations were usually a gilded cross with a crown of thorns and shroud or a classically framed altarpiece, while the organ dominated the west end of the church.

The main features of the architectural styles of the various epochs are easily discernible, but there have always been regional and local differences which have set their mark on churches in various ways, from medieval times up to the present day. Builders, masons, carpenters, wood sculptors and church painters—all had their special backgrounds and their geographically delimited regions. Thus no two churches are exactly alike. These variations are to be found even during the centrally-controlled neoclassical period.

CHANGING IDEALS

In the mid–19th century a new type of church with style imitations like new Gothic and Romanesque began to emerge. Alongside imitations of styles the design of churches and church interiors at the close of the 19th century expressed more and more the ideals and ambitions of individual architects.

At the end of the last century a thorough restoration of old church interiors, especially the neoclassical, was embarked upon. This desire to modernise churches not only functionally but also in style continued during the 20th century, so a well-preserved neoclassical or late 19th-century church interior is quite rare today. New liturgical demands, decreasing congregations in country parishes and heavy maintenance costs are other present-day complications in the conservation and repair of old churches.

The interior of Rappestad Church in Östergötland, built in the first few years of the 19th century, still has characteristic Neoclassical features. Pehr Hörberg painted the altar piece in 1802. At that time he was living in Östergötland, but he was from Småland and his roots were in the West-Swedish tradition of church painting. He was the first classically-trained artist to devote himself to altar pieces. His first was painted in 1786 and his last, No. 87, in 1815.

Around 1900 a new style of wooden architecture developed in upper Norrland. Stensele Church, called the cathedral of Lappland, was designed by Fredrik Ekberg and consecrated in 1886. The nave is like a light, three-aisled basilica, with room for 2,000 people.

NUMBER OF BELFRIES PER PROVINCE

1:10 000 000

100-

40-99

10-39

1-9

LAPPLAND 3

NORRBOTTEN 9

VÄSTERBOTTEN 7

JÄMTLAND 11

ÄNGERMANLAND 14

HÄRJEDALEN 3

MEDELPAD 4

HÄLSINGLAND 14

DALARNA 8

GÄSTRIKLAND

VÄRMLAND 4

VÄSTMAN-LAND 11

UPPLAND 115

DALSLAND

NÄRKE 9

SÖDERMANLAND 45

BOHUSLÄN 6

VÄSTER-GÖTLAND 101

ÖSTERGÖTLAND 19

HALLAND 6

SMÅLAND 59

GOTLAND

ÖLAND

BLEKINGE 10

SKÅNE 9

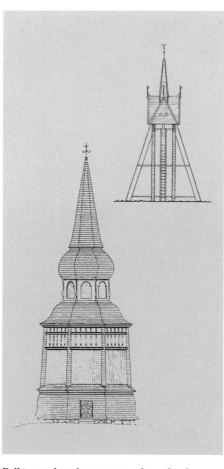

Bell towers have been preserved mostly where churches without towers are in the majority; there are none on Gotland, for example. The plans are of the bell tower at Granhult, 19 m high and built in 1703 for two bells, and the octagonal belfry at Borgsjö in Medelpad, 33 m high and built in 1782 for three bells by the church builder Pål Persson from Stugun. (L69)

Bell Towers

In districts where churches without towers are predominant, the lofty bell tower is a characteristic feature of church settings. In the 17th century there often seem to have been separate bell towers even when the church had a tower, because the new bells were considered too heavy for medieval towers. In 1759, however, the government decreed that wooden bell towers should be avoided and the bells moved back into the stone towers wherever possible. For this reason the tower became an important feature of the new, classical church.

Today somewhat more than 450 old bell towers are still standing, mainly from the 18th century, but some date back at least in part to medieval times. Their construction bears witness to great carpentry skills with roots in the early Middle Ages.

The oldest type consisted of a *belfry*, a type which has survived mainly in northern Sweden and in the old Danish provinces. A belfry is built up on a number of standing beams on a square or octagonal base and is built and ornamented with many old-style details.

Bell spires, which are considered to have been developed under the influence of Gothic architecture, used to be spread over the whole country but are now found mainly in southern and central Sweden. They may be open or completely or partly covered with boards. The characteristic feature of old bell spires is the crossing saddle roof with a tall central spire.

Churchyards

Our country churchyards are today usually surrounded by dry walls of granite blocks. This uniformity dates back to a circular letter from the government in 1764 in which parishes were urged to avoid the expensive maintenance of brick walls and wooden fences from Catholic times.

For the same reason, most of the lychgates that led into the churchyard were gradually replaced by ordinary gates. Stone lychgates of medieval origin are still preserved, while the oldest timbered lychgates date from the 17th and 18th centuries.

In olden times the churchyards themselves consisted of a grassed enclosure with a few grave memorials and were very different from today's

Tombstone in Linköping Cathedral made in the 17th century but resculptured in 1793. There are some 300 tombstones in the floor of the cathedral. In "Suecia Antiqua" shows the state of the churchyard in the 17th century (picture p. 155).

Stävie churchyard in Skåne has its traditional design preserved, including the box hedges typical of the landscape. The oldest parts of the churchyard are from the mid–19th century.

The church site at Kållerstad, Småland (above) was abandoned in 1858, and the timber church from 1764, which had replaced a stave church, was pulled down. In the deserted churchyard are some 18th-century wrought-iron memorials. At Åsenhöga, Småland, (below), too, the present stone church was preceded by two wooden churches. The deserted churchyard still has some 17th-century double gravestones typical of the district.

well-kept park-like churchyards. Right up to 1819 churchyards were used for grazing the parish clerk's cattle. Wealthy persons, who chose to be buried inside the church beneath the floor or in certain cases in private sepulchres, were not interested in the way the churchyards were kept. Towards the end of the 18th century, however, the custom of burying people inside churches was restricted, mainly for reasons of hygiene, and in 1783 it was forbidden to sell new graves there. At this time the new churchyard began to take shape, with burial plots, paths and trees. The simple grave memorials of the peasants, often made of wood, were joined by the more richly decorated tombs of the upper classes. Thus the design of gravestones and tombs reflected both social structure and changing artistic styles.

The now dominant park landscape style has in the past few decades radically changed many old churchyards. Large stretches of grass have replaced gravel on the graves and iron fences, hedges and stone surrounds have been removed.

The churchyards of churches in towns were usually replaced in the 19th century by cemeteries outside the town. One of the largest 20th-century cemeteries is Skogskyrkogården (The Forest Cemetery) in Stockholm, whose crematorium was built in 1940 to the design of Gunnar Asplund.

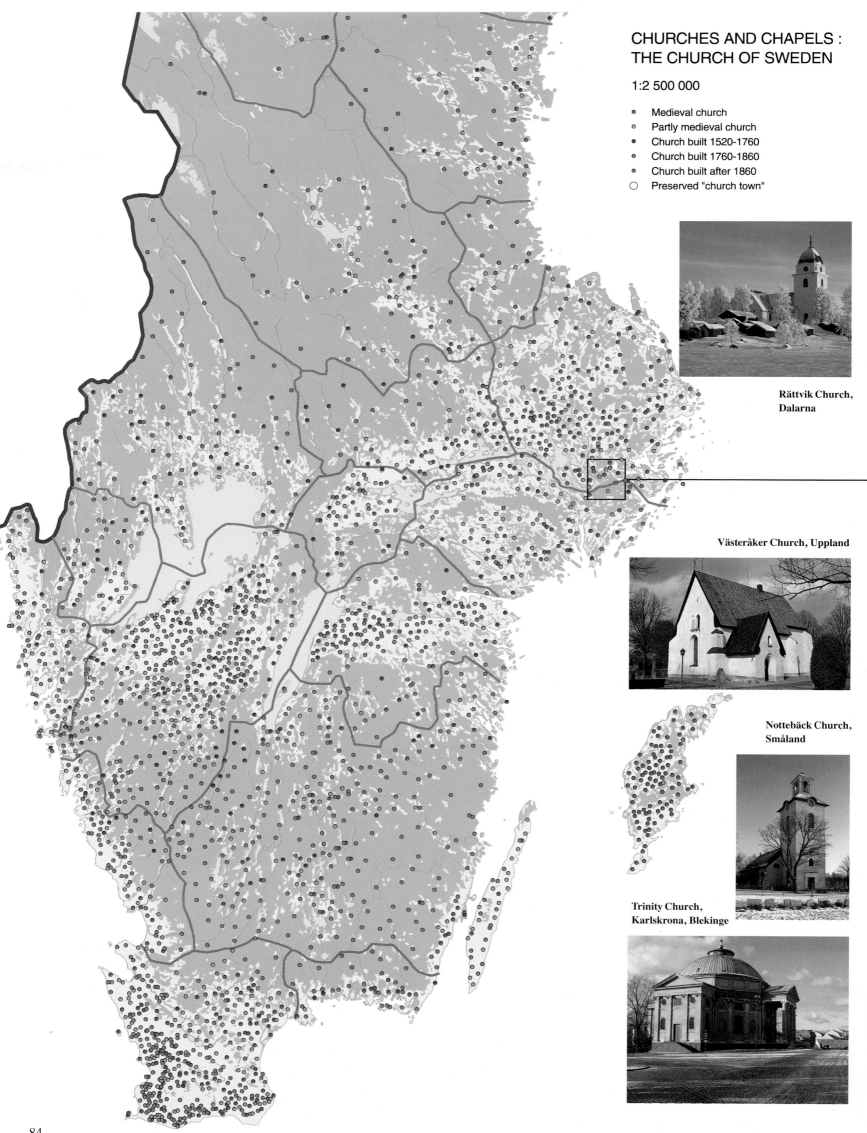

CHURCHES AND CHAPELS : THE CHURCH OF SWEDEN

1:2 500 000

- Medieval church
- Partly medieval church
- Church built 1520-1760
- Church built 1760-1860
- Church built after 1860
- Preserved "church town"

Rättvik Church, Dalarna

Västeråker Church, Uppland

Nottebäck Church, Småland

Trinity Church, Karlskrona, Blekinge

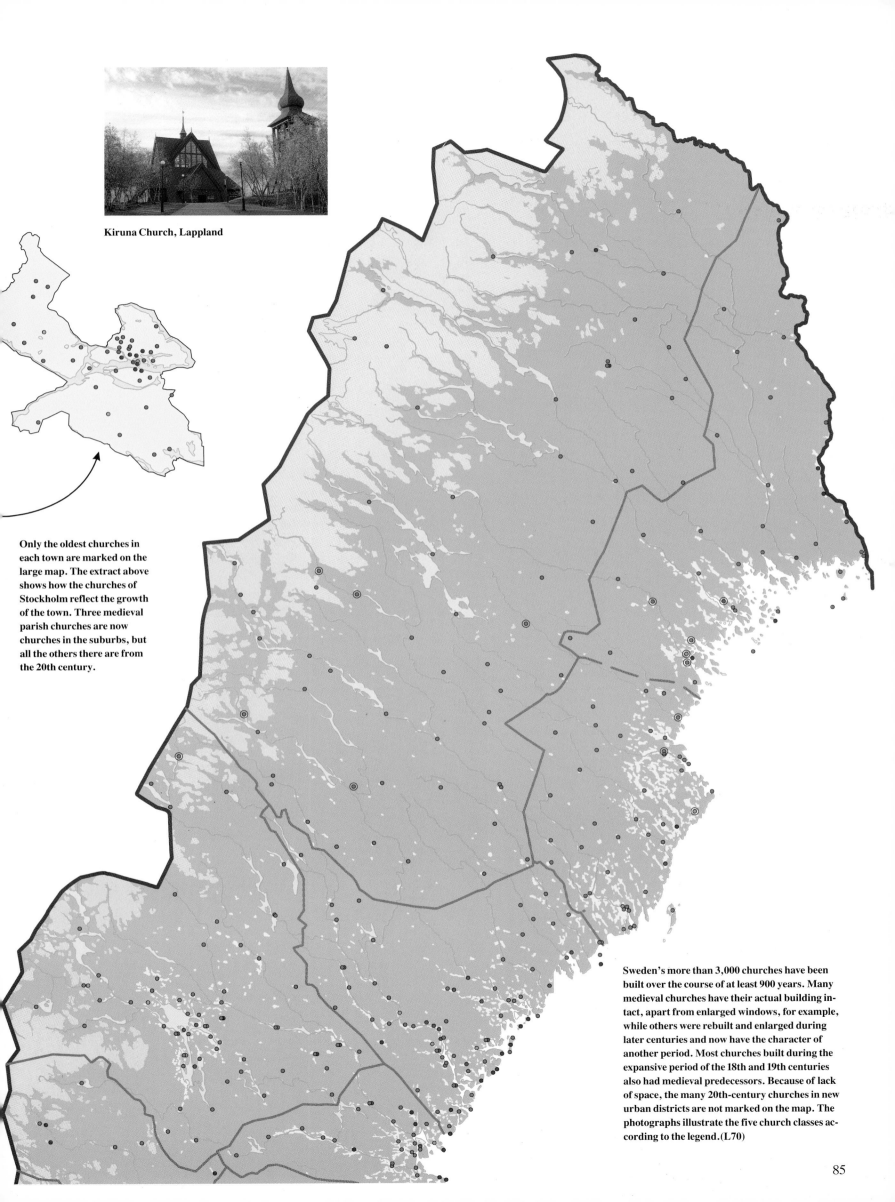

Kiruna Church, Lappland

Only the oldest churches in each town are marked on the large map. The extract above shows how the churches of Stockholm reflect the growth of the town. Three medieval parish churches are now churches in the suburbs, but all the others there are from the 20th century.

Sweden's more than 3,000 churches have been built over the course of at least 900 years. Many medieval churches have their actual building intact, apart from enlarged windows, for example, while others were rebuilt and enlarged during later centuries and now have the character of another period. Most churches built during the expansive period of the 18th and 19th centuries also had medieval predecessors. Because of lack of space, the many 20th-century churches in new urban districts are not marked on the map. The photographs illustrate the five church classes according to the legend.(L70)

Buildings and Farms in Rural Areas

Our knowledge of agrarian building environments is limited. No central register of such buildings exists and systematic surveys were not started until 1968.

For many years ethnological research concentrated mainly on the oldest or "best" buildings, so we know more about old buildings than the present-day stock. Methodical investigations started in 1912 under the aegis of the Nordic Museum. In 1925 Sigurd Erixon organised extensive surveys of villages and farms.

Almost all agricultural buildings are privately owned, and changes take place rapidly. Buildings that are no longer in use are neglected, while others take over new functions or are modernised. Few such buildings are protected by the Cultural Heritage Act, but in practice buildings owned by local archeological societies and open-air museums are protected. However, most local Folk Museums—

about 1,000 in number—consist of collections of buildings; there are only a few dozen museum farms standing in their original environments. To this list may be added sawmills, windmills, watermills and the like that have not been moved.

The appearance of peasant architecture varies according to the supply of building materials and local building traditions. When a certain style has been adopted by the upper classes it tends to be copied. Architecture may also be influenced by legislation and the recommendations of authorities. Factors like the size of the farm, the type of household, the kind of farming and the need for storage space also play a significant part. In addition the location of buildings is always dependent on the topography.

Our stock of agricultural buildings comprises almost one million houses. Here we shall concentrate on those built before 1900.

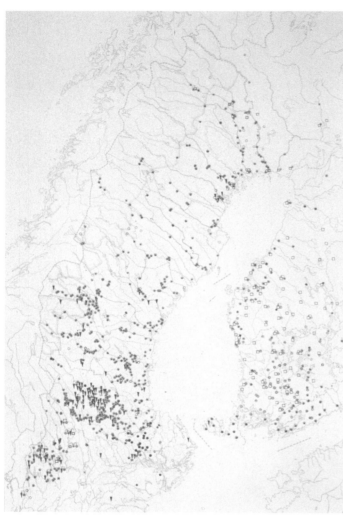

One of many examples of ethnological documentation of buildings: Sigurd Erixon's map (1957) of log post storehouses. The symbols indicate four different kinds of foundations (posts, horizontal planking, blocks, timbered chest) combined with two different types of entrances (on the short and on the long side).

A well-preserved double cottage on one floor at Lundby near Bergaholm in Salem, Södermanland, still has the same traditional ground plan and appearance as it had in 1930, when it was documented. The log walls are panelled and the corners built in. The kitchen functions as a living room.

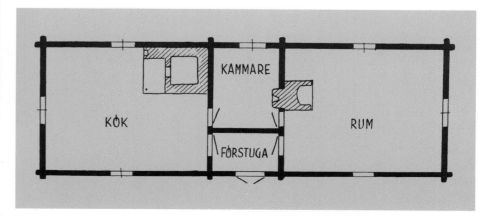

The church storehouse at Älvdalen, Dalarna, is not only a superb example of a log post storehouse using old corner dovetailing techniques but is also the oldest known profane log house in Sweden, dated by dendrochronology to about 1280.

DISTRIBUTION OF THE THREE PREDOMINANT BUILDING TECHNOLOGIES

1:10 000 000

- Timbered buildings with dovetailed corners
- Timbered buildings, some post and plank buildings
- Timbered buildings, post and plank buildings
- Post and plank buildings, timbered buildings (ca. 60/40%)
- Post and plank buildings, some timbered buildings, some half-timbered buildings
- Post and plank buildings, half-timbered buildings (50/50%)
- Half-timbered buildings, some post and plank buildings
- Half-timbered buildings

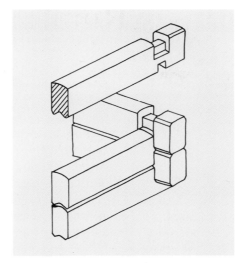

Distribution of the three most frequent building techniques during the late 19th century, in approximate frequencies. (L71)

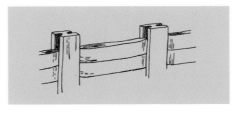

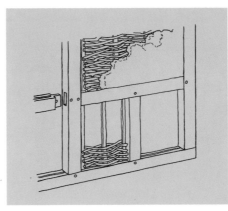

The drawings explain the principles of the three most common old building techniques using wood; from top, dovetailed logs, post and plank building and half-timbering.

Post and plank constructions are nowadays mostly found in old farm buildings in southern Sweden; here, a barn in Skåne.

Materials and Technology

Country buildings in Sweden are in the main built of wood. *Timbered* farm buildings of the traditional log-cabin type were constructed until 1880–1900, and outhouses as late as 1890–1910.

Where oak was in good supply, *post and plank* buildings were common. Further north the same technique used pine planks in small buildings. This method fell out of use at the end of the 19th century.

Staves, that is, vertical planks, were used mostly in western Sweden.

Half-timbering is a mixed technique: a frame of wood is filled with wattles, between which straw or small branches are woven and then coated with mud. In later buildings the filling is often bricks. To the north half-timbering is more common in urban areas than in rural districts, and it is predominant in Skåne.

Stone is used as building material mainly on Öland and Gotland, where limestone was reintroduced after the middle of the 18th century. Stone is also used for barns and stables in combination with wood. Before 1840 *bricks* were used in agrarian settings only in Uppland; thereafter this material became more common, mainly in Mälardalen and Skåne.

In the mid–19th century the new steam sawmills produced large quantities of planks. *Board buildings* using various post, plank and stud constructions were now built and timbered houses were faced with boarding.

The *red paint* which is so typical of Swedish buildings first came into use in country districts in the mid–18th century. Before that buildings were a natural grey colour.

Half-timbering has been used for houses and buildings, both in towns and in the country; here, an old farmhouse in Stehag, Skåne.

Northern Swedish farms with their traditional system of many buildings arranged in a square sometimes looked like a small hamlet. At Tomtan Farm in Klövsjö, Jämtland, the farmhouse can be seen in the background to the right, with the summer cottage and the cowsheds in the square. In the foreground, a log shed and a baking house outside the square.

The enclosed four-sided Skåne farms often combined half-timbered farmhouses with farm buildings of natural stone. Glimmeboda Farm in Brösarp, Skåne, is also characteristically situated in the terrain.

Types of Buildings and Farms

Agrarian architecture has several dozen types of buildings. Most of Sweden has traditionally had a *multi-building system*, that is, one building for each function. There are exceptions in southern and western Sweden where several functions were gathered under one roof—because it is easy to build long half-timbered and plank houses. Log cabins, however, are often limited by the length of the logs, because logs were not joined lengthwise.

TWO-ROOM COTTAGES

The typical country cottage in Sweden was the two-room cottage—in principle two identical, mirror rooms placed side by side with a joint porch. The original form is a one-storeyed building in which one room was used as a kitchen and living room and the other as a parlour.

Two-room cottages were the usual type on farms from Norrbotten down to northern Götaland, with the exception of Dalarna, until the mid–19th century. Then two-room cottages also came into use on smallholdings and crofts and as labourers' cottages for two families. As late as the turn of the last century at least one third of farm cottages in central Sweden followed the basic design of the two-room cottage.

LOG STOREHOUSES

Log storehouses raised above the ground were used for storing clothes, household utensils, corn and food. The log store house and the loft cabin are the two types of buildings which were given the most conscious esthetic design. Consequently, and as a result of careful timberwork, log storehouses have often been preserved. Some 50 of them are known to date from before 1500.

Many log storehouses have an overhanging upper storey. The main gable often has a gallery. On large farms in northern Jämtland and Norrbotten there are three-storeyed storehouses. Farms in the Torne and Kalix valleys have storehouses with a curved upper storey—the result of influence from Russian church architecture. Several log storehouses have been turned into holiday cottages and guest cottages.

TYPES OF FARMS

Different types of farms have their buildings placed in different patterns on the farm site. Ethnologists have used the distribution of these different types during the later part of the 19th century to divide Sweden into cultural regions, but the types date back to conditions as long ago as the Iron Age. They have also been influenced by other cultural environments and by the need for protection.

Today, when the multi-building system is no longer practised, the old farm types are rare except for the West Swedish type and the square Skåne farm. However, the principle of having farmhouse and cattlesheds either separate or combined lives on in various districts. The number of farms with separate cattlesheds increases the further south you go, Skåne excepted.

DISTRIBUTION OF TRADITIONAL FARM TYPES

1:20 000 000

South Swedish farm	Geatish farm
North Swedish farm	Middle Swedish farm
Central Swedish farm	West Swedish farm

The distribution of traditional farm types was quite evident as late as the early 20th century. The southern Swedish farm was enclosed. The northern Swedish farm was in a closed or open square with separate buildings. The central Swedish farm was divided into a farmyard and cattleshed yard with a row of sheds separating them. The Geatish farm was in a long row, with farmyard and cattleshed yard separated by a fence. The middle Swedish farm had a farmyard which were separate from the cattle yard and surrounded by the farmhouses. The western Swedish farm was loosely planned with few rows of buildings. (L72)

Samples of farm types taken in the 1970s show that the traditional arrangements of buildings were in a process of dissolution.

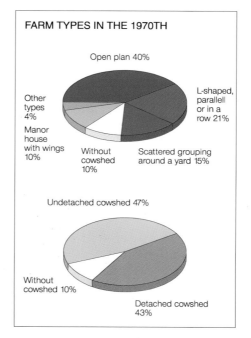

FARM TYPES IN THE 1970TH

Open plan 40%

Other types 4%

Manor house with wings 10%

L-shaped, parallell or in a row 21%

Without cowshed 10%

Scattered grouping around a yard 15%

Undetached cowshed 47%

Without cowshed 10%

Detached cowshed 43%

How Old are the Buildings?

It is difficult to date the older agrarian buildings; there is often no historical data available. The C^{14} method gives unreliable results for wood that is less than about 1,000 years old. Instead it has been necessary to estimate age by means of stylistic criteria or the design of constructions such as timber joints. These methods can result in errors of up to 100 years either way. Rebuilding and additions make dating more problematic.

Sample tests in the 1970s showed that nearly all dwelling houses in the countryside were built after 1800, and

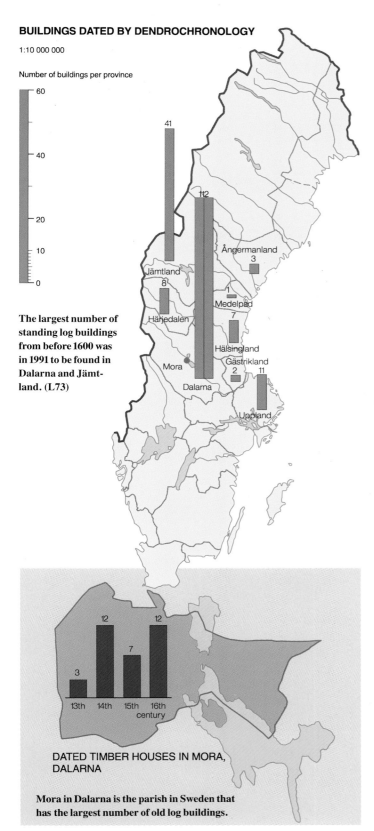

BUILDINGS DATED BY DENDROCHRONOLOGY

1:10 000 000

Number of buildings per province

The largest number of standing log buildings from before 1600 was in 1991 to be found in Dalarna and Jämtland. (L73)

DATED TIMBER HOUSES IN MORA, DALARNA

Mora in Dalarna is the parish in Sweden that has the largest number of old log buildings.

that 84 per cent were built after 1875. The oldest houses are in the north, but there are wide variations throughout the country. A good number of the houses have been rebuilt since 1940. The outhouses are on average of a later date; 36 per cent were built after 1940, often using quite new techniques.

DENDROCHRONOLOGY

The introduction of the dendrochronological method in the mid–1970s made it easier to get exact datings. A graph of annual rings based on many trees from the same district is constructed and its chronology is determined by comparison with samples of wood of a known date.

There is a basic graph for pine in southern Norrland and northern Svealand. Up to the summer of 1991 samples had been taken from about 400 old buildings, most of them in Jämtland and Kopparberg counties. The majority of dated buildings are earlier than 1600. The oldest known profane building is the church storehouse at Älvdalen in Dalarna, for whose walls logs were cut in the winter of 1285/86, while the timber church of Granhult in Småland was built as early as 1217.

Hamlet Settlements

Before the land reforms of the 18th and 19th centuries most agrarian settlements were in villages or hamlets, that is, a group of farms and their buildings on a hamlet toft surrounded by enclosed fields and meadows, which were divided into strips owned individually, and by common pastureland, fences and roads and often common forestland as well. The sequence of cultivation and use of pastures, together with the maintenance of roads, fences and other common property, was regulated by rules and by decisions made by the landowners at the village meetings.

Archeological investigations have shown that farms on the plains in the Iron Age changed their location and that hamlet settlements also existed. At the beginning of the Middle Ages farms often moved together to form villages. An important reason was the

The row village of Äppelrum in Räpplinge, Öland, to this very day shows the links between each farm's field plots and the farm site in the village, which was not normally split up on Öland.

introduction of cultivation systems by which one field were left fallow every second or third year (two-field and three-field systems).

In later periods villages were formed by the successive division of isolated farms, through inheritance, for example. There are many quite large villages in Dalarna, Småland and Norrland which began as pioneer settlements in the Middle Ages or modern times. Gotland, on the other hand, has had scattered farmsteads for as long as settlement history there is known.

THE LOCATION OF HAMLETS

Villages had varying structures in different parts of the country. Usually hamlets consisted of a few farms, with the exception of those on Öland and in Skåne, Västergötland, Dalarna and parts of Norrland. Large villages in northern Sweden have a different structure from those in the south, however. They consist of groups of farms with small fields without mixed ownership. Fishing waters and the forest were the main sources of livelihood.

Some hamlets became church villages, thus developing a special character with a church, vicarage, school, parish hall, almshouses and so on.

The terrain was the most significant factor for the location of a settlement. Old terms such as cluster village, shore village, road village, ridge village and the like give only a superficial description. Below the highest coastline the typical location of a hamlet is on south-sloping parts of tilly and rocky hills or the sides of valleys beside clayey soils. On the till plains of Skåne and Västergötland the large villages lay in the dales with the fields around them. Above the highest coastline the fine-grained till on hilltops was used and in northern Sweden frost-free locations on high slopes or along shores.

VILLAGES WITH "VILLAGE GREENS"

For the location of hamlets there are in various parts of the country structural features that arose intentionally. In southern Sweden many villages had a sack-shaped enclosure, in Västergötland called a "toe", around which the farms were built. This green, often with a pond in the middle, was for the cattle and was connected with the outfield pastures by a cattle track.

1:10 000 000

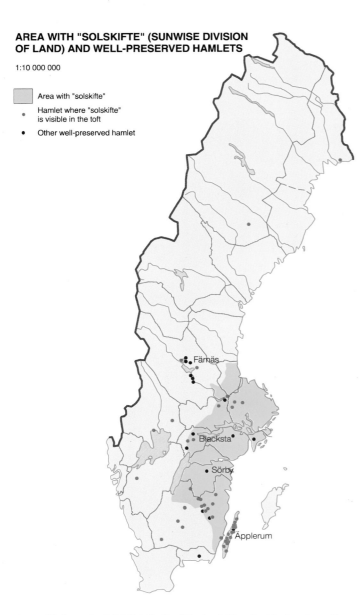

Area with "sunwise field distribution" (or lawful location) before the redistribution of land in the 19th century, a limited selection of well-preserved row villages "lawfully located", and a few other well-preserved villages ("cluster villages"), all listed as being historic areas of national interest. (L74)

BLACKSTA IN GÅSINGE-DILLNÄS, SÖDERMANLAND

Blacksta began as an Iron Age settlement; there is a cemetery north of the village. In the Middle Ages Blacksta developed into a regulated row village on an esker with four units of taxable land (Sw. mantal, hides). The land was redistributed in 1857, when there were seven farms in the village, but this led to only a few changes in the buildings, probably because there were no other suitable building plots available.

VILLAGES WITH "LAWFUL LOCATION"

Another distinct type of village in Sweden was planned or regulated. This was the characteristic "row village" of eastern central Sweden, with single or double rows of farms, built according to the "sunwise" system (Sw. solskifte). How a village should be planned is described in the provincial laws from the Middle Ages. The width of the farmhouse plots along the village street should reflect the size of the farms in the village. The sequence of the farms in the village toft should reappear in the sequence of the strips in the village fields. The sunwise system was a means of creating a fair system for the distribution of the village's resources and land ownership.

The hamlets in eastern central Sweden were small. Sörby in Landeryd, Östergötland, still has the same plot division as in 1690, and the five farms have old-fashioned features including twin cottages for two farms.

THE DISSOLUTION OF VILLAGES

Most villages were dissolved during the 19th century as a result of the repeated redistribution of land by acts of parliament. Countless farms were moved out into amalgamated fields to be cultivated individually within the former village land. Two or three farms might have been left at the old site, which can also be identified by its location in the terrain and by deserted farm plots. In areas with hamlets or scattered settlements, the settlement picture was not much affected by land redistribution. The relocation of farms was greatest in Skaraborg county, Skåne and western Östergötland.

The original village character of "sunwise" areas is best preserved on Öland, with its large row villages

FÄRNÄS VILLAGE IN MORA, DALARNA

The village may be described as an extreme example of a cluster village, where the farmsteads are grouped together without any apparent order on a large piece of land. It is first mentioned in 1325. As early as 1571 it had 40 taxpayers, increasing to 45 in 1627. At the great land redistribution in 1850 it had just over 100 farms. The village has developed seven clusters, which have now grown together. The buildings are begining to spread out into the fields; there are detached houses in a previous gap at the centre and on the outskirts. In other respects the village has retained its old-time character. But the enclosed farmyards are disappearing.

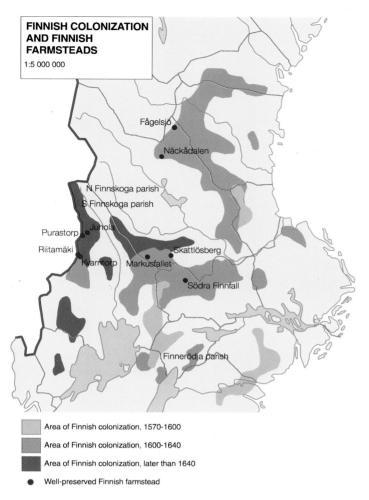

FINNISH COLONIZATION AND FINNISH FARMSTEADS

1:5 000 000

Fågelsjö

Näckådalen

N. Finnskoga parish

S. Finnskoga parish

Purastorp   Juhola

Riitamäki

Kvarntorp   Markusfallet

Skattlösberg

Södra Finnfall

Finnerödja parish

▢ Area of Finnish colonization, 1570-1600

▢ Area of Finnish colonization, 1600-1640

▢ Area of Finnish colonization, later than 1640

● Well-preserved Finnish farmstead

The Finnish districts lie in forest areas around the old province borders. North of the area shown here there are several in the border districts between Ångermanland/Medelpad and Ångermanland/Jämtland. Many Finnish farms are now ordinary farms or small hamlets, others have been abandoned. (L75)

Ritamäki in Lekvattnet, Värmland, is a Finnish farm with a multi-building system and a well-preserved smoking shed. The farm has a typical hilltop localisation.

along the natural elevated beach ridges. In Dalarna the concentrated settlement in the large villages with widely scattered land ownership was preserved by exceptions to the land redistribution laws. The villages in both these provinces have great cultural-historical value. In the rest of Sweden there are well-preserved villages here and there.

The farms which were moved out in the 19th century built houses of the then modern type, for example a farmhouse of the six-partitioned plan. Outhouses were often built of stone or brick.

Three Waves of Colonisation

Isolated farm settlements, on Gotland and in Bohuslän, for example, may go back to prehistoric times. In most areas, however, such settlements are the result of colonisation in historical times, where the original settlement could not, for some reason or other, be divided. Three waves of colonisation will be described here; these led normally, after a time, to the establishment of taxed farms (freehold farmsteads).

EARLY MIDDLE AGES

A powerful wave of colonisation swept across Europe, including Sweden, during the first half of the Middle Ages. It was a result of a large increase in population and both church and king supported an increase in the number of taxable farms. Farmers in the old villages, however, did not welcome the new settlers on their land, since they might encroach on their new cultivation and forest grazing grounds. The provincial laws in southern Sweden were more restrictive towards new farms on common land than the Hälsingland law in the north. Nevertheless many people moved out into the forests, often to village and parish commonland, cultivating hay meadows, burn-beaten land or other suitable land. Hence up to about 1,300 settled districts grew thanks to the colonisation of high-lying land of till;

Gudmundstjärn Farm in Indal, Medelpad, is an isolated, 18th-century settler's farm in the forest away from the older settlement. It has a multi-building system consisting of 23 preserved buildings and ancient meadow and arable land.

there was also some growth in the old settled areas. There is clear evidence of colonisation—not least in place names—in Småland and parts of Västergötland and Värmland. The use of low-technological iron manufacturing was a contributory factor in certain areas, and in Bergslagen colonisation was mainly due to mining.

In the 14th century the situation changed. Repeated outbreaks of the plague and agricultural crises resulted in many new farms being deserted in the late Middle Ages. The new medieval settlements in Småland and Värmland, for example, are today mostly small hamlets.

FINNISH DISTRICTS

Finnish districts appeared in several parts of Svealand and southern Norrland in the period 1570–1660 as a result of immigration from Finland. These districts were often located on high, uninhabited ground along the provincial boundaries where there was sandy heathland without shealings. The land in these areas above the highest coastline was suitable for slash and burn cultivation, since it was not drained of nutrients. The Finnish settlements lie in frost-protected locations on slopes and hilltops.

In northern and western Värmland this 17th-century Finnish culture lived on until the mid–19th century, with the river Klarälven as a boundary to the shealing settlements to the east. Today there remain only seven well-preserved Finnish farms on their original sites.

COLONISATION OF NORRLAND

New settlements in inner Norrland had started as early as the Middle Ages—in some areas, like Jämtland, on a large scale. After the late medieval crisis and before the Lappland regulations of 1749, which encouraged new settlement, there was little colonisation. Farms were located on hilltops or slopes with fine-grained till in less frost-exposed positions or along shores. Good fishing was an essential factor. Making a livelihood from hunting and mire meadows required large areas, so settlements were scattered. Establishing this form of settlements came to an end in the 1860s. They often developed later into villages when freehold farms were divided. The buildings were simple; more sophisticated farmhouses were not built until the expansion of forestry.

Buildings on Non-freehold Land

In the old peasant society those who had no property lived in simple circumstances. Those who had the use of a patch of land they could cultivate had the highest status.

At Åsle tå in Falbygden in Västergötland stands one of the best-preserved building environments for the propertyless people of country districts, typically located along a stream.

The most usual form of building on non-freehold land was the croft. Crofts were built on private land of the manor estates during the 17th century. It was not until 1743 that crofts were allowed to be built on peasant land. After the redistribution of land a peasant farmer could establish a croft without hindrance from the other inhabitants of the village, and there was a boom in building. There were also soldiers' crofts built for the conscript system.

Crofters lived under varying conditions. The contractual periods varied greatly. The landowner was paid by daywork, often complemented by mi-

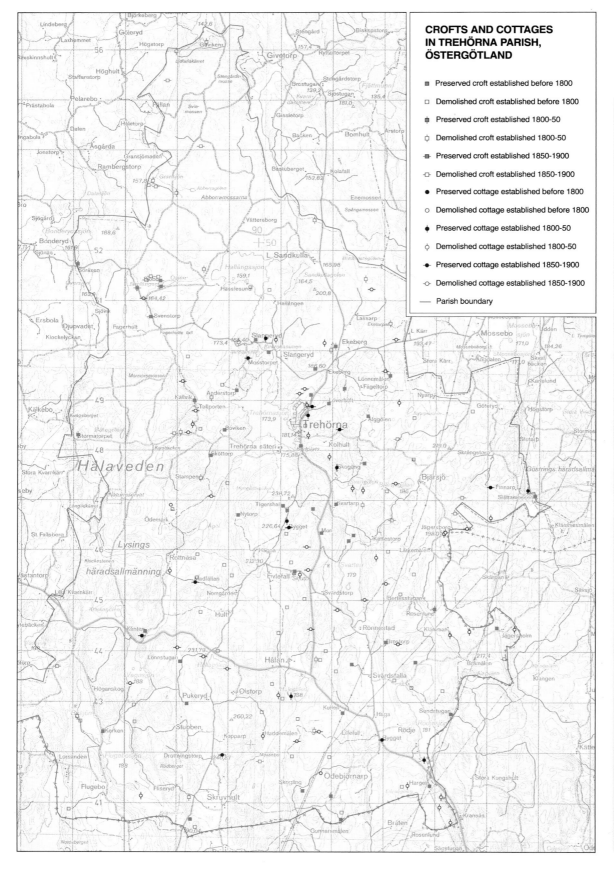

CROFTS AND COTTAGES IN TREHÖRNA PARISH, ÖSTERGÖTLAND

- ■ Preserved croft established before 1800
- □ Demolished croft established before 1800
- ▤ Preserved croft established 1800-50
- ▢ Demolished croft established 1800-50
- ▦ Preserved croft established 1850-1900
- ▫ Demolished croft established 1850-1900
- ● Preserved cottage established before 1800
- ○ Demolished cottage established before 1800
- ◆ Preserved cottage established 1800-50
- ◇ Demolished cottage established 1800-50
- ◆ Preserved cottage established 1850-1900
- ◇ Demolished cottage established 1850-1900
- — Parish boundary

DEFINITIONS

Cottar (Sw. backstugusittare): a person who lives in a cottage on some other person's land.

Crown farmer (Sw. kronobonde): tenant of a farm belonging to the Crown, held with right of tenure which is transferrable.

Tenant farmer (Sw. landbonde): person who in return for labour and an annual fee has the right to use farmland owned by a nobleman.

Tax farmer (Sw. skattebonde): private owner of a farm for which taxes according to the size of the farm are paid to the Crown.

Plot of land (Sw. lägenhet): part of a property which has been leased with usufruct (right of use).

Croft (Sw. torp): early meaning— a new dwelling on common land, which later was taxed and became a farmstead; later meaning— a small, untaxed farm on private land, occupied in return for labour. (Sw. **statare**): an agricultural labourer engaged for the whole year with payment in kind and dwelling.

TREHÖRNA, ÖSTERGÖTLAND

The forested parish of Hålaveden is an example of a district rich in crofts and cottages. The crofts are generally speaking about 50 years older than the cottages. They lie closest together round Lake Trehörnasjön, at the centre of the parish, where some have survived as permanent dwellings. The crofts usually lie on the edge of the farm properties. There are only a few on the commons in the north and west, except where there is marsh and bogland. The buildings here are relatively late, most of them built later than 1850.

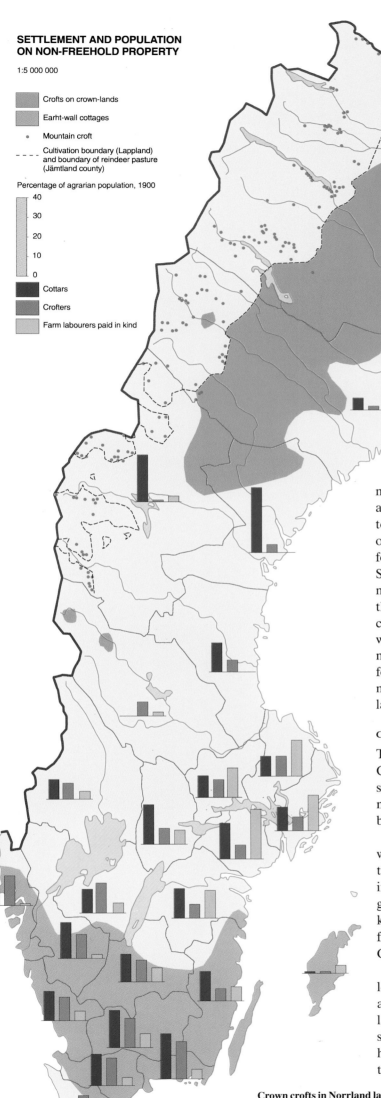

SETTLEMENT AND POPULATION ON NON-FREEHOLD PROPERTY

1:5 000 000

Crofts on crown-lands

Earht-wall cottages

• Mountain croft

- - - Cultivation boundary (Lappland)
and boundary of reindeer pasture
(Jämtland county)

Percentage of agrarian population, 1900

40
30
20
10
0

Cottars

Crofters

Farm labourers paid in kind

As late as 1926 this barrack for farm labourers was still standing at Hammarby, in south Stockholm.

nor services. The croft consisted of a simple dwelling house, often built together with outhouses at an angle or in a row. Most crofts were to be found in the counties of Östergötland, Skaraborg and Kristianstad. The number began to decrease just before the middle of the 19th century. The croft system came to an end in 1943, when daywork as a method of payment for rent was forbidden. The foundations of crofts are amongst the most common remains in the cultural landscape.

CROWN CROFTS

There were several types of crofts on Crown land in northern Sweden. The state ownership of Crown land have meant that these environments have been preserved.

Many settlements already existed when the first regulation concerning the leasing of Crown land was passed in 1891. Various forms of tenancy gradually developed, with various kinds of obligations: forest crofts, farming cottages, colony cottages and Crown crofts.

Mountain cottages involved the leasing of Crown land for farming above the "cultivation limit" in Lappland, where the land had in principle since 1867 been reserved for reindeer husbandry, and in the reindeer mountain pastureland in Jämtland.

Crown crofts in Norrland lay below, and mountain cottages above the cultivation line. Earth cottages were a typical southern Swedish type of home for poor people. Crofts and crofters existed in most counties with a few notable exceptions, while farm labourers paid in kind lived mostly in the large agricultural counties. (L76)

COTTAGES

In 1772 peasants were granted the right to build "hillside cottages", or cots. The number of cottars reached its peak around 1870 and were mostly in the counties of Malmöhus, Skaraborg and Kristianstad. These cotters made a living as daily labourers, craftsmen and makers of handicraft products. The cots were of the simplest possible kind, often standing in groups on the outskirts of villages, on village greens, on commonland or along the parish boundaries.

Some of these cots were earth cots, that is, were dug into a hillside. Usually one end was underground. The advantages were protection from the wind, saving of timber and some degree of warmth. Earth cots are thought to be no older than the 18th century, and they were abandoned as permanent dwellings in the 1920s or earlier. This type was mostly found in Götaland, and some 50 have been preserved.

LABOURERS' DWELLINGS

The "statare" system, that is, working for payment in kind, is a Swedish institution with certain parallels abroad. This form of employment started in the 1750s and by 1900 the majority of such labourers were in the counties of Södermanland, Östergötland and Malmöhus. In the two following decades their number increased but then fell rapidly. The "statare" system disappeared as a result of a collective agreement in 1945.

These labourers lived in some part of the farm buildings, on old farms, in crofts and cottages or in long barrack-like buildings specially built for the purpose. These usually housed four families and could be on a street.

The shealings of the large Dalarna villages were also extensive. The cots at Ljusbodarna in Leksand consist of two clusters, each with a number of buildings of various types.

The distribution and variants of the shealing system about 1900 covered a much larger area than the living shealing system today. The small map shows the decline of the shealing system in Dalarna in the 20th century. Many shealings are used today as second homes, while others have been demolished, but quite a few are still used for grazing cattle. (L77)

Shealings

The shealing system means that cattle spend the summer months on pastureland fairly close to or a long way from the farms in the village. The milk was processed on the spot into products that would keep; since 1960–70, however, it has usually been sent to dairies. If the milk is brought home daily, the term half-shealing is used. Sometimes farms used two or more shealings, switching between nearby home shealings and more distant, shealings. The two-shealing system also existed in the form of spring and autumn shealings. Most of the people on a farm would move to the home shealing for hay-making, foliage collection and sometimes cultivation. Up at the distant shealing a dairymaid would look after the cattle.

There is evidence of a shealing system in the Middle Ages in Dalarna and Hälsingland. About the end of the 16th century it developed rapidly and by the end of the 19th century, when it was at its peak, the shealing boundary line stretched from northern Uppland across to northern Bohuslän. The heart of the area was in northern Dalarna, Härjedalen and western Jämtland, the centre of the multi-shealing system. New shealings were established as late as the end of the 1960s at Klövsjö in Jämtland.

A shealing has one or more cowhouses, a shed for milk products and a cot. A few dozen huts, the predecessors of the cots, have been preserved; they have an earth floor, a hearth in the middle and a hole in the roof for the smoke. There might also be a simple cookhouse, a barn, a storehouse, a mill and so on. At some shealing sites with arable land permanent dwellings were later built. Such shealings were common in eastern Dalarna and northern Hälsingland. Half-shealings were simpler and were mostly found in Norrbotten and Västerbotten. At the shealings along the Gulf of Bothnia pastures rather than hayfields were predominant.

The Nordic Museum's register of shealings comprises 7,390 names; not all of these were in use at the same time, and certainly a few are missing. Most of them have now disappeared, are falling down or have in part been turned into leisure areas. A few dozen have been restored.

SHEALING SYSTEM AROUND 1900 AND TODAY

1:10 000 000

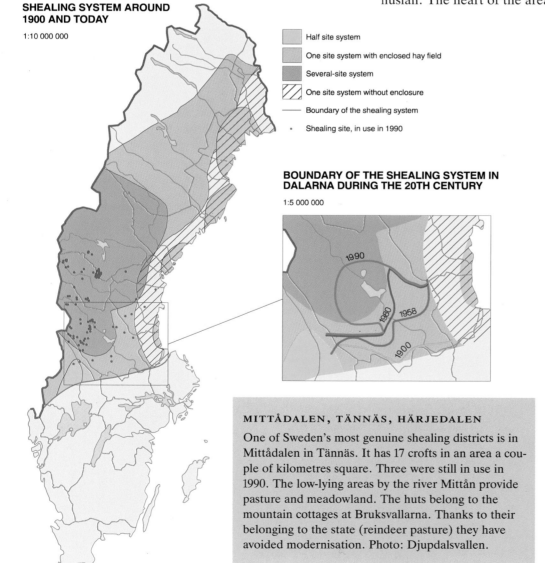

- Half site system
- One site system with enclosed hay field
- Several-site system
- One site system without enclosure
- Boundary of the shealing system
- Shealing site, in use in 1990

BOUNDARY OF THE SHEALING SYSTEM IN DALARNA DURING THE 20TH CENTURY

1:5 000 000

1990
1980
1958
1900

MITTÅDALEN, TÄNNÄS, HÄRJEDALEN

One of Sweden's most genuine shealing districts is in Mittådalen in Tännäs. It has 17 crofts in an area a couple of kilometres square. Three were still in use in 1990. The low-lying areas by the river Mittån provide pasture and meadowland. The huts belong to the mountain cottages at Bruksvallarna. Thanks to their belonging to the state (reindeer pasture) they have avoided modernisation. Photo: Djupdalsvallen.

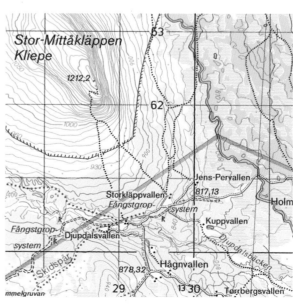

Castles, Palaces and Manor Houses

Stegeborg on an island in Slätbaken bay, Östergötland, was originally a medieval fort, which became an enclosed defensive castle during the late Middle Ages and was used as fee castle. During the Vasa Period it was rebuilt as a Renaissance castle, which was ruined in the 1730s.

CASTLES, STRONGHOLDS AND RUINS FROM BEFORE 1530

1:5 000 000

Building still standing

Ruin

Middle Ages before 1530

The right conditions for the building of manor houses arose when the temporal class of noblemen was created in the second half of the 13th century. The number of manors seems to have been large during the 14th century but thereafter decreased and was estimated at about 470 during the union between Sweden, Denmark and Norway (1397–1521).

Most of the manor houses were in the cultivated districts of central, western and southern Sweden. The high nobility had large estates, so their houses were far apart. The low nobility or gentry were in the majority in Västergötland and Småland, which accounts for the large number of manors in these provinces.

Medieval manor houses, especially those belonging to the low nobility, were not very different from ordinary farmhouses. They were the same timbered dwelling houses with two rooms and a porch. The larger manors were often protected by wooden palisades, moats and stone towers. There was a ban on fortifications between 1396 and 1483. The number of fortified houses increased when the ban was lifted.

At the end of the 15th century manors began to be fortified with stone houses. The best example is Glimmingehus, but medieval fortified manors can also be seen at Vanås, Bergkvara

There are only a few preserved medieval forts, castles and manor houses left. Those mapped here have a clear medieval character. Others were rebuilt or abandoned and ruined. Among those were private castles, for example, Vädursholm and Lindholmen. More evident are the ruins of forts or strongholds which were the central point of a county or a sheriff's castle but were burnt down, for example, Axevall, Rumlaborg and Faxehus. A third category are the border forts placed on the roads along river valleys, for example the Viskan (Öresten), the Ätran (Oppensten), the Lagan and the Mörrumsån, including a few on the Danish side in Skåne and Blekinge.

(ruins), Torpa, Örbyhus and Wik. Several other manors have parts of late medieval stone forts incorporated in later buildings. A fort was a rectangular building, often with a double-room plan on each floor and defence systems in the form of machicolation, firing galleries and portcullisses. Some of them also had overhanging corner towers.

No medieval manor house built of wood has survived. The famous Ornäs loft, built between 1470 and 1490, probably belonged to a manor house, but it is not a main building but a storehouse.

During the second half of the 13th century a reform of defence and administration took place which meant that castles were built at administratively and strategically important places. Castles were built to protect the most important towns and became centres of the king's administration. During the second half of the 14th century the number of such castles increased and they were better constructed. The reason was that the Crown had borrowed money and given the lender a castle and its fee as security. The holders of these fees built new castles or improved existing ones to strengthen his position.

The increase in the number of fees reduced their financial bases, which led to increased taxation. This was one of the causes of the Engelbrekt Revolt of the 1430s, which resulted in

Vik in Balingsta, Uppland, has been both a defensive tower and a house. The castle was built in the 15th century on four floors with hanging corner towers and is one of Sweden's best-preserved medieval fortified houses.

Per Brahe the Elder's ancestral home, Sundholmen, at Lake Tolken, Västergötland, was built in the 1540s in a typical late-medieval location, and was destroyed by fire in 1706. The ruins have been restored.

several castles being burnt down. Many of them were not rebuilt, because developments in the art of war required better fortifications. The administration was centred on fewer but better castles. The fee castles that were retained were Stockholm, Nyköping, Stegeborg, Stegeholm, Kalmar, Borgholm, Älvsborg, Örebro and Västerås.

A third category of fortified manor houses were those belonging to the bishops. These, too, were turned into castles at the end of the Middle Ages. The best-preserved one is the bishop's castle at Strängnäs and Tynnelsö, while Linköping, Läckö and Arnö were incorporated into later buildings and Biskopstuna and Stäket remain as ruins.

CASTLES AND MANOR-HOUSES FROM 1530-1630

1:5 000 000

- ■ Building from this period
- ■ Rebuilt medieval house
- □ Ruin of building from this period

The Vasa Period, 1530–1630

"To build is our greatest delight", said King Johan III. The sons of the Vasa dynasty set their mark on the castles of the 16th century and inspired the building ambitions of the nobility. However, it was King Gustav Vasa who ushered in the new epoque with the massive Gripsholm castle, which is medieval in character, a ring-wall castle with an irregular plan and towers of different sizes.

At the Riksdag assembly of 1544 in Västerås it was decided that national castles should be built. One of these was Vadstena, a new castle, while the others were rebuilt and extended medieval castles. Vadstena Castle was the most characteristic renaissance building but was excelled in splendour and richness by both Kalmar and Borgholm (ruin), Svartsjö (ruin), Gävle and not least Stockholm's Old Castle.

The fortified manor houses of the renaissance had many variants: twin buildings with diagonal towers (Penningby), high, rectangular forts (Bråborg and Eksjö hovgård, both ruins), rectangular or square buildings with diagonally-placed towers (Åkerö—demolished, Stora Sundby—rebuilt) or four corner towers (Grönsö—rebuilt), castles with three or four buildings in a square (Tullgarn—demolished, Linköping—rebuilt) or an irregular, towered castle (Hörningsholm, rebuilt, Stegeborg—ruin).

Both location and design were determined by defence requirements. Castles were often placed on an island in a lake and had additional walls and embankments. The diagonally-placed towers made it possible to cover the four sides of the castle with fire.

Renaissance castle building in Danish Skåne continued the tradition of the late medieval fortified house, which was complemented with two or three rows of buildings to make a three or four-row castle, surrounded by moats or placed on an island created by driving piles into a lake bed. In its complete form the Skåne renaissance castle was provided with diag-

The map shows the buildings that were built during this period as well as older buildings that were so radically rebuilt that they have the characteristic features of this period. The original date is given in colour. Relatively few but usually very valuable castles and manor houses have preserved features from this time. (L79)

onally-placed towers, as at the particularly well-preserved castles of Vittskövle and Torup or in the rebuilt castle of Trolleholm. Svenstorp is a more palace-like building, similar in style to Vadstena Castle.

The plan was still basically the extended double-room design. The ground floor contained the kitchen and storerooms, the first floor the living quarters and the second floor a banqueting hall and guest rooms.

The number of manor houses in Sweden in the mid–16th century has been estimated at about 370. Most of these were, as in the late Middle Ages, only built of wood, sometimes provided with primitive fortifications. None of these houses have been pre-

A manor farm (Sw. sätesgård/ säteri) is a farm where a nobleman lived and made his living. The term is from the 15th century, but there were manor farms from the 13th century. The system of nobility means that a nobleman was exempt for paying tax on his land. In return he provided horses for the king's cavalry. A manor had to be built in accordance with its status. The right to own a manor farm was formalised at the coronation of King Erik XIV in 1561. The right to establish manors was abolished in 1686, and the sole right of the nobility to own them disappeared in 1810.

A *fort* (Sw. borg) is a fortified manor house, a fortified royal residence or a fortress that was part of Sweden's defence and administration. Forts may consist of a tower surrounded by walls, fences and moats. Within a fort there are wooden dwelling houses and storehouses. It may also have a stone house. This building was often extended in the 16th and 17th centuries, so that a multi-sided Renaissance castle was formed.

Castle (Sw. slott) is the term for all royal residences and for medieval forts functioning as centres of administrative districts. Castles developed from the stone forts used for both dwelling and defence. The magnificent buildings built by the nobility in the 17th century and the many replicas of late-medieval castles built in the latter part of the 19th century are also called castles.

Manor house (Sw. herrgård) is the term for the main building of a manor, great estate or an ironworks. The Swedish term is also used for the whole estate.

Vittskövle, the largest castle in Skåne, was built by the Danish Brahe family in the 1550s as a square three-storeyed fortress with two diagonally-placed corner towers round a courtyard and surrounded by a moat.

"Torpa Stonehouse" in Västergötland is the only preserved example of the medieval forts along the roads to Halland, but it was rebuilt in the 16th century. It contains a Renaissance banqueting hall and a Baroque chapel.

Penningby in Länna, Uppland, is a rectangular castle built of stone with two diagonal corner towers from the late 15th and/or 16th century.

The map shows the buildings built during this period as well as older buildings that were so radically rebuilt that they have the characteristic features of this period. The original date is given in colour. The period when Sweden was a great power has left many superb examples both of Baroque palaces and Caroline manor houses and of buildings completely rebuilt in the style of the period. (L80)

served in their entirety. The ground floor at Erikssund in Uppland is that of a 16th-century house with preserved decorative paintings from about 1600.

Wooden manor cottages also usually had the same double-room plan. The porch was often extended to make a hall and sometimes the room behind the porch was enlarged so that the ground plan looked like a cross — a cruciform cottage. This cruciform part might have two floors even though the rest of the cottage had only one floor.

Great Power Period, 1630–1730

The 17th century was the era of the great stone buildings, at the same time as the typical Caroline wooden manor house was developed. Economically and politically Sweden was a great power and the nobility grew in number and power.

The Chancellor of Sweden, Axel Oxenstierna, had new buildings erected at his ancestors' home, Fiholm, in 1640. He was assisted by the French architect Simon de la Vallée, who had come to Sweden in 1637 and created the foremost model for Swedish manor houses in the 17th century—the House of Nobility in Stockholm. At Fiholm, based on French and Dutch designs, he showed what a Swedish country mansion should look like. Previously, manor-house buildings could be placed freely or stand in a line, but now the main building and the wings were placed at right angles to each other round a courtyard along whose central axis an approach road was built. Axel Oxenstierna's second mansion, Tidö, is older in style, with a totally enclosed courtyard.

Simon de la Vallée was the first member of a prominent family of architects. He and his son Jean left their mark on the manorial architecture of the late renaissance and early baroque periods. A fellow architect at Fiholm was Nicodemus Tessin the Elder, an immigrant from Stralsund who also introduced a dynasty of architects to Sweden.

Most of the stone houses built in the first half of the 17th century still bore the mark of the late renaissance. They were high, rectangular buildings with steep roofs and curved gables, decorated with roof lights and rich window frames and doorways. The ground plans were in general those of the renaissance.

CASTLES AND MANOR-HOUSES FROM 1630-1730

1:5 000 000

	Building from this period
	Rebuilt medieval house
	Rebuilt building from 1530-1630
	Ruin of building from this period

The upper picture is of one of the two one-storeyed wings of Fiholm in Söder-manland, built in brick by Axel Oxenstierna in 1640–42. The castle itself was never built; the material is said to have been used instead to rebuild Jäder Church as Oxenstierns's memorial church.

The picture beneath is of Salsta Castle in Lena, Uppland, built in the 1670s in three storeys, with wings and corner pavilions designed by Nicodemus Tessin the Elder.

The Peace of Westphalia in 1648 made Sweden a great power, and this position was reflected in an unparalleled building boom. Great stone houses built in the first half of the 17th century were extended, rebuilt and richly decorated (Nynäs, Karlberg and Ericsberg). Others were built from scratch on the same scale and with the same richness of decoration (Salsta, Sjöö, Skokloster, Mariedal, Steninge and Finspång).

These buildings were given a richer facade, either in stone or in stucco or painted to give the illusion of hewn stone. Facades with painted decorative or symbolic images also occurred. The high, steep roofs were replaced by various types of elegantly curved or straight hipped roofs modelled on the House of Nobility.

First among the noblemen who built these manors was Queen Kristina's favourite, later the Chancellor of Sweden, Magnus Gabriel De la Gardie. He rebuilt all his manor houses and properties and was only surpassed by the Dowager Queen Hedvig Eleonora. During her long period as Dowager Queen (1660–1715) she probably built more than anyone else in Sweden, either before or after her. Drottningholm Palace was built so large and decorated so magnificently that it is a remarkable piece of architecture even by European standards.

During Hedvig Eleonora's time the old castle of Stockholm, Three Crowns, burnt down, and plans for a new palace inspired by Bernini's Italy were drawn up by Nicodemus Tessin the Younger. Building commenced but was not completed until the middle of the 18th century.

The building of splendid stone houses for the nobility came to an

Salnecke in Gryta, Uppland, is a three-storeyed castle built of stone and a wing. It was built in the 1640s and has an old-style ground plan with a hall running through the whole building.

Rotenberg in Vikbolandet, Östergötland, is a typical small Caroline manor house with a hipped roof and two wings of plastered timber from about 1700.

abrupt end in the 1680s with Karl XI's reduction, which radically reduced the land ownership of the nobility and weakened their economic power. At the same time the right to form new manor estates was abolished.

It was primarily the power of the high nobility that was broken, whereas the low nobility in fact emerged from the battle with new strength. The representatives of the low nobility built the physical image of the Caroline period: the wooden manor house with a hipped roof. The Caroline manor house was broader than the double-room type and had double suites of rooms. A possible relic from the double-room design was a hall running right through the house. It was more common, however, to have a room in the middle of the house, after the hall. The appearance varied, but the ideal seems to have been a projecting room that allowed light to come in from three sides. Sometimes the design was enriched by adding side projections into the courtyard, or corner pavilions. Caroline manor houses mostly had one floor. Occasionally only the hall and the central part were two-storeyed.

In general 17th-century stone houses were plastered and limed, with corner chains, fillets and frames painted grey or red and with red-tarred or yellow or grey window casements and frames. Alternatively, the plaster was painted red, often with white pointing to make it look like brickwork. Brick buildings could also be painted red and given white pointing, to reinforce the effect. At the end of the century yellow began to be used for facades, in combination with grey or white fillets and frames. Wooden Caroline manor houses were painted red directly on the timber and had grey corners, fillets and frames.

In Danish Skåne building continued at a lively pace up to the Swedish conquest of 1658. The building material at that time, as in the 16th century, was brick, combined with details in light sandstone. The models were Dutch and the style was called after King Christian IV. Plans followed the old pattern of two or more wings round a courtyard. The twin manor house of Marsvinsholm, built in the 1640s, is a notable exception, with its diagonally-placed square towers.

The reduction and the wars led to a decline in building during the period 1680–1720, even though there are conspicuous exceptions such as Sten-

Drawing of Åkerö Manor, built in the 1750s by Carl Gustaf Tessin. The castle, which stands on an island in Lake Yngaren, Södermanland, was portrayed here from the lake by G Silfverståhle in 1812.

CASTLES AND MANOR-HOUSES FROM 1730-1830

1:5 000 000

■ Building from this period

■ Rebuilt medieval house

■ Rebuilt building from 1530-1630

□ Rebuilt building from 1630-1730

The map shows the buildings that were built during this period as well as older buildings that were so radically rebuilt that they have the characteristic features of the period. The original date is shown in colour. Castles and manor houses from this period were first built in the Rococo style and later in the Neoclassical style. (L81)

inge and Sturefors, created by Nicodemus Tessin the Younger. In the 1720s, however, building increased again. Three large three-storeyed palaces (Tullgarn, Björksund and Bergshammar) were started in Södermanland. Along the east coast several manor houses had been destroyed by Russian raids in 1719, and they were partly restored in the 1720s, but mainly at a later date. A few still stand in ruins.

Liberty Period to Karl Johan Period, 1730–1830

Just as the hipped roof is typical of the 17th century and the Caroline period, so is the mansard roof characteristic of 18th century manor-house architecture. The first preserved example of this new roof design is at Bergshammar, completed in the 1730s. This palace, like Tullgarn and Björksund, was designed by the French-born architect Joseph Gabriel Destain.

The rococo manor house was designed by the architect Carl Hårleman and set the style for many years. The

models, like that for the mansard roof, were taken from France. Hårleman's plans were engraved by Jean Eric Rehn and were widely distributed. These plans presented a two-storeyed stone building with a plastered facade under a mansard roof. The facades were livened up by a broad, middle projection and smaller side projections, all decorated with broad rustic work, painted grey or white on the yellow or pinkish plaster. The upper part of the mansard roof is covered with iron sheeting, while the lower part is tiled. All the sheeting is painted red to give the whole roof a uniform appearance.

The inhabitants of manor houses had now changed their life style. A large class of country gentry needed more practical solutions for their daily life, for guests and for parties. The leading lights when it came to improving housing standards seem to have been a new class of manor-house owners. This included successful merchants and millowners who built perhaps the most notable manor houses of the epoque. All the large Uppland ironworks were rebuilt at this time; not only the manor house and its wings but also the whole township was designed in one uniform spirit.

Carl Hårleman created not only the ideal rococo manor house and model plans for official residences but was also—after the death of Nicodemus Tessin in 1728—the architect of the royal palace in Stockholm. At his death in 1753 he was succeeded as director by Carl Johan Cronstedt, who carried on the rococo traditions and designed a number of manor houses. Cronstedt's colleagues, Jean Eric Rehn and Carl Fredrik Adelcrantz, also worked in the rococo style to begin with, but they gradually became more Gustavian in their designs. Adelcrantz designed the Chinese pavilion at Drottningholm and Sturehov, while Rehn was the architect of Gimo and Forsmark, Erstavik, Ljung and Lambohov, some of the finest creations of the "young Gustavian" era.

King Gustav III inaugurated yet another lively period of palace and manor-house building, which moved towards neo-classicism after the king's visit to Italy in 1783–84. The King's pavilion at Haga, Hylinge and Elghammar are delightful examples of this late Gustavian classicism.

A large number of manor houses were built, rebuilt and refurnished in

Övedskloster in Skåne was rebuilt for Hans Ramel in the 1760s and 1770s to the design of Carl Hårleman. The castle, which is seen here from the garden, has an enclosed courtyard with four wings and very rich Rococo interiors.

the late 18th century. Many Caroline houses were now given a second floor and were plastered "to raise their status". Those Caroline manor houses which were not extended or plastered were at least given a facade of planed wood painted yellow on top of the red timber frame.

The red-brick ideal of the 17th century had been replaced by French sandstone as the highest fashion. An impression of French sandstone was achieved either by using wooden pan-

The castle at Gimo ironworks in Uppland was built in the 1760s to the design of Jean Eric Rehn. His plans show the courtyard surrounded by wings and walls and the garden.

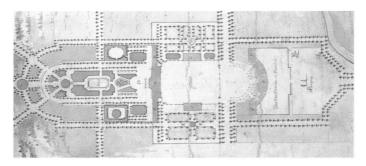

elling and oil paint, or, a somewhat more complicated method using plaster and limewash, or the most expensive method of plastering and painting brick walls. All these methods were used widely. Throughout the period the yellow facades were combined with grey or white fillets and frames. The windows were painted ochre or grey and at the end of the century mahogany-red.

Napoleon's strict, cold imperial style never reached Sweden's manor houses although one of the emperor's field marshals became king of Sweden. The Swedish Empire or Karl-Johan style was a milder form of classicism, often realised in wood but strongly influenced by French models. The pure Empire-style buildings are few in number; mention may be made of Sperlingsholm, designed by Gustaf af Sillén, Broby, Gyllebo, Krontorp and Ribbingsholm, built by unknown architects, Aske by Charles Bassi, Stjernsund and Skottorp by Carl Fredrik Sundvall, Ekensholm by Knut Kurck and finally the orthodox Rosendal, the king's private country residence, designed by Fredrik Blom. The characteristic features of this style of architecture are its colossal columns or pilasters, rotundas and low gabled roofs.

Karl Johan Period to Modern Times, 1830–1930

The great political, social and economic changes that the 19th century brought also affected the building of manor houses to a high degree. At the beginning of the period the Empire style was still viable, but was be-

ginning to meet competition from various medieval styles, especially Neo-Gothic, above all in the south of Sweden. If the Empire style may be said to express power, the Gothic revival may rather be termed contemplative.

In Skåne Carl Georg Brunius was the leader of the Neo-Gothic movement. He rebuilt palaces and manor houses, but perhaps his greatest achievement was to create magnificent stables and barns. Visions of the Middle Ages inspired the most remarkable Romantic building in Sweden, Stora Sundby, a 16th-century castle rebuilt in the 18th century which, in the 1830s, was clothed in 12th-century Norman dress with the help of Sir Walter Scott's favourite architect, Peter F Robinson.

After 1850 the doors were opened to all the styles of history. The French architect Viollet le Duc was admired for his principle that a building should be restored to its original form or completed in the way that was originally planned. With the help of architects like Helgo Zettervall, Isac Gustaf Clason, and two Danes, Christian Fredrik Zwingman and Ferdinand Meldal, Sweden was given southern French renaissance palaces, Vasa castles, Dutch or French Baroque palaces and English country houses, all created with lively imagination and technical skill. It is easy to see all this hectic and splendid building activity as a way for the old nobility to show its status after having lost its political power. At the same time the new class of manor house owners, succesful mill owners and merchants, wanted to demonstrate their status in the same way.

Älghammar was built about 1810 on a headland by Lake Lockvattnet, Södermanland. Both its exterior and its interior are in typically Empire style.

Trolleholm in Torrlösa, Skåne, was originally a Renaissance castle which burned down in 1678 but was rebuilt. The castle was restored in brick in early Renaissance style by F Meldahl in 1886–88; it has four corner towers, a stair turret, a moat and an outer courtyard with three wings.

CASTLES AND MANOR-HOUSES
FROM 1830-1930

1:5 000 000

- Building from this period
- Rebuilt medieval house
- Rebuilt building from 1530-1630
- Rebuilt building from 1630-1730
- Rebuilt building from 1730-1830

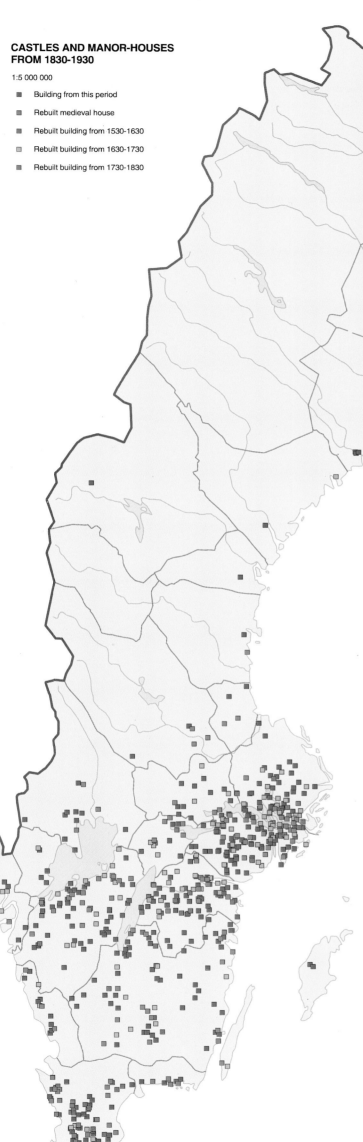

Stora Sundby on Lake Hjälmaren in Södermanland was built in the 1540s and rebuilt in the 1830s and 1840s in the style of a Norman knight's castle.

The map shows the buildings that were built during the period as well as older buildings that were so radically rebuilt that they have the characteristic features of this period. The original date is shown in colour. During this period at first the Empire style was dominant, being used for many years for smaller buildings; after 1850 various historical styles took over; and in the early 20th century the Art Noveau was introduced. (L82)

Alkvettern ironworks manor on the lake of the same name in Värmland was built in 1804–09 and represents the many Swedish Empire-style manor houses.

The middle-class town-style of living influenced the plan of 19th-century manor houses. It became more complex, there were more drawing rooms and clear lines were drawn between the rooms for the gentlefolk and for the servants.

There are many splendid examples of buildings in every possible style in history, but in the ordinary manor house the Swedish Empire style lived on until the 1870s. These were simple and strict two-storeyed houses, mostly built of wood, panelled or plastered, painted white or grey, with classical door and window frames painted grey or mahogany-red, a classical roof edge and a low gabled roof covered with sheet iron or slate.

After the 1870s the Swiss style and gingerbread decorations dominated the simpler kinds of manor-house architecture. This was made possible by developments in the new wood industry which could supply a variety of factory-made carpentry work at a reasonable price.

Fredrik Lilljekvist's controversial restoration of Gripsholm Castle in the 1890s gave rise to a debate as to whether it was right to restore buildings according to historistic principles. This resulted in a loss of interest in Gothic and Renaissance styles. Instead Art Nouveau, Swedish baroque and Swedish 18th-century styles became fashionable in the last epoque of manor-house building in Sweden, which took place during the first three decades of the 20th century. Influence from the English arts-and-crafts movement is also discernible in manor houses, particularly in the largest building of the epoque, Adelsnäs.

Public Buildings

There was no real political and administrative centre in Sweden during the Middle Ages. Royal demesnes, castles and sheriffs' estates were used as administrative centres for collecting state taxes and as seats for its fee lords. The castle in Stockholm was one of those bases which increased in importance during the Late Middle Ages thanks to its strategic location. Not until the time of Gustav Vasa, however, was it possible to speak of a capital city with a central administration.

During the Middle Ages there was also a regional division of the system of justice which had its roots in old traditions of self-government. Defence included strategically placed forts constructed by the Crown, bishops or private lords, but in general it relied on citizen bands, later supplemented by cavalry provided by the nobility.

State Administrative Buildings

The constitution of 1634 formed the basis of a modern civil and military administration based on county divisions which partly corresponded to the old medieval fees and which generally speaking have survived to the present day. The Lord Lieutenant was often allowed to reside in one of the Crown castles, but in due course special residences were built to provide both living quarters and offices. Their architecture was intended to demonstrate the presence of authority.

The central administration in Stockholm developed from the old Castle, Three Crowns, and particularly after it was burnt down, spread in the first place to the surrounding parts of the Old Town and Riddarholmen, where several fine 17th-century

nobility palaces now house government offices. Other buildings have been specially constructed for administrative purposes up to the present day—in both Stockholm and other towns (relocated offices).

"A Courthouse shall be built in every Hundred" said the Civil Law of 1734. In the course of time other buildings grew up round these small courthouses: a jail, stables and storehouses. Quite often there was an inn nearby. During the 20th century the amalgamation of court districts led to a need for larger courthouses, so new monumental court buildings were erected in many towns and central places, at the same time as the State sold several of the old courthouses.

The breakthrough of modern communication systems created a need for new public buildings such as customs houses, railway stations, post offices

CASTLES, COUNTY RESIDENCES AND POST OFFICES

1:10 000 000

▲ Royal castle or palace
■ Other castle owned by the State
● County governor's residence
◉ Post office

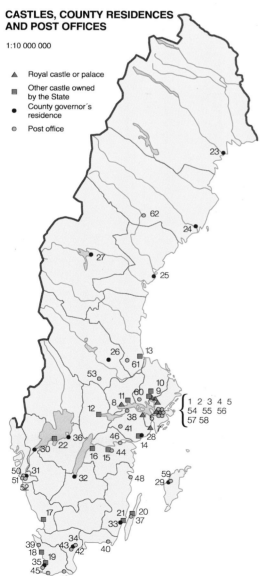

Royal castles and palaces	
1	Rosersberg
2	Ulriksdal
3	Stockholm
4	Drottningholm
5	Haga
6	Gripsholm
7	Tullgarn
8	Strömsholm

Other state-owned castles and palaces	
9	Skokloster
10	Uppsala
11	Västerås
12	Örebro
13	Gävle
14	Nyköpingshus
15	Linköping
16	Vadstena
17	Halmstad
18	Landskrona citadell
19	Malmöhus
20	Borgholm (ruin)
21	Kalmar
22	Läckö

County residences	
23	Luleå
24	Umeå
25	Härnösand
26	Falun
27	Östersund
28	Nyköping
29	Visby
30	Vänersborg

31	Göteborg
32	Jönköping
33	Kalmar
34	Kristianstad
35	Malmö
36	Mariestad

Post office buildings	
37	Borgholm 1941
38	Eskilstuna 1930
39	Helsingborg 1903
40	Karlskrona 1944
41	Katrineholm 1906
42	Kristianstad 1917
43	Kristianstad 1916
44	Linköping 1918
45	Malmö 1906
46	Norrköping 1916
47	Trelleborg 1913
48	Västervik 1911
49	Ystad 1901
50	Göteborg 1924
51	Göteborg 1940
52	Göteborg 1941
53	Ludvika 1921
54	Stockholm Central-posten 1903
55	Stockholm 1932
56	Stockholm 1936
57	Stockholm 1929
58	Stockholm 1938
59	Visby 1942
60	Enköping 1945
61	Storvik 1911
62	Åsele 1926

In addition to the royal palaces and other castles owned by the state country residences and post office buildings of cultural-historical value are showed here as examples of the rich administrative building stock. (L83)

Kalmar Castle was perhaps the most important national fortress in the Middle Ages, but in its present form it has the characteristic features of the Vasa period. The walled medieval town grew up under the protection of the castle. It was abandoned after the move to Kvarnholmen in the 17th century. The great medieval Kalmar Church used to stand in the park in the foreground.

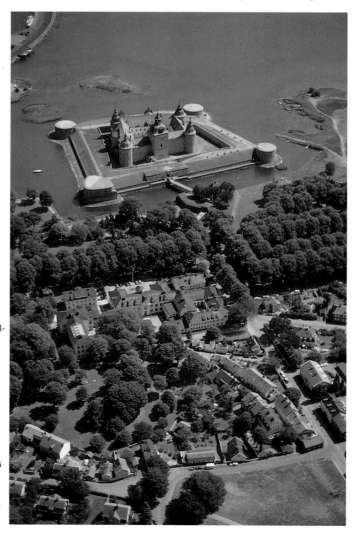

and telegraph offices. Previously postal offices had been housed in various types of buildings and when the telegraph service was introduced it was often placed in the town hall. Towards the end of the 19th century the growing post and telegraph services required more space and in the decades round the turn of the century the government built impressive and lavish post and telegraph offices designed by prominent architects.

The universities have some of the most valuable buildings in the education sector. Among them are several monumental buildings at Lund and Uppsala which also have links with the old cathedrals there. An unusually rich environment of the same type is to be found at Strängnäs.

Municipal Administrative Buildings

Before the middle of the 19th century towns had only a limited number of public buildings. The foremost of these was, of course, the town hall, often used both by the judiciary and the local administration. Usually there were also schools, poorhouses, hospitals and a fire station.

A change took place after the 1850s, when great social, political and economic developments led to an extensive increase in public building. The Municipal Reform Act of 1862 was of great significance because it strengthened the whole of the municipal administrative system, emphasising the independence of towns from the state.

In the later part of the 19th century the old town halls became quite inad-

equate for the ever-swelling municipal authorities. New town halls or city halls—both terms were used—were built in the early 20th century in many Swedish towns, usually designed by prominent architects. The increasing demands for premises for official town functions led to these being combined with the compulsory inn facilities in the form of town hotels, which were also given special architectonic treatment to emphasise their official status. If a State grammar school was also established, this was a feather in the town's cap, and the school's buildings, designed by skilful architects, would be located centrally in the town and given an impressive appearance.

In the course of time further municipal buildings of a more or less lavish design were erected—fire stations, public baths, libraries and the like.

The old town hall in Jönköping (upper picture) was built in the 1690s to the design of Erik Dahlbergh, who was county governor there at the time. Together with the 17th-century court-of-appeal it creates a very valuable setting.

The old town hall in Nyköping (lower picture) is also part of a valuable setting, including the governor's residence and St Nikolai Church. To the right there is a glimpse of the present municipal hall, an example of the way in which our own time has set its mark on old environments.

COURT HOUSES LISTED AS BEING OF HISTORIC IMPORTANCE

1:10 000 000

- ☐ Court house
- ☐ District Court house
- ■ Court of Appeal or Supreme Court building

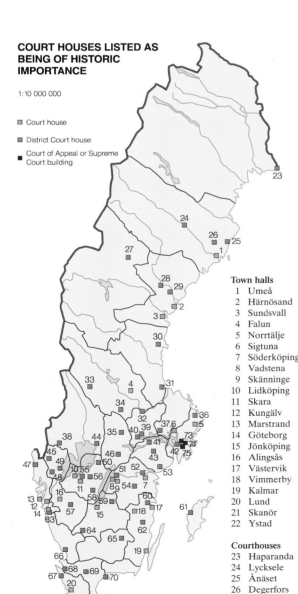

Several of the listed town halls and courthouses no longer function as such today. The terminology for town halls and municipal offices (municipal halls), which are not shown on the map, may also vary from place to place. (L84)

Town halls
1 Umeå
2 Härnösand
3 Sundsvall
4 Falun
5 Norrtälje
6 Sigtuna
7 Söderköping
8 Vadstena
9 Skänninge
10 Lidköping
11 Skara
12 Kungälv
13 Marstrand
14 Göteborg
15 Jönköping
16 Alingsås
17 Västervik
18 Vimmerby
19 Kalmar
20 Lund
21 Skanör
22 Ystad

28 Sollefteå
29 Nyland
30 Hudiksvall
31 Gävle
32 Krylbo
33 Malung
34 Ludvika
35 Lindesberg
36 Häverödal
37 Enköping
38 Långelanda
39 Kolbäck
40 Köping
41 Eskilstuna
42 Haga
43 Malmköping
44 Kristinehamn
45 Alltorp
46 Hallsberg
47 Tanumshede
48 Tångelanda
49 Mellerud
50 Valla
51 Motala

58 Tidaholm
59 Tranås
60 Gamleby
61 Visby
62 Ishult
63 Mölndal
64 Reftele
65 Lenhovda
66 Halmstad
67 Helsingborg
68 Ängelholm
69 Hässleholm
70 Sölvesborg
71 Hammenhög
72 Ystad

Courthouses
23 Haparanda
24 Lycksele
25 Ånäset
26 Degerfors
27 Strömsund
52 Norrköping
53 Nyköping
54 Fillinge
55 Kållängen
56 Binneberg
57 Gäsene

Higher courts
73 Högsta domstolen Stockholm (Bondeska palatset)
74 Svea Hovrätt Stockholm (Wrangelska palatset)
75 Göta Hovrätt Jönköping

The former courthouse at Ånäset was built for the Nysätra district-court area in Västerbotten to the design of C F Sandgren in 1896. The courtroom is clearly marked, even in the panelled exterior.

Johannisborg Castle in Norrköping was built from 1613 onwards for Duke Johan and was fortified with five bastions, a bank and a moat. It was burnt down by the Russians in 1719, and two of the bastions were demolished when the State Railways built their locomotive sheds there. The gateway tower remains and one can see the castle foundations as dark "crop marks" in the field. Many 17th century fortresses have the same star-shaped ground plan.

A fortress has stood in the sound at Vaxholm since the mid–16th century to protect the sea entrance to Stockholm. A new fortress was built in 1833–63, but even then it was obsolete and replaced by forts placed elsewhere. The citadel now houses a military museum.

Fortifications

In the early Middle Ages, up to the mid–13th century, the Swedish kingdom was a loosely-united collection of provinces. The permanent castles which were subsequently built at strategic spots served both for defence and for administration. But it was not until the time of Gustav Vasa that the defensive system was fortified on a more long-term basis. He strengthened forts that were in disrepair and had new strongpoints built at strategically important places. He created a permanent army that could be reinforced at need by recruitment in Sweden or the employment of foreign mercenaries.

During the later part of the 17th century King Karl XI created a part-time army recruited by allotment. The constitution of 1634 had already set up province or county regiments using an organisation which was to last for almost 300 years. In return for exemption from taxation groups of farms and estates could hire and maintain cavalry. Parishes were divided into military sections, each of which maintained a soldier who lived in and tilled a croft of a certain type. On officers' farms, houses graded in size according to rank were built according to plans drawn up by Erik Dahlbergh; however, consideration was paid to "local customs and the special features and traditions of each province". Several new designs were made before 1800. As a result of this and in combination with other archi-

tects' designs a kind of Swedish architectural style was developed during the 18th and 19th centuries which also influenced rural buildings in general.

When, after a long debate, the old allotment system was abolished by acts of parliament in 1892 and 1901, it had made a permanent contribution to the cultural heritage of the Swedish countryside.

KALMAR COUNTY, AN EXAMPLE

There are reasons to believe that to-day's estates and manor houses have developed from the farms of the medieval lords. Some of these farms were fortified during the Middle Ages; they usually stand at strategic places along the coast, at river mouths or on important roads.

Gustav Vasa rebuilt and fortified the two most important castles in the county, Kalmar and Borgholm. Forts were built and beacons placed along the coast and on Öland. 17th-century army reforms created regiments like Småland's cavalry regiment, which consisted of eight companies.

The sections for the Småland regiments were relatively small—only one and a half assessment units. Each section was to provide board and lodging for one soldier, which meant providing a croft with a piece of land on the outskirts of the village/section. In the coastal parishes the population had to maintain the alloted seamen, the boatswains. The part-time army was a force made up of peasant farmers comprising all in all some 30,000 soldiers and 3,000 officers. Many cot-

The barracks of the Royal Uppland Regiment at Polacksbacken in Uppsala were inaugurated in 1912. They stand on the regiment's old camp grounds and parts of those buildings are preserved behind the barracks.

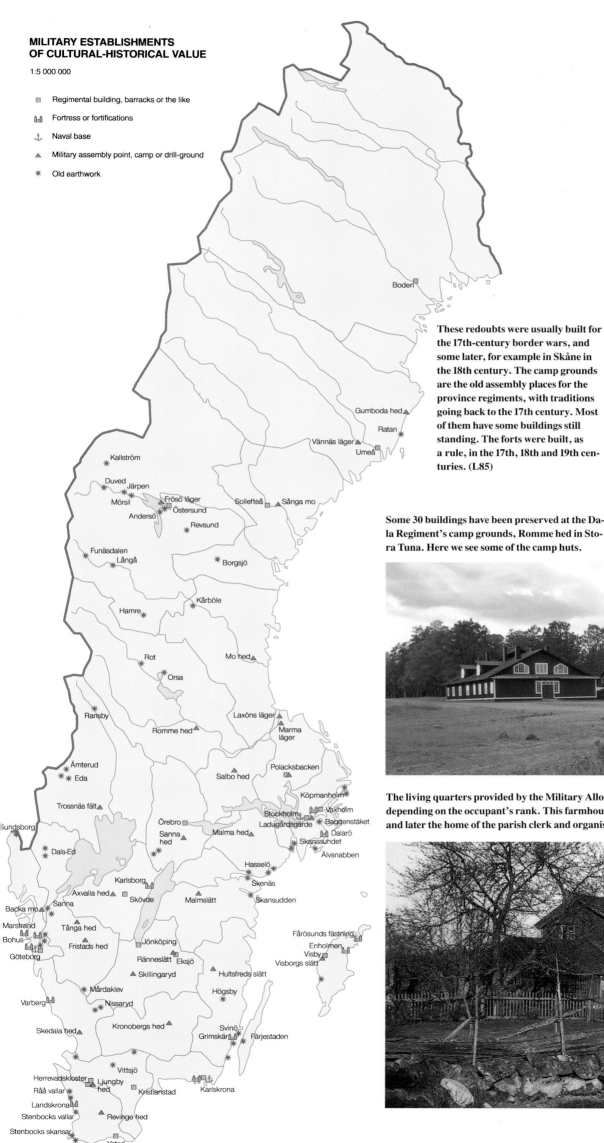

MILITARY ESTABLISHMENTS OF CULTURAL-HISTORICAL VALUE

1:5 000 000

- ▫ Regimental building, barracks or the like
- ⛫ Fortress or fortifications
- ⚓ Naval base
- ▲ Military assembly point, camp or drill-ground
- ✳ Old earthwork

Boden

Gumboda hed
Ratan
Vännäs läger
Umeå

Kallström
Duved
Järpen
Mörsil
Frösö läger
Andersö
Östersund
Sollefteå
Sånga mo
Revsund

Funäsdalen
Långå
Borgsjö

Kårböle
Hamre

Rot
Mo hed
Orsa

Ransby
Laxöns läger
Romme hed
Marma läger

Ämterud
Eda
Salbo hed
Polacksbacken

Trossnäs fält
Köpmanholm
Stockholm
Vaxholm
Örebro
Ladugårdsgärde
Baggenstäket
Sanna hed
Malma hed
Dalarö
Skanssundet
Älvsnabben

Sundsborg
Dals-Ed
Hasselö
Skenäs
Karlsborg
Axvalla hed
Skövde
Malmslätt
Skansudden

Backa mo
Sanna
Marstrand
Tånga hed
Bohus
Fristads hed
Jönköping
Fårösunds fästning
Göteborg
Ränneslätt
Eksjö
Enholmen
Visby
Visborgs slätt
Skillingaryd
Hultsfreds slätt

Mårdaklev
Högsby
Varberg
Nissaryd
Svinö
Kronobergs hed
Grimskärr
Färjestaden
Skedala hed

Vittsjö
Herrevadskloster
Ljungby hed
Råå vallar
Kristianstad
Karlskrona
Landskrona
Stenbocks vallar
Revinge hed
Stenbocks skansar
Ystad
Skåre

---

tages inhabited by soldiers, grenadiers, cavalrymen and boatswains have survived and are often used now as second homes.

Military training was held regularly at special camps. The companies first assembled at their appointed places for roll call and then marched to the camp. The Kalmar Regiment, which moved from Staby to Mariannelund in the 1780s, was transferred in 1796 to Hultsfred Plain. This camp was in use between 1797 and 1918. Military buildings from this period are still standing in the area round the river Silverån, a hussar's croft and trenches used in maneouvres. A hospital now occupies the old regimental buildings.

The Småland regiments remained at their camps until they were placed in barracks between 1906 and 1920. The Defence Regulations of 1925 dissolved the Småland cavalry, the Småland grenadiers were absorbed by the Kronoberg regiment and the Jönköping and Kalmar Regiments were amalgamated and placed at Eksjö. Between 1942 and 1979 an air squadron was based near Kalmar.

These redoubts were usually built for the 17th-century border wars, and some later, for example in Skåne in the 18th century. The camp grounds are the old assembly places for the province regiments, with traditions going back to the 17th century. Most of them have some buildings still standing. The forts were built, as a rule, in the 17th, 18th and 19th centuries. (L85)

Some 30 buildings have been preserved at the Dala Regiment's camp grounds, Romme hed in Stora Tuna. Here we see some of the camp huts.

The living quarters provided by the Military Allotment Board were of varying sizes and standards depending on the occupant's rank. This farmhouse was a piper's quarters for the Kalmar Regiment, and later the home of the parish clerk and organist of Lönneberga.

Higher education has many valuable and historic buildings, in Lund mainly grouped round the University Square. The main university building, whose assembly hall can be seen in the picture, was built in 1878–82 to the design of Helgo Zettervall.

The obligation for country sections to provide soldiers and boatswains had its equivalent in the towns; in the 1740s boatswains' cottages were built in Västervik, some dozen of which are now preserved as historic buildings.

Vicarages

Vicarages have a special place in the cultural history of Sweden. They were created by legislation whose main features remained unchanged for more than 600 years. Vicarages have reflected both changes in architectural fashion and local building traditions.

Each vicarage had a farm, and vicarages often had a great deal in common with other farms. It is usually the main house that gives a vicarage its special character, looking like an upper-class residence.

In the 16th and 17th centuries vicarages were notable for their many buildings which the parishioners were obliged by law to build. A vicarage in Njurunda in Medelpad, for example, had 18 buildings in 1724. The priest himself was responsible for their maintenance.

Listed vicarages of historic national or regional interest are compared here with the number of "old" parishes (i.e. before urban expansion and administrative reforms). Not every parish had its own vicarage, and some had several. These sources of error cancel each other out. Over 900 vicarages are recorded, and there are about 2,450 parishes. The names on the map indicate the vicarages that are listed as historic buildings. In Norrköping there is Hedvig's Vicarage, in Växjö the Old Deanery, in Köping the Dean's House and in Västerås the Deanery and the Assistant Rector's House. (L86)

VICARAGES

1:10 000 000

- Vicarage listed as historic building

◀ Vicarages of national interest, %

◀ Vicarages of regional interest, %

Number of parishes per county

270
200
100
50

The vicarage at Västra Tunhem near Hunneberg in Västergötland is an unusually complete old vicarage consisting of twelve buildings. The main house dates back to 1722; the wings are also from the 18th century and other buildings from the 19th century.

Increasing prosperity and better heating systems in the 18th century meant that the dwelling houses began to look more and more like manor houses, as, too, did the houses of officers and other persons in authority in the countryside. This new type of house is usually called a six-part house. It has a large reception room behind the hall, with the kitchen and bedrooms on either side.

During the 19th century vicarages retained the old division between dwelling house yard and cattleshed yard, but the dwelling houses were

Transtrand
Videbo Skuttunge
Fläckebo Länna
Holmedal Västerås Ängsö
Väse Köping Ed
Nor Veckholm
Edsleskog Risinge
Västra Tunhem Norrköping
Korsnäs
Bönared Gränna Västervik
Seglora
Dädesjö
Råshult Växjö Kalmar
Ausås
Österslöv
Everöd
Burlöv

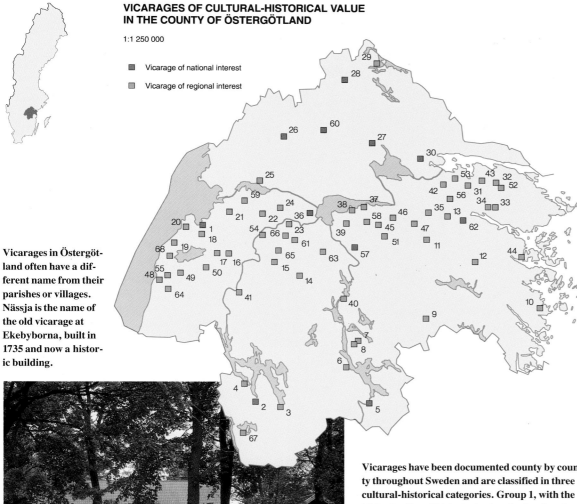

VICARAGES OF CULTURAL-HISTORICAL VALUE IN THE COUNTY OF ÖSTERGÖTLAND

1:1 250 000

■ Vicarage of national interest

□ Vicarage of regional interest

1	Vadstena	35	Västra Husby
2	Asby	36	Vreta Kloster
3	Norra Vi	37	Östra Skrukeby
4	Torpa	38	Östra Harg
5	Horn	39	Rystad
6	Västra Eneby	40	Vårdnäs
7	Kättilstad	41	Åsbo
8	Hägerstad	42	Styrstad
9	Gärdserum	43	Östra Stenby
10	Gryt	44	Sankt Anna
11	Östra Ryd	45	Gistad
12	Ringarum	46	Skärkind
13	Drothem	47	Gårdeby
14	Nykil	48	Västra Tollstad
15	Östra Tollstad	49	Rök
16	Högby	50	Väderstad
17	Appuna	51	Örtomta
18	Strå	52	Häradshammar
19	Rogslösa	53	Dagsberg
20	Örberga	54	Normlösa
21	Västra Stenby	55	Heda
22	Fornåsa	56	Tingstad
23	Björkeberg	57	Landeryd
24	Klockrike	58	Törnevalla
25	Kristberg	59	Ask
26	Tjällmo	60	Hällestad
27	Risinge	61	Rappestad
28	Regna	62	Skönberga
29	Skedevi	63	Slaka
30	Kvillinge	64	Stora Åby
31	Konungsund	65	Viby
32	Östra Husby	66	Västerlösa
33	Östra Ny	67	Västra Ryd
34	Å	68	Väversunda

Vicarages in Östergötland often have a different name from their parishes or villages. Nässja is the name of the old vicarage at Ekebyborna, built in 1735 and now a historic building.

Vicarages have been documented county by county throughout Sweden and are classified in three cultural-historical categories. Group 1, with the highest cultural-historical value, is of national interest; Group 2 is of regional interest; and Group 3 covers other vicarages. These are not recorded here, but there are probably some 85 of them in the county. All vicarages in Östergötland were documented in 1978–79 and 1984–85. (L87)

In the parish of St Anna in the archipelago, originally a chapel parish, the vicarage is called Korsnäs. The old main house (left), now a wing, is a one-storeyed double cottage from 1745, and the present timbered one (above) has one and a half storeys, and was designed in 1809.

larger, often with two storeys, more rooms and modern conveniences. In the late 19th century they were more and more influenced by the panelled facades of town and country houses. The farm buildings began to be placed as wings separated from the main building, and many different functions, which had previously occupied an equally large number of buildings, were gathered there.

During the 18th century most vicarages had orchards and hopyards. During the 19th century flower gardens with paths, herbaceous borders and lilac-bush bowers were added. Avenues of deciduous trees were planted at many places along the approach roads, which further accentuated the vicarage's status in the parish.

The ecclesiastical reforms of the 20th century affected vicarage environments badly. The new law of 1910 concerning priests' salaries put a definite end to the ancient system by which the priest was also a farmer. The church's land was separated from the house and let out to a tenant-farmer by the parish. Today more and more vicarages are being sold off as private houses.

The railway station at Vansbro, Dalarna, from 1899, was given a more luxurious appearance, because it was expected that the town, now that it had a railway junction, would prosper.

Railway Buildings

In the mid–1850s it was decided that major railways lines should be built by the state, while minor lines should be run by private enterprises approved by the state. Five major routes were planned; the western line, Stockholm-Falköping-Göteborg, and the southern line, Falköping-Jönköping-Malmö, were completed in 1864. The Gävle-Dala railway, built as early as 1859, was the first private railway of any importance. In 1939, when almost half the railway network was privately owned, it was decided in principle that the whole network should be nationalised. In 1967 The Swedish State Railways administered 95 per cent of the railways in Sweden.

A large number of station buildings, workshops, locomotive sheds and the like were built. Sweden's railway station buildings developed what might be called multiple uniformity. The principle throughout the 19th century was that station buildings should set a modern architectonic example, thus becoming a public face, a proud trademark.

The incomparably greatest builder was the Swedish State Railways (SJ). Between 1855 and 1895 A W Edelsvärd was the chief architect at SJ. He was succeeded by Folke Zettervall, who remained in charge until 1931. Edelsvärd and Zettervall together created most of the railway stations.

Private railway companies built about 340 lines, and the buildings on these lines varied greatly in appearance.

Sweden's 1,580 or so railway stations were documented between 1968 and 1980, and were classified in four categories, as shown in the diagram. Of the 120 or so in the first class, 55 have now been declared historic buildings, and are shown on the map. (L88)

LISTED RAILWAY STATIONS

1:10 000 000

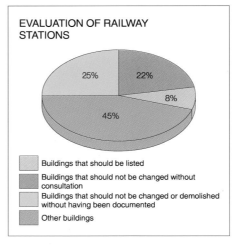

EVALUATION OF RAILWAY STATIONS

25%   22%

8%

45%

- Buildings that should be listed
- Buildings that should not be changed without consultation
- Buildings that should not be changed or demolished without having been documented
- Other buildings

The station buildings along many railway lines had a uniform design. This is true of the Inland Line, built at the beginning of the century, exemplified here by Fågelsjö in Orsa Finnmark, Dalarna.

■ Prison in use

□ Prison not in use

■ Hospital

The prisons of cultural-historical value were built between 1847 and 1878 in a design typical of its time and in many cases later rebuilt or enlarged. Only a few hospital buildings are protected by the Cultural Heritage Act because hospitals in continuous use are enlarged, rebuilt and modernised to serve their purpose. (L89)

Very few of the very earliest station buildings from the 1850s and 1860s are still standing. Those preserved from 1855 to the early 20th century are heterogenous in style, which can primarily be explained by the continual changes in style in late 19th-century architecture. One new style followed the other. Another explanation is the large number of different builders.

Prisons

There were 35 prisons in Sweden at the end of the 18th century, all of which were common prisons where the prisoners lived communally in barrack rooms. These prisons were in fortresses, castles, town halls or in special buildings. As a result of a parliamentary decision in 1840–41 that the prison-cell system should be adopted, several large prison buildings and state jails were erected between 1840 and 1890. They followed standard plans drawn up by the Prison Board, using highly standardised ground plans and facades, one type

for the large county prisons and another for the smaller ones. In both cases the Philadelphia system was adopted, with day cells along the outer walls and a central corridor running as an open gallery through all the floors. Most of these buildings have been preserved and many of them are still in use, with minor changes since they were first built.

Hospitals

The Municipal Reform Act of 1862 transferred responsibility for health care from the state to the newly-formed county councils. The result was an intensive construction of new hospitals throughout the country. Previously hospitals had mainly been situated in the county towns, but they were now built in other towns as well. In 1861 there were 47 large and small hospitals; by the end of the century the number had risen to 141.

The new hospitals, like the prisons, were built according to almost identical plans, so there were great similarities between hospital buildings. After 1874 a permanent architect was employed by the Hospitals Board, but town architects and other well-known architects were also commissioned, which resulted in some new artistic ideas. Axel Kumlien (1833–1913), for example, had designed at least 36 new hospital buildings by the turn of the century. More than half the hospital beds that were added between 1880 and 1910 were in buildings designed by him. A good example of his architecture is the private hospital Sophiahemmet in Stockholm, built in 1889.

The prison in Kalmar (left) was built in 1852. It is characteristic of its period and relatively well preserved.

The old hospital in Umeå (below left) was built on one floor in 1785 and is one of Sweden's oldest preserved hospitals. Its catchment area was the whole of upper Norrland, and it was extended in the 1860s in typical panelled style.

The former sanatorium at Österåsen in Ed, Ångermanland has a location and style typical of this type of building. It stands on a wooded hill by the river, was designed by Fredrik Lilljekvist, inaugurated in 1902 and consists of several pavilions joined together.

Towns

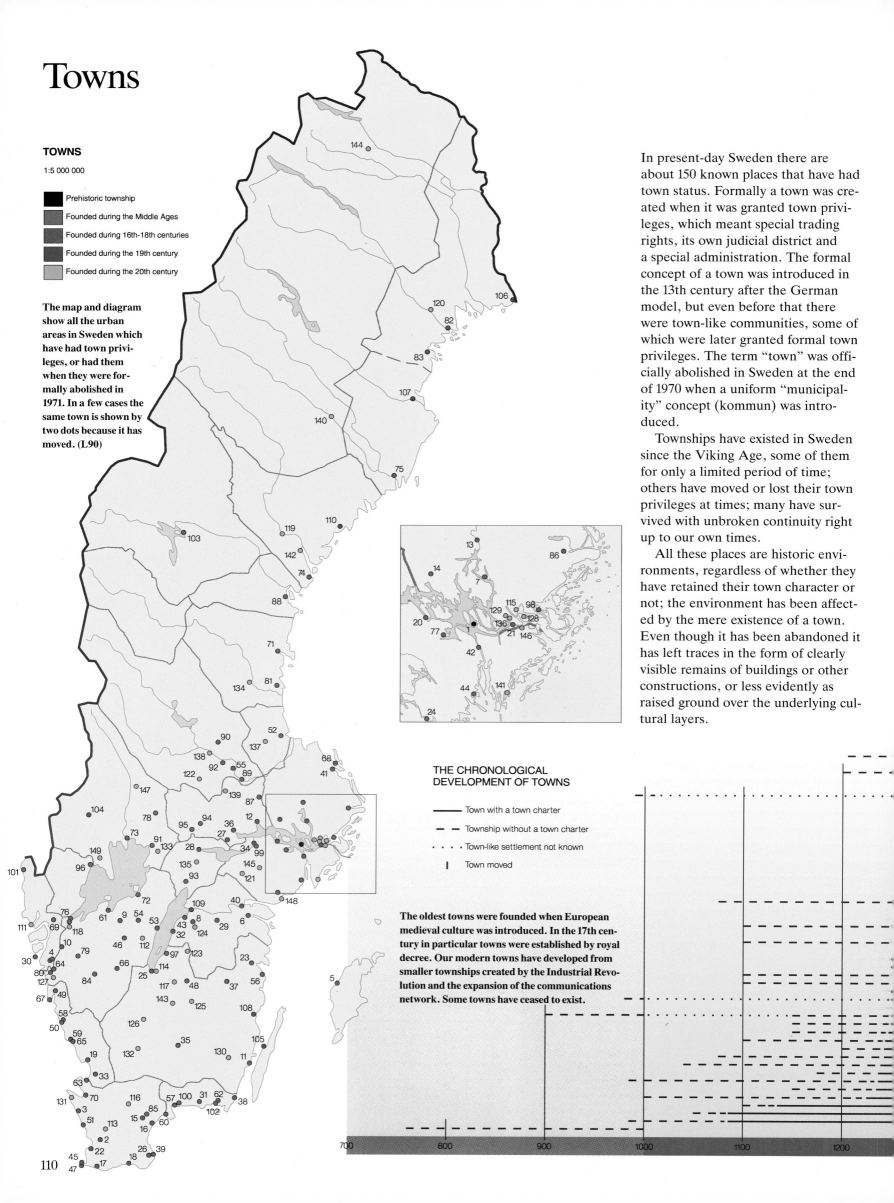

TOWNS

1:5 000 000

- Prehistoric township
- Founded during the Middle Ages
- Founded during 16th–18th centuries
- Founded during the 19th century
- Founded during the 20th century

The map and diagram show all the urban areas in Sweden which have had town privileges, or had them when they were formally abolished in 1971. In a few cases the same town is shown by two dots because it has moved. (L90)

In present-day Sweden there are about 150 known places that have had town status. Formally a town was created when it was granted town privileges, which meant special trading rights, its own judicial district and a special administration. The formal concept of a town was introduced in the 13th century after the German model, but even before that there were town-like communities, some of which were later granted formal town privileges. The term "town" was officially abolished in Sweden at the end of 1970 when a uniform "municipality" concept (kommun) was introduced.

Townships have existed in Sweden since the Viking Age, some of them for only a limited period of time; others have moved or lost their town privileges at times; many have survived with unbroken continuity right up to our own times.

All these places are historic environments, regardless of whether they have retained their town character or not; the environment has been affected by the mere existence of a town. Even though it has been abandoned it has left traces in the form of clearly visible remains of buildings or other constructions, or less evidently as raised ground over the underlying cultural layers.

THE CHRONOLOGICAL DEVELOPMENT OF TOWNS

— Town with a town charter

- - - Township without a town charter

· · · · Town-like settlement not known

| Town moved

The oldest towns were founded when European medieval culture was introduced. In the 17th century in particular towns were established by royal decree. Our modern towns have developed from smaller townships created by the Industrial Revolution and the expansion of the communications network. Some towns have ceased to exist.

700   800   900   1000   1100   1200

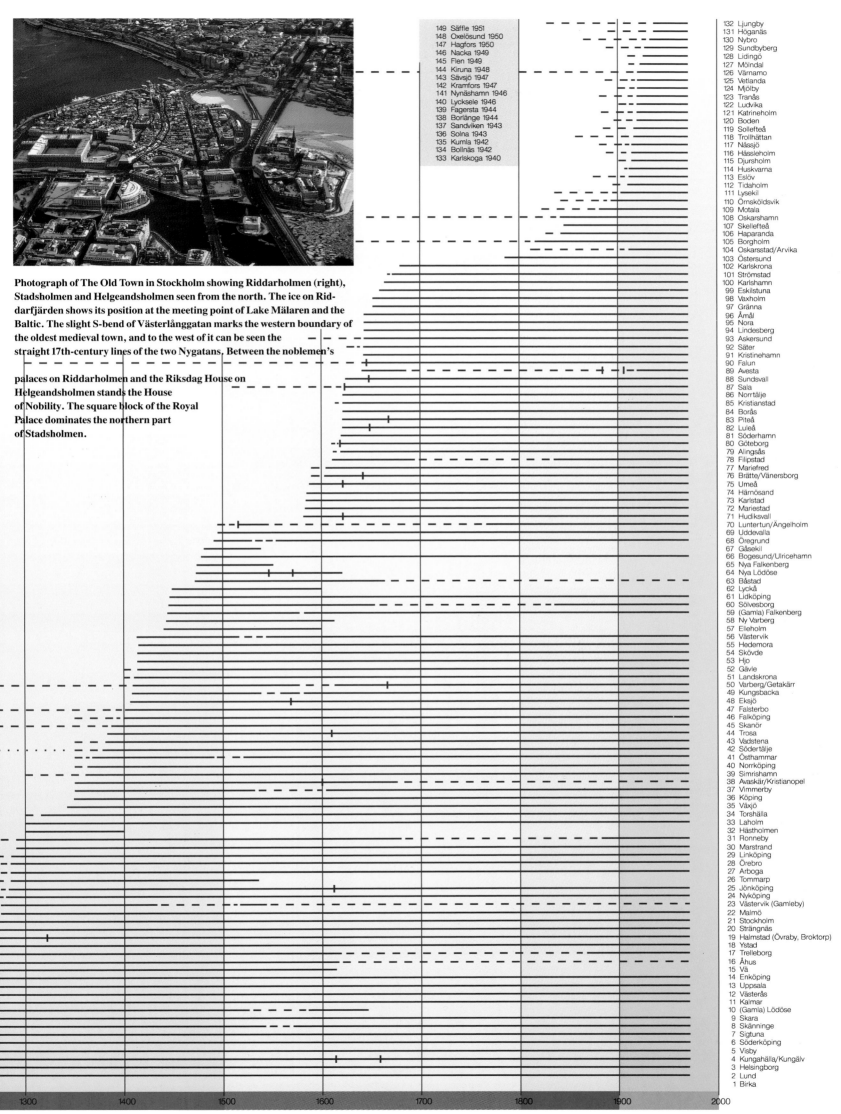

Photograph of The Old Town in Stockholm showing Riddarholmen (right), Stadsholmen and Helgeandsholmen seen from the north. The ice on Riddarfjärden shows its position at the meeting point of Lake Mälaren and the Baltic. The slight S-bend of Västerlånggatan marks the western boundary of the oldest medieval town, and to the west of it can be seen the straight 17th-century lines of the two Nygatans. Between the noblemen's

palaces on Riddarholmen and the Riksdag House on Helgeandsholmen stands the House of Nobility. The square block of the Royal Palace dominates the northern part of Stadsholmen.

149 Säffle 1951
148 Oxelösund 1950
147 Hagfors 1950
146 Nacka 1949
145 Flen 1949
144 Kiruna 1948
143 Sävsjö 1947
142 Kramfors 1947
141 Nynäshamn 1946
140 Lycksele 1946
139 Fagersta 1944
138 Borlänge 1944
137 Sandviken 1943
136 Solna 1943
135 Kumla 1942
134 Bollnäs 1942
133 Karlskoga 1940

132 Ljungby
131 Höganäs
130 Nybro
129 Sundbyberg
128 Lidingö
127 Mölndal
126 Värnamo
125 Vetlanda
124 Mjölby
123 Tranås
122 Ludvika
121 Katrineholm
120 Boden
119 Sollefteå
118 Trollhättan
117 Nässjö
116 Hässleholm
115 Djursholm
114 Huskvarna
113 Eslöv
112 Tidaholm
111 Lysekil
110 Örnsköldsvik
109 Motala
108 Oskarshamn
107 Skellefteå
106 Haparanda
105 Borgholm
104 Oskarsstad/Arvika
103 Östersund
102 Karlskrona
101 Strömstad
100 Karlshamn
99 Eskilstuna
98 Vaxholm
97 Gränna
96 Åmål
95 Nora
94 Lindesberg
93 Askersund
92 Säter
91 Kristinehamn
90 Falun
89 Avesta
88 Sundsvall
87 Sala
86 Norrtälje
85 Kristianstad
84 Borås
83 Piteå
82 Luleå
81 Söderhamn
80 Göteborg
79 Alingsås
78 Filipstad
77 Mariefred
76 Brätte/Vänersborg
75 Umeå
74 Härnösand
73 Karlstad
72 Mariestad
71 Hudiksvall
70 Luntertun/Ängelholm
69 Uddevalla
68 Öregrund
67 Gåsekil
66 Bogesund/Ulricehamn
65 Nya Falkenberg
64 Nya Lödöse
63 Båstad
62 Lyckå
61 Lidköping
60 Sölvesborg
59 (Gamla) Falkenberg
58 Ny Varberg
57 Elleholm
56 Västervik
55 Hedemora
54 Skövde
53 Hjo
52 Gävle
51 Landskrona
50 Varberg/Getakärr
49 Kungsbacka
48 Eksjö
47 Falsterbo
46 Falköping
45 Skanör
44 Trosa
43 Vadstena
42 Södertälje
41 Östhammar
40 Norrköping
39 Simrishamn
38 Avaskär/Kristianopel
37 Vimmerby
36 Köping
35 Växjö
34 Torshälla
33 Laholm
32 Hästholmen
31 Ronneby
30 Marstrand
29 Linköping
28 Örebro
27 Arboga
26 Tommarp
25 Jönköping
24 Nyköping
23 Västervik (Gamleby)
22 Malmö
21 Stockholm
20 Strängnäs
19 Halmstad (Övraby, Broktorp)
18 Ystad
17 Trelleborg
16 Åhus
15 Vä
14 Enköping
13 Uppsala
12 Västerås
11 Kalmar
10 (Gamla) Lödöse
9 Skara
8 Skänninge
7 Sigtuna
6 Söderköping
5 Visby
4 Kungahälla/Kungälv
3 Helsingborg
2 Lund
1 Birka

1300   1400   1500   1600   1700   1800   1900   2000

Early Towns

Seventy of the town sites in present-day Sweden originated before 1520 and are counted as medieval. One of them, Birka, had already been abandoned at the beginning of the Middle Ages, and some important medieval communities were not granted town privileges until the 17th century. Seven towns date from the very earliest Middle Ages, before 1100. These had central or strategic locations in the three medieval kingdoms. Five were centrally located: Birka and Sigtuna in Mälardalen, Skara in western Sweden and Lund and Helsingborg in Danish Skåne. Two towns had forward, offensive positions: Lödöse in western Sweden and Kongahälla in southern Norway. Visby probably played a fairly independent role at an early stage but later it became an outpost in the Swedish kingdom.

Many towns were established later in the Middle Ages, especially in the 13th and 15th centuries. In the central districts—Mälardalen, Östergötland, Västergötland and the Danish Skåne provinces—towns seldom lay more than 30 km apart at the end of the Middle Ages. The economically and politically dominant area within the Swedish kingdom was marked by the location of its towns along an axis running from the Gulf of Finland (Viborg) through Åbo and the towns in Mälardalen to the mouth of the Göta älv (Lödöse). Outside this zone further towns were created later, initially along the Baltic coast in the south and the north and then in the neighbouring forest districts and through concentration in the central areas. A similar development in the Danish

The town wall at Visby is Sweden's most impressive medieval monument and one of the best preserved of its kind in northern Europe. View from the north-eastern wall, "Nordergravar".

area led to the creation of towns along the coast in the more peripheral provinces of Blekinge and Halland. In the Norwegian kingdom Marstrand (late 13th century) and Uddevalla (ca. 1500) represent a corresponding attempt on the part of the central power to secure economic and political control of coastal zones.

There are today at almost all of the 70 town sites at least a few visible remains of medieval settlement. However, the extensive replanning of Swedish town centres after the Second World War in particular destroyed large parts of these medieval traces—both above and below the ground.

TOWN PLANS

Although research long claimed the opposite, there were in fact no uniform principles for the organisation of town settlements in the Middle Ages. It was topography that determined how a town was modelled; however, attempts to steer these developments were made at an early date. The system of building plots in particular was strictly regulated: the size and location of these plots followed a common pattern. It has even been possible in some cases to trace continuity from medieval times up to the present day. Boundary lines, for example, could be preserved for a very long time. In Visby and Stadsholmen in Stockholm it is possible to study the medieval character of the building plots in the design of the street facades. In many cases the width of a building corre-

sponds to the width of the plot.

The square as an idea and a reality is one of the fundamental elements of the medieval town. It was the town's public place and was mentioned early in source material on towns. This was where goods were sold, official announcements were made, justice was done and social intercourse took place. Many present-day squares in medieval towns originated in the Middle Ages, but most of them have been enlarged, altered and adapted to the needs of later times. To begin with they were very different in shape: triangular, square, rectangular or simply a broadened street.

TOWN WALLS, TOWN RAMPARTS

The medieval town was separated from the surrounding countryside by ditches, fences, ramparts or walls. These demarcations emphasised the special legal, social and economic status of a town and had both a practical and a symbolic function. In a few cases they functioned as defence systems against attack. The custom of marking off a town's boundaries was practised at an early date; at Birka there are large parts of an earth rampart which was constructed in the 10th century. Such ramparts are found at other places such as Västergarn on Gotland and Löddeköpinge in Skåne (late Viking Age) and Lund (early Middle Ages). A few town moats and fences are mentioned in written sources, but none has been preserved. Town walls are still standing, however. The best-preserved one is at Vis-

The Middle Ages constantly make their presence felt in Visby, both in the streets' lines, in the preserved profane buildings and in the dominant church ruins.

MEDIEVAL TOWNS	Town plan	Streets	Square	Building plots	Town wall/earthwork/moat	Town gate	Stone building	Brick building	Cellar	Town hall	Church	Monastery/convent	Public building	Castle
Birka														1
Lund									5		2			
Helsingborg											1			1
Kungahälla														
Visby					158						8	2	2	
Söderköping											2			
Sigtuna											4			
Skänninge											1			
Skara											1			1
(Old) Lödöse														1
Kalmar														1
Västerås							2				1			1
Uppsala							8				2			
Enköping											1			
Vä											2	2		
Åhus											1	2	1	
Trelleborg											1			
Ystad											1			
Halmstad: Övraby											1			
Broktorp														
Strängnäs							3				1			
Stockholm					<200			1			2			
Malmö							14				1			
Västervik/Gamleby											1			
Nyköping											2			1
Jönköping														
Tommarp														
Arboga							1	5			2			
Örebro											1			1
Linköping								5			2			1
Marstrand											1			
Ronneby											1			
Hästholmen														
Laholm											1			1
Torshälla											1			
Växjö											1			
Köping											1			
Vimmerby														
Avaskär/Kristianopel														
Simrishamn											1			
Norrköping														
Östhammar														
Södertälje											1			1
Vadstena					17	2					1	2		
Trosa											1			
Skanör											1			1
Falköping											1			
Falsterbo											1			1
Eksjö														
Kungsbacka														
Varberg-Getakärr											1			1
Landskrona														
Gävle														
Hjo														
Skövde											1			
Hedemora											1			
Västervik											1			1
Elleholm														
New-Varberg														
(Old) Falkenberg											1			1
Sölvesborg											1			1
Lidköping											1			
Lyckå														
Båstad											1			
New Lödöse														
New Falkenberg											1			
Bogesund/Ulricehamn											1			
Gåsekil														
Öregrund														
Uddevalla														
Luntertun/Ängelholm											1			

Most cultural remains from the Middle Ages are normally beneath the ground, but some of them are also preserved above the ground, most evidently in Visby and in The Old Town of Stockholm, where the number of medieval buildings is largest but difficult to specify. The churches are the best preserved category, but remains of castles, streets and the town plan may also be seen.

by, which surrounds the whole medieval town. This wall is mainly from the 13th century, but the Gunpowder Tower dates from the 12th century. Visby, like Kalmar, Stockholm and Viborg, has been besieged; at these times the wall had a real defence function. Besides those towns Åhus also had a town wall.

FORTS

In many cases forts were placed close to a town. There were early royal demesnes that were later transformed into castle-like forts, becoming centres of the royal administrative counties (Kalmar, Nyköping, Stockholm, Örebro). The king's interests in a town were protected by a sheriff.

TOWN ARCHITECTURE

Buildings in medieval Scandinavian towns did not differ greatly from those in the countryside. Log houses and other wooden houses were grouped together like farms; cattle-sheds, workshops and dwelling houses were also more or less alike. Town buildings stood closer together, however, and followed an organised plan. There are no medieval wooden houses preserved in towns today, but in a few towns there are stone cellars of a medieval character whose upper wooden storeys were rebuilt at a later date. In southern Sweden—the old Danish provinces—there were more buildings constructed of various materials (half-timbering), as archeological investigations have shown.

Preserved medieval buildings built of brick are mainly found in southern Sweden. It is only Visby and Stockholm (the Old Town), however, that can be said to be complete medieval towns built of stone. In both of them later building partly changed their medieval character, but large parts of existing buildings contain medieval walls. Their characteristic features are the high gables facing the streets which were equipped with hoists under the roof to make it possible to take in goods at every floor. The often very richly decorated gables may be seen as an expresssion of the citizens' desire for status. But the stone buildings in towns are to a great extent the result of the presence of the nobility. The desire to build in stone and brick expresses status, the need for better protection against fire and theft and in some cases a lack of wood for building. The stone houses of Visby and Stockholm clearly reflect the importance and power of these towns.

Every medieval town had a town hall or at least some sort of building for town business. Today only one medieval town hall remains, at Vadstena. In a number of other towns there is mention of a town hall, and in a few cases these were documented in later times.

CHURCH ARCHITECTURE

Preserved church buildings—parish churches, and religious institutions (monasteries, pious foundations and societies)—were generally built of stone or brick. The religious societies in medieval towns reflected their corporative nature; various groups of people created places where they could meet and take care of each other. Not many traces remain today; the Reformation swept away the social safety net which had been created during the Middle Ages. A few abbeys and ruins of monastery buildings are all that is preserved today. At Skänninge, Vä, Visby and Åhus there are remains of the chapels of charity institutions; at Uppsala a building which is presumed to have been a priests' retirement home has been preserved.

The early churches in the oldest towns did not differ in design from those in the countryside, though they may have been larger and more impressive (for example, Falköping, Vä and Simrishamn). From the 13th century onwards a more specific town-church style of architecture developed, characterised by the need for many side chapels. The towns' guilds found a natural way of expressing their faith by donating money for masses and altar societies. So the typical architecture of town churches arose, usually built in brick, with richly decorated exteriors and separate side chapels. Sometimes originally Romanesque churches were rebuilt to meet these needs (Söderköping, Nyköping). Later rebuilding led to changes, but there are, nevertheless, several examples of well-preserved medieval town churches. In many towns the churches are the only visible sign above ground of the medieval period.

All the medieval cathedrals that have been preserved are in towns—except for Gamla Uppsala and Dalby, which have different functions today. Some of them were built before the place became a town.

The west end of St Laurentii Church in Söderköping is a typical example of the Baltic brick Gothic style.

113

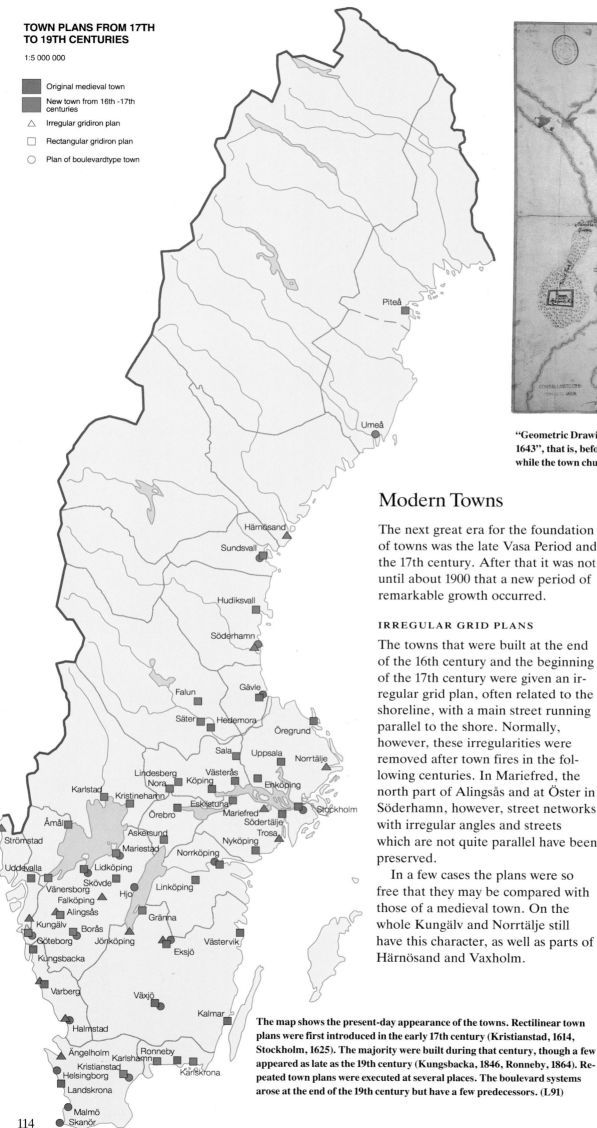

TOWN PLANS FROM 17TH TO 19TH CENTURIES

1:5 000 000

- Original medieval town
- New town from 16th -17th centuries
- △ Irregular gridiron plan
- □ Rectangular gridiron plan
- ○ Plan of boulevardtype town

Piteå

Umeå

Härnösand
Sundsvall

Hudiksvall

Söderhamn

Falun
Gävle

Säter
Hedemora
Öregrund

Sala
Uppsala
Norrtälje

Lindesberg
Västerås
Nora
Köping
Karlstad
Enköping
Kristinehamn
Eskilstuna
Åmål
Örebro
Mariefred
Stockholm
Strömstad
Askersund
Södertälje
Trosa
Mariestad
Nyköping
Uddevalla
Norrköping
Lidköping
Skövde
Vänersborg
Hjo
Linköping
Falköping
Alingsås
Gränna
Kungälv
Borås
Göteborg
Jönköping
Västervik
Kungsbacka
Eksjö

Varberg
Växjö

Kalmar
Halmstad

Ängelholm
Ronneby
Karlshamn
Kristianstad
Helsingborg
Karlskrona
Landskrona

Malmö
Skanör

"Geometric Drawing of the Town of ASKERSUND . . . drawn . . . Anno 1643", that is, before it was built. On the left, the country parish church, while the town church is as yet only mentioned as "Site of Church".

Modern Towns

The next great era for the foundation of towns was the late Vasa Period and the 17th century. After that it was not until about 1900 that a new period of remarkable growth occurred.

IRREGULAR GRID PLANS

The towns that were built at the end of the 16th century and the beginning of the 17th century were given an irregular grid plan, often related to the shoreline, with a main street running parallel to the shore. Normally, however, these irregularities were removed after town fires in the following centuries. In Mariefred, the north part of Alingsås and at Öster in Söderhamn, however, street networks with irregular angles and streets which are not quite parallel have been preserved.

In a few cases the plans were so free that they may be compared with those of a medieval town. On the whole Kungälv and Norrtälje still have this character, as well as parts of Härnösand and Vaxholm.

RECTILINEAR GRID PLANS

The ideal of the age was a regular grid-plan town. The first completely rectilinear grid plans appeared in Sweden in the early 17th century. The earliest preserved example is probably Norrköping, where Johannisborg Castle and a new town district were built at Saltängen, north of the river Motala Ström, in accordance with a plan which was probably drawn up in 1613.

The best conditions for applying a regular plan occurred, of course, when an old town was moved or enlarged, as at Varberg and Lidköping, and in the new towns. The first Swed-

The 17th-century town of Kungälv is built along the old main road and displays certain irregular grid-iron features.

The map shows the present-day appearance of the towns. Rectilinear town plans were first introduced in the early 17th century (Kristianstad, 1614, Stockholm, 1625). The majority were built during that century, though a few appeared as late as the 19th century (Kungsbacka, 1846, Ronneby, 1864). Repeated town plans were executed at several places. The boulevard systems arose at the end of the 19th century but have a few predecessors. (L91)

■ Preserved medieval streets and monumental buildings

■ Preserved parts of the 1643 gridiron plan

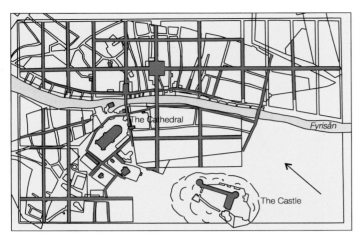

The street system in Uppsala was radically altered in 1643. Some lines of streets, monumental buildings and the inner structure of certain street quarters are from the Middle Ages.

ish town with a rectilinear street plan was probably Sala, dating from 1624. It was not until the 1640s that this design became the normal one.

TOWN PLAN CHANGES

Adjustments to town plans involved far-reaching consequences for private persons and could normally only be undertaken after a fire in the town. In several cases 17th-century plans were not enforced until the mid–19th century. Nor is it unusual for medieval streets to have survived town rebuilding. Perhaps it was precisely that part of town that did not suffer from the fire. Opposition from the townsfolk was often so strong that the town was rebuilt with only minor changes. Skänninge, which burnt down several times in the 18th century, is one example.

Only in a few cases, and in places where the Crown had special interests, were extensive adjustments made without a fire having devastated the town. This is true of Norrmalm and Södermalm in Stockholm (1637 and 1642 respectively), Uppsala (1643) and possibly Falun (1646).

FORTRESS TOWNS AND CANAL TOWNS

One category of towns that received special attention was the dozen or so towns, which were surrounded by fortresses, or were planned so, in the 17th and 18th centuries.

When Göteborg was planned in about 1620, a Dutch-inspired plan was used with rectilinear streets, canals and powerful fortresses. Apart from the fact that most of the canals have been filled in to make streets and that the forts have been demolished, the town plan is remarkably well preserved. The names of the streets — Östra and Västra Hamngatan (Harbour Street) — and their great width, which distinguishes them from other streets, reveal that they were originally canals. Karlskrona has a special status, as it was built to be Sweden's foremost naval base with a town plan in the Baroque style which is unique in Sweden.

THE BOULEVARD TOWN

The town fortresses in Malmö were pulled down from 1806 onwards and those in Göteborg two years later, but those in most other towns were not demolished until after 1850. The fortress zones were gradually replaced by belts of broad tree-lined streets, parks and public buildings.

Tree-lined streets had already been

introduced in a number of towns, partly under Finnish influence — Borås in 1827, Växjö and Lidköping in the 1840s, Norrköping in the following decade and Umeå in 1864. After fires towns were transformed into twin streets with a park in between, called boulevards.

THE BUILDING STATUTE OF 1874

The rapid expansion of towns after the Industrial Revolution led to a series of laws, in particular the Building Statute of 1874. Town plans were to be drawn up. Great attention was paid to fire prevention and hygiene. The rectilinear street plan was still applied, but now with clearly differentiated streets. Broad, tree-lined main streets were a characteristic feature of the epoch. Uniform districts of five-storeyed stone or brick apartment houses with shops on the ground floor grew up along the broad streets and lower buildings along the narrower streets.

THE 20TH CENTURY

A new ideal town plan was introduced after the turn of the century — an irregular network of streets which followed the terrain and buildings on a smaller scale. This type of architecture is mainly to be seen in outer suburbs and garden cities. Kiruna and Nynäshamn were special in this respect, since they were built on "virgin land".

Since the 1930s town architecture has been characterised by modifications to the enclosed town ideal. Suburban building increased rapidly and in combination with extensive clearances in the centre it has been the main trend since 1945.

Up until the 17th century Kalmar was a border fortress on the coast. The castle's fortifications were strengthened during the 13th–15th centuries to protect the medieval town. After the war of 1611–13 the town was rebuilt with radial streets and bastions, but these soon became obsolete, and the town moved in the mid–17th century to Kvarnholmen, which was fortified. In 1822 the fortifications were replaced by parks and public buildings.

The plan for the development of Umeå in 1864 is an early example of a differentiated street system consisting of broad long streets crossed by narrow ones. Boulevards were built in 1879 for fire protection. After the fire in 1888 the old heart of the town was replanned with a central axis. When the town expanded in 1898, a star-shaped open place was created with a monumental railway station. In 1922 the grid-iron plan was abandoned in favour of a scheme that was more suited to the natural conditions.

**TOWN PLANS
IN UMEÅ**

■ 1864
■ 1879
■ 1888
■ 1898
■ 1922

HOUSES IN TOWNS

1:5 000 000

□ Predominance of painted wooden houses

△ Many plastered wooden houses

■ Old stone buildings

■ The stone architecture of the 19th century

The map shows towns with fairly homogeneous environments with old buildings of a specific type. Towns with several symbols have as a rule various types of environments in different parts of the town. (L92)

The 16th-century town area round Norra Storgatan in Eksjö contains one of the best examples of a well-preserved "wooden town" in Sweden. It dates back to the 18th and the 19th centuries.

The stone buildings along Brännkyrkagatan in Stockholm were built after a fire in 1759 and up to the mid–19th century.

Town Architecture

Wooden buildings were in the majority in most towns right up to the present century; there were, however, exceptions in the southernmost parts of Sweden, in Stockholm and Göteborg and in a few other towns.

In the mid–18th century the more impressive buildings were clad with wooden panelling, which in form resembled stone, and it was at this time that pale oil-based paints became fashionable. The older building tradition of unpainted or red timber is sometimes found in storehouses, but normally these two were clad in simple, red panelling. Gradually local variants of panel architecture developed and new styles in combination with industrial manufacturing led to increasingly decorated facades in the late 19th century.

The Skåne provinces as well as Visby and Stockholm had an old tradition of building with bricks, half-timbering and to some extent stone. From the time of Johan III onwards pressure was put on citizens to build in brick or stone, but the result in general was disappointing.

Brick houses are often plastered. The tradition of panelling houses, even half-timbered houses, spread right down into Skåne and during the course of the 19th century plastered houses became more common further north.

At the end of the 19th century many large towns could boast brick or stone buildings resembling those in the big cities. Outside Stockholm, Göteborg and Malmö, Sundsvall and Norrköping are the best examples.

The pace of growth accelerated and changes in style left their marks: rich, classical plaster facades in the 1880s, more brick and stone in the 1890s, Nationalist, Romantic and Jugend styles at the turn of the century and so on. The "Lord Lieutenant Houses", as they were called, were one way of getting round the building regulations, with a ground floor built of stone and two upper storeys of wood. Such buildings are common in Göteborg but also occur with plastered facades at other places.

More and more the industrial town separated home from work; apartment houses became the dominant form, which led to a new type of social segregation. In one and the same building there were often apartments for different social classes—the second and third floors overlooking the street were the finest and the apartments on the far side of the inner courtyard the least attractive.

The fortress Kärnan is the central point in medieval Helsingborg, above the cliff. Below, remains of the irregular, medieval streets round the church of St Mary are visible.

Helsingborg

Helsingborg is one of the towns where it is possible to follow a long continuity in architecture and trace the various stages of development, like rings in a tree trunk. Thanks to its topography and its strategic position for shipping and defence this town has a character all of its own. Political and administrative factors, whereby local industry and commerce have been the driving force without the assistance that other towns received as administrative centres, have also left their mark on Helsingborg.

THE MEDIEVAL TOWN

The oldest, early medieval Helsingborg was situated on a height close to a royal castle consisting of a circular central tower surrounded by a wall. Today a square tower erected in the early 14th century stands on this site. The fragments of the medieval town plan which have been preserved in the form of a few streets which still follow their original lines are on the coastal plain below the height and are the relics of the centre of the high-medieval town. A road running towards the north-east coincides with the present Långvinkelsgatan. The church of St Mary was built in the 14th century and is a typical high and late medieval town church.

THE FORTRESS TOWN

After Helsingborg was transferred to Sweden in 1658, extensive work was commenced on a modern bastion, but as early as 1680–81 these defences were demolished. All that remains above ground are a few small ruins, some of them in Öresundsparken. But it is also possible to trace the fortress in the form of street lines and the names of streets and districts such as Norra Vallgatan (North Rampart Street), Bröstvärnet (The Parapet)

and Bastionen (The Bastion). The main square was constructed in 1693 on the site of the fortified route down to the harbour. The previously fortified area is visible today in the line of parks and public buildings that were built in the late 19th century. In this respect Helsingborg follows an international pattern, of which the Ringstrasse in Vienna is the foremost example.

During the period from the mid–17th century, which we can see on the oldest map, up to the mid–19th century the town developed slowly in other respects. The old street network was extended somewhat to the west and a few streets in the centre were altered.

THE INDUSTRIAL TOWN

During the 19th century a large modern harbour was gradually created, and Helsingborg also became an important railway junction. New blocks were built on filled-in land outside the old town in a grand style of city architecture. The town expanded in all directions, and in the old town streets were altered and new roads opened up. The old buildings were modernised or restored and new types of buildings made their appearance: public buildings, industrial buildings, municipal utilities, buildings for the popular movements.

THE EARLY 20TH-CENTURY TOWN

The population doubled in the first decades of the 20th century and the town area increased sixfold as a result of incorporating outlying areas. A town plan adopted in 1909 greatly augmented the planned area. This plan was adapted to existing circumstances such as old buildings and streets, property boundaries and so on and developed an irregular shape typical of its time.

OLD ROADS AND BOUNDARIES

A good many traces of the cultural landscape at the time before the town expanded have been preserved in Helsingborg. A network of country roads and lanes, estate boundaries and town boundaries, remains of villages and early cottage settlements can be distinguished in today's streets and blocks. Odd angles, dead ends and apparently illogical features in the townscape can tell us a great deal about the town's history, as can the names of streets and districts and individual buildings.

The development of the town can be traced in the preserved street network. The location of the old fortresses is partly indicated. The map to the right shows remains of old roads which led into the town, and old boundaries visible in the street network.

THE HISTORY OF HELSINGBORG IN ITS TOWN PLAN; OLD ROADS AND BOUNDARIES

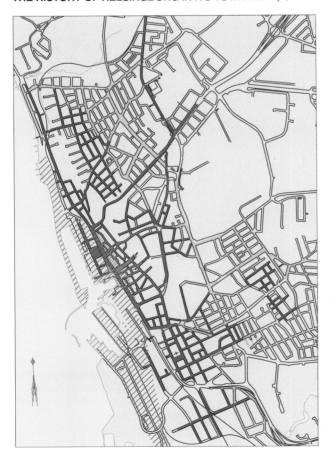

▬▬▬	Preserved medieval streets
▬▬▬	Streets from the period 1500-1850
▬▬▬	Streets from the period 1850-1900
▬▬▬	Streets from the early 20th century
//////	Fill-in land from the same period as the streets, respectively
――――	Old road
――――	Old boundary

Townships

Even though towns are important, small places are in the majority, and they present a more specialised cultural-historical aspect of urban Sweden. They have arisen and developed as a result of local factors such as trade by land and sea, natural resources, communications and services. But altered styles of living also gave rise to or changed communities; seaside resorts, spas and tourism are examples of these factors.

The preservation of cultural environments has always been interested in special communities, places whose history has been acknowledged as important. These include places that have retained their pre-industrial character. There has also been great interest in well-preserved, often esthetically attractive environments or isolated objects. This, together with other factors, means that we enjoy many well-preserved places that show what cultural environments looked like before the Industrial Revolution. There are fewer places that have been recognised for their continuity of development and change, and the numerous places that have arisen or been altered during the past hundred years have aroused little interest.

Many originally small places grew and became townships, urban districts and towns. New communities were formed, others stagnated or lost their importance. There are traces of historical development left in the architecture of most places, and in several cases they represent something of the best among our cultural attractions.

Statistically speaking small towns are those with between 200 and 2,000 inhabitants, but we make no such restrictions here. Instead it is the contents of the cultural environment and the special history of places that have determined our choice.

The cultural environments of small towns have been created by hard work and care interacting with nature and its resources. The shaping of the environment has often been accomplished with small means but with full control over the potential and with esthetic aims.

SELECTED BUILT-UP PLACES

1:5 000 000

✝ Church "town" (overnight accomodation for churchgoers)
● Fishing village
■ Spa
⚓ Seaside resort
● Old market town
● Railway town or village
— Railway

A limited selection of six different categories of small places which are of national historic interest. Other small places which have been destroyed or altered beyond cultural-historical evaluation are poorly documented. **(L93)**

The special atmosphere of the tightly-packed "church towns" is clearly seen at Lövånger, Västerbotten, where the area containing 117 church cottages differs strikingly from the modern part of the town.

A special kind of urban development in both form and function is the Norrrland "church town". Over 70 church towns are known, the great majority of which were in upper Norrland, as far down as northern Ångermanland and Jämtland, with a few in Hälsingland-Härjedalen. A dozen or so have been preserved either completely or partly, all of them in upper Norrland.

The largest and best-preserved are in the coastal parishes in the counties of Västerbotten and Norrbotten. It is there that they remained in use longest, the last ones being built in the early 20th century. The early ones are now presumed to have arisen after the Reformation in connection with the growth of religious education and compulsory church-going. In Luleå and Piteå the oldest towns were located in the same area as the church towns.

Church cottages were owned by registered land-owning farmers and were inherited together with their land. They stood close together in alleys or sections, which originally were spontaneous but later sometimes regulated. Hamlets from a certain part of the parish had their cottages in the same area. Originally they were combined with stables and sheds.

The cottages were mainly used as accomodation at the major church festivals, and were kept locked at other times. Originally "church towns" may also have been used for market days, court sessions and taxation days. They had great social significance. In certain cases they may have been used for permanent residence.

There was no need for "church towns" in the small parishes in the southern and central parts of Sweden, but stables were needed for the horses on Sundays. The long row of stables at Ljuder Church in Småland are post and plank buildings from the early 19th century.

The "church-town's" rows of cottages clearly converge on the medieval church at Lövånger.

Fatmomakke "church town" in Vilhelmina, Lappland, was built in the late 18th century. It was divided at an early date into separate sections for Saami, settlers and merchants. The Saami section contained store sheds and cots, the other sections log cabins.

The largest of the "church towns" is at Nederluleå Church in Gammelstad, Norrbotten, which is also Norrland's largest medieval church. This was also a market place, and for a short period in the 17th century Luleå's oldest town stood here.

In the mid–1940s there were fishing villages spread all along the coast. Although fishing has lost a great deal of its importance, being replaced by tourism and pensioners' homes, most of the villages still retain their fishing atmosphere. (L94)

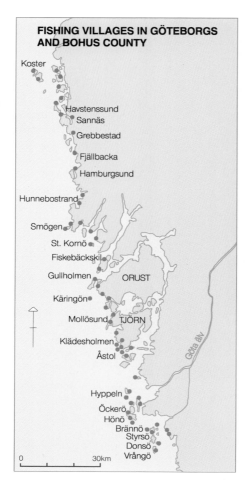

FISHING VILLAGES IN GÖTEBORGS AND BOHUS COUNTY

Koster
Havstenssund
Sannäs
Grebbestad
Fjällbacka
Hamburgsund
Hunnebostrand
Smögen
St. Kornö
Fiskebäckskil
Gullholmen
ORUST
Käringön
Mollösund TJÖRN
Klädesholmen
Åstol
Hyppeln
Öckerö
Hönö
Brännö
Styrsö
Donsö
Vrångö

Göta älv

0   30km

The fishing villages of Gotland are some of the smallest places in Sweden. But the small huts and sheds huddle close together on the flat sea shores, as here at Helgumannen on Fårö.

The cottages on Käringön lie close together round the harbour in a sheltered position facing away from the open sea. The panelled houses used to be painted with train-oil, yellow ochre or red ochre; some one-room cottages have been preserved.

Harstena in Gryt, Östergötland, is an example of the east-coast combination of farming and fishing village — an archipelago village with unpartitioned land and with mainly 19th-century cottages clustered round a harbour.

Fishing Villages

The first fishing communities were inhabited seasonally or lived in by people with several occupations, a small plot of land with a few cows, hunting and so on. In due course most fishing communities turned to fishing as their only means of livelihood. Nowadays tourism is an important source of income.

KÄRINGÖN

Pure fishing communities developed at a very early date in Bohuslän, mainly because of the rich sea harvests but also due to lack of good agricultural land and a good supply of naturally protected harbours.

Three great herring periods led to a high degree of specialisation. The first was in the second part of the 16th century, the second began in the mid-18th century and the third in the late 19th century. Several fishing villages grew up during the first intensive fishing period, among which was Käringön, an island far out to sea beyond Orust. Käringön was established in the early 17th century.

It is not until one approaches the harbour that one sees that this bleak island of bare rocks and heather-covered heaths conceals a fishing village. The first sight that meets one's eyes is the tightly-packed lines of jetties and boats, the red huts for fishing tackle and the frames for drying and cleaning the nets. Then come the white cottages standing directly on the rocks, placed where they are best protected from the wind, yet with a clear view of the sea. Like most of the fishing villages along the coast of Bohuslän, the land there was once owned by the Crown, so paths and tracks wander among the tightly-packed cottages without any fences or enclosures.

What we see today as a typical Bohuslän fishing village is an environment created at the end of the 19th century. Earlier these fishing villages were dominated by low, grey cottages with small outhouses, enclosed fields and boat moorings on the shore itself.

ULVÖHAMN

The fishing villages along the east coast of Sweden, which from the Middle Ages onwards were seasonal fishing places for the townsfolk, form another cultural environment. This system, whereby certain fishing waters and harbours were linked to individual towns along the coast, was particularly common along the coast of Norrland. The citizens of Gävle travelled farthest, from Örnsköldsvik in the north to Älvkarleby in the south. The largest and best-known of their 80 or so known harbours is Ulvöhamn.

Farmers and townsfolk made their way out to this fishing village in the summer to fish for Baltic herring but also to do a bit of farming and cattle rearing. Along the water's edge fishing huts and jetties lie close together; above them are the cottages, packed tightly together with their gables facing the sea and often joined together with toolsheds and saltsheds. The cottages and their gardens stand in rows along the harbour street, which runs parallel to the shore. On the other

At the fishing village of Ulvöhamn in Nätra, Ångermanland, there are clearly visible zones along the shore: fishing sheds, cottages, net-drying frames and outhouses. Originally this was a place for seasonal fishing, and the chapel from this period can be seen in the background.

side are the net frames, followed by simple barns for the cows, sheds for the goats and other outhouses. One of the communal buildings in the fishing village was the chapel. The old chapel, from 1622, is the oldest building at Ulvöhamn today.

Like many other similar villages Ulvöhamn developed at the end of the 19th century into a permanent fishing village inhabited all the year round by fishermen. The simple cottages were rebuilt to become larger and more comfortable. After the Second World War fishing along the coast became less and less profitable, and instead tourism has become an important industry. A well-known speciality for many years was the preparation of fermented Baltic herring.

Market Towns

One type of community that grew up in a uniform social environment similar to that of the fishing villages was the market town, where merchants played a leading role.

Trading and markets before the 19th century free-trading regulations were a privilege closely linked to towns. When market towns were developed, trading could be carried on there by traders from those towns that had that privilege since the 17th century. These markets gradually developed into permanent settlements.

PATAHOLM

There were several market towns along the coast of Småland. The place that has preserved its character better than any other is perhaps Pataholm, at the mouth of the Alsterån.

Pataholm belonged to the citizens of Kalmar, and it was merchants from Kalmar that traded with the local farmers from the countryside round "Pata". Timber and firewood, pitch and tar were the main products that the farmers brought in wagons to be sold. In return they bought salt and herring from the merchants.

If one travels along the old country road north from Kalmar, one suddenly has a view of the small islands that line the channel into Pataholm. Not long ago sailing barges lay at anchor here, waiting for cargo and wind. The road down to the little village was lined on both sides with old skippers' houses and craftsmen's cottages. The latter formed Pataholm's "shanty town", an area for the poor just outside the traditional village boundary.

The cottages in Pataholm date mostly from the 19th century, in simple Empire style, painted in light colours. The cobbled square, the green gardens with their tall trees and the red outhouses and warehouses make a picture which is as close as one can get to the little wooden township. Today the barges, the timber and most of the inhabitants are gone. The hustle and bustle of commerce have been transformed into a pastoral idyll.

Many Norrland fishing villages began as seasonal fishing harbours for the townsfolk of Gävle and other towns in central Sweden. Several were abandoned while others were used as long as fishing continued. Most of them are now used for holidays. (L95)

OLD FISHING VILLAGES, "GÄVLEBOHAMNAR"

Skagshamn
ÖRNSKÖLDSVIK
Trysunda
Ulvöhamn
Norrfällsviken
Bönhamn
Berghamn
HÄRNÖSAND
Barsviken
SUNDSVALL
Skeppshamn
Lörudden
Brämön
Gran
Bergö
Bålsö
HUDIKSVALL
Kuggören
Kråkö
Hölick
Agö
SÖDERHAMN
Skärså
Prästgrundet
Storjungfrun
Iggön
Bönan
GÄVLE
0   25   50 km

The market village of Pataholm in Ålem stands on a headland jutting out into Kalmar Sound. During its heyday at the end of the 19th century it was a centre for the timber trade and shipping, with its own shipyard. Drawing of the merchants' houses round the square by Oscar Hullgren, 1884.

The Club House at Lysekil has burnt down, but its equivalent at Marstrand, built in 1866 to the design of A C Peterson, has a very similar appearance with its panelled facade and gingerbread wood decorations—"carpenter's delight". The House had its heyday during the reign of Oscar II.

Bathing Resorts, Spas and tourist Towns

Bathing as medical treatment and physical recreation has been practised both in the sea and at spas inland.

LYSEKIL, A BATHING RESORT

Lysekil lies in the central Bohuslän archipelago. When a doctor, Professor Huss, proposed to a merchant in Lysekil that they should establish a bathing resort there, he knew what he was talking about. Experience from spas in Germany could be utilised in the "brisk and healthy" climate of the West coast. Not far from the old fishing village a complete institution quickly sprang up, with hot baths and cold baths.

In time the institution expanded; a large company was launched in 1860 by Carl Curman, the physician at the health resort. He took responsibility himself for the overall planning, the architecture and the design of the site. A new building for hot baths was constructed together with a club house, a cold-water bathhouse, a restaurant and several impressive villas for the clientele.

Dr Curman's own villas form part of the same milieu. He created a home in the then-popular Neo-Gothic and Old Norse style, using ornamentation borrowed from old log houses and the Viking Age. After consultations on the veranda of the hot bathhouse at which he prescribed medicines and discussed his patients' state of health, Dr Curman would retire to this atmosphere.

The guests stayed at the resort's hotel or lodged at some merchant's or tradesman's house after the owners had temporarily moved down to the basement with their families. This interest in the archipelago is explained as a reaction to the dirty and overcrowded conditions in the industrial cities. Today Lysekil is no longer as important a resort as it was in the late 19th century. It was made an urban district as early as 1836, but did not attain town status until 1903. As a summer-holiday town—even without its baths—it has, however, retained its attraction.

MEDEVI SPA

The history of Medevi Spa began when Dr Urban Hiärne, Karl XI's personal physician at the time, "discovered" the health waters at Medevi in 1678. The chalybeate water had been used since time immemorial for medical and magical purposes. But Hiärne systematised and organised the taking of the waters, and the community that grew up round the activities became—to use an anachronism—"a model health farm".

People travelled to Medevi during the spa season to cure all kinds of aches and pains, to bathe and to be revitalised, but also to socialise. Social life followed a strict routine, and the term "the porridge parade" is still in use. But it was not just the upper classes that came to Medevi. Hordes of poor people also came in search of treatment and relief from pain, particularly to the hospital, which was enlarged during the 18th century.

Medevi Spa is today Sweden's best-preserved cultural environment created for recreation and taking the waters. The buildings are a hotch-potch from different centuries. Here are examples of the sober style of the 1690s alongside early 19th-century Empire facades and lavish gingerbread work in the Swiss manner from the middle of the same century.

The community was strictly planned to start with, but as the decades passed the plan was ignored, so that buildings were placed more freely. But after more than 300 years the Promenade (the main street) still passes straight between the renovated old houses. The group of houses at the Spa Square still creates the same intimate atmosphere.

An arrival at Medevi Spa in Östergötland is depicted in a tale from about 1910: "Before us lies the prospect of the long summer full of spa music, the bells summoning us to meals and promenades, the bowling alley, bathing in Lake Vättern, rides in horse-drawn carts—excursions to Övralid, Hålaberget and Hulta . . . . The cab draws up, we are there. Our entry into the Inspector's House is by candlelight. Down between cool sheets. What happiness life can offer!"

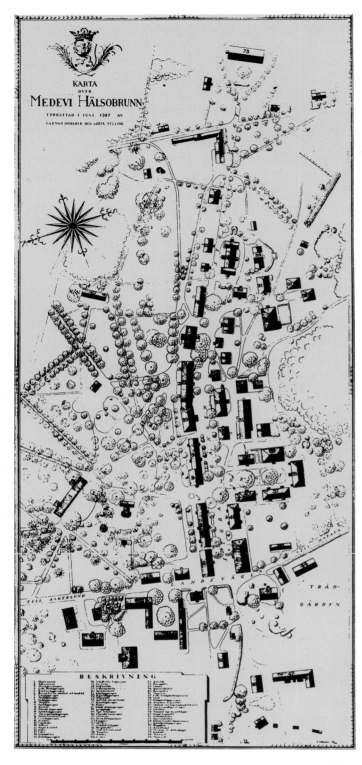

The plan of Medevi Spa cannot be reproduced here on a legible scale, but it gives some idea of the placing of the buildings along Stora Gången (the Promenade) with the spa square to the right and the high well to the left. This historic monument comprises about 50 buildings of various ages and styles from the 17th century onwards, situated above (east of) the old country highway.

ÅRE — A TOURIST RESORT

Fresh air was important for western Jämtland and Åre. The clear, fresh mountain air, "filled with oxygen", was considered healthy and rehabilitating. Fresh-air fiends followed those seeking treatment. The tourists were more important in the long run, and they, too, were a new feature in the mountain landscape. The Swedish Touring Club was founded in 1885 and concentrated its efforts to begin with on the Norrland mountain districts.

Around the turn of the century and during the preceding decades adventurous excursions into the wilderness, the beautiful views and the "pastoral idyll" attracted new groups of travellers. The railway between Östersund and Trondheim, which opened in 1883, made it possible to exploit the Jämtland mountains on a large scale. Åre soon became a central point for this early phase of tourism. Hotels and other facilities were quickly built to meet the needs of these new groups.

The starting point was the railway station, built to a model design of the Swedish State Railways' architect, A W Edelsvärd. The station is relatively simple but must have seemed remarkable in contrast to the log-cabin style of the surrounding farmers'

hamlets. The station was followed by restaurants and large hotels, all built in an impressive panelled style with decorative woodwork.

There was a new building phase after the turn of the century, based on a new town plan drawn up by P O Hallman. The extensive range of large buildings that grew up between 1910 and 1930 had a more obvious national-romantic style, creating a more striking atmosphere. A monumental community was created in a short time during these two periods, and it still forms the heart of the tourist resort of Åre. But this early cultural environment no longer dominates the winter sports resort. Nevertheless, Åre can boast more than 100 years of continuity as a tourist centre, a good example of Sweden's "tourist" history.

Åre is seen here from the west when the central part of the town and its hotels had been built up round the station, but the district still has an old-fashioned, rural appearance. The photograph is probably from 1910 or soon after. The view today (below) from an adjacent point gives some idea of the explosive development the resort has undergone during the last few decades.

The square at Teckomatorp as it was planned, showing the impressive railway station with its characteristic brick architecture to the right.

"Ordinary" Townships

The latest important period in urban development in Sweden is closely connected with the changes that took place towards the end of the 19th century in commerce, transport and industry. When free-trading was introduced, new commercial centres could be established away from the traditional ones, which lay inside towns. Commerce and markets were able more effectively than before to attract permanent shopkeepers and craftsmen. The development of transport systems—more and better roads, canals and above all the new railway lines—led to the establishment of many new communities. Swedish industry was to a large extent in the initial phase localised in the countryside, where there were good supplies of raw materials and water power. It is among water mills, spinning mills, sawmills, mines and engineering workshops that the origins of many small townships are to be found.

These places became the goal of many of those people who could no longer make a living on the land; here they could find jobs and services. Many of the townships combined a number of different functions. Industrial townships, for example, are often administrative centres and commercial centres as well.

Many of these "ordinary" towns developed in a similar way in the 20th century. We see traces of various epochs in the development of a community: commerce and services as the basis, new industries, the municipal centre, suburban estates, apartment blocks and the car-based society. Especially in rural areas an old parish centre and a church often form part of the oldest district of a township. The different epochs are very often clearly visible.

Today we look upon small towns as a rural phenomenon or even a rural problem. Commerce has moved from many small shops to larger and more concentrated stores. Trains no longer stop at as many stations as they used to. Several towns dependent on one industry have suffered as a result of industrial competition. When we recognise these threats, we realise even more the great value of the cultural environments of small towns, both as a historic background and as a valuable social factor for local identity.

Railway Townships

When the main railway lines between Malmö, Göteborg and Stockholm were built, the tracks were laid in straight lines without much regard for the old places along their routes. All the new communities that grew up along the new railway lines contributed greatly to the restructuring of the Swedish countryside.

TECKOMATORP

A railway halt was created in 1865 at Teckomatorp on the new private line between Landskrona and Eslöv. At that time Teckomatorp consisted of two farms, but more buildings soon grew up and in 1872 it was granted the status of a post and railway station. The real leap forward came in 1885, when the line between Malmö and Billesholm ran through the village. Teckomatorp was now joined to the West coast line and had become a railway junction.

The village expanded during the next few hectic decades. Since it was now a central junction, a new brick railway station was built in something

approaching medieval splendour. The spacious square was planned to be lined with grandiose buildings, but only the town hotel lived up to these expectations. Instead the shopkeepers, tradesmen and workers were housed in buildings of an elaborate but sober character. The biggest employer was the sugar factory, which soon owned large areas of land round the town. It was the area south of the railway line that was developed, and the site north of the railway which started in such great style remained little more than a decorative facade.

The clearly distinguished town is surrounded by the plain, with fields running right up to the buildings. The great plans that were made for Teckomatorp at the beginning of the century are still quite visible in its uniform buildings.

Progress continued during the first half of the 20th century, and the town's expansion was crowned with municipal privileges in 1915 and the status of a municipal centre in the 1950s. But the winds changed in the 1970s, when Svalöv became the municipal centre; services disappeared and there were fewer jobs.

New housing estates of bungalows and apartment blocks were established as an independent community without any connection with the old centre. Services were gathered in a new commercial estate on the outskirts of the old town. Commuting to jobs at other places became more and more important. Teckomatorp lives on in new and somewhat different circumstances, while its inhabitants have a large and valuable resource in the old, well-built houses, the mature gardens and the human scale that characterise the small town.

The main western railway line built in the mid–19th century crosses the somewhat older Göta Canal at Töreboda in Västergötland, which aroused great expectations for the new township. The railway station and town plan show traces of these hopes; it was not easy to realise that the canal was already obsolete.

Industrial Monuments

The conservation of industrial monuments has become an increasingly urgent question for cultural preservation as rationalisation and closures have become more and more frequent. Such changes have always occurred, of course, leaving more or less evident traces in the cultural landscape, but in our times we have realised the need to document changes as soon as possible after the event.

Industrial monuments are here taken in the first place to mean buildings—whether still in use or with new functions—and ruins of buildings. But they can also be a wide range of other things: machinery and other equipment, documents, photographs and plans that show a company's growth and development, as well as transport systems of various kinds. Other significant objects are sites that throw light on working conditions and workers' homes, as well as personal memoires. Documenting industrial monuments covers the whole environment in an industrial community.

Documented industrial environments are valuable both from a technical-functional viewpoint and from a general cultural-historical viewpoint. The choice of objects should show what is typical in a certain industry and in a certain era. The laws and regulations controlling the preservation of cultural monuments play a part when these evaluations are made, as do its methods and practicalities and even ideological considerations. Since the objects are in many cases not comparable, there is no general scale of values to refer to.

Industrial closures that affect whole regions have led to difficulties in preserving or finding new uses for often very extensive plants. It is not possible—or even desirable—to preserve everything, in view of the limited private and state financial resources that are available. Thus surveys and documentation are necessary as the basis for making decisions.

We have very varying levels of relevant knowledge at present. There are no adequate national surveys of every industry. We must therefore choose our examples in the first place from industries or areas where we have some form of information. Where we lack such information, priority has been given to those objects or environments that are considered to have been of decisive importance for our industrial development or valuable for other reasons.

Power Stations

Wind and water power were important sources of energy in olden times. Wind power was used primarily for grinding mills. Water power was able to provide a continuous and high level of energy, for ironworks, sawmills and water mills, for example, but this was dependent on changes in the level of the water supply. Power supplies increased greatly when turbines were introduced in the early 19th century. When steam engines were invented, industry no longer had to be located close to rivers.

Water power superseded steam power as a producer of electric energy when a functional generator of electric current was constructed. At the beginning of the 20th century approximately 60 per cent of all electrical plant ran on hydro-electric power. The technology for transmitting energy over long distances meant that heavy industry could be electrified.

Electric energy for the public was first produced by water power in southern Sweden. The exploitation of the Trollhätten falls, which began in 1907, raised questions concerning the state's rights to water power. The State Power Board was established in 1909, after which many of the large power stations were built by the state.

In 1914 most hydro-electric power stations were in Bergslagen. North of Gävle there were only 32 hydro-electric power stations producing more than 500 horsepower. The Porjus station on the Stora Luleälv, which is of technical-historical interest, was one exception. As late as 1923 most of the large power stations were on the Dalälven.

The Indalsälven with its huge natural lake reservoirs was an attractive choice for water power construction. At the end of the 19th century smaller power stations began to be built. Hissmofors was built between 1894 and 1897, and plans to regulate lakes were initiated in 1920. With the ex-

One kilometre of rapids falling some 20 m in height created this concentrated industrial landscape on the river at Norrköping. Mills from the Middle Ages were already there; later came armourers' workshops and a brass foundry, but from the 17th century onwards it was the textile industry that was dominant. The factory buildings are mainly from the late 19th century, with the well-known "Smoothing Iron" on Laxholmen (now the Museum of Work), from 1917, as one of the last to be built. In the foreground the Old Square, to the left the gateway tower of Holmen's Mill (1750) and in the background Bergsbron (bridge). It is no easy task to preserve industrial settings when the buildings' original functions have disappeared.

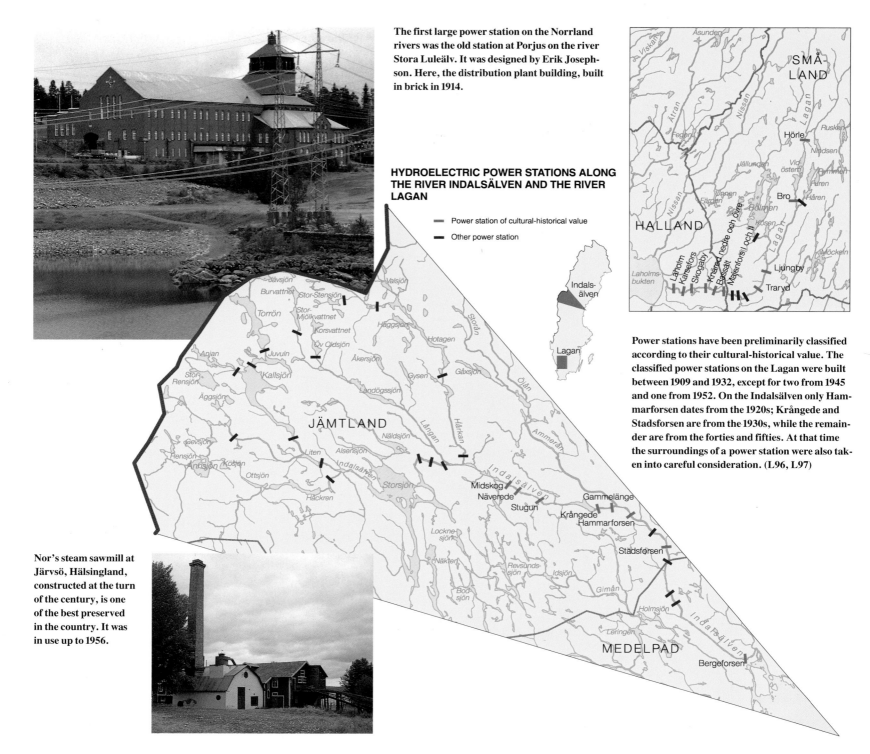

The first large power station on the Norrland rivers was the old station at Porjus on the river Stora Luleälv. It was designed by Erik Josephson. Here, the distribution plant building, built in brick in 1914.

HYDROELECTRIC POWER STATIONS ALONG THE RIVER INDALSÄLVEN AND THE RIVER LAGAN

— Power station of cultural-historical value

— Other power station

Power stations have been preliminarily classified according to their cultural-historical value. The classified power stations on the Lagan were built between 1909 and 1932, except for two from 1945 and one from 1952. On the Indalsälven only Hammarforsen dates from the 1920s; Krångede and Stadsforsen are from the 1930s, while the remainder are from the forties and fifties. At that time the surroundings of a power station were also taken into careful consideration. (L96, L97)

Nor's steam sawmill at Järvsö, Hälsingland, constructed at the turn of the century, is one of the best preserved in the country. It was in use up to 1956.

ception of certain tributaries the river was completely exploited during the 1940s and 1950s. These power stations are typical of the technology and construction work of the period.

One of the most powerful rivers in southern Sweden is the Lagan, which was successively exploited at many points and which has several power stations of great cultural and technical-historical interest.

The Forest Industry

The forest industry is historically speaking the second and today the most important of Sweden's basic industries. In the absence of nation-wide evaluations the Sundsvall region has been chosen to represent this industry.

This region may be considered the largest and most concentrated forest-industry area in Europe. The history of the industry here is based mainly on the rich forests of the highlands, on good harbours along the coast and on the fact that the two large rivers that meet the sea close to each other were suitable for timber floating.

The oldest industries here were ironworks and glassworks, which were located in this part of Sweden because of its good supply of fuel. After the iron era there were in the central Sundsvall area 22 shipyards, 43 steam sawmills, and eight paper pulp mills. The shipyard at Sundsvall was one of the largest in Sweden in the mid–19th century.

Industrial buildings cannot usually be judged on purely esthetic grounds;

their function and their social importance are more significant. The plants belonging to the cellulose and paper industries are very large and complex and it is difficult and expensive to preserve them.

SAWMILLS

Water sawmills were the predecessors of steam sawmills. Very few of these mills have been preserved in toto. Most water sawmills were small plants placed directly by a waterfall. They consisted of a sawhouse, water and floating channels and other buildings.

The steam engine made sawmills independent of water power, so they were located instead at the harbours. Tunadal's steam sawmill, built in 1849, was the first in Sweden and is now the only remaining sawmill in the

Skönvik's steam saw-
mill north of Sundsvall
was built by F Bünsow
in 1861. At one time
the mill employed
more than 500 men.
All that remains of the
mill are the boiler-
house, the smithy and
the workshop. Several
large wooden houses
for the workers stand
on the slopes above the
mill.

Sundsvall district. After the strong increase in demand for sawn timber in
the 19th century there was a reconstruction period around the turn of
the century when many sawmills were
combined with or replaced by a pulp
mill.

THE PAPER AND PULP INDUSTRY

The development of the paper industry may be divided into three phases.
The proto-industrial period when pa-

per was made by hand with rags as
the raw material lasted from the late
16th century to the end of the 19th
century. Mills at that time were located in southern and central Sweden.
Ösjöfors hand paper mill in northern
Småland, which was founded in 1777
and continued to operate until 1926,
is the oldest one to be preserved on
its original site with its interior and
equipment in good order.

Phase two, which involved mechanisation and a transition to large-scale
industry with wood as the raw material, lasted from about 1830 to 1950.
Frövifors paper mill in Västmanland,
built in 1902, is a good example of
early mechanical paper manufacturing. We are now in phase three,
which involves a concentration of
operations and expansion.

The mechanical pulp industry was
located in western Sweden and the
chemical pulp industry in Norrland.
The turning point for the Norrland
cellulose industry came in 1890–1910.
The more modern factories were
large, palace-like buildings built of
red brick. Reinforced concrete was
first used about 1905. The now-de-
molished Svartvik sulphite factory in

Njurunda, built in 1907, had dark,
completely smooth brick walls with
broad strips between windows with
small panes.

The Mining Industry

The oldest mines in Bergslagen have
been in use since the Middle Ages.
The Lappland iron-ore fields were
discovered in the 17th century, but it
was not until the Thomas process had
made it possible to exploit the phos-
phorous ore and the transport problems had been solved with railways
that mining could be undertaken on
a large scale. Production in Lappland
soon exceeded that in the mines in
central Sweden. The discovery of rich
and easily-accessible deposits of ore
in other parts of the world weakened
Sweden's iron exports after 1950.
Practically the whole of the mining industry in central Sweden disappeared
in the 1980s; the last iron-ore mine,
Dannemora, was closed in April 1992.

PLANT AT A MINING FIELD

The most important of the many
buildings at a mine is the pithead,
built on top of the mine shaft. The
mined ore was brought to the surface
here, and it was here that the miners
ascended and descended the mine. It
may be built of wood, brick, iron or
reinforced concrete. The winder

**INDUSTRIAL AREA
OF THE SUNDSVALL
DISTRICT**

- Ironworks
- Shipyard
- Water sawmill
- Steam sawmill
- Pulp mill or
  groundwood mill
- Paper mill
- Partially-preserved
  industry
- Partially-preserved
  dwellings

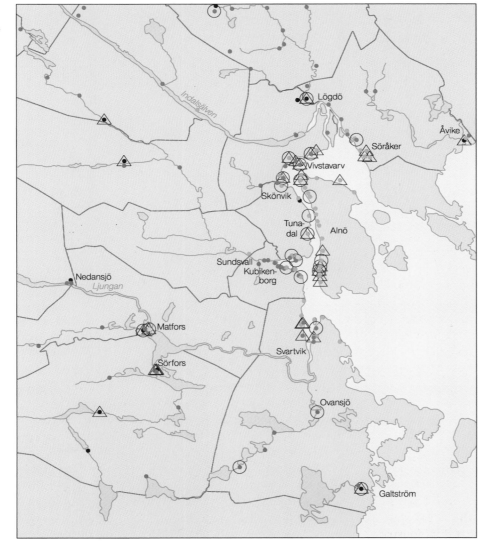

Only a small number of the many
industries that have existed in the
Sundsvall area have been in operation at the same time. The ironworks have the oldest-preserved
settings, best of all at Galtström
and Lögdö. In the forest industries
bankruptcies and reconstructions
were common, for example the
sawmills on Alnön, and more modern industries have replaced obsolete ones on the same spot, like the
sequences of shipyard-sawmill-
pulpmill at Vistavarv and Svartvik.
Well-preserved and well-main-
tained old industrial buildings are
unusual; in many industries all that
remains is some well-constructed
building such as a boilerhouse or an
enginehouse. There may still be
remains of the surrounding community in the form of mansions,
workers' dwellings, buildings used
by the popular movements etc, as
at Vistavarv, Skönvik, Eriksdal on
Alnön, Svartvik and to some extent
at Matfors.

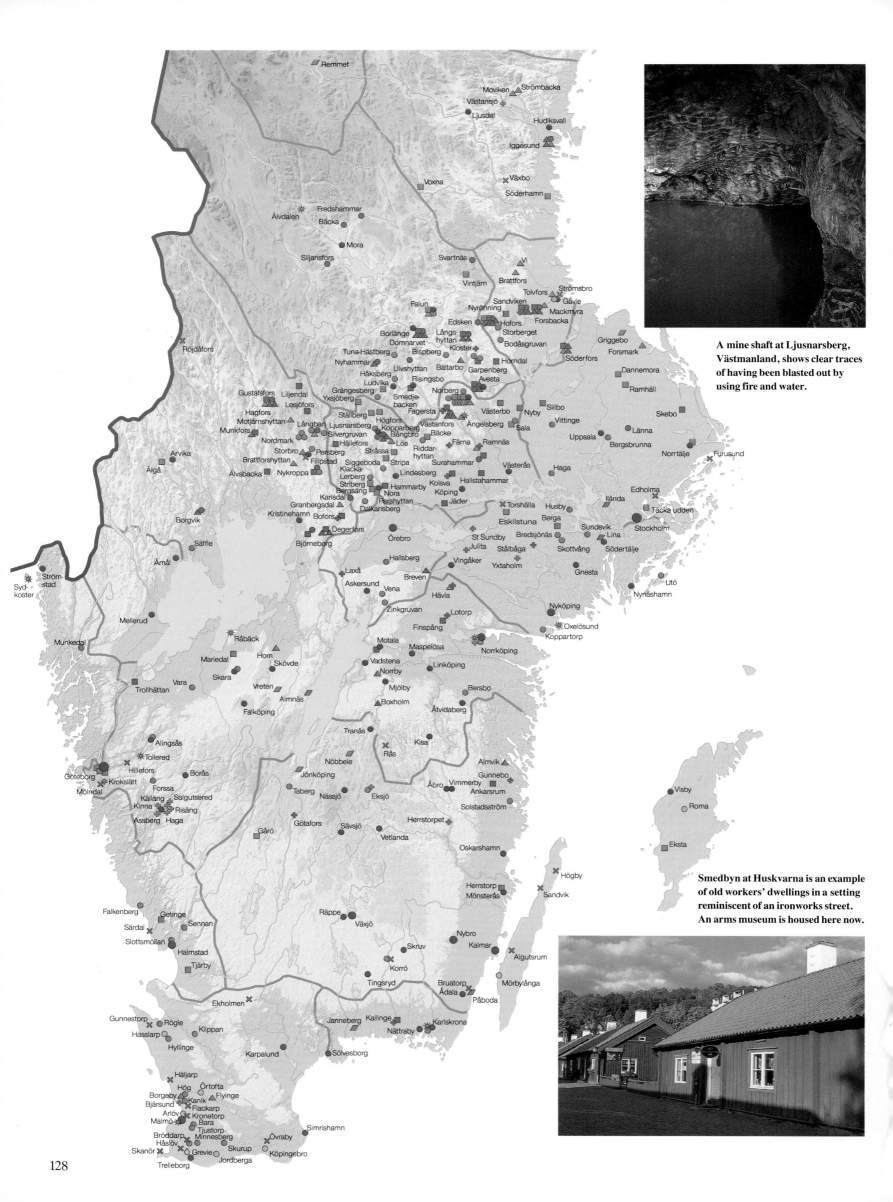

A mine shaft at Ljusnarsberg, Västmanland, shows clear traces of having been blasted out by using fire and water.

Smedbyn at Huskvarna is an example of old workers' dwellings in a setting reminiscent of an ironworks street. An arms museum is housed here now.

Remmet

Moviken Strömbacka
Västansjö
Ljusdal
Hudiksvall
Iggesund

Voxna
Växbo
Söderhamn

Älvdalen Fredshammar
Bäcka

Mora

Siljansfors
Svartnäs
Vi
Vintjärn Brattfors
Tolvfors Strömsbro
Falun Nyrönning Sandviken Gävle
Edsken Hofors Mackmyra
Borlänge Långs- Storberget Forsbacka
Domnarvet hyttan Bodåsgruvan
Tuna-Hästberg Bispberg Kloster Griggebo
Nyhammar Bältarbo Hörndal Forsmark
Håksberg Ulvshyttan Garpenberg Söderfors
Ludvika Risingsbo Avesta Dannemora
Gustafsfors Liljendal Grängesberg Norberg Ramhäll
Lesjöfors Yxsjöberg Smedje- Västerbo Nyby Sillbo Skebo
Hagfors Ställberg backen Nyby Vittinge
Motjärnshyttan Långban Högfors Fagersta Ängelsberg Sala Länna
Munkfors Ljusnarsberg Kopparberg Västanfors Uppsala Bergsbrunna
Nordmark Silvergruvan Bångbro Bäcke Färna Norrtälje Furusund
Arvika Storbro Persberg Hällefors Stråssa Löa Ramnäs
Älgå Brattforshyttan Filipstad Siggeboda Stripa Riddar- Surahammar Västerås Edholma
Älvsbacka Nykroppa Klacka- hyttan Haga Ilända
Karlsdal Lerberg Lindesberg Kolsva Hallstahammar Täcka udden
Borgvik Granbergsdal Striberg Hammarby Köping Stockholm
Kristinehamn Bergsäng Nora Jäder
Säffle Bofors Nora Pershyttan Torshälla Husby
Degerfors Dalkarlsberg Eskilstuna Berga
Ämål Björneborg Örebro St Sundby Sundsvik
Hallsberg Julita Bredsjönäs Lina
Strömstad Laxå Breven Stålbåga Skottvång Södertälje
Sydkoster Askersund Vena Hävla Vingåker Gnesta
Mellerud Zinkgruvan Yxtaholm
Munkedal Råbäck Finspång Lotorp Nyköping Utö
Mariedal Horn Motala Oxelösund Nynäshamn
Skövde Maspelösa Norrköping Koppartorp
Skara Vadstena Koppartorp
Vara Vreten Norrby Linköping
Trollhättan Almnäs Mjölby Bersbo
Falköping Boxholm Åtvidaberg
Tranås Visby
Alingsås Kisa Roma
Tollered Rås
Göteborg Hillefors Borås Nöbbele Almvik Eksta
Krokslätt Forssa Jönköping Gunnebo
Mölndal Källäng Salgutsered Taberg Åbro Vimmerby
Kinna Risäng Nässjö Eksjö Ankarsrum
Assberg Haga Götafors Sävsjö Solstadsström
Gårö Vetlanda Herrstorpet
Oskarshamn
Falkenberg Högby
Getinge Herrstorp Sandvik
Sennan Räppe Mönsterås
Särdal Växjö
Slottsmöllan Nybro
Halmstad Skruv Kalmar
Tjärby Korrö Algutsrum
Tingsryd Mörbylånga
Gunnestorp Rögle Bruatorp
Hasslarp Klippan Janneberg Kallinge Ådala Påboda
Hyllinge Nättraby Karlskrona
Häljarp Karpalund Sölvesborg
Hög Örtofta Ekholmen
Borgeby Kanik Flyinge
Bjärsund Flackarp
Arlöv Kronetorp
Malmö Bara Simrishamn
Bröddarp Tjustorp Övraby
Håslöv Minnesberg Skurup Köpingebro
Skanör Ö Grevie Jordberga
Trelleborg

128

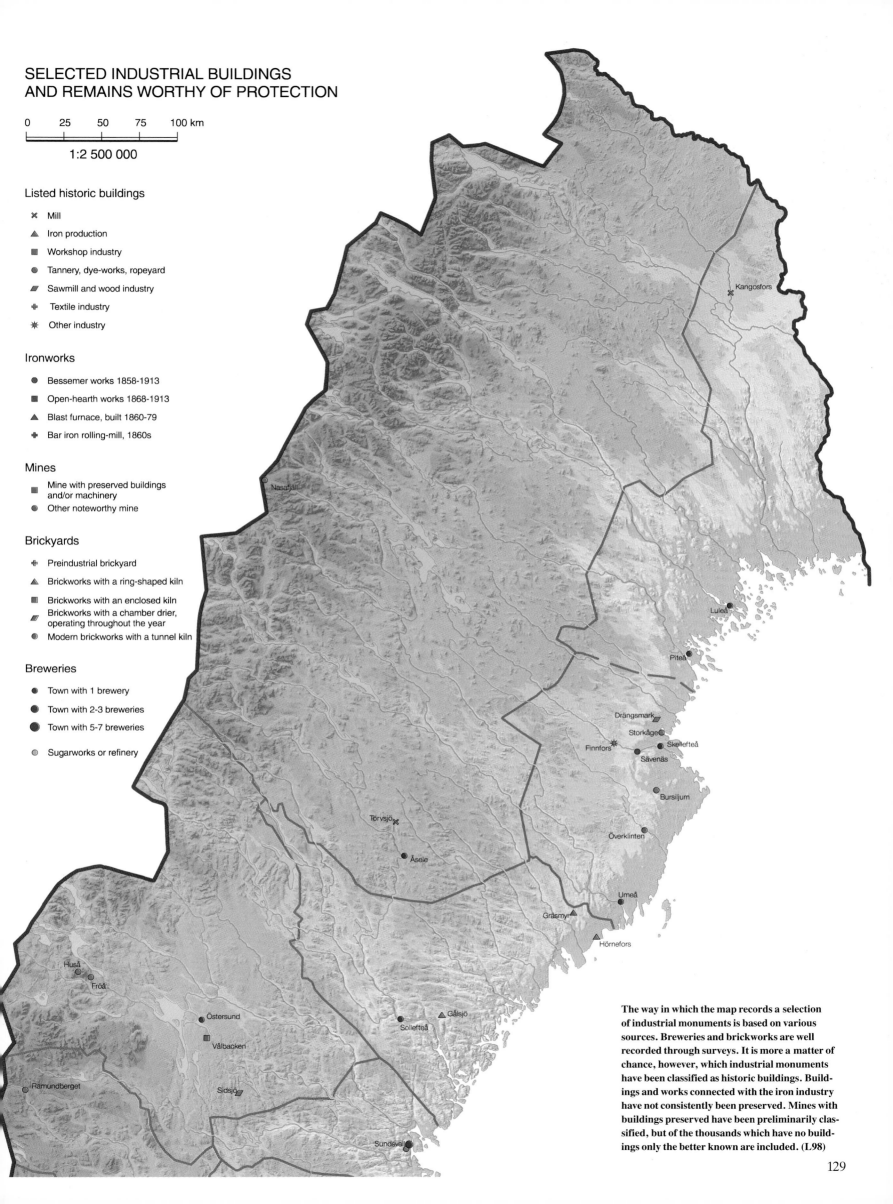

SELECTED INDUSTRIAL BUILDINGS AND REMAINS WORTHY OF PROTECTION

0   25   50   75   100 km

1:2 500 000

Listed historic buildings

✖ Mill
▲ Iron production
◼ Workshop industry
● Tannery, dye-works, ropeyard
◢ Sawmill and wood industry
✚ Textile industry
✳ Other industry

Ironworks

● Bessemer works 1858-1913
◼ Open-hearth works 1868-1913
▲ Blast furnace, built 1860-79
✚ Bar iron rolling-mill, 1860s

Mines

◼ Mine with preserved buildings and/or machinery
● Other noteworthy mine

Brickyards

✚ Preindustrial brickyard
▲ Brickworks with a ring-shaped kiln
◼ Brickworks with an enclosed kiln
◢ Brickworks with a chamber drier, operating throughout the year
● Modern brickworks with a tunnel kiln

Breweries

● Town with 1 brewery
● Town with 2-3 breweries
● Town with 5-7 breweries
◉ Sugarworks or refinery

The way in which the map records a selection of industrial monuments is based on various sources. Breweries and brickworks are well recorded through surveys. It is more a matter of chance, however, which industrial monuments have been classified as historic buildings. Buildings and works connected with the iron industry have not consistently been preserved. Mines with buildings preserved have been preliminarily classified, but of the thousands which have no buildings only the better known are included. (L98)

129

house where the lifting gear is housed has to be close to the pithead. After being mined the ore has to be crushed and sorted. Stamping mills, where the rock is crushed, used to be driven by water power. There is a stamping mill preserved at Pershyttan. Picking sorted the granite from the ore in the crushed rock. There are picking houses preserved at Långban and Sala. The ore was then washed to remove earth and grit. A washing house is preserved at Falun. Ore-dressing plants were first built in the late 19th century.

Keeping mines dry was a problem for many years. The water was pumped up by water power. Devices for mechanical power transmission between a waterfall and the mine were introduced in the late 16th century at Stora Kopparberget. As late as the 20th century these lever systems were still in use and are preserved at Pershyttan and Norberg.

It was not until electric power was introduced in the 20th century that water could be pumped up from very great depths; electricity also made it easier to bring the ore to the surface, of course. Mine ventilation was another long-lasting problem. The first fans came into use in the 1860s.

The miners had their changing rooms and so on in the mine sheds, which also housed the mine office, stores, a drill smithy, repair shops and later on a powerhouse.

A mining village containing miners' cottages, supervisors' houses, the manager's house, perhaps a chapel and a People's House, and a village store usually stood close to the mining field.

The Iron and Engineering Industry

Iron manufacturing played by far the most decisive role in Sweden's industrial development. Apart from its being the largest export industry for many years, many forest industries and engineering works have their origins there. However, the iron industry has seen great changes since the later part of the 19th century onwards.

BLAST FURNACES

The construction of blast furnaces changed in the mid–19th century as a result of English influence. The new blast furnace at Långshyttan, built by Håkan Steffansson in 1859, was the start of a new era. During the following 20 years modern blast furnaces were built at a number of ironworks.

INGOT-STEEL PROCESSES

The introduction of ingot-steel processes led to large-scale iron manufacturing. The Bessemer process was brought into use in 1858. The Bessemer furnace preserved at Hagfors began production in 1880.

The Martin open-hearth process was brought into use at Munkfors in the 1860s. This oldest works is preserved. Steel could be produced in

The pithead building at "Queen Christina's Shaft" at the silver mine in Sala is one of several buildings of cultural-historical value here.

large quantities at low cost by these methods. They required large plants with a suitable location. Many small works with old furnaces and hammer smithies in Bergslagen had to be closed down.

ROLLING MILLS

Rolling-mill technology developed during the 1860s and led to an enormous increase in production. Ingot steel was rolled for the first time at Smedjebacken in 1861. Ten years later a mill was started up at Munkfors. In the same year Steffansson constructed a reversible rolling mill at Forsbacka. Rolling mills were also built at Iggesund and Långban at the same time.

ENGINEERING

Cast-iron goods were manufactured both directly at the blast furnaces and in special furnaces in which the pig iron was remelted. Stavsjö, Åker and Finspång all had cannon and ammunition moulds alongside the blast furnaces.

Ironware manufacturers, such as Huskvarna Weapon Factory (dating from 1689) and companies in Eskilstuna, made products for the home market and for export. Engineering workshops developed from the 18th century onwards. Baltzar von Platen's workshop at Motala, established in 1822 when the Göta Canal was being built, was of vital importance. The production of ironware at mills expanded, but independent workshops were also established. The engineering industry grew in importance and size with the production of internal combustion engines, electric motors, sewing machines, bicycles, agricultural machinery and other such goods.

After the 1870s larger factories were built, some of them looking like medieval castles, others in new, imported styles with sawtooth roofs, for example.

Rademacher, a merchant from the Baltic province of Livland, established 20 manufactories at Eskilstuna in the 1650s. They were built of timber and housed both workshops and workers. Six of these forges are still standing today, forming part of an industrial park.

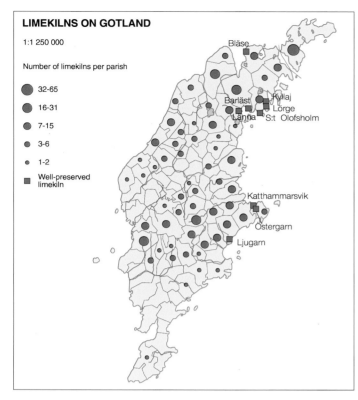

LIMEKILNS ON GOTLAND

1:1 250 000

Number of limekilns per parish

- 32–65
- 16–31
- 7–15
- 3–6
- 1–2
- ■ Well-preserved limekiln

Bläse

Barläst · Kyllaj
· Lörge
Lanna · S:t Olofsholm

Katthammarsvik

Östergarn

Ljugarn

The number of lime kilns per parish is primarily dependent on the supply of limestone; where the limestone does not crop out, there are none. The largest plants are as a rule on the coast, since they export their products. (L99)

One of Gotland's largest lime works is at Bläse in Fleringe, with two high shaft furnaces, wood furnaces, lime stores, a silo and other buildings.

Kronetorp's Mill in Burlöv was built in 1841. It is one of the largest windmills in Skåne, a four-storeyed Dutch mill with a rotatable cap. The miller's house is from the same date. The windmill happens to be placed next to a Bronze Age barrow.

The Stone and Soil Industry

The stone and soil industry covers the quarrying and processing of rock and earth with the exception of ore.

Granite of various colours and coarseness has been quarried in many places to provide building stone. The stone industry was most extensive in Bohuslän and Blekinge, where it has transformed parts of the landscape, for example on Malmön and Tjurkö. Stone was quarried in other parts of the country, too: granite in the Stockholm archipelago, porphyr in Älvdalen and marble in Kolmården and Närke.

LIMEWORKS

Ever since the Middle Ages limestone has been quarried for building. A few medieval quarries preserved on Gotland which provided stone for churches are almost unique.

The most common use of limestone, however, was to produce lime for building, agriculture and other purposes. The burning of lime goes back many centuries on Gotland. It was first practised by farmers, then by lime "barons" and later by companies.

In the Middle Ages lime was burnt in small stacks. The lime kiln that was built at St Olofsholm in Hellvi in the 17th century began the expansion of lime production on the island. Firewood was piled up at the bottom of kilns and limestone placed on top. The kiln was lit and allowed to burn for three to four days, after which it was raked out. The lime was slaked in boxes down by the water. Shaft kilns, in which limestone and wood were fed in from the top, operated continuously.

The lime kilns on Gotland have now been registered as ancient monuments. Others are to be found elsewhere in Sweden, for example on the edge of Hunneberg and in the Silurian district of Västergötland. Many have been destroyed, of course, by later quarrying, at Kinnekulle, for example.

THE BRICK INDUSTRY

Bricks have been used in Sweden since the Middle Ages. For a long time bricks were made and fired on the actual building site. At the beginning of the 19th century brickworks were usually attached to a country estate. The growth of the industry was

in part due to the need for drainage pipes for agriculture and bricks and tiles for the new towns.

Five phases may be distinguished in the development of the brick industry: a pre-industrial stage on estates and farms, three industrial stages with improvements to kilns and a fifth at modern brickworks where bricks are fired in a tunnel kiln.

In the olden days bricks were fired in small field kilns, a process which took about three weeks. The first ring kiln in which the fire is moved round, permitting continuous operation, was built at Lomma. A flame kiln, in which the goods are stationary and the fire moves, was developed for roof tiles and pipes. Unfired bricks were originally dried in the summer in boxes which allowed the air to circulate freely, but later they were dried on top of the kilns, which made use of waste heat.

Around 1900 there were about 500 brickworks in Sweden; 15 years later more than half of them had closed down. Only twelve were left in 1992.

THE GLASS INDUSTRY

Glass was being manufactured in Sweden as early as the 16th century, mainly in Mälardalen. There were 15 glassworks in the 17th century, eight of them in the Stockholm area. Glass production was stimulated during the 18th century, when 16 glassworks were established in various places; Kosta was one of them. When the Småland ironworks were closed down, the farmers started selling charcoal to glassworks, since glassmaking also requires large quantities of fuel. Ten new glassworks were established in eastern Småland in the 1870s, and another 26 in the following two decades, so a specialised industrial region has grown up here. When machine glass production and other modern methods were introduced, the result was over-production and rationalisation.

There are cultural layers to be found under the surface at several early glassworks that were closed down long ago. The buildings at glassworks were designed along the same lines as those at ironworks, with workers' cottages lining straight streets and the manor house in the background. Kosta, Orrefors, which replaced an ironworks, and Pukeberg offer well-preserved glassworks environments.

131

The steam mill at Kalmar is a typical example of the monumental architecture of the early 20th-century food industry.

The Food Industry

The windmills and watermills, farm dairies and co-operative dairies, slaughterhouses and the like that were part of the old farming society represent the earliest stage of the food industry.

The large mills built in Gothic-style architecture are characteristic features in towns. The steam mill at Kalmar and two mills in Stockholm provide good examples.

BREWERIES

The brewing industry was organised as a guild in the 17th century and was practised as a craft. After the introduction of free-trading in 1846 it was transformed by industrialisation and urbanisation.

Steam power was used for the first time in Göteborg after 1810, which led to the mechanisation of many processes. A large number of Bavarian breweries were established in towns, requiring large premises for fermentation and cooling. At the end of the 19th century there were 13 breweries in Stockholm, nine in Göteborg, and five in both Norrköping and Gävle. A peak of 240 breweries was reached in 1905–6, followed by a period of rapid concentration.

The buildings' functions controlled the architecture, but a conscious esthetic design was nevertheless evident. A medieval-type facade with impulses from the renaissance and Gothic styles developed after the 1860s. Stone, brick and various types of plaster were used.

Buildings containing both malthouses and brewhouses were both tall and long. The facades had several rows of small windows and there were ventilation stacks near the eaves. Brewhouses had high, wide windows to let in the daylight and to display the interior with its large copper mash and wort vessels.

THE SUGAR INDUSTRY

Imported cane sugar was refined in Sweden as early as the 17th century. There were ten such refineries in the country in 1741. When sugarbeet began to be cultivated in the 1830s, the situation changed. The refinery and raw-sugar factory at Landskrona, established in 1838, was a forerunner for the whole sugar industry. Many modern raw-sugar factories, most of them in Skåne, were built in the 1880s.

The combined factories had a refinery and a raw-sugar factory of about the same size alongside each other or in a row. The refineries had large, tall factory buildings with a ground plan, storeys and windows that were regular. Dwellings for the office and factory workers were built round the plants.

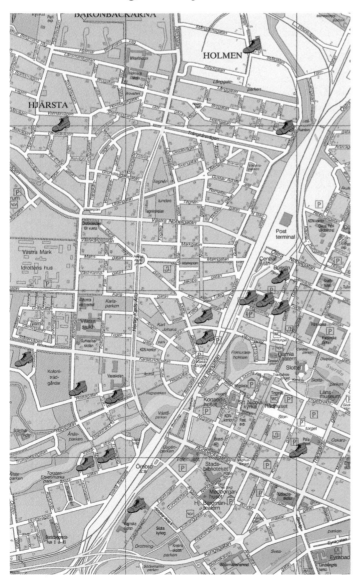

The shoe-making industry in Närke was one of the most purely local specialisations in Swedish industry. In 1938 more than 50 per cent of all Swedish shoes were manufactured here. It had grown up from shoe-making in the Kumla district. Industrialisation began in the 1890s and the industry expanded greatly up to 1914. In 1934 there were in Örebro 17 large and 56 small factories and in Kumla 6 large and 23 small ones, employing altogether some 5,000 workers. The decline started in the 1950s. The large companies had custom-built factories, often fine pieces of architecture. The largest ones in Örebro are shown on the map. The last factory closed down in 1981. The photograph shows the Örebro Shoe Factory in 1916, with its typical factory facade of 1907. Some shoe factories have now been demolished, and most of them are used for other purposes. For a few decades the shoe industry set its mark on both the town's architecture and its social life.

Rydal's spinning mill on the river Viskan was founded in 1854 and has valuable industrial architecture. There is a well-preserved mill community round the factory. The municipality runs a museum project here now.

The merchant's house at Källäng in Örby is typical of the well-built houses of this kind, functioning as a merchant's house from the 1840s up to the beginning of the 20th century. There also used to be a weaving mill here.

The Textile Industry

The "Seven Hundreds District" in Västergötland, the district of cottage industries, clothes factories and travelling salesmen, is characterised more than others by the textile industry. Local crafts, cottage industries and factory industries are three stages in the growth of this industry.

Making of home-woven cloth for sale grew in importance in the 17th century. Flax was introduced at many places as a new spinning material and was cultivated in most of the villages in Hälsingland and Ångermanland. The preparation of flax became a useful source of income, which is evident in the large, timbered farmhouses that grew up. Flax was superseded by cotton in the early 19th century.

In the Seven Hundreds District water-powered cloth stamping machines were also developed, and later dyeing shops. Merchants in Alingsås and Borås and later in the countryside paid women to weave cloth in their homes. As early as 1840 the Seven Hundreds District, with about 4,000 home-workers, accounted for 78 per cent of Sweden's total production of cotton goods.

The first mechanical weaving mill was opened at Rydboholm in 1834. The water power of the river Viskan was important for its location. The spinning mill at Rydal, established in 1854, was the first one to be electrified; it still has spinning buildings from various epochs, as well as offices and factory workers' dwellings.

By 1860 there were twelve mechanised cotton spinning mills in or near towns. These large spinning and weaving mills introduced the factory system, which meant extreme specialisation of work. Göteborg, Norrköping, Malmö, Uddevalla, Borås and Gävle are central examples of towns with important textile industries. Now that they have more or less disappeared it is a great problem to preserve the bulky specialised factory buildings in a meaningful way. The remarkable industrial landscape round the river in central Norrköping, for example, contains mainly old textile industries, all now closed down.

In the Seven Hundreds District the old merchant farms influenced the location and design of factory buildings. Many textile industries were modelled on English brick-built factories, while others have continental features. The buildings were either several storeys high with pillar-and-beam constructions or on one floor with a hall with a sawtooth roof. The location of the factories in an open agricultural landscape still creates a special atmosphere in Viskadalen. Jonsered in the valley of the Säveån was built as a model town on a strict plan.

There were 38 textile firms, 28 knitwear firms and 31 ready-made clothes firms in Mark in 1951. With its small-scale industrial environment Mark has survived the crises better than other regions.

TEXTILE INDUSTRY BUILDINGS IN MARK

■ Cloth merchant's mansion
■ Weaving mill
□ Spinning mill
■ Clothing or knitwear factory
— Municipality boundary

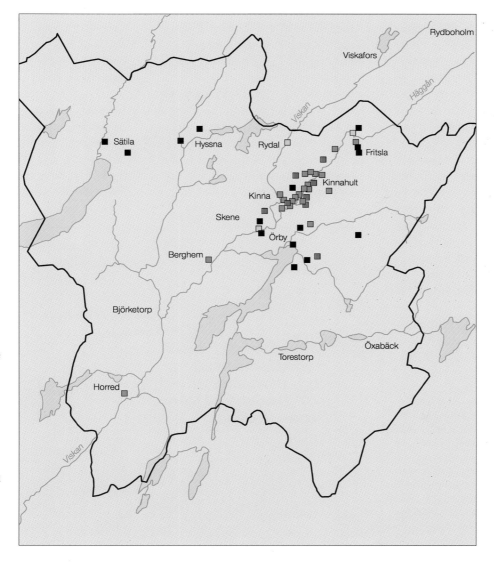

Merchant's houses are historic buildings. They also influenced the design of early factories. A couple of the spinning mills are of the Lancashire type, while the weaving mills are one-storeyed halls or multi-storeyed buildings of the German type, all more or less rebuilt over the years.

Place Names

Place names in Sweden tell us something about the people who named the places and about the places at the time they were named. Names are invaluable clues when we are trying to find out how people lived and what the old landscape looked like. Not only the names of settlements but all place names have something to tell us about olden times.

Place Name Research

Research into Swedish place names was originally a branch of history. The first serious researcher in the subject was Andreas Stobaeus, a professor at Lund University, who noted in the early 18th century that many place names could be grouped according to their final elements, for example -löv, -inge and -torp. He used this observation to date various names. In the late 19th century this research became a linguistic discipline, in which the history of language and etymology had central positions. Norway was a pioneer country in this respect; in 1897 Oluf Rygh began to publish "Norwegian Farm Names". This work was the model for the Swedish equivalent "Swedish Place Names" which was initiated in 1902. In the first half of the 20th century Jöran Sahlgren emphasised both the topographical and the linguistic aspects of the subject. In more recent years an applied form, name preservation has grown up.

The main task of place-name researchers is to interpret names, that is, to explain what elements they consist of, what the names mean and what they referred to when they were given. This is a typical interdisciplinary subject.

The method of interpretation requires the oldest possible written forms of the name (medieval forms

for old names), a genuine dialect pronunciation, factual knowledge of what the name referred to and linguistic competence. Researchers see, for example, that Frövi cannot contain the name of the god Frö, as it would then be called *Frösvi, but the goddess Fröja instead. Understanding of the dialect may help to explain that the name of a lake like Gårlången in Dalarna has nothing to do with a farm (Sw. gård) but contains a word for dirt, mud (Sw. gorr).

PLACE NAMES AS A LINGUISTIC SOURCE

Place names are a part of language and change with it. One evident trend in language is for long words to be shortened and simplified, in many cases so that they become unrecognisable. Gunnersta, for example, might originally have been *Gunþiharjashuso(n)staðiR. With the help of place names it is possible to reconstruct lost words, old ways of making words and inflections. A reconstructed word is shown by placing * before the word. An example of a lost word is *thora, height, which is in the names Toran and Långtora. This is closely related to another lost word *thiur, height, corresponding to Early English þeor, a cyst, which is found in the name of the island Tjörn and in Tjurbo in Västmanland. Another lost word of great antiquity is in the name of Lake Vättern. A thousand years ago the lake was called Vaetur, which includes

a word which is closely related to English water and German Wasser. Two parish names in Norrland, Undersvik in Hälsingland and Undersåker in Jämtland contain another lost word, undorn, which refers to a certain time of the day. The factual background is probably that the bay (vik) and the field (åker) were in the sun at that time. In olden times the collective word yxn was used to denote a herd of oxen, which is to be found in the name of an island in Östergötland, Yxnö, and Yxenhult in Skåne.

An important way of forming new words and names was to add a suffix to a root. Many of our old nature names were formed in this way. The most common form seems to have been an n-suffix, which is found in old names of islands like Adelsö (*Alsna) and Solna, and in old river names like Ljusnan (*Lusn) and Ljungan (*Oghn). Old inflections are preserved in place names. Today Swedish only has one genitive marker, -s, but earlier there were other forms such as -ar, -u and in the plural -a. Thus the place name of Stering comes from the old form Stigharäng. The first element is the genitive of the word stig, road, path. The dative case form has disappeared from modern Swedish but is found in two old names which are common in Norrland, Åkre and Hamre, which go back to archaic dative singular forms Akri and Hambri.

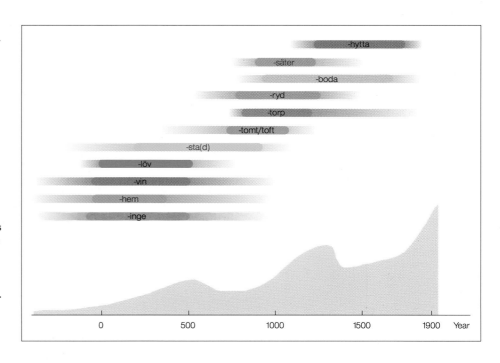

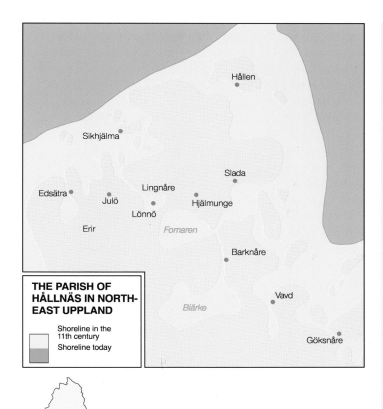

THE PARISH OF HÅLLNÄS IN NORTH-EAST UPPLAND

Shoreline in the 11th century

Shoreline today

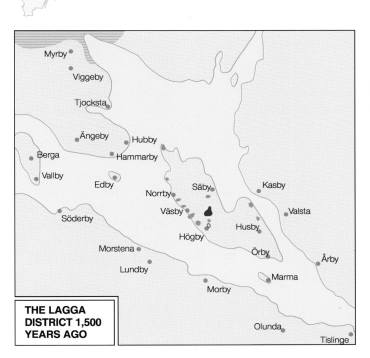

THE LAGGA DISTRICT 1,500 YEARS AGO

Cemetery, Late Iron Age

Cemetery, Early Iron Age

Bronze Age barrow

PLACE NAMES AS HISTORICAL SOURCES

A place name carries historical information about the time when the name was given. A description of a place becomes at some point in time a name. In order to get historical information from names, however, it is necessary to be able to date them reasonably accurately. It is usually impossible to say the year in which a name was created, but in general we can relate place names to long periods

HÅLLNÄS

The parish of Hållnäs in northern Uppland consists of a large headland which, some 1,000 years ago, was a scattered archipelago. The oldest nature names today are the names of villages. Hållen (*Huld*) was an island, like Julö, Lönnö and Sikhjälma (*Sädholm*). Vavd and possibly Slada were the names of bays. The names also tell us that there were lakes which have now disappeared: *Fomaren, *Bjärke* (in the name Barknåre), *Erir* (in Edsätra) and *Linge* (in Lingnåre). The main elements in Barknåre, Lingnåre and Göksnåre is *nor*, 'a stream connecting lakes or bays'.

LAGGA

1,500 years ago the district of Lagga south-east of Uppsala was a system of shallow bays. Lagga, from *lagg*, 'edge', was the name of an island. On the island there was, during the early Iron Age, a settlement with a cemetery. The settlement then gradually moved downhill as the shoreline receded. All the new farms were given names ending in *-by*, a popular type in the late Iron Age. Väsby lay to the west and Norrby to the north, Säby contains the word *sä*, 'lake', and Örby *ör*, 'sandbank'. Högby lies near an old Bronze Age barrow, and Husby was later the name of a royal demesne. Names on the original mainland may also be of the same type: Viggeby, 'the hamlet by the bay', and Hammarby, 'the hamlet on the rocky hill'.

of time such as prehistoric times, the Middle Ages or modern times. This is particularly true of names with the same final element, for example *-sta(d), -säter, -böle*, and *-torp*.

The methods for dating place names may be divided into linguistic and non-linguistic methods, and absolute and relative methods. Using our knowledge of how the language has developed, we can sometimes say that a name ought to be older than a certain date; but the non-linguistic dating methods are more important. Elevation of the land, ancient monuments, the location of a settlement and its size and so on can give us information about the age of the settlement and its name. Archeological finds and pollen analysis can give us even more definite evidence. The ex-

istence or absence of certain types of names on Iceland and the Faroes and in the Danelaw in England tell us whether they were in use during the early Viking Age (800–900 A.D.), when these areas were colonised.

Some types of names were used as early as the early Iron Age, while others were formed principally in the Viking Age/Middle Ages; yet others appeared exclusively in the Middle Ages. New settlement names are created particularly at times when the population and number of settlements increase. In many cases old field names or nature names were adopted, in other cases new names were created, often with main elements in common use at that time. Thus about 2,000 years ago many old names of fields ending in *-vin* were taken as the names of farms. In the same period the element *-hem* was used to name a settlement. During the expansive period of the Viking Age *-by*, which is also found in the Danelaw, and *-sta(d)*, which occurs on Iceland, were used, while *-torp* and *-ryd* were common particularly during the expansive medieval period. This "fashionable" occurrence of certain place-name elements during certain periods is fundamental for dating place names.

The Structure of Names and the Landscape

Place names are linguistic relics. A piece of cultivated land may be called *storåkern, rågåkern, torråkern, Svens åker* and so on. At some point in time one of these names sticks, so everyone who knows the place calls it by that name, for example Storåkern (Great Field). Storåkern is no longer just a word, it is a name. The original meaning of the name is not of interest any more. Storåkern may be covered with tarmac and used as a carpark, but the name can still be used.

Thus a name may be conserved and live a fairly long life. Yet there is a continual exchange of names; names are born and die. The decisive factor for how long a name survives is how many people use it. The name of a meadow which few people use has less chance of surviving than the name of a village, which is well known and is used by many people. The reason why so many old nature names are preserved today is that at some time they became the names of settlements, thereby being conserved.

SELAÖN

Selaön in northern Södermanland is unusually rich in old place names which are connected with prehistoric religion and cult. Names of gods appear, like *Frö* in Fröslunda, *Oden* in Odensicke (*-eke*), *Ull* in Ullunda and the names of goddesses like *Fröja* in Fröberga and *Njärd* in Nällsta— probably **Niaerdharstaver*. *Lytir*, 'pagan priest' is found in Lytislunda. Several names may refer to administration: Tuna and Husby, and Karleby close by—probably *karlar* 'lifeguard, military unit'.

Taking elevation of the land into consideration, it is possible that these names were formed around the birth of Christ, but not all of them are related to the shoreline. This may also be the case with the two original island names Runsö and Algö to the north. The two villages called Viggeby (*Vikby*) are also interesting. To find a bay that reaches up as far as the western Viggeby one has to go back almost 2,000 years.

SKYTT'S HUNDRED

The village names on Söderslätt in Skytt's Hundred, Skåne, around the year 1570, are typical of a plain in Skåne. The parishes are small, often with only one or two villages in each parish. There is an old group of place names on Söderslätt which contain final elements like *-inge*, *-löv*, *-stad*, *-lösa*, and *-ie* (barrow). The names in *-ie* refer to Bronze Age barrows. Names like Räng and Gylle are also certainly old. Round these names are grouped later, medieval place names in *-torp*, *-arp* and *-rup*, as well as *-köpinge* (market place).

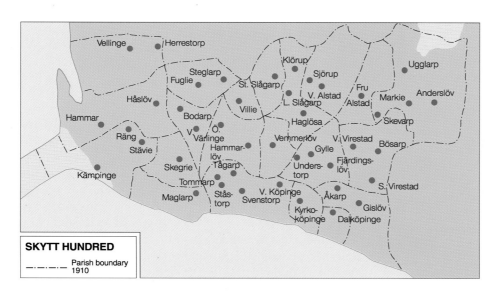

SKYTT HUNDRED
—·—·— Parish boundary 1910

Another decisive factor for the survival of names is that they are recorded on some occasion and thereafter more regularly in writing. When the written forms became more common, for example on maps, they set the standard for everyday use.

SPECIAL STRUCTURES

The place names of central places, for example demesnes with a royal sheriff within an administrative district, have a special structure. The best-known of these is probably *Husby* (<*Husaby*). It occurs particularly in the central parts of Svealand. Their equivalents in Norrland are often called *Kungsgården*. Also the names *Bo* and *Bosgård(en)* are a reminder that society used to be socially and economically stratified and under government control. Many researchers maintain that names ending in *-tuna* should also be interpreted as old central places or administrative estates for a central power.

A name structure is also evident in the sphere of religion. Cult place names are found throughout prehistoric districts, but in certain areas there are concentrations of such names. One of these districts is Lake Storsjön in Jämtland, in which the two largest islands, Frösön and Norderön, contain the names of the god *Frö* and the goddess **Njärd*. Adjacent to the churches and near several churches in the neighbourhood one finds the name *Hov*, which in all probability was the name of a pre-Christian cult place. Another district characterised by cult names is the headland that runs out into Lake Vättern west of Vadstena in Östergötland. Here we find Järnevi and Järnberga, probably containing the name of the goddess **Härn*, and Ullevi and Ullnäs, evidently containing the name of the god *Ull*. The element *-vi* in Järnevi and Ullevi may be translated as "pagan cult place". Cult activities must have been particularly connected with these places.

REGIONAL VARIATIONS

Some types of names become characteristic and typical of particular regions during certain times. The reason for this is that certain words and elements were popular within a culturally homogenous region, that is, where cultural contacts were lively. In other words it is possible to delimit cultural areas with the help of place names.

Thus certain areas and parts of Sweden have a particular set of names. The appearance of the names immediately signals that one is in, for example, Skåne, Västergötland, Gotland or Västerbotten. In the same way as Sweden's topography, fauna and flora and its ancient monuments vary in appearance, so do place names change their appearance. Certain place names are typical of certain parts of the country, for example *-rup* (*-torp*) and *-tofta* in Skåne; *-ryd*, *-skruv* and *-måla* in Småland; *-arve*, *-brya* and *-vät* on Gotland; *-ene* (*-vin*), *-um* (*-hem*) in Västergötland; *-tuna*, *Husby* and plural names like *Berga* in Mälardalen; *-benning* and *-hyttan* in Bergslagen; *-mur* in Gästrikland; *-um* (*-hem* and dative plural ending) in Ångermanland; *-mark* in Västerbotten.

Names of Fields

Cultural landscape research studies how man has utilised natural resources and shaped the landscape. Place names can also provide information in names of villages and farms, and nature names, but above all in field names.

Since the names of fields usually have the smallest number of users, they tend very often to be lost and changed. However, many field names are several hundred years old, and if they have become the names of a set-

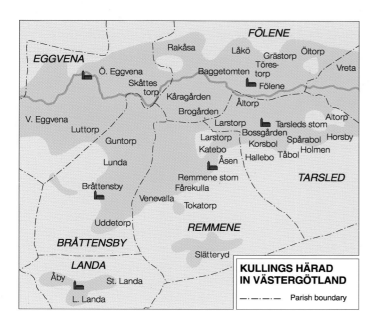

Map labels (Kullings Härad): FÖLENE, EGGVENA, Rakåsa, Låkö, Grästorp, Öltorp, Ö. Eggvena, Töres-torp, Vreta, Skåttes-torp, Baggetomten, Fölene, V. Eggvena, Kåragården, Åltorp, Luttorp, Brogården, Altorp, Guntorp, Larstorp, Tarsleds stom, Bossgården, Horsby, Larstorp, Spårabol, Lunda, Katebo, Korsbol, Holmen, Åsen, Hallebo, Tåbol, Bråttensby, Remmene stom, TARSLED, Fårekulla, Venevalla, Tokatorp, Uddetorp, REMMENE, BRÅTTENSBY, LANDA, Slätteryd, Åby, St. Landa, L. Landa

KULLING'S HUNDRED

Central Västergötland is characterised by small parishes. Sometimes a parish consists of just one village, which will have an ancient name. A farm in the church village can be called *stom*, 'vicarage', as in Tarsled's stom. In some cases the old village name is not used for the vicarage, being replaced by Stommen. Kulling's Hundred includes the parishes of Bråttensby, Eggvena, (*-vin*), Fölene (*-vin*), Remmene (*-vin*), Tarsled (*-löv*) and Landa. All of these are old village names. Round these old villages there are usually later and smaller settlements with medieval names ending in *-torp*, *-boda*, *-bol*, *-hult*, *-ryd* and *-gården*.

ARDRE

The hallmarks of Gotland names are ancient and obscure parish names and farm names in the genitive form. The name Ardre may contain the word *årder*. A characteristic farm-name element is *-arve*, 'heir', in which the first element is a personal name; *-städe* and *-gårde* are also frequent. Farm names in the genitive normally consist of a personal name, such as Botvalde and Mullvads, but also of an occupational name, such as Smiss, 'smith's'. Two typical Gotland names are Kaupungs, 'market place' and Stenstugu.

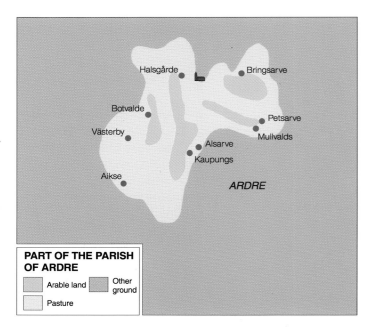

Map labels (Ardre): Halsgårde, Bringsarve, Botvalde, Petsarve, Västerby, Mullvalds, Alsarve, Kaupungs, Aikse, **ARDRE**

tlement, they may be more than a thousand years old. A wide definition of a field name is: the name of any kind of land used for agriculture. This includes names of permanent or sometimes cultivated land, meadows, enclosed grazing lands, natural hayfields on mires and marshes and so on. Other such types of land are burnt-beaten land, hunting grounds, fishing places, places for extracting raw materials and so on.

All these types of land had different names in different regions. Large cultivated fields might be called: *åker*, *land*, *teg*, *täkt* and *vång*, while small fields and patches of land cleared in forests were called: *horv(a)*, *värva*, *hump*, *spjäll*, *stycke* and *vret*. Meadows and hayfields may be divided into two types of land, those that lay mainly close to a village on well-drained land and those that were marshy and often lay among the outfields. The former were usually called *äng*, *änge*, or *vall(a)*. Marshy hayfields in Norrland often had names containing *-myr(a)* or *-flo*, while those in the south might contain the element *-mad*. Hay land were created in the forests by felling trees and burning the undergrowth. Burn-beaten areas were called *bråne*, *bråte*, *fall*, *göle*, *kas(e)*, *ranning*, *rossel*, *ruda*, *rödja*, *sved* and *svedja*. Grazing ground was mainly forestland, so the various pastures were given the nature names where they lay, but special pastures were also regionally called *hag(e)* or *bet(e)*. Many fields have names containing *hage*, *gärde*, *lycka* and *lock*, which in principal means that they were enclosed.

Old Types of Names

Names used by many people have had a good chance of surviving to the present day. A handful of place-name elements date fairly definitely from prehistoric times, that is, they are at least 1,000 years old, such as: *-löv*, *-lösa*, *-vin*, *-hem*, *-tuna*, *-inge*, *-sta(d)*, *-land(a)* and some names ending in *-by*, *-åker*, *-säter*, *-rum* and *-tomt/-toft*. In a few cases the elements may be even older, so that many names ending in *-hem*, *-vin*, *-inge* and perhaps *-tuna* and *-sta(d)* may be about 2,000 years old.

Some of the oldest settlement names include those which originally were the names of fields of various kinds. Among them are *-vin*, pasture,

åker, and probably *-land(a)* as well. It is also probable that certain names ending in *-rum*, meaning open place, clearing, may be very old names of hayfields and pastures. The element *-lösa* has a similar meaning. The element *-löv* or earlier *-lev*, evidently referred to land that had been inherited. It is related to the modern Swedish verb *lämna* (leave). The element *-hem* probably also referred to a habitation. It is the same word as modern Swedish *hem* (home), but place names show that it could refer to large districts as well as individual farms. Place names containing the element *-inge* contain old folk names, like *hämringar* 'those who live at the hammer'. It was more likely to be a tribe rather than a family that was referred to.

The three elements *-tuna*, *-sta(d)* and *-by* have all been discussed at

Both western Swedish and central Norrland place names in *-vin* represent a westerly cultural region and are related to Norwegian names in *-vin*. (L100)

THE PLACE-NAME ELEMENT *VIN*

1:10 000 000

● 10 place-names

● 5 place-names

· 1 place-name

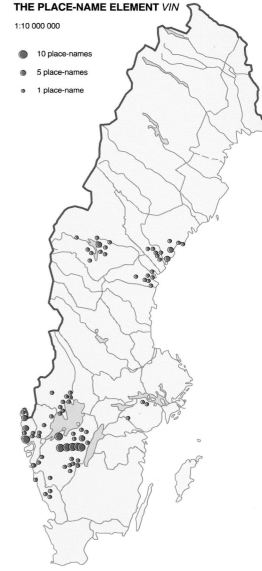

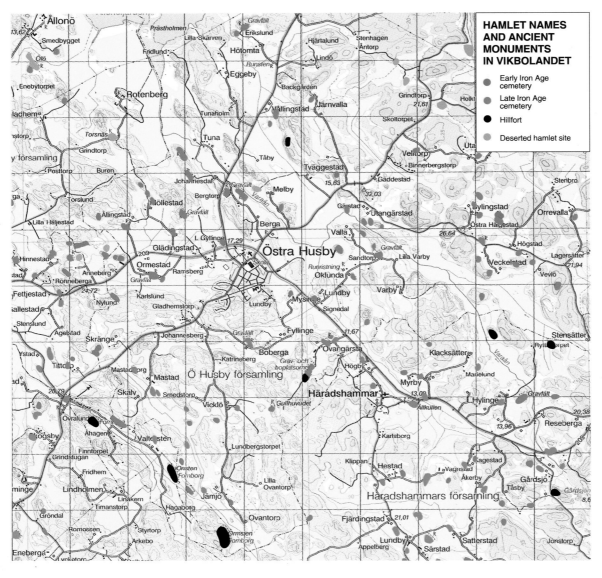

length. The word *tun* means 'fence, enclosure', but in place names it is considered to have a special meaning, that of a central function in a district. The element *-sta(d)* contains a word that may be translated as 'place, habitation', but its meaning in place names has been the subject of lively discussions. The same is true of *-by* (group of farms), which may be translated as 'farm or hamlet'. The element *-tomt*, which in the south of Sweden is *-toft*, seems in many cases to have referred to deserted farm sites. Thus it would not indicate a period of expansion, as do the other examples above, but of desertion.

PLACE NAMES AND OLD CULTURAL DISTRICTS

When various name elements and dialect words are entered on a map, it is apparent that several of them show the same distribution. If it is also possible to date them, the existence of certain cultural provinces at various times can be proved. Such investigations show that Sweden has by no means been a homogenous and uniform cultural area. Instead, other patterns emerge, in which different regions show cultural affinity at various periods.

With the help of place names— here the final elements *-löv/-lev*, *-tuna* and *-vin* are used as examples—one discovers at least three overall cultural provinces in Scandinavia during prehistoric times. One is the southern Scandinavian (*-lev/-löv*), covering Denmark, Skåne, Halland, Västergötland and sometimes even Bohuslän and southern Norway, that is, the area round the Kattegatt. Another eastern Scandinavian province, (*-tuna*) lies along the Baltic, with Mälardalen as its central district and including Östergötland, eastern Småland, Öland, Gotland and the coast of Norrland. The third is a Norrland/ Norwegian province (*-vin*), comprising Norway, central Norrland and sometimes even Bohuslän, Dalsland, Västergötland and southern Norrland. Archeological finds can also be interpreted along these lines. Characteristic names within each area are supplemented to varying extents by other types of names.

Agvallen
Järvsö

Östra Husby

Hörninge

VIKBOLANDET

The Vikbolandet peninsula has many cemeteries from the Early Iron Age on higher parts of the land. Most were abandoned in the Late Iron Age when the hillsides around the clayey plains were colonised. Place names are of a uniform Iron Age type. Names ending in *-stad* predominate, but names ending in *-inge*, *-by* and of the *Berga* type also occur. The large cemeteries at the mouth of the Varaån belong to Tuna, Berga and Gyllinge, and there was a rune-stone bridge at Lönnbro. Hill forts may have names ending in *-sten*. A few farms ending in *-torp* have small, late cemeteries. Names ending in *-säter* have in one case a cemetery, while the majority lie outside the Iron Age district, representing medieval colonisation.

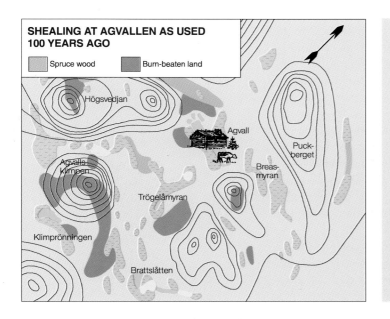

SHEALING AT AGVALLEN AS USED
100 YEARS AGO

Spruce wood   Burn-beaten land

AGVALLEN'S SHEALING

Agvallen's shealing lies in Färila, Hälsingland. What today is nothing but forest was only a hundred years or so ago cultivated grazing land and hayfields. There was also a grazing meadow. All the mires were used for hay, and wherever possible areas were enclosed and cleared as mire fields, for example *Brattslätten*. The marshy spruce forest, rich in herbs, made excellent pasture. The most notable features, however, were the many burn-beaten areas. Memories of these are found to this very day in the form of names ending in *-svedja, -fall* etc.

VILLAGE OF HÖRNINGE

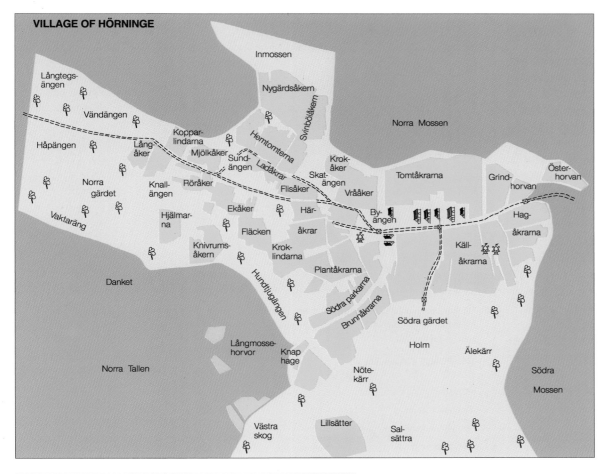

Inmossen

Långtegs-
ängen

Nygårdsåkern

Vändängen

Norra Mossen

Håpängen

Koppar-
lindarna

Hemtomterna

Lång-
åker

Mjölkåker

Sund-
ängen

Ladåkrar

Krok-
åker

Skat-
ängen

Österhorvan

Norra
gärdet

Knall-
ängen

Röråker

Flisåker

Vrååker

Tomtåkrarna

Grind-
horvan

Vaktaräng

Hjälmar-
na

Ekåker

Här-
åkrar

By-
ängen

Hag-
åkrarna

Knivrums-
åkern

Fläcken

Krok-
lindarna

Plantåkrarna

Käll-
åkrarna

Danket

Hundtjugängen

Södra parkarna

Södra gärdet

Brunnåkrarna

Långmosse-
horvor

Knap
hage

Holm

Älekärr

Södra

Norra Tallen

Nöte-
kärr

Mossen

Västra
skog

Lillsätter

Sal-
sättra

THE JÄRVSÖ DISTRICT

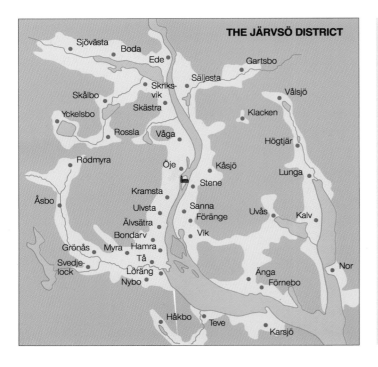

Sjövästa

Boda

Ede

Gartsbo

Skriks-
vik

Säljesta

Skålbo

Skästra

Vålsjö

Yckelsbo

Rossla

Våga

Klacken

Rödmyra

Öje

Kåsjö

Högtjär

Kramsta

Stene

Lunga

Åsbo

Ulvsta

Sanna

Uvås

Kalv

Älvsätra

Föränge

Bondarv

Vik

Grönås

Myra

Hamra

Svedje
lock

Tå

Löräng

Änga

Nor

Nybo

Förnebo

Håkbo

Teve

Karsjö

HÖRNINGE VILLAGE

The map shows names of infields at Hörninge Village on Öland in 1647. Apart from -*åker* (field) the elements -*linda* (fallow field) and Hjälmarna and Fläcken also occur. Two small plots in the outfields have names ending in -*horva* and outfield meadows in -*säter*/-*sätter*. It is of particular interest that an old village site can be reconstructed for Hörninge Village with the help of the names Hemtomterna and Ladåkrar.

The distribution of names ending in -*löv* is to the south and west. They indicate an old cultural area round the Kattegatt, where Denmark/Skåne played a leading role. Names ending in -*tuna*, on the other hand, indicate an eastern Scandinavian cultural area, the centre of which was eastern central Sweden. The element -*tuna* is presumed to have related to administrative centres within a district. In Uppland, and to some extent in Södermanland, -*tuna* places seem to have been connected with old Hundred divisions. They are also often parish names. In other parts of Sweden -*tuna* places had strategic importance. (L101)

THE PLACE-NAME ELEMENTS
LÖV **AND** *TUNA*

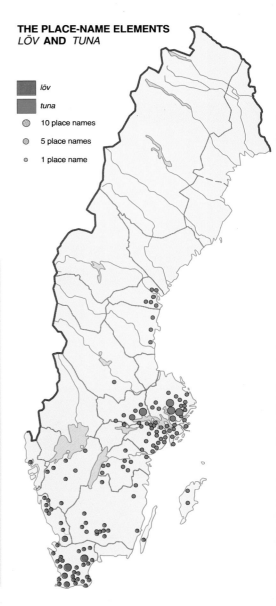

löv

tuna

⬤ 10 place names

◔ 5 place names

∘ 1 place name

JÄRVSÖ

In southern Norrland central place names often end in -*sta*(*d*) and -*säter*. In Järvsö we find Säljesta, Kramsta, Ulvsta, Skästra (Skärsätra) and Älvsätra. Simple nature and field names are Haga, Gärde, Öje, Sanna and others. Names ending in -*boda* like Gartsbo, Förnebo, Håkbo, Åsbo and Boda are characteristic of inland districts. These names were used for a kind of secondary farm called "bodland". These -*boda* villages lie round the older centres of cultivation. There are also villages with names ending in -*myr* (mire), -*äng* (meadow), -*sved*(*ja*) (burn-beaten area), and so on. Most of them are probably medieval names.

Medieval Types of Names

Settlement expanded greatly in the early Middle Ages (11th, 12th and 13th centuries), but stagnated, in certain areas to a high degree, during the 14th century, when the Black Death struck Sweden; finally, there was a certain recovery in the late Middle Ages. These developments are reflected in new place names.

Many new settlement names were created during the early Middle Ages, for which the words and elements that were modern at that time were used; for the southern parts of Sweden these were mainly -torp and -ryd, in the north -boda, -böle and -mark. We also got new categories of names which were not the result of expanding agriculture. We got small administrative units which closely affected ordinary people; church parishes. Other industries than agriculture created settlements, above all mining and iron manufacturing. Two medie-

Häradshammar in Vikbolandet has a typical topography for -stad names in eastern central Sweden. Round the bowl-shaped plain in the background lie Hestad, Fjärdingstad, Särstad, Satterstad, Vagnstad and Kagestad.

THE PLACE-NAME ELEMENT
STA(D)

1:5 000 000

- ● 20 place names
- ● 10 place names
- • 5 place names
- · 1 place name

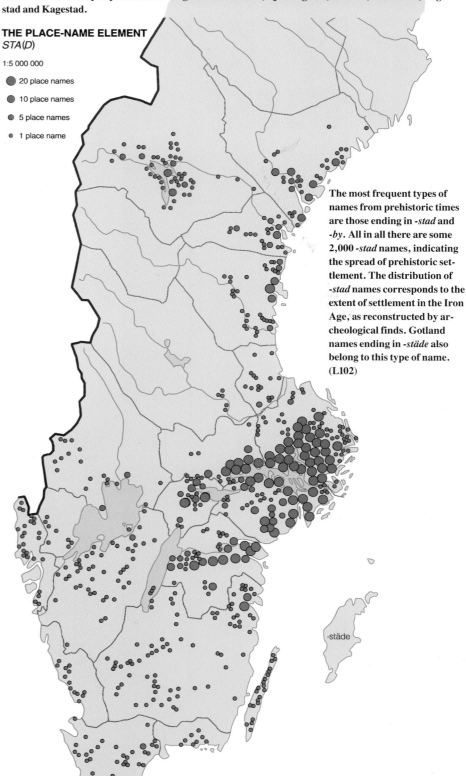

The most frequent types of names from prehistoric times are those ending in -stad and -by. All in all there are some 2,000 -stad names, indicating the spread of prehistoric settlement. The distribution of -stad names corresponds to the extent of settlement in the Iron Age, as reconstructed by archeological finds. Gotland names ending in -städe also belong to this type of name. (L102)

-städe

FRÖSÖN

In the central districts of central Norrland there are old names ending in -hem and -vin which are not found in southern Norrland. On Frösön and the surrounding district we find Mjälle (*Mjeldhem*), Tanne (*Tandhem*), Vagle (*Vaglhem*), Undrom (*Underhem*), Sem (*Sähem*), and Grötom (*Grythem*); and Rödön (*Rodvin*), Ösa (*Os-* or *Åsvin*), Härke (*Harkvin*) and Knytta (*Knyttvin*). Characteristics of the Jämtland names are Önet and names ending in -lägden, which indicate abandoned settlements. *Hov* is probably the name of a pagan cult centre. Typical Jämtland name structures are a church village called Hov, a few centrally situated villages with names in -hem and -vin, a number of villages ending in -sta(d) and -säter and further away Önet and names ending in -lägden, as well as numerous medieval nature names.

FRÖSÖN

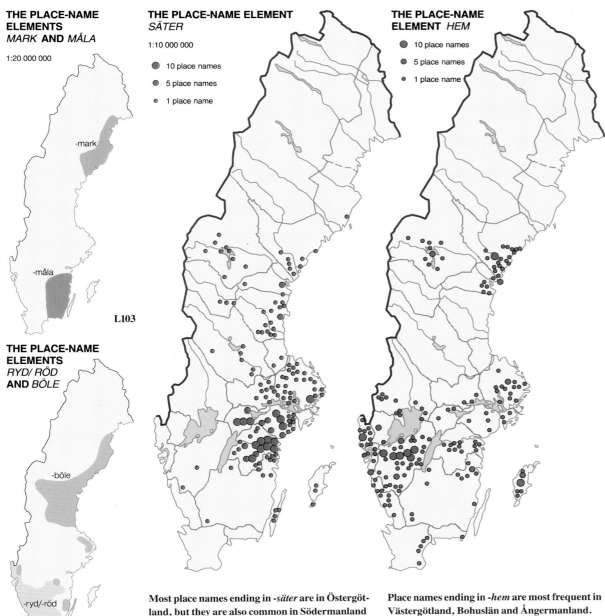

THE PLACE-NAME ELEMENTS
MARK **AND** *MÅLA*

1:20 000 000

-mark

-måla

L103

THE PLACE-NAME ELEMENTS
RYD/ RÖD **AND** *BÖLE*

-böle

-ryd/-röd

L104

THE PLACE-NAME ELEMENT
SÄTER

1:10 000 000

- 10 place names
- 5 place names
- 1 place name

Most place names ending in *-säter* are in Östergötland, but they are also common in Södermanland and Närke. These names indicate the extent of an eastern Swedish cultural area during the Viking Age and the earliest Middle Ages. (L105)

THE PLACE-NAME ELEMENT *HEM*

- 10 place names
- 5 place names
- 1 place name

Place names ending in *-hem* are most frequent in Västergötland, Bohuslän and Ångermanland. Nowadays they often have the form "Lerum" and are difficult to distinguish from simple names in the dative plural like "Högom". Many *-hem* names on Gotland have unique and obscure first elements. (L106)

Arnemark

Lill-Pite

Böle

Sjulnäs

Öjebyn

Långnäs

Pite

Gammel-staden

Roknäs

Svensbyn

Piteå

Bergsviken

Pitholm

Nybyn

Hortlax

Blåsmark

Hemmingsmark

Högsböle

Jävre

PITEÅ AND SURROUNDINGS

PITEÅ

Sweden's northernmost districts are characterised by ancient names for rivers and bays. The Piteå district has the old name for the river Piteälven, *Pita*, (probably Saami), river or bay names like Jävre, and the many nature names which were transferred to places such as Bergsviken, Roknäs and Långnäs. The three place-name elements *-böle*, *-mark* and *-byn*, often have a personal name in the genitive as the first element, for example Hemmingsmark and Svensbyn. Finnish (or Saami) features are seen in Hortlax (Finnish hurrta, 'wolf' or 'dog' and *-lahti*, 'bay').

val name categories with a new background are the names of trading places and markets, above all *-köping*, and the names of castles and fortresses, where apart from *-borg* and *-gård* the elements *-hus* and *-holm* became common, as in Dalaborg, Stegeborg, Bohus, Gripsholm and Rydboholm.

The type of place name that best demonstrates the extensive new colonisation of the early Middle Ages in the south of Sweden is *-torp*. This type of name comprises for the main part a late Viking Age and medieval group of names. It is presumed to have come from the south along with new cultural, social and agricultural impulses from the continent. The countries round the south Baltic Sea were transformed into a feudal society at this time, built up round main farms and vassal farms. Feudal elements in society and agriculture and a noble class gradually developed in Sweden, too. One way of understanding Scandinavian village names in *-torp* is to relate them to north German names in *-dorf*. The element *-torp* may have come to Scandinavia with the sense of "vassal farm", from which meanings such as "new habitation" (in general) arose. It is striking how the distribution of *-torp* names in general coincides with the distribution of the nobility in Sweden.

Other, predominantly medieval types of names are those mainly from Götaland: *-ryd, -red, -röd* and *-rud*, which are all closely related to the Swedish verb *rödja*, meaning to clear and referring to cleared forest areas. In Småland, however, quite a few places with *-ryd* names have late Iron Age cemeteries and are thus older. The element *-måla*, which has a very limited distribution in south-east Sweden, is connected with *mål* (measure) and by all accounts meant "marked-off, measured plot of land". The element *-hult* in Götaland meant "wood, grove", probably for cattle grazing or foliage fodder. Place names of this kind prove to have been used originally for sites that were of economic importance for agriculture. The more widely-used *-bol* and *-böle* are usually translated as "farm, new habitation", where *-böle* was particularly characteristic in parts of Norrland. This is also the case with *-mark*, which occurs in Värmland and at isolated places in the rest of central Sweden in an older meaning of "boundary (forest)". Several of these names are for

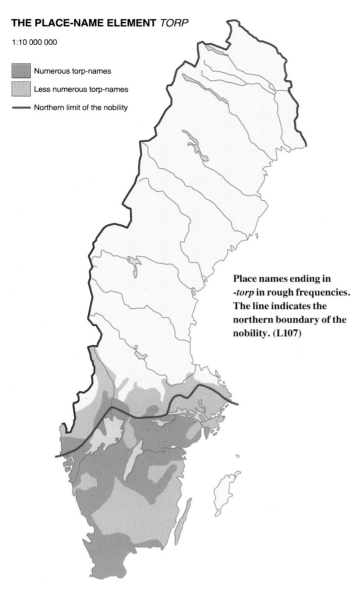

Numerous torp-names

Less numerous torp-names

Northern limit of the nobility

**Place names ending in
-*torp* in rough frequencies.
The line indicates the
northern boundary of the
nobility. (L107)**

**Place names ending in -*hyttan* and -*benning* (building) occur within a limited
area in central Sweden where there was workable iron ore. The map shows
names which were originally connected with iron but later became names
of settlements. (L108)**

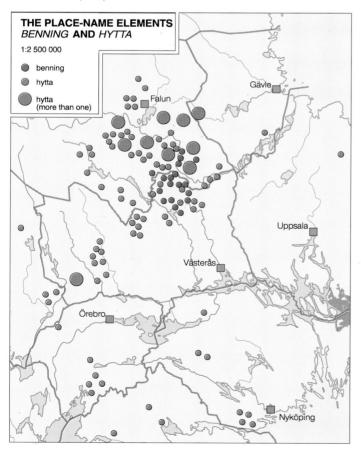

THE PLACE-NAME ELEMENTS
BENNING **AND** *HYTTA*

1:2 500 000

● benning

● hytta

● hytta
(more than one)

Gävle

Falun

Uppsala

Västerås

Örebro

Nyköping

areas like Mark's Hundred in Väster-götland and a few parish names in Värmland. The northern Swedish names with -*mark* (forest, new culti-vation in the forest) were given to new medieval settlements. A typical medieval name type in central Swe-den and southern Norrland contains -*boda*, the plural of *bod*. If one ig-nores the late names of shealings con-taining -*bodarna*, these names refer to sheds of various kinds which were used for storing fodder in the out-fields, to pastures in the outfields or to fishing huts. In Hälsingland -*boda* later came to mean a farm where peo-ple lived during the summer.

What is characteristic of medieval settlement names is also the large number of person's names in the first element, many of which names ar-rived with Christianity. The fact that the individual owner/farmer lent his name so often to a habitation may have to do with new forms of owner-ship and cultivation. It is also striking that many names contain words that are related to the Swedish verbs *sved-ja* (burn-beat), *rödja* (clear), *fälla* (fell), *hugga* (chop), all of which refer to colonisation.

During the 12th and 13th centuries Christianity gained such a strong posi-tion that the church began to divide the country into parishes. There were a large number of privately-owned churches in southern Sweden, where-as further north various village coun-cils seem to have gathered round church buildings. The names of par-ishes are of great interest. A large majority of those in the south are old village and farm names—the name of the village or farm where the church was built gave its name to the parish. Farther north old district names are more common as parish names. Here one also finds church place names, which in many cases may have earlier had some sort of central function as meeting places for a district. In isolat-ed cases completely new names were created when a parish was formed.

In the old mining area of central Sweden the element -*hyttan* (smelting house) occurs in many names of such settlements which later developed in-to villages. They originally referred to furnaces for processing the iron ore. These names seem to date back to the late Middle Ages (after 1300). In a small area in northern Västman-land, the old Norberg mining district, names ending in -*benning* (proto-Swedish *bygning*, building) occur,

which probably go back to a smelting house. The first elements in these names are often personal names. The number of German names is worth noting, such as Änglika in Änglikben-ning (now Ängelsberg), Gerike in Jörkhyttan and Könike in Königs-hyttan.

Names of Districts

The name *Sverige* (Sweden) earlier *Svearike*, may be translated as "the kingdom of the Sveas". The tribal name Svear has not yet been given a definite interpretation. The heart-land of the Sveas was Mälardalen. During the Middle Ages in the Ice-landic sagas the Uppland part of Swe-den was called *Svíþjóð*, that is, the Svea people. The term *Svíaveldi* is al-so used but with an extended mean-ing, including Västergötland and Värmland. The Geatish people had their heartland in Östergötland and Västergötland: the name *Götar* is also shrouded in mystery. The reason for the name Sverige was probably that the old heartlands of the Sveas were the centre of power when a united kingdom grew up. Norrland is a com-paratively new collective term for the provinces in the north of the country.

Names of districts and administra-tive units are widely distributed. This group includes counties, provinces, parishes and hundreds. The division of the provinces of Götaland and Svealand into hundreds is an ancient one. The term hundred originated in the troop that was connected with the old sea military organisation. The hundreds of Götaland may have got their names from the hundred's court places or be the name of an ancient district, for example "small lands" as-sociated with the province name Små-land.

Several province names originally referred to a smaller area, like Dal, Halland, Värmland or Härjedalen but later covered a larger area. The names of smaller areas or "lands" which did not become provinces are very difficult to interpret, which is an indication of great age. Many nature names, of lakes, streams, rivers and islands, for example, belong to this ancient group, too.

A large number of old names of is-lands are found today as names of set-tlements. As a result of the elevation of the land, channels have disap-peared and the names have been

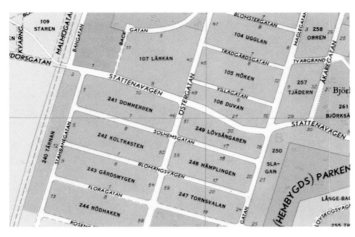

An extract from a town-planning map of Hässleholm provides an example of the way in which street and quarter names were allocated in categories.

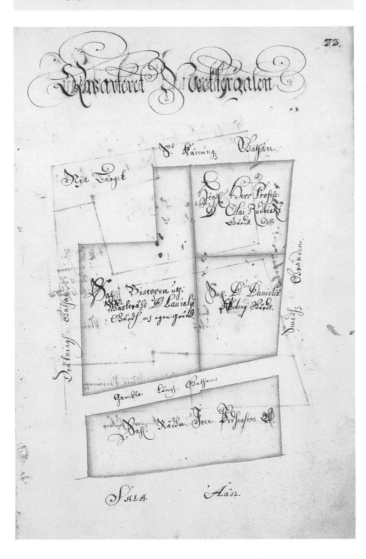

transferred to the settlements on the former islands. In Norrland many names of lakes have become names of settlements as a result of later colonisation.

Names in Towns

STREET NAMES

Medieval towns often had no street names. A street might be called the one "when you go from the square to the monastery" (Uppsala, 1396), and the position of a farm might be given as "north of the stream west of Birger Larsson's cabbage patch south of Lars Olofsson's barn and down to the road" (Arboga, 1458). There were, however, street names at an early date. These might, for example, describe the street (Långa strätet, Söderköping), or its position (Östergatan, in Örebro and other towns), tell what tradesmen lived along the street (Skomakaregatan, in Stockholm, for example), give the name of a well-known building in the street (Klostergatan, a common name) or the name of someone who lived there (Staffan Västgötes gränd in Stockholm).

A large number of these spontaneously-created street names went out of use after the Middle Ages, partly because of the great changes in town plans which many towns introduced. Ever since then streets have been named officially, but the medieval type still lives on. The growing power of the king in the 17th century was manifested in names like Drottninggatan (Queen's Street) and Kungsgatan (King's Street); Drottningatan in Stockholm (1639) was named after the young Queen Kristina, while the contemporary Regeringsgatan referred to her guardians. A new type of name, memorial names, celebrated the memory of generally or only locally-known persons (for example, Tegnérgatan and Linnégatan, which were common, Karin Boyegatan in Uppsala, Sköna Gertruds väg in Katrineholm) or important events (Fredsgatan in Stockholm in memory of the Peace of Westphalia in 1648). A characteristic feature of modern street names is the way they are arranged in groups, so that in a particular area they belong to the same category, for example names of famous scientists, mill terms, names of birds or types of weather.

NAMES OF QUARTERS

In the Middle Ages towns were normally divided into four parts, in the beginning called *fourths* and later *quarters*. After many towns had followed foreign models in the mid–17th century and had regular street networks with a rectilinear grid plan, the word quarter was used for the square blocks of buildings in the street network. Names of such quarters are known from the central parts of Stockholm as early as the 1640s. In Uppsala, which seems to have been the first town after Stockholm to introduce quarter names, such names are known from 1671 onwards. This naming of quarters is a Swedish phenomenon. The names, which were given officially, were first used in fire protection and proved to be useful for the registration of people and property.

Several principles were used in the naming of quarters. Many of the oldest names have a local association. Kronkvarnen (Crown Mill) in Stockholm was called after a windmill and a pistol maker lived in the quarter called Pistolen in Uppsala (1671). The Stockholm quarters called Havsfrun (Mermaid), Sjöhästen (Seahorse) and Sjömannen (Seaman) (1648–49), whose names are connected with marine life, are in the old Admiralty parish in Östermalm. Group naming is also evident here, often without any local associations, which has become such a prominent feature of modern street and quarter names. A special group contain personal names, Erik, Nils and so on. Because of their purely official character, quarter names are not usually very well known and are therefore seldom used in everyday conversation.

OTHER NAMES

Not only streets and quarters are given names, but also bridges, squares, parks, districts and so on. Apart from all the official names, there is a rich flora of unofficial, popular names. These are often given to individual buildings and may refer to an owner or be descriptive, like Kullberg House and the Smoothing Iron in Katrineholm. They are quite often joke names or pejorative, for example Sillhovet (Herring Court) near Hovgatan in Köping, an impressive edifice built by a person who sold herring.

Saami and Finnish Place Names

Original Saami place names are found above all in inner Norrland, and Finnish place names are found in Norrbotten County and, especially earlier, in the 17th-century Finnish districts as well.

PLACE NAMES AND POPULATION

If one travels through inner Norrland from south to north, one notices that the place names gradually change in character. The Saami names increase in number. In the far north there are also Finnish place names, while the Swedish ones are almost entirely absent. But even many relatively southerly place names have Saami equivalents. Examples of these are Tännäs (*Neassah*), Funäsdalen (*Biengendaelie*), Strömsund (*Straejmie*), Åsele (*Sjeltie*) and Vilhelmina (*Vualtjere*). Further north there are, for example, Lycksele (*Likssjuo*), Malå (*Málage*), Storuman (*Lusppie*) and Arvidsjaur (*Árviehávrrie*). Famous tourist resorts closer to the mountains are Gäddede (*Tjeedtege*), Fatmomakke (*Faepmie*), Tärnaby (*Dearnna*) and Arjeplog (*Árjepluovve*).

Towns in old Saami districts often have double names. Jokkmokk (*Jåhkåmåhkke*) is usually called *Dálvvadis* by Saami because of the old winter settlement at this place. Kvikkjokk comes from the Saami *Guojkkajåhka*, river rapids. In Saami the place is now usually called *Huhttán*, the smelting house, because of the 17th-century mining operations there.

LIGUISTIC INFLUENCE ON NAMES

The pronunciation and meaning of Saami and Finnish names have often been obscured by Swedish influence. In the far north Saami names have been made Finnish or Swedish. *Giron* (Kiruna), *Čohkkeras* (Jukkasjärvi) and *Vazáš* (Vittangi) are examples of names which in a now trilingual area have a pronunciation that deviates from Saami. The Swedish population, which last colonised the area, gave the Finnish name a pronunciation and spelling that were adapted to Swedish. Saami *Gárasavvon* corresponds to *Kaaresuvanto* in Finnish, which became Karesuando in Swedish. The Finnish dialect *-suanto*—in standard Finnish *-suvanto* (calm water between rapids)—has been preserved in the Swedish form of the name.

In Tornedalen Finnish names were

SAAMI AND FINNISH LANGUAGE AREAS

1:5 000 000

- Northern Saami area
- Lule-Saami area
- Ume-Saami area
- Southern Saami area
- Area with a few Saami elements
- Finnish colonization from the 16th and the 17th century
- Southern limit of the Finnish language

Gárasavvon
Giron • Cohkkeras
Vazás
Váhtjer/Jiellevárre
Huhttán/Guojkkajåhkå
Dálvvadis/Jåhkåmåhkke
Hietaniemi
Vitsaniemi
Árjjepluovve
Salvis
Deärnná
Árvviehávrre
Luleju
Suorssá
Málåge
Faepmie
Lusppie
Vualtjere
Likkssjuo
Tjeedtege
Sjeltie
Straejmie
Ubmeje
Biengenvoemie
Neassah

Although the Saami people are only about 18,000 in number, they have four dialects. Finnish used to be spoken in a far larger area than today—mainly as a result of colonisation from Savolaks in the 16th and 17th centuries. (L109)

SAAMI TERMS

The hiker may find on his maps the following Lule-Saami terms: *áhpe*, (large) mire, *badje-*, upper, *bákte*, cliff, *duottar*, mountain, *gájsse*, mountain peak, *giedde*, dwelling, *gielas*, heath, *gábbå*, knoll, *gárttje*, waterfall, *jávrásj*, small lake, tarn, *jávrre*, lake, *jiegge*, mire, *jåkha*, beck, river, *luokta*, bay, *oajvve*, rounded mountain, *skájdde*, headland in a river, *suoloj*, island, *tjåhkkå*, mountain top, *várre*, mountain, *vuolle* or *vuolep*, lower.

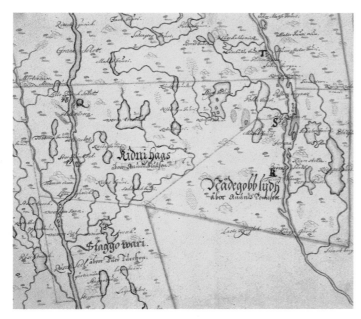

Extract from a map of Lappland dated 1671 by Gedda, a surveyor. It includes the river Vindelälven between Ruskssele and Vindelgransele to the left and Malån from the Lappland boundary to Koppsele to the right. Lycksele, Malå and Norsjö meet at the bend in the boundary line. Scattered Swedish names occur, such as the present-day villages along the Vindelälven, but Ume-Saami names are in the majority. Some of them have been given Swedish forms; Slepa Jauri, for example, has become Släppträsk.

Extract from a map of Tornedalen dated 1736 by Hackzell, a surveyor, which covers the Torne valley up to Pajala. Among the many names are two Swedish ones: Biörckön near Torneå and Helsingebyn opposite Hietaniemi Church. The surveyor, however, was Swedish, which is evident in expressions such as Öfwer Torneå (Upper Torneå) and Korpikylä Forss (Rapids).

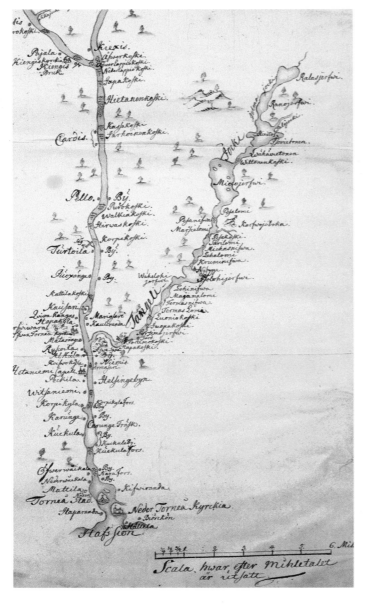

made Swedish in an attempt to interpret or translate them. Such names are Hedenäset (*Hietaniemi*, hieta, sand), Risudden (*Vitsaniemi, vitsa* or *vitta*, withy, rod) and Bäcksta (*Päkkilä*, containing the personal name *Päkki*). The Finnish names in Tornedalen are from the coast inland. Saami names in other river valleys do not appear until the boundary of Saami territory. They then increase in number and are in a clear majority in the mountains. Of 2,500 names on five sheets of the mountain map (Scale 1:100,000) of Lule "lappmark", only about 30 are Swedish.

PLACE-NAME RESEARCH AND HISTORY

Saami and Finnish place names in Sweden are linguistic and cultural material of great value. Saami names prove that Saami were already living along the Arctic Sea coast about the birth of Christ. One example is the name *Máhkarávju* for the Norwegian Mageröya. Its sound shows that it was formed in proto-Nordic times. The Saami names for the rivers *Lule, Pite, Skellefte* and *Ume* älv, which were adopted with Swedish pronunciations, are a sign of the importance of the Saami population even along the coast in olden times.

River names sometimes suggest cultural differences between coast and inland. The lower reaches of the river Kalix älv, for example, have the Finnish name *Kaihnuunväylä*. The upper reaches are called *Gáláseatnu* by Saami and by the Finnish-speaking population *Kaalsasväylä* (*-eatnu* and *-väylä* both mean river). The rivers Pite and Skellefte älv have different Saami name forms depending on which dialect areas they run through. The river Lule älv is connected with the Saami *lulle*, meaning east and was perhaps earlier the name for its course below where the rivers meet at Vuollerim.

The rivers Torne and Muonio älv and their surrounding districts in Sweden have a special status. When Abraham Hülphers was travelling in Lappland in 1758 and was approaching Torneå, he writes: "At Saifvits (Säivis), the first village in Torneå, we came to the first Finnish inns. The people did not understand our language." To this very day the boundary of Finnish along the coast runs between Sangis and Säivis, about 30 km from the Finnish border. Inland the boundary runs all the way up

to the river Stora Lule älv. Finnish place names south of this boundary must be interpreted as an indication of more widespread Finnish settlement in olden times. There are many place names in Kalix that end in Finnish *-järvi*, lake. *Morjärv, Niemisel, Rosvik* and *Hortlax* in Norrbotten county and *Jörn* in Västerbotten are just a few names that are thought to be Finnish outside the present-Finnish-speaking area.

On Olaus Magnus' map Carta Marina (1539) the name Hälsingeby, *Helsigaby* is found north of Torneå. In sources from the same century onwards this village is also called *Kai(h)nuunkylä*. The name's connection with people from Hälsingland and "kväner" (Finnish *kainulaiset*) led to archeological investigations there. These showed that there had been settlements from the 11th century, and that cattle had been reared there at least from the 13th century.

Finnish place names in Tornedalen have also been used in investigations of the origin of the first immigrants. It has been possible to prove that Tornio names (Finnish *tornio*, spear) in Finnish areas probably spread north from Tavastland as early as the 11th century. Place names in Tornedalen, vocabulary and pronunciation also suggest influences from both eastern and western districts in the Finland of that time.

In many forest districts in southern Norrland and the central parts of Sweden there are old place names which date back to the Finnish immigrations of the 16th century and onwards. Many of them are in well-known "Finnish districts", while others are near the province boundaries in previously uninhabited country where the Finns settled down.

PLACE NAMES AND MULTILINGUALISM

Place names show that the three populations were in contact with each other. Traces of a language that was superseded is preserved in place names. Where the village of *Vuono* (north-Saami *vuotna* bay) lies west of Haparanda there was a deep bay about 1,000 years ago. Tornedal names containing the element *Keräs* (Saami *geres*, sledge), *Kaarti-* (Saami *gárdi*, reindeer enclosure) and *Kaiti-* (*skáidi*, spit of land in a river) lie very close to the coast. Early Saami-Finnish bilingualism has helped to preserve the names.

Historic Areas of National Interest

The National Project

The Göta Canal runs like a band of history between the lakes through Östergötland and Västergötland. This is a whole system of locks, bridges, tree-lined avenues and houses for canal workers which reveal its age. The canal was built between 1810 and 1832. It is easy to see that it stands for much more than engineering and communications.

A domestic waterway between the Baltic and the North Sea had been a grand vision for Sweden's political leaders for centuries. This vision was directed at first against Denmark, which was still imposing tolls in the Sound, but it was not realised until after the upheavals of 1809. It saw the end of enlightened despotism; the middle class and later parliamentary democracy were allowed to develop. The canal was built when Sweden's dream of being a major power had finally been abandoned.

Two places express the utopian concept of the canal project extremely well. Motala was to be the heart of the canal functions to which the most modern English engineering skills were to be imported. Karlsborg was to be the ideal military centre, to which the king and the government could retire in times of unrest. By combining old royal centralism with new technological and commercial ambitions, the canal became a symbol of a new national identity, a realisation of the idea of "recapturing Finland within the frontiers of Sweden", as Tegnér expressed it in 1810 in his poem "Svea".

When the railways were built in the second half of the 19th century, the Göta Canal quickly lost its importance. The Motala workshops were still there, however, and this small town in Östergötland remained a technological centre until late in our age of radio communication. The idea of a central defence system never needed to be tested, since Sweden was now entering its almost 200-year-long era of peace. The canal project was deeply rooted in the old system, but without it Sweden's modern history would have been quite different.

A HYPOTHESIS

For how many Swedes does the Göta Canal mean anything today? How many people are glad that it is still there and can still be used? Many Swedes have travelled along it, crossed it and been irritated by the red lights at its bridges, or stopped and found the old technology interesting.

For a remarkably large number of people it actually means much more. Perhaps a million or so of us are the descendants of those who constructed it. Even more probably have their roots in places that depended on the employment it created. Many of us should perhaps thank it for being here today, because without it our great-great grandmother would never have met our great-great grandfather . . .

OUR HERITAGE IN ITS ENVIRONMENT

The Göta Canal is a well-preserved communication system dating from

The 678-metre-long defence wall at Karlsborg's Castle with its cannon emplacements was probably intended both to be and to look like an almost impregnable defence system for the heart of the kingdom.

A 27-metre stairway of eleven locks in three stages leads from Lake Roxen up to the plain at Vreta kloster. The lowest part, which is the highest stairway, is still called Carl Johan's Locks. In and round these locks there is a busy hustle and bustle of both canal boats and privately-owned holiday craft during the summer tourist season.

the early 19th century, which, thanks to its continuing existence, can inform us directly of a great many things that were of importance in this vital phase in our history. In other words, it is a *culture environment*.

This term refers to any traces of human appliances for production, consumption and social life seen as entities and contexts. Any unforeseen effects that mankind's activities have had are also included, as well as the cultural importance that can be ascribed to natural elements and ideological features. Thus it comprises mankind's interplay with nature and the surrounding world. In other words cultural environments are *the historical dimension of today's landscape, defined from mankind's point of view*.

The cultural environment is recognised as a resource of great general importance. It is in some way everyman's heritage—as well as everyman's responsibility. With knowledge and practice we can learn to "read" in the landscape what our forefathers invested there in the form of work, knowledge and experience, decipher the way things have developed and get a perspective of our own role in the whole story. This gives us an identity and a general understanding of our times. Once one has learnt to "read", one has a source of insight and enjoyment.

ONE OF 1,700 AREAS OF NATIONAL INTEREST

The Göta Canal is a reference point in the landscape for a phase in history, or even a national symbol. It is a priceless part of our cultural heritage, so it is natural that it forms one of the 1,700 or so areas that were selected in 1987 as being "Historic Areas of National Interest according to the National Resources Act".

The task for culture environment preservation in this context concerned not only the particularly old and the particularly fine but the whole of Sweden's history, with its enormous economic, cultural and social breadth and countless regional nuances. The same thought lay behind the physical national planning of the early 1970s, but now the overall concept was more detailed and carefully worked out.

CAN 1,700 ENVIRONMENTS REPRESENT HISTORY?

What is history? Is it more than "a series of wretched events, one following the other", as the British historian Arnold Toynbee wondered? But no one event is quite like the other—nor is it independent of the others; nor is any one cultural environment quite like the others. How then is one to make a representative choice? Fernand Braudel distinguishes between three different rhythms in history: the rapid pulse of *events*, the short and long waves of *economic and social cycles*, and finally the long *durations*.

It is difficult to imagine that a cultural environment can be the outcome of one event *alone*. Just like every event, the environment in which it has occurred is also bound up within a cycle or *sign of its time*. Every environment always occupies a position in the *structure* of the long durations, which primarily seem to be determined by nature's distribution of different types of soil, water and other such factors, and which lead to long sequences in mankind's use of the landscape.

The selection of historic areas of national interest must in the first place reflect the slow, underlying and structural rhythms in our country's development, its regional features and the transitional periods. Below we summarise a few of the main features of what has been included in the national sample of Swedish cultural history. In other words: here is the cream of Sweden's cultural heritage—in the landscape!

This map highlights environments where village tofts and buildings, ancient forms of cultivation and shealings provide strong arguments for preservation. As a rule the large environments are more complex, that is, their preservation is justified by relics of various kinds from various periods. (L110)

Cultural Environments of Industries

THE HISTORY OF FARMING IN TIME AND SPACE

The map shows the environments of national interest, allowing one to see the long history of farming in three broad phases of development. The cultivation of grain began more than 6,000 years ago. In environments in Skåne and western Sweden there are stone chamber graves which seem to bear witness to the surplus of energy that the improved food supply gave. In southern and central Sweden we can follow the gradual development of agriculture during the Bronze and Iron Ages in traces such as clearing cairns, stone walls, field systems and the like. The richly-preserved graves give the best picture of the distribution of farming culture over large areas.

In the centuries before and after 1000 A.D. great, permanent cultural features in the landscape were being established through the formation of villages on the plains and colonisation in the forests. By that time the classical, fairly steady type of farming using fertilised fields and fallow, cattle rearing and hunting, fishing and other such activities had achieved a considerable degree of stability. This kind of farming gradually spread to practically all the cultivable parts of Sweden. Implements were improved and social organisation changed radically, but it retained its ecologically-based methods right up to the 19th century.

In this century more sophisticated farming methods were introduced. Village life was broken up by the re-distribution of land and new land was sought by cultivating meadows, lowering the level of lakes and ditching. Farmers experimented with crop rotation and the cultivation of fodder crops, mechanised production and became more market-oriented.

TRACES OF THE OLD PEASANT SOCIETY

It was not until the cultivator had learnt to combine cattle rearing with cultivation to create an integrated production system that he became a *farmer* (Sw. bonde). What is important in this respect is not the means of livelihood itself but the state of being permanently settled. Permanent settlement gave a more long-sighted character to the effort that was invested in clearing land, digging ditches and building barns, stables, storehouses and dwelling houses. The farmer worked for future generations. But it was more than that; the graves of one's ancestors lay close by. The farmer saw himself as a link in a long chain. As a result the pattern became more and more fixed and has in many cases survived later changes.

The map shows almost 400 historic areas of national interest, including well-preserved old villages, ancient field forms and/or preserved shealings. If one studies them carefully, one sees a picture showing clear regional differences. The four-sided farms of Skåne with their lines of pollarded willows, the strict order of the farms of Öland with their lines of cottages facing up to the wind and foreign incursion, the hilltop locations of the highland villages above the highest coastline, the many medieval showpieces and scattered farmsteads of Gotland, the small villages of Mälardalen in the valleys, the impressive farmhouses of Hälsingland, the closely-packed cottages of Dalarna and its system of property inheritance—all of these are important examples. Some of them bear traces of over-population, like the large cottar settlements

There are many areas in Småland where agrarian environments are interwoven with ancient forms of cultivation. Krokshult in Kristdala is characterised by small-scale farming and old-style cattle-grazing in open pastureland, still fenced in the traditional manner.

in Skåne, in the Falbygden and on Öland from the 18th and 19th centuries.

SOCIAL-HISTORICAL CONTENT

One of the main tasks when selecting areas of national interest is to survey the history of every social class. The fact that the relics of the upper classes may be both better built and more worthy of preservation from an esthetic point of view creates a problem. The castles and manor houses which are valuable for architectural and historical reasons are, however, only the stylish centres of complete systems of fields, farm buildings, dwelling houses, crofts, parks, ponds, harbours and the like. From an *overall* point of view a manor-house environment has far-reaching social implications, since far more Swedes are descended from farmhands and crofters than from the gentry and castle builders.

The selection shows how economic and new agricultural methods were introduced during the early Middle Ages, which made it possible to separate ownership from cultivation. Land ownership became more and more centred on cathedrals, monasteries and powerful families. Up to the 17th century the tenant system prevailed. Tenant farms often belonged to the hamlet communities and had to be managed according to their traditional annual cycle. From this period there are remains mainly of upper-class buildings, often at places where there are still manor houses. The villages also remain, but their character has been changed by later developments, when they were often abandoned.

The manor laws of the 17th century gave estate owners the possibility of rationalising their estates and increasing their own management. At the same time the church estates which had been confiscated in the reformation were redistributed to the Crown's creditors and given away as rewards during the Great Power period. This resulted in exclusive castle and manor-house environments growing up on a large scale.

The social distribution of the selection mainly reflects the 18th and 19th centuries. The reduction of nobility estates at the end of the 17th century destroyed the power of the nobility. From the 18th century onwards it was money and not rank that counted. Many confiscated estates were used as official state residences. Towards the 19th century the shortage of cultivable land—with the methods available at that time—became more acute. Land reforms were passed so that both farmers and estate owners could amalgamate their land holdings. The removal of privileges made it possible for farmers to acquire land owned by the Crown and the nobility. Most of our crofts and cottages grew up now and later the barrack-like buildings for agricultural labourers and their families.

TRAPPERS AND NOMADS

Before the farmers there were trappers in Sweden for thousands of years. There are many, though often not very marked traces of this form of culture. In the interior of northern Sweden there was a living mobile trapping culture which survived among the Saami until the 17th and 18th centuries. Since the Middle Ages it has been successively replaced by reindeer nomadism.

The selection of Saami environments bears witness to the fact that they migrated over much greater distances up to a very late date than they do today. How old Saami reindeer husbandry is, how it arose and why it has retained its special features are much-discussed questions. From the point of view of environmental usage it is interesting to compare Saami cultural environments with the choice of trapping pit environments.

FISHING ENVIRONMENTS

Maritime connections are evident in many areas of national interest. The oldest of them are found in the coastal environments of the Stone and Bronze Ages. A map of fishing villages shows the environments that can be directly explained by fishing in a more diversified society.

The historically most remarkable of these are to be found round the coast of Skåne, where large seasonal fishing camps were established around 1200. The demand for cheap food in the towns on the continent was the driving force. Later it was the fishing in Bohuslän that was most important.

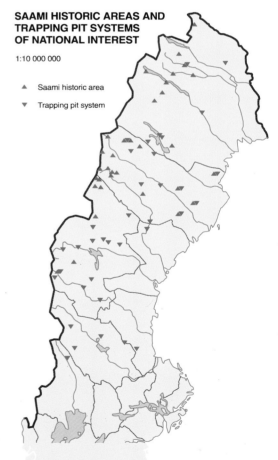

SAAMI HISTORIC AREAS AND TRAPPING PIT SYSTEMS OF NATIONAL INTEREST

1:10 000 000

▲ Saami historic area

▼ Trapping pit system

The area of Saami culture is in part the same as that of the prehistoric hunting and trapping culture in Norrland. This includes a large number of trapping pits. Saami environments and trapping pits—especially those used for trapping wild reindeer—often occur in the same type of landscape. (LIII)

The diagram shows the number of historic areas of national interest where varying types of settlement are one reason for preservation. In fact they may occur either together in complex environments or singly in more uniform environments.

SOCIAL CLASSES IN THE AGRARIAN AREAS OF NATIONAL INTEREST

Crofts and cottages 16%

Castles and manors 31%

Peasant villages 53%

There are also many similar but more modest fishing settlements along the whole coast of Sweden from Strömstad in the west to Haparanda in the north-east. Here the townsfolk-fishermen from the small towns competed with the country population. One notable example is provided by the seasonal fishing camps of the people from the Mälardalen towns and Gävle far up in the Sea of Bothnia.

Industrial Cultural Environments

It is not easy to select industrial environments so that a fair historical picture is presented. Considering its peripheral location Sweden has a long industrial history. But its industries have in recent years been transformed very rapidly. Many environments which are now of primarily historical interest formed only fifty years ago the backbone of Sweden's economy and its future hope. In other environments closures and rationalisation have resulted in the disappearance of many traces of old industries.

The environments of mining and forest industries have a special place in Sweden's economic history and hence in its cultural heritage. Our selection is coloured by our emphasis on totality and context. Environments of national interest may have been chosen because they throw light on communications, living conditions or social conditions as well as technological or industrial-historical—or preferably all aspects at the same time.

The rows of poles in the water are the remains of old wooden piers belonging to the wharf at Skönvik's Sawmill in Medelpad. On the far side of the bay stands Östrand's modern pulp mill.

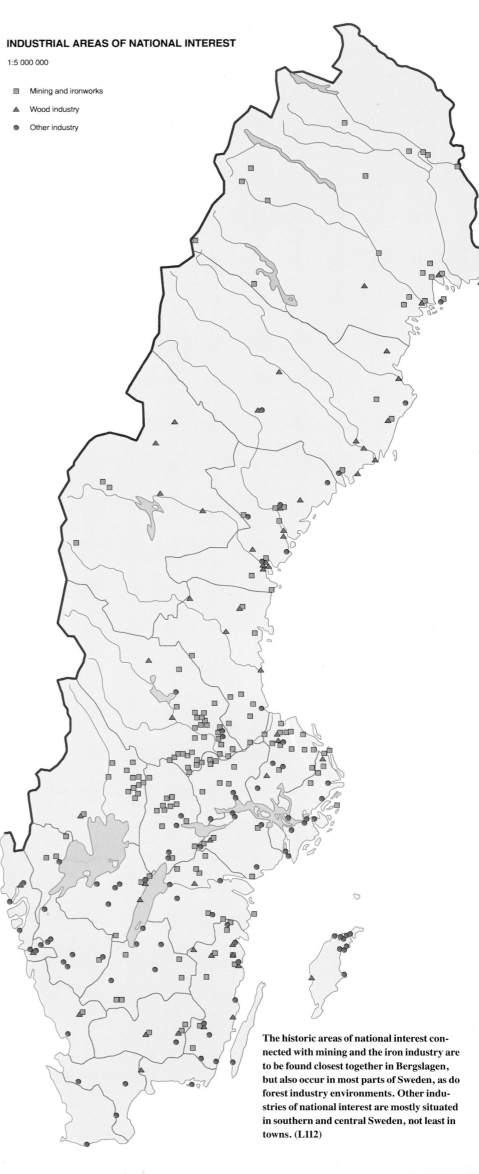

INDUSTRIAL AREAS OF NATIONAL INTEREST

1:5 000 000

◻ Mining and ironworks

▲ Wood industry

● Other industry

The historic areas of national interest connected with mining and the iron industry are to be found closest together in Bergslagen, but also occur in most parts of Sweden, as do forest industry environments. Other industries of national interest are mostly situated in southern and central Sweden, not least in towns. (L112)

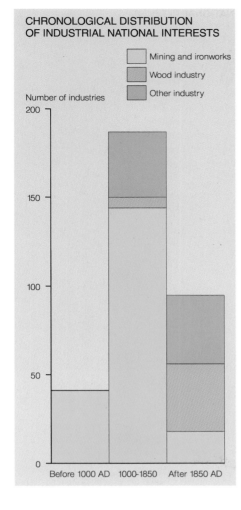

CHRONOLOGICAL DISTRIBUTION OF INDUSTRIAL NATIONAL INTERESTS

☐ Mining and ironworks
▨ Wood industry
▨ Other industry

Number of industries
200

150

100

50

0

Before 1000 AD   1000-1850   After 1850 AD

What above all symbolises the mining town of Falun in our times — the giant hole called "Stora Stöten" — is not an open-cast mine but the result of what must have been one of the greatest disasters in Sweden's mining history, the collapse of the mine in 1687. Sala silver mine also has a similar but earlier giant hole.

Mining industries are predominant in a belt running between the river Klarälven and Roslagen. The classic regions of forest industry are reflected in the examples, which are taken largely from the river valleys of Norrland.

Among other industries we find the many different kinds of stone quarrying, windmills and watermills and many classical places associated with the growth of the engineering industry. These include power generation and relics of its early predecessors in the form of the many waterwheels which powered factories along our rivers.

Environments cannot be dated as precisely as their component parts. Continuity is a prominent feature of Swedish industrial history.

What research has taught us in recent years about low-tech iron manufacturing has affected our selection but the classic period of iron manufacturing from the Middle Ages up to the 19th century predominates. As mining decreases in importance, the forest-industry environments increase, which is undoubtedly a fair reflection of developments. It was in fact by taking over the charcoal-producing forests of the mines and ironworks that the forest industries gathered momentum. The fact that what here are called other industries occur precisely before and after 1800 is more of a coincidence.

STORA KOPPARBERG

There are good reasons for highlighting Falun in our industrial history. It contains remains of a thousand-year-old mining industry, including old smelting works, enormous slagg heaps and Stora Stöten, the hole that resulted from a cave-in in 1687. Falun represents so much in our history of the Middle Ages and the 17th century, mainly of course for financial reasons. The copper-clad roofs of Stockholm, Amsterdam and other towns are eloquent symbols of this. Falu red paint, which was first manufactured in the 1760s from a byproduct of mining, has almost become a symbol of Sweden since it conquered the Swedish rural environment.

Town Environments

Most Swedish towns have environments of national interest. The first great wave of urbanisation, which reached its full strength in the early Middle Ages, after a couple of archeologically famous proto-forms, had resulted by 1500 A.D. in some 70 towns. About half of them belonged to Sweden then as now, while the remainder are in provinces that belonged to Denmark or Norway.

During the Middle Ages those characteristics developed that have ever since symbolised town life: the square, the town hall, the merchants' houses, the craftsmen's districts, the town gates, the toll fence and so on. In towns where streets and buildings still reflect something of their medieval origin, the whole town centre has in general been declared a historic area of national interest.

The second wave of urbanisation in the 16th and 17th centuries took place mainly north and west of the regions where the medieval towns had arisen. After Skåne, Halland, Blekinge and Bohuslän had become Swedish, towns were founded to replace others that were abandoned. It was central power that lay behind the rise of these early modern towns. Many of them, with their geometric patterns of straight streets and large squares, suggest the political power. Almost all the towns from this period are of national interest, which may be due to the fact that they are well preserved.

What is called the Swedish "wooden town" is also well represented — that is, the middle and lower-class living and working districts, mostly from the 18th and 19th centuries, which are found in some 60 old towns. The county towns are also represented.

The third wave of urbanisation came with the Industrial Revolution, at the end of the 19th century. This was when the proportion of people living in towns grew and Sweden developed a few large cities. Not quite half the towns contain areas of national interest: railway and street systems and residential districts which illustrate new social patterns.

The urbanisation of Sweden would not be adequately depicted, however, if the smaller towns in Sweden were not included. The historic areas of national interest include a large selection of specifically Swedish urban areas: small market towns and municipalities, fishing villages, "church towns", spas and other urban districts with special features. At the lowest level central places are represented by parish centres with churches and the like in agrarian environments.

TOWNS AND TOWNSHIPS OF NATIONAL INTEREST

1:5 000 000

- ■ Medieval town
- ■ Town from the 16th or 17th centuries
- ☐ Town from the 19th or 20th centuries
- ■ Other town or township

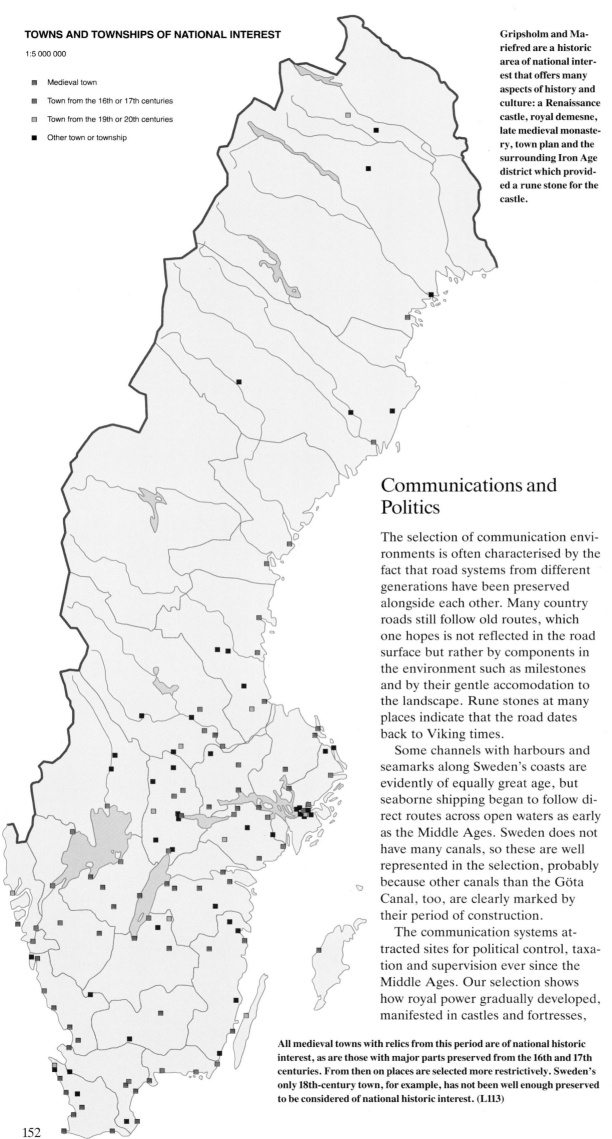

Gripsholm and Mariefred are a historic area of national interest that offers many aspects of history and culture: a Renaissance castle, royal demesne, late medieval monastery, town plan and the surrounding Iron Age district which provided a rune stone for the castle.

Communications and Politics

The selection of communication environments is often characterised by the fact that road systems from different generations have been preserved alongside each other. Many country roads still follow old routes, which one hopes is not reflected in the road surface but rather by components in the environment such as milestones and by their gentle accomodation to the landscape. Rune stones at many places indicate that the road dates back to Viking times.

Some channels with harbours and seamarks along Sweden's coasts are evidently of equally great age, but seaborne shipping began to follow direct routes across open waters as early as the Middle Ages. Sweden does not have many canals, so these are well represented in the selection, probably because other canals than the Göta Canal, too, are clearly marked by their period of construction.

The communication systems attracted sites for political control, taxation and supervision ever since the Middle Ages. Our selection shows how royal power gradually developed, manifested in castles and fortresses,

how the number of such installations decreased rapidly when the balance of power had become clearer after the Peasants' Revolt in the 15th century, and how the 17th-century nation state primarily felt the need to strengthen its outer defences.

The Interplay of Areas of National Interest

The rise of central places marks an important stage in the development of every region. In the selection of areas of national interest one can see how crafts, industry and the exercise of power gradually separated out from the peasant landscape and step by step became centralised.

Country highways form part of most country landscapes, as do fairways in coastal districts. In the environments recorded here roads and fairways provide an important argument for preservation. Most canals are worth preserving for their own sake.

All medieval towns with relics from this period are of national historic interest, as are those with major parts preserved from the 16th and 17th centuries. From then on places are selected more restrictively. Sweden's only 18th-century town, for example, has not been well enough preserved to be considered of national historic interest. (L113)

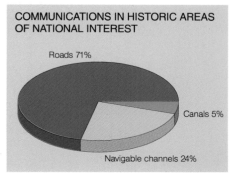

COMMUNICATIONS IN HISTORIC AREAS OF NATIONAL INTEREST

Roads 71%
Canals 5%
Navigable channels 24%

AREAS OF NATIONAL INTEREST ON GOTLAND

1:1 250 000

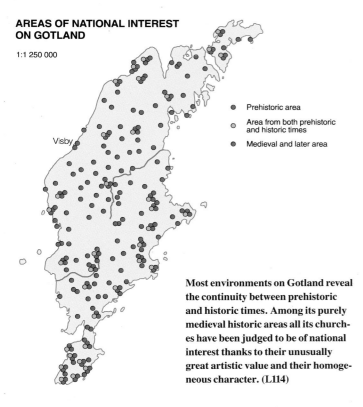

Visby

- ● Prehistoric area
- ○ Area from both prehistoric and historic times
- ● Medieval and later area

Högom

Most environments on Gotland reveal the continuity between prehistoric and historic times. Among its purely medieval historic areas all its churches have been judged to be of national interest thanks to their unusually great artistic value and their homogeneous character. (L114)

Most forts and fortresses or their ruins create their own environments; the largest or best preserved of them are considered to be historic areas of national interest. Others may form part of medieval town settings, for example, or be connected with communication routes. (L115)

CASTLES AND FORTIFICATIONS OF NATIONAL INTEREST

1:10 000 000

- ■ Medieval castle or stronghold
- ■ Fortress or fortification from modern times

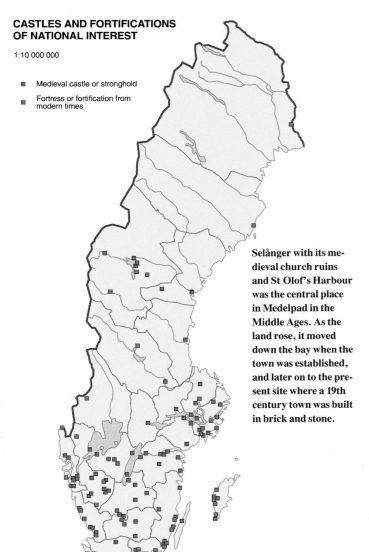

Selånger with its medieval church ruins and St Olof's Harbour was the central place in Medelpad in the Middle Ages. As the land rose, it moved down the bay when the town was established, and later on to the present site where a 19th century town was built in brick and stone.

AREAS OF NATIONAL INTEREST ROUND SUNDSVALL

1:1 250 000

- Area with Iron Age landscape
- Iron Age chief settlement
- Medieval area
- Area with ironworks
- Area from the Industrial Age

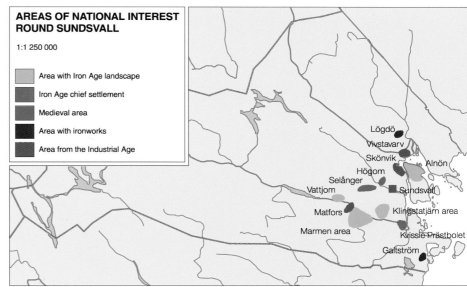

Lögdö
Vivstavarv
Skönvik
Alnön
Högom
Selånger
Vattjom
Sundsvall
Matfors
Klingstatjärn area
Marmen area
Kvissle Prästbolet
Galtström

Medelpad has small but densely-packed Iron Age districts, one of which formed a central place in the Middle Ages. A town proper developed only with the arrival of the wood industry. (L116)

TWO EXAMPLES

Gotland has a specially rich prehistorical landscape, from which Visby emerged in the early Middle Ages. This richness is evidently connected with the transport of goods across the Baltic. Visby became a town of international fame in the 13th century, with a large German-speaking population alongside the native Gotlanders. The town acquired special privileges.

The remarkable thing about Gotland is that the countryside also continued to develop for a very long time. There is, so to say, "a second Visby" in the shape of farmers' ports, warehouses, stone buildings and superb churches. In the course of time, however, the town got the upper hand, and the country population often became dependent on its citizens.

The selection of historic areas of

national interest on Gotland attempts to reflect the tension between town and country and includes, apart from the town, all parish centres with their characteristic monumental churches, several harbours and almost all farms with preserved medieval buildings.

Medelpad had during the Iron Age the most distinctive farming settlements along the Norrland coast from a social point of view. The selection here comprises two prominent Iron Age chieftains' farms at Njurunda and Selånger, and a few larger districts. The Middle Ages is represented by the province's legal centre with a royal demesne, a harbour and the church ruins at Selånger.

Sundsvall was founded in 1621 on a site which, with respect to the elevation of the land, is a clear parallel to the older central place. A royal warrant ordered 37 Medelpad farmers and a handful of blacksmiths to move to an appointed site by the river Selångersån. The landscape was at the time self-sufficient for the necessities of life and got hold of other things by small-scale barter.

Not until the mid–18th century did the town achieve a certain importance when a few citizens managed to launch some large-scale businesses. A couple of ironworks also represent this period.

During the 19th century Sundsvall became the centre of the sawmill industry—a battlefield for legendary wood barons and a centre for the growth of the labour movement. The second main focus of the selection illustrates how the economic boom was manifested in Sundsvall's "stone town" and in the network of shipyards, sawmills, wharves and workers' environments which made it possible.

The Cultural Heritage in Society

The Development of Cultural Monument Preservation

In Renaissance Europe classical culture was the focus of attention for the scholarly world. But the more remote countries in Europe also paid attention to their own cultural heritages in the form of their prehistory, sagas of varying origins and the like. These nationalistic currents existed in Sweden as early as the 15th century.

THE ARCHEOLOGICAL CULTURAL HERITAGE

The foremost of the early antiquarians was Johannes Bureus (1568–1652), who began Sweden's long anti-

quarian tradition. He devoted his main attention to rune stones, but also played an important role as tutor to King Gustav II Adolf (Gustavus Adolphus). In 1630 the king appointed Bureus and two of his colleagues to be "National Antiquarians", with the task of surveying monuments in accordance with a royal memorandum.

His cousin, Andreas Bureus, organised the Swedish Land Survey. In repeated and detailed surveying instructions during the 17th century surveyors were also ordered to make note of ancient monuments on their maps of villages and farms. Thus the tradition of recording cultural monuments on maps is a long one.

Sweden passed its first Law on Ancient Monuments in 1666. The protection included all ancient monuments on Crown land and taxable land, while the nobility were presumed to look after them on their land. The definition of ancient monuments was very broad and there were few possibilities of actively applying the law. The best protection was afforded, as previously, by the stability of land use and traditions in the peasant-farmer landscape.

In 1667 an antiquarian institute was inaugurated at Uppsala for research into "antiquities". An ordinance regarding prehistoric finds was issued in 1684, aimed principally at coin hoards.

Thus the foundation stones on which the preservation of the archeological cultural heritage still rests were laid as early as the 17th century: documentation, research, legal protection, cooperation with map-makers and information.

Thanks to the Romantic movement the antiquarian interest was revived around 1800. A circular letter was issued in 1805 pointing out the need to preserve ancient monuments during the current land reforms. The Gothic Association and its magazine Iduna increased people's interest.

A new ordinance on ancient monuments was issued in 1828, which proved, however, to be far too vague and toothless. It reappeared in a new form in 1867 with the order that "all permanent ancient monuments preserving the memory of the inhabitants of the fatherland in prehistoric times"

were to be protected. This meant that rules for how prehistoric remains could be moved had to be introduced. The Royal Academy of Letters, History and Antiquities was entrusted with the power to issue licences.

Scientific archeological research from the mid–19th century onwards introduced a completely new attitude towards the historical importance of ancient monuments.

The Ancient Monuments Ordinance of 1867 soon proved to be inadequate and its observance left much to be desired. After several commissions a new law was passed in 1942, which was one of the most radical of its kind: all ancient monuments were to be "placed under the protection of the law". Every permanent monument had a right to a protective area. Anyone who wanted to "disturb, alter or move" an ancient monument had first to obtain permission and then pay for a scientific investigation. This law, and the 1937 parliamentary decision on cooperation between a systematic survey of ancient monuments and the publication of the Economic Map, which made it possible to protect and investigate ancient monuments, laid the foundation of modern archeological cultural preservation. This law was complemented in certain respects in 1988, when all the regulations concerning antiquarian protection were gathered into Culture Heritage Act.

BUILDING CULTURE

As early as the 16th century there was royal interest in protecting certain "historic" buildings. There was an inscription on the royal demesne at Biskops Arnö: "The Great King Johan the Third of that Name Has Rebuilt and Improved Me, as so many other Fallen Houses and Deserted Churches. Anno 1586." However, it is not possible to speak of building conservation at that time.

In 1618 a "Chamber Order" was issued regarding the management of the Crown's property and buildings. The first "survey" of the more important buildings of the country was Eric Dahlbergh's "Suecia Antiqua et Hodierna" (1661–1717).

Apart from fortresses and castles the state was interested in churches.

Eric Dahlbergh's "Svecia Antiqua" contains illustrations of well-known ancient monuments. Here we see the great barrow "Inglinge Hög" at Östra Torsås in Småland. There is also a fanciful drawing of the famous great stone ball on the barrow. The illustrations of the oval stone settings which dominate the cemetery round the barrow are rather more accurate.

Templum Chathedrale Lincopenſe.

Dahlbergh's print of Linköping Cathedral gives an idea of what the cathedral looked like before the additions of the 19th century; it also illustrates a 17th-century town churchyard.

The drawing by Dahlbergh of Finsta in Roslagen from the east gives a broad landscape picture. Skederid Church stands on the left and the manor house in the centre. Beyond it there is a gravel ridge with several cemeteries, the southernmost of which have now disappeared. On the right, the village of Simlunda and at the bottom an ancient burial ceremony.

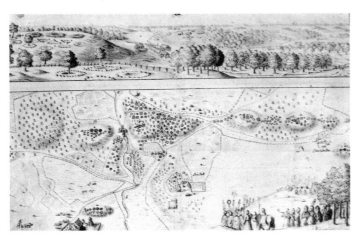

The 1686 Church Law laid down that the king should supervise the parishes' responsibility for the churches and approve the building of new churches. A royal letter in 1759 contained directives for preservation and maintenance.

An ordinance in 1776 extended this administrative responsibility for public buildings. The Royal Inspectorate was to scrutinise plans and calculations, in practice from a functional and esthetic point of view, and the king was to approve them. No antiquarian viewpoints are expressed. The 1867 Ancient Monuments Ordinance required government permission for demolishing or rebuilding old churches. But the development of the population in the 19th century, combined with a lack of antiquarian insight, was disastrous for the medieval churches in many areas. A modern view of old churches as documents of their whole historical development did not arise until the 20th century. A first important survey of church effects was carried out about 1830.

It is hardly possible to speak of the antiquarian conservation of any other buildings until the 1920 directives concerning public buildings. Now, for the first time, a state building could be protected by law if it had special artistic or cultural-historical value. A law passed in 1942 made it possible for buildings remarkable from a cultural-historical viewpoint owned by others than the state to be protected as historic buildings. This law was brought up to date in 1960 and was included in this form in the 1988 Culture Heritage Act.

ENVIRONMENTAL ASPECTS

"Natural environments" were the subject of state consideration around the beginning of this century which was expressed in the first nature protection laws and national parks. It was to be a long time, however, before the realisation that "cultural environments" needed legal protection gained general acceptance.

The term *culture environment* refers to cultural elements and qualities in a landscape influenced and utilised by mankind. These landscapes and environments include places that are protected by the Culture Heritage Act mainly ancient monuments and historic buildings. But a culture environment that is worthy of protection need not contain remarkable places of this kind. It may just as well contain many everyday and typical things, providing good examples of human-ecological relations, ancient forms of work, typical cultural "period pictures" or continuous chronological sequences. Place names are also of great importance in the cultural landscape. It is the *totality* of the environment that characterises its value.

The 1942 laws give some protection to local environments. At that time more radical changes in the culture environment were hardly expected. But the massive expansion of society in the post-war period led to a need to participate in planning in larger-scale and more preventive forms than the laws on cultural monuments allowed.

Antiquarian methods for working with the totalities of the cultural environment were developed in conjunction with national physical planning. The breakthrough for this new way of approaching the problems was the 1972 Bill on the management of land and water. This included reports on cultural environments which were later followed up in municipal and regional planning.

There was a debate in connection with the new Culture Heritage Act as to whether cultural protection needed its own "Cultural Reserve" system to safeguard the cultural environment. The decision in the end was that it should be taken into consideration in general planning, in the first place through the 1987 Natural Resources Act, which, together with the Planning and Building Act controls the state's planning and development of the landscape. The Culture Heritage Act safeguards the heart of cultural-environmental protection—the places protected by law and their local environments, while planning laws meet the overall interests of the culture environment.

THE MODERN ORGANISATION

The municipalities are today the primary authorities for cultural-environmental protection. They have the economic resources and the main responsibility for planning. Several municipalities also have expert knowledge in the form of municipal museums or municipal antiquarians. The responsibility for churches lies with the parishes.

The main responsibility for the legal supervision of cultural-environmental questions lies with the county administrative boards, which deal with most matters covered by the Culture Heritage Act. Their internal organisation varies, but there are experts in various fields, which makes it possible for them to weigh different interests against each other. An unusual construction is the informal responsibility for the cultural environment and cultural monuments borne by the county museums. They receive some state grants for their work in assisting the county boards in these matters.

The overall supervision of cultural-environmental protection is the responsibility of the Central Board of National Antiquities, which also cooperates with other central authorities and boards, is responsible for development work and looks after the interests of the sector in general.

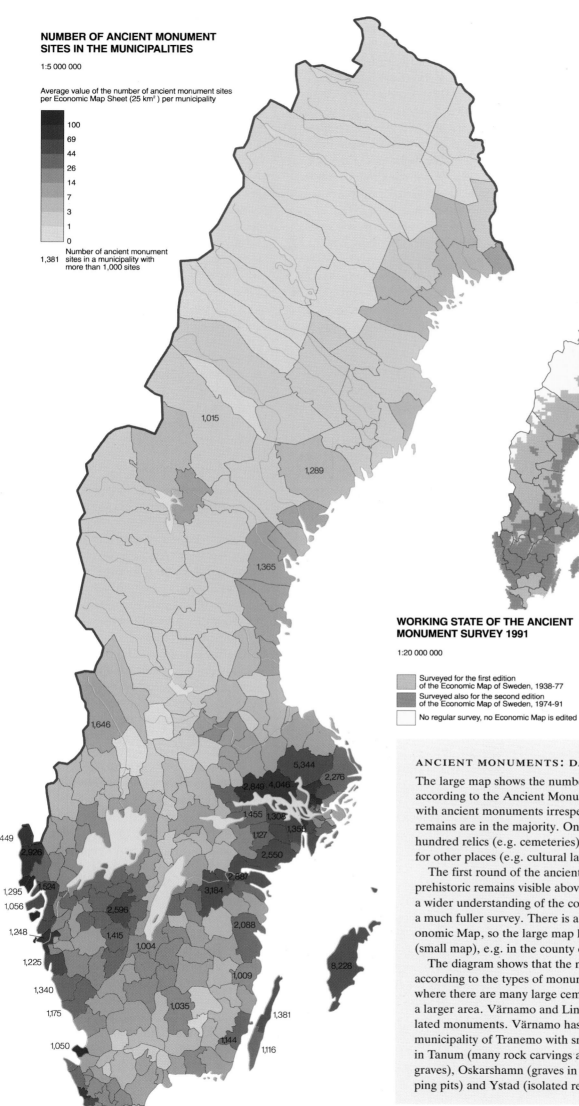

NUMBER OF ANCIENT MONUMENT SITES IN THE MUNICIPALITIES

1:5 000 000

Average value of the number of ancient monument sites per Economic Map Sheet (25 km²) per municipality

	100
	69
	44
	26
	14
	7
	3
	1
	0

1,381 Number of ancient monument sites in a municipality with more than 1,000 sites

WORKING STATE OF THE ANCIENT MONUMENT SURVEY 1991

1:20 000 000

Surveyed for the first edition of the Economic Map of Sweden, 1938-77

Surveyed also for the second edition of the Economic Map of Sweden, 1974-91

No regular survey, no Economic Map is edited

Recording Ancient Monuments

The most important conditions for ensuring that the protection and conservation of ancient monuments are firstly that the authorities have expert knowledge of ancient monuments and secondly that the public can share this knowledge.

EARLY RECORDINGS

Three weeks after Sweden's first ancient monuments law was passed in 1666, a royal letter was sent to the clergy requesting them to " . . . diligently and discreetly search out and discover all Antiquities. . . " These "Inquiries on Antiquities" which were made between 1667 and 1693 have been preserved in part. They record only a small number of the prehistoric remains, but are still of great value.

Many reports were made during the 19th century. The surveys carried out by scholars paid by the Academy of Letters, History and Antiquities and by regional archeological societies in the 1840s and onwards are particularly valuable, because they cover such wide areas. The first presentation of ancient monuments in general map form was made at the same time by the Geological Survey of Sweden. The most complete survey so far was carried out in western Sweden around 1900.

ANCIENT MONUMENT SURVEY

The Central Board of National Antiquities began detailed surveys in the 1920s. In 1937 the Riksdag decided

ANCIENT MONUMENTS: DATA

The large map shows the number of sites with ancient monuments per unit area according to the Ancient Monuments Register, 1991. The figures refer to all sites with ancient monuments irrespective of time or type, although prehistoric remains are in the majority. One site may contain anything from one to several hundred relics (e.g. cemeteries), while the number of relics cannot be specified for other places (e.g. cultural layers, sites beneath the ground, deserted villages).

The first round of the ancient monument survey was devoted almost entirely to prehistoric remains visible above the ground. Thanks to better resources and a wider understanding of the concept ancient monument, the second round led to a much fuller survey. There is a great lack of information in areas without an Economic Map, so the large map has to be seen in the light of these circumstances (small map), e.g. in the county of Kronoberg and the interior of Lappland.

The diagram shows that the number of ancient monuments per site varies according to the types of monuments in each area. It is largest in Vallentuna where there are many large cemeteries. Uppsala has a similar picture within a larger area. Värnamo and Linköping have many cemeteries but also many isolated monuments. Värnamo has larger (later) cemeteries than the comparable municipality of Tranemo with smaller (earlier) cemeteries. The lowest average is in Tanum (many rock carvings and dwelling sites), Falköping (mostly isolated graves), Oskarshamn (graves in a coastal environment), Torsby (scattered trapping pits) and Ystad (isolated remains in a totally cultivated area). (L115)

WHAT IS AN ANCIENT MONUMENT?

The ancient monument concept is treated in the 2nd chapter of the Culture Heritage Act. After general prerequisites a specification is given in eight points.

"Permanent ancient monuments are the following traces of human acitivity in past ages, having resulted from use in previous times and having been permanently abandoned:

1. graves, funeral buildings and burial grounds, together with churchyards and other cemeteries,

2. raised stones and stones and rock bases with inscriptions, symbols, marks and pictures, as well as other carvings or paintings,

3. crosses and memorials,

4. places of assembly for the administration of justice, cult activities, trade and other common purposes,

5. remains of homes, settlements and workplaces and cultural layers resulting from the use of such homes or places, e.g. traces of working life and economic activity,

6. ruins of fortresses, castles, monasteries, church buildings and defence works, and also of other remarkable buildings and structures,

7. routes and bridges, harbour faciliets, beacons, road markings, navigation marks and similar transport arrangements, as well as boundary markings and labyrinths,

8. wrecked ships, if at least one hundred years have presumably elapsed since the ship was wrecked.

Permanent ancient monuments also include natural formations associated with ancient customs, legends or noteworthy historic events, as well as traces of ancient popular cults."

that prehistoric remains should be entered on the Economic Map of Sweden. The first survey was carried out with limited resources up until 1977, covering the whole country except for the mountain districts, for which no Economic Maps were made. Since 1974 a new survey has been in progress, using the knowledge and experience from the first one, to meet new concepts and to fill previous gaps in information.

In practice the work consists in systematically surveying the terrain on the basis of previous surveys and topographical conditions and in recording and describing the remains that are observed. Field supervisors are responsible for judging the remains according to the law and deciding whether they should be included on the Economic Map, and for storing in the map database of the National Land Survey, which is becoming more important with time. Field record books, field photography maps and a printed map to keep the information up to date are stored in the register of ancient monuments, and copies are circulated to the regional cultural preservation authorities.

THE ANCIENT MONUMENT REGISTER

The sites are registered in numerical order for each parish. A site may consist of one single relic, a small group of remains or a larger number reported within a common area, such as a cemetery, a deserted village. Each site is marked with the traditional symbol for ancient monuments—a runic R—on the map, sometimes combined with an informatory text or name. All sites are also reported to the Central Board for Real Estate Data, where they can be identified by coordinates. A selection of the most visible and most interesting monuments is also marked on the Topographical Map.

The Ancient Monument Register now contains some 700,000 separate items, on almost 150,000 sites. A dozen municipalities have more than 2,000 sites each. They are all large in area and consist of old cultural districts, dominated by prehistoric remains. Many smaller municipalities have the same density.

The most numerous category of ancient monuments comprises prehistoric graves, which dominate the old cultural districts. Prehistoric dwelling sites are another large category in, for example, the muncipalities in Bohuslän and inland municipalities in Norrland. Rock carvings, in Enköping and Tanum, for example, may have a local dominance. Trapping pits are frequent in municipalities like Torsby and Strömsund. Remains from historical times such as castle and church ruins, village tofts, road signs and iron manufacturing sites occur at varying numbers.

A register of this kind can never be complete, and the map reveals two serious sources of error. One is the large Lappland municipalities, which have only partly been surveyed. This means that remains of the trapping and nomad cultures are under-represented. The other source of errors is seen primarily in the totally-cultivated districts of Götaland, where remains have been removed by cultivation over hundreds of years and many have disappeared for ever.

The Yellow Map marks ancient monuments with an R. Along the ridge of Fjärås bräcka in Halland there are scattered barrows and other prehistoric remains. There is a well-known cemetery at Li on the hillside to the west. Along the shore of Lake Lygnern there are Stone Age sites with no visible remains and a hill fort on the headland in the lake.

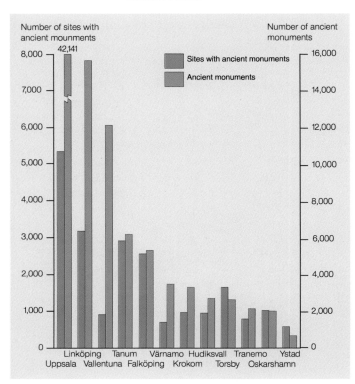

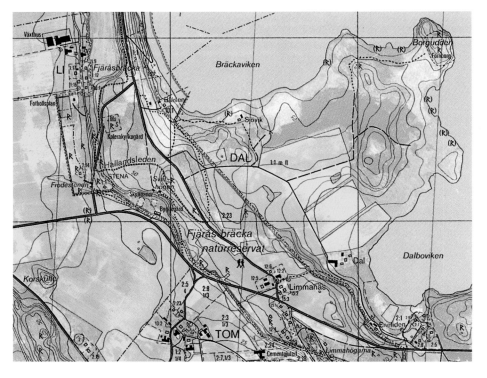

ARCHEOLOGICAL EXCAVATIONS IN 1964-88

1:10 000 000

Number of excavations per county

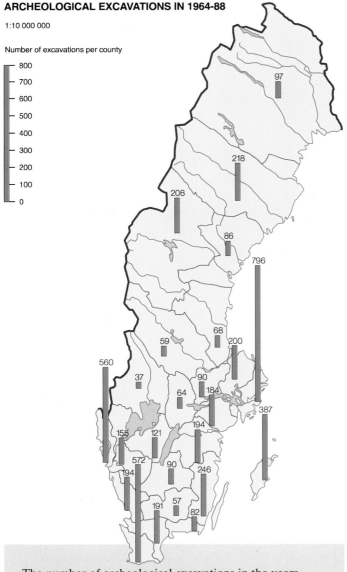

The number of archeological excavations in the years 1963–88 amounts to almost 5,000. The statistics include only final surveys; test surveys are not included. Not all of them cover whole ancient monument sites but only explored parts. Some have gone on for several seasons at one place but are counted as one survey. Frequency refers in the first place to changes in land use, but obviously the density of monuments in a county is also of importance. The number of purely scientifically motivated excavations is limited but can affect the values in certain cases, such as for Gotland. The big-city counties have the highest frequency, but the surveys prior to the exploitation of water power in Norrland took place in part before this period.

Archeological Field Investigations

Archeological investigations have been carried out in Sweden with scientific aims since the late 19th century. Until the 1930s archeology concentrated on investigating individual monuments in order to have a supply of prehistoric material for research and museums. Since then the science has broadened its scope to include studies of cultural environments from both social and human-ecological aspects—"mankind in the landscape".

Whenever land has been exploited since the 1940s, various types of ancient monuments have been investigated by archeological teams on commission in many parts of Sweden: Stone Age dwelling sites in Norrland, Iron Age cemeteries in central Sweden, dwelling sites in totally-cultivated districts in southern Sweden and medieval town centres. Many investigations have resulted from land exploitation for modern suburbs, and earlier for hydro-electric power stations. Since the 1970s more and more large-scale investigations have been carried out in the countryside as a result of the need for modernisation and the extension of the communications network.

BUILDING UP KNOWLEDGE

To be meaningful and to live up to the Culture Heritage Act, field archeology on commission has to work with modern scientific aims. When this is the case, every investigation is a step towards building up our store of knowledge.

Every archeological dig bears a special responsibility, since it inevitably involves an irrevocable removal of source material. The removed remains and their content of cultural-historical facts must be documented when excavated. Documentation then replaces the remains and can be used for future research. The need for completeness, carefulness and objectivity is great, as is the need to be able to evaluate and give priority to archeological data.

SOURCES

Archeological source material falls into two categories: artefacts, i.e. mankind's material products; and eco-facts, traces in nature of human activities. The former consist partly of prehistoric remains in the landscape and partly of prehistoric objects. Eco-facts consist of, for example, pollen, phosphate levels in the ground and radioactive charcoal. The breadth of scope between the smallest and the largest objects, between the macro and the micro perspective, is therefore often very large in an archeological investigation.

Consequently archeologists are also dependent on several other sciences such as osteology for bone analysis, pollen analyses and Quaternary geology for landscape studies, place-name research, human geography and so on. Statistical studies are vital for quantitative analyses of large amounts of data. The methods of laboratory archeology give more detailed knowledge of raw materials and manufacturing processes, but also of recent decomposition caused, for example, by air pollution.

The "strip cartoon" below gives a summary of the normal sequence of events in a commissioned archeological investigation, in this case a planned new road. There is often feedback from the various stages of the work as well.

1. Information from town planning, for example the National Road Administration, legal management and antiquarian plan scrutiny

2. Studies of archives, maps, texts, a possible archeological survey

3. Pilot investigation to establish the extent and type of prehistoric remains.

158

PLAN DOCUMENTATION

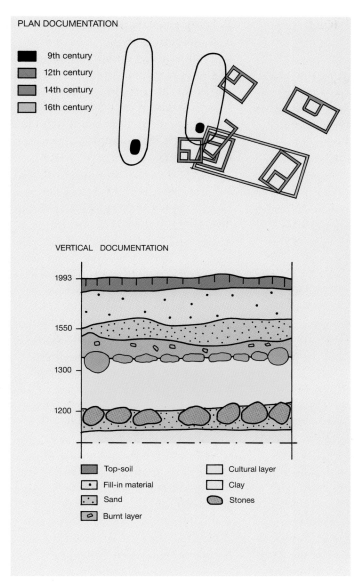

- ■ 9th century
- ▦ 12th century
- ▤ 14th century
- ▢ 16th century

VERTICAL DOCUMENTATION

1993
1550
1300
1200

- ▨ Top-soil
- ⬚ Fill-in material
- ⬚ Sand
- ⬚ Burnt layer
- ▢ Cultural layer
- ▢ Clay
- ⬭ Stones

Top, a model of plan documentation showing the development of various building phases; beneath, a model of cross-sections of soil layers with encapsulated layers of medieval buildings.

Partly excavated 11th-century house foundation at Skabersjö, Skåne

Stone surrounds of a stone ship, the Viking Age, Stångebro, Linköping, Östergötland

Town wall and cultural layers from the Middle Ages, Helgeandsholmen, Stockholm

DOCUMENTATION

In practical fieldwork excavating with a digger is combined with digging by hand, and with manual drawing and photography using digital systems for measuring and registration.

The time factor is vital for studies of prehistoric development. An important basis for chronology is the formation of cultural layers, stratigraphy, which can occur when different activities succeed one another in a settlement. The fact that houses within a farm are relocated or that new graves are placed successively within a cemetery also make it possible to study chronological development. Investigations are therefore documented both horizontally in plans and vertically in sections. Processing the information will then reveal chronological horizons formed by the information from to the same periods.

Each excavation results in an archeological report consisting of text, drawings, photographs, lists of finds and so on. This accompanies the finds for conservation and registration at a museum, after which it is filed for future research.

Ruins of a 17th-century silver blast furnace, Silbojokk, Arjeplog, Lappland

Cemetery, dated 300 B.C.–200 A.D. at Annelund, Visby, Gotland

4. **Excavations and documentation of the site and finds**

5. **Analysis and evaluation of drawings, observations, photographs, samples etc**

6. **Conservation of objects, publication of report etc**

7. **Distribution of information to commissioners, municipalities, the public etc**

The 16th-century writer Olaus Magnus gave the preservation of antiquity its motto in his history of the Scandinavian people. Above the flame is written in runic script in Latin: Preserve the Old!

The number of preservation plans per county varies not only with respect to the number of ancient monuments but also as a result of financing by means of labour market funds, and other state, municipal and private grants. Consequently, the number of objects that can be preserved varies according to the level of (un)employment. In the current year there was a total of 3,805 preservation plans; 2,938 objects were preserved, 641 of them by municipalities and 168 privately. A total of SEK 14.64 million was allocated in the form of labour market funds and SEK 3.66 million in direct state grants. (L119)

PRESERVATION OF ANCIENT MONUMENTS 1991-92

1:10 000 000

- Preservation projects
- Preserved sites
- Sites preserved by local authorities

Number of projects and sites respectively

450
400
300
200
100
0

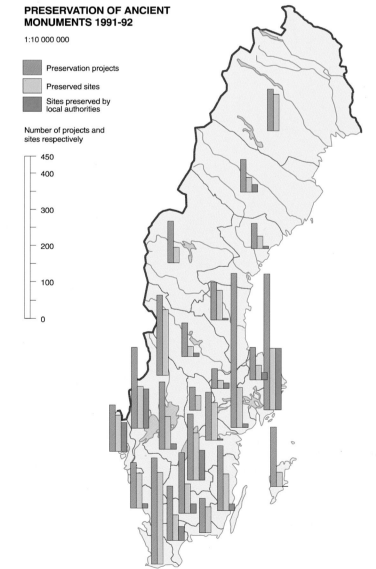

Preservation of Ancient Monuments

The aim of the Culture Heritage Act is to protect the country's ancient monuments and preserve them for future generations, and this is also the most important aim of ancient monument preservation. It should also reflect in an educational and many-facetted way ancient developments in our country and its regions. Information on ancient monuments is therefore important.

MOTIVATION

In the old peasant landscape all uncultivated infields were used for hay and grazing, and as a rule the forests were also grazed. In "the landscape formed by the scythe and the muzzle" the conservation of ancient monuments was a result of traditional land usage. It has often been reported how easily ancient monuments could be seen in the open landscape.

Around the turn of the century a romantic vision of nature grew up. The ideal was a natural landscape, and land that was left uncultivated was thought to be able to maintain such a state or return to it. This opinion was also put forward by the growing nature conservation movement. Meadows and pastures, for example, were declared protected land, so that they would be able to develop their beautiful flowers without interference. Prehistoric sites were also to be planted with trees, preferably spruce, which was one of the symbols of nature romanticism.

One of the areas that suffered from this policy was the island of Björkö in Lake Mälaren. Parts of the island were purchased by the Crown in 1912, and not only felling but also grazing and preservation were forbidden. The prehistoric sites on the island soon became overgrown with a thick forest. This state of affairs gave a strong incentive to develop modern conservation methods.

Another motive of quite a different calibre is provided by the transformation of agriculture. The closing down and amalgamation of farms, rationalisation and mechanisation of farming methods, farming without cattle and a general decrease in natural grazing, resulting in tree plantations on a large scale, a final end to all meadow hay-making and the removal of obstacles to cultivation—all these are examples of a trend which has had inevitable consequences for old cultural land with prehistoric remains. They rapidly become overgrown—to begin with often by an impenetrable scrub of blackthorn and dogrose or by brushwood, followed by an ugly forest of mixed trees. Ancient monuments are damaged both directly by the vegetation and indirectly because they become difficult to detect. It becomes difficult or even quite impossible for people to enjoy seeing them.

PROGRESS AND METHODS

Modern conservation as we know it today began in the early 1930s with manual and traditional hay-making methods to protect prehistoric remains, and make them accessible, visible and easy to understand. The first places to be tackled were national monuments like the mounds at Uppsala and not least Björkö. It was also

The best conservation both of prehistoric remains and of many other relics is by means of grazing of the same kind as has always been used in natural pastureland. A grazed prehistoric barrow cemetery at Ovangärstad in Östra Husby, Östergötland.

Conservation of ancient monuments is important if the public are to understand them properly. Above, an overgrown barrow cemetery at Roslags-Kulla, and below, a grazed and conserved cemetery of the same type at Rimsjö in Husby Sjuhundra, Uppland.

realised that continuous management was needed, and methods for this purpose were worked out as conservation plans proceeded.

The conservation of prehistoric remains on a large scale was established after the Second World War, when people became aware of the changes in agriculture. At this time many prehistoric remains were still well preserved and easily visible. One important method was therefore to try to maintain traditional cattle rearing by means of grants to certain districts.

Up to the mid–1960s conservation aimed at preserving or recreating meadows and pastures in selected areas by manual methods, since many prehistoric remains lay on this kind of land. When these activities grew rapidly in the 1970s, machinery was brought more and more into use. It

Left, the overgrown ruin of a fortified medieval tower at Totra in Hamrånge, Gästrikland, and below, the uncovered and conserved ruin of a small medieval, private church at Prästbolet in Njurunda, Medelpad.

Traditional conservation work, as here on Björkö in Uppland, was carried out with the same manual methods that previously were used for meadows. This also encouraged the growth of rich and valuable plant life.

was also realised that old cultural landscapes cannot be recreated, but only imitated. Gradually an understanding of the special fauna and flora of various areas played a more important role, and there has been growing cooperation with nature conservation. Prehistoric remains which have always, or for a long time, lain in forests should also be preserved in such environments.

Up until the mid–1970s the selection of objects for conservation comprised almost only prehistoric remains like cemeteries and hill forts. A broader, comprehensive view of the cultural environment has now led to a more representative selection, which also includes dwelling sites, notable roads, industrial monuments and the like.

ORGANISATION

Conservation has meant cooperation with many partners. During the 1950s a great deal of work was done by teams of mental patients. Agreements with the National Labour Board made conservation work an important occupation for the unemployed. The county administrative boards took over direct responsibility for preservation work in 1978, while responsibilty for planning and development remained with the central authorities.

Each county has a regional conservation programme, in which the selection of objects is made with consideration to representativity, accessibility, current threats and the like. There is a programme for every object. This is executed on commission by the county administrative board with cooperation between the county forestry boards and the county museums. Increased cooperation also takes place with the municipalities, which in some cases take responsibility for both financing and execution. In 1990 there were maintenance plans for almost 4,000 objects, over half of which were in operation. The need may, however, best be described as incalculable.

Graves and cemeteries are the most common relics and represent more than half the objects to be preserved. Among the rest, the spectacular hillforts are more strongly represented than their actual number would justify. Dwelling and settlement sites are under-represented, which is only natural since many do not have visible remains above the ground. Ruins are clearly visible, requiring more conservation work, and the same is true of industrial remains. Considering the large number of ancient monument sites that exist (almost 150,000), the number that receive preservation work is remarkably small.

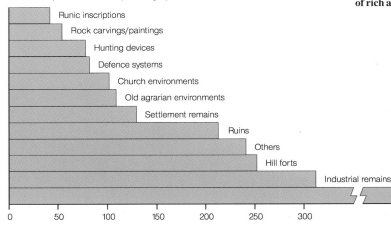

Number of preservation sites per category

Runic inscriptions
Rock carvings/paintings
Hunting devices
Defence systems
Church environments
Old agrarian environments
Settlement remains
Ruins
Others
Hill forts
Industrial remains
Graves and cemeteries

0   50   100   150   200   250   300   2,200   2,250   2,300

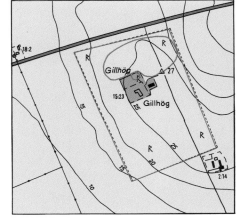

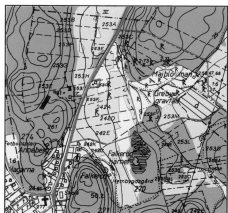

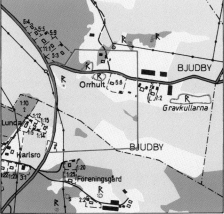

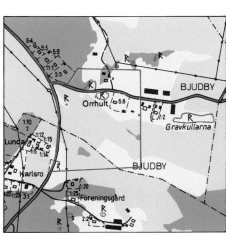

Tureberg in Sollentuna, Uppland has the remains of a cemetery with a large barrow, "Kungshögen", but they are surrounded by roads, railways and modern buildings quite out of tune with their setting. This weakness in planning is of an early date, but the result would have been different if the ancient monument area of the site had been registered.

The passage grave called "Gillhög" at Barsebäck in Skåne stands together with a dwelling site on a ridge in arable land and needs a comparatively wide field of vision. Its boundaries have been fixed to prevent further building. The structures are marked in blue, the fixed boundary in red.

The large cemetery from the early Iron Age at Greby in Tanum, Bohuslän, characteristically lies on a moraine between hills which ought to be kept completely open. To the west the boundary follows the country highway.

At Blacksta in Södermanland there stands a rune stone, originally where a road crossed a hollow. A boundary line ought to keep this hollow open, as well as a view of the roads. The two small cemeteries form part of the setting, but no decision has been reached about the larger one to the east.

Ancient Monument Areas

Every ancient monument has, in accordance with the law, a protective area surrounding it. The protective area should be as large as is necessary to preserve the remains and give it adequate space. It is intended to give the remains environmental protection.

The aim is to protect the area necessary for understanding the remains, their significance and their relationship with the natural surroundings. The boundary should be large enough to give an idea why people in ancient times chose that particular place. When assessing the size of the area, consideration should be paid to topography and other local conditions, for example the supply of raw materials, land use, relics of orig-inal vegetation and functional relations with other ancient monuments.

A rune stone that stands on its original site, for example, is often connected with an ancient road. It may have been erected by a ford or to mark a bridge. Today the previous marshland may have been drained and turned into fields. In order to preserve the rune stone and remains of the road or sunken ways in a meaningful way, it is important to preserve the traces of the original topography which may remain. Only then will it be possible to understand the function and significance of the rune stone.

Each type of ancient monuments has as a rule its special relationship with other remains and with the natural environment. Hill forts were created where the natural conditions were optimal for defence, so the whole strategic system should be included in the protective area. The monumental Bronze Age barrows of southern Sweden are dependent on the open landscape with free lines of sight, since they were built on hill tops to enhance their monumental character and to be visisble from far away. The same is more or less true of the cairns along the coast which are connected with channels and may have marked associated territories. Trapping pits in Norrland were dug where the terrain attracted animals or forced them to go. Headlands and ridges, passes between mountains and mires or along the banks of rivers are examples of trapping places where the whole pass ought to be included in the ancient monument area.

Protection for ancient monument areas is a direct consequence of the law which needs no special decision. The same regulations apply within the area as to the remains themselves. This means that all changes to the area are regulated by the Culture Heritage Act.

In order to determine the size of an area it may be necessary to decide how to draw its boundaries. Such decisions are made by the county administrative boards. Up to now only about 175 such boundaries have been determined. This low figure has to be seen in relation to the fact that the majority of decisions are made when planning housing areas, roads, gravel pits and other changes to the environment, but it may also indicate that the concept of ancient monuments is supported by public opinion.

Protection for Churches

The parishes of the Swedish church have about 3,000 church buildings. All of those built before 1940 are protected by the Culture Heritage Act. The law states that church buildings and the land around them are to be conserved and maintained so that their cultural-historical value does not diminish and so that their appearance and character do not deteriorate. Rebuilding and alterations to the exterior or interior must be approved by the Central Board of National Antiquities. Churches built later than 1940 may be protected in the same way if the Central Board so decides; of the 600 or so churches built after this date, 83 are now protected. This legal protection also applies to the land round a church, where it is forbidden to build or demolish buildings or the like without permission. If the church has a graveyard round it—which is the case with most old churches—the county administrative boards are responsible for these decisions.

There is a large and valuable collection of treasures in Swedish churches which is also protected by law. Among them are altar screens and altar pieces, crucifixes, wood carvings, fonts, chandeliers and candlesticks, epitaphs and shields, votive ships, organs, bells, textiles of various kinds and many other types of objects which have been purchased for or donated to the church for its religious services, for its decoration or for day-to-day maintenance. Thus articles for everyday use are also included. Other church treasures are old gravestones, including those in churchyard. The 1940 time limit does not apply to church treasures. In a modern church that is not protected by law there may therefore be both ancient and modern treasures that are protected.

Church treasures are to be well protected and cared for. Every parish must keep an inventory of objects of cultural-historical value. Responsibility for this inventory lies with the vicar and a church warden. Permission is required if a parish wishes to dispose of an object or remove it from the inventory. The same applies to repairs or alterations to an object, or if it is to be moved. The Central Board has the right to inspect church treasures and decide whether they should be included in the inventories.

The aim of the law is to give secure protection to the great cultural-historical values which churches and their treasures represent. They form a national cultural heritage which reflects almost 900 years of social development, spiritual life and religious activity, as well as artistic creativity. Swedish churches have an inestimable artistic and historical value even by international standards.

The primary responsibility for the conservation of churches and their treasures lies with the parishes. When work is to be done on buildings or their interiors which requires permission, the parishes have to draw up a proposal which is sent to the Central Board of National Antiquities for approval. This is usually done in cooperation with the county museum, which also usually provides cultural-historical assistance, supervision and documentation of the work. It may also be necessary to carry out scientific investigations, when, for example, old walls or wall paintings are revealed. When work is done under the ground—including under the floor of the church—the regulations concerning ancient monuments apply.

Some work requires the assistance of experts, for example, murals, textiles, organs and so on, and heavy costs are often involved in conservation and restoration work.

It is in the nature of things that the aims of the law to protect cultural-historical, artistic and architectural values may conflict with the wishes of the parishes to make changes which meet with the needs of today's religious services and parish life. This applies above all to church buildings and their permanent fixtures, for which changes and additions within reasonable limits have been accepted.

CHURCHYARDS

Churchyards and graveyards are protected by regulations in the Culture Heritage Act. As for churches, the general protection applies to churchyards and graveyards created before 1940. If the Central Board so decides, this protection may also be extended to establishments of a later date. State supervision and inspection are only to concern themselves with cultural-historical interests, which include artistic values. Supervision is the responsibility of the county administrative boards. General suitability, on the other hand, is the concern of the local building departments, as is permission in accordance with the Planning and Building Act to build a new cemetery.

Old churchyards and graveyards often have great cultural-historical value—apart from their value as the site of a church. Both the location of graves and the design of memorials may provide clear social-historical clues. Regional features are common, such as the wrought-iron crosses of the blacksmiths of Bergslagen and the granite monuments of the stonemasons of Bohuslän. A strict selection of gravestones and other memorials can be protected as church treasures by law.

Deserted churchyards, that is, churchyards that are no longer used for burials and where old graves are no longer maintained properly, are ancient monuments, and are subject to the relevant regulations.

When old churches are being restored, mural paintings often require specialist attention. Here late medieval ceiling paintings are being restored at Stora Skedvi Church in Dalarna.

Adolf Fredrik's Church in Stockholm was built between 1768 and 1787. Its facade, which for many years was greyish-yellow in colour, was painted white in typical Neo-classical style when the church was restored in 1992.

Acharius-Bergenstråhle's house in Vadstena is an example of a private historic building with a long history. The ground floor dates back to the 17th century and the upper floor to the late 18th century. The house was rebuilt in 1836 by C U Bergenstråhle, giving it its present appearance. After being used as a factory and an office it has now been restored.

At the end of 1991 1,041 privately-owned buildings and 385 state-owned buildings were listed as historic buildings—a small number compared to all the valuable cultural-historical buildings that exist. Apart from their richness, value and form, their distribution among counties and between town and country also depends on other factors; a historic building may have been listed, for example, because of potential threats to its existence or local initiative. Each historic building may include one or quite a number of buildings. (L120)

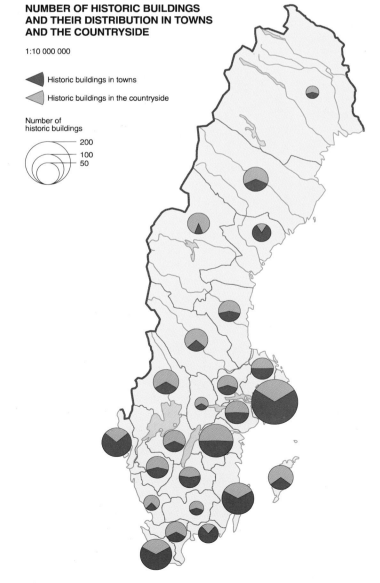

NUMBER OF HISTORIC BUILDINGS AND THEIR DISTRIBUTION IN TOWNS AND THE COUNTRYSIDE

1:10 000 000

◢ Historic buildings in towns

◣ Historic buildings in the countryside

Number of historic buildings
- 200
- 100
- 50

Historic Buildings

Most buildings are, of course, in some sense or other, of cultural-historical value—for example for those who built them or lived there or have other associations with them. The regulations protecting profane buildings are, however, in contrast to the general protection for ancient monuments and churches, extremely selective. This is mainly because the stock of buildings, in contrast to ancient monuments, is constantly being renewed, improved and altered, but also because the great range of forms, functions and designs is of great importance.

If one excludes traditional monumental buildings, it is true that for the great mass of everyday buildings the criteria for selecting and protecting them must be formulated clearly. One common criterion is their building-historical value, which is often connected with great age and rarity. Usually it is also demanded that they represent something more than themselves; they should be typical of their period and place, which as a rule means that they have to be in a fairly original state, preferably also well preserved. These simple factors alone limit the choice.

Thus there is between architectonic monuments and everyday houses a wide spectrum ranging from the unique to the representative, and from the original to those which have successively been changed. In addition, social, esthetic, functional and

Axel Oxenstierna's Palace in Storkyrkobrinken is one of the noblemen's palaces in Stockholm that is now a state-owned historic building. It was built 1653.

technical scales of value are of great importance, as are personal factors concerning builders and architects, owners and occupiers. Finally, most buildings form part of a whole of some kind, whose origin, design and condition also affect their cultural-historical value.

Of the total stock of built-up real estate in Sweden about five or six per cent is roughly calculated to be of cultural-historical interest in a limited sense. This may seem to be a small percentage, but it corresponds to about 150,000 objects, which gives some idea of the size and difficulty of the problem of evaluating them. It is also difficult to judge how many of them might be considered for listing as historic buildings, since no complete inventories exist. However, a preliminary estimate seems to suggest that between 4,000 and 5,000 objects meet the cultural-historical requirements for listing. This also shows that the requirements of the law are restrictive.

LEGISLATION

European legislation concerning building protection is based on French legislation in this field. The bill of antiquities of the 1660s was an expression of interest in monumental buildings. In the 18th and 19th centuries institutes and regulations were further developed, but they were for the same categories of buildings.

The 1920 government directives concerning public buildings gave a limited number of state-owned buildings—mainly of a monumental character—permanent protection. These buildings and the like varied greatly in character, ranging from the royal palace and the royal theatre in Stockholm to lighthouses and military storehouses.

Not until 1942, later than in Norway and Denmark, for example, did Sweden pass a law protecting noteworthy buildings owned privately or by municipalities. This law required the owner's agreement before a building could be listed.

An enquiry was followed by a new law on historic buildings that was first enforced in 1961. If a building or the like was to be listed, it had to be "particularly noteworthy". Now, however, it was possible to list a building against the owner's will, but this could, in certain cases, entitle the owner to compensation from the state.

1 Utmeland, the Vasa monument erected in 1860 at the 300th anniversary of the death of Gustav Vasa.

2 Ornäs, a loft house connected with Gustav Vasa's adventures in 1520.

3 Uppsala: Geijersgården. The home of Erik Gustaf Geijer, 1837–46.
Linnaeus' garden: Carl Linnaeus (von Linné) restored this garden, created by Olof Rudbeck in 1635.

4 Linnaeus' Hammarby, a country house purchased by Carl Linnaeus in 1758.

5 Mora Stones, an 18th-century building with memorial stones of royal elections.

6 Växjö: Östrabo Bishop's Palace, the home of Esaias Tegnér, 1824–46.
The Old Deanery: Pär Lagerkvist's father grew up here, described in the novel "Gäst hos verkligheten".

7 Höjentorp, the country home of Jonas Alströmer and his family, 1735–1832.

8 Isala, the King's Barn, connected with Gustav Vasa's adventures.

9 Rankhyttan, The King's Barn; Gustav Vasa stayed here in 1520.

10 Grisslehamn, Albert Engström's studio, 1906–40.

11 Stockholm: Bellevue House, built in 1757 for the royal painter Johan Pasch; in the park Carl Eldh's studio, built in 1918.
Södermalm, Christian Eriksson's house and studio.
Bellman's House, the home of Carl Michael Bellman, 1770–74
The Thielska Gallery, built in 1906 by Ernest Thiel.
The Old Town, Latona 11, where the artist Carl Larsson was born in 1853.

12 Solna, Annelund, bought in 1822 by Per Henrik Ling, "the father of Swedish gymnastics".

13 Saltsjöbaden, "the Bee Hive", a summer villa built in 1922 for Ernest Thiel.

14 Dalarö, Eva Bonnier's summer home and studio.

15 Vaxholm, Villa Akleja, the home and studio of JAG Acke, 1901–24.

16 Torsvi, JAG Acke's summer home, 1914–20.

17 Vadstena: The Convent of St Birgitta, begun in the 1380s and consecrated in 1430.
Acharii-Bergenstråhle's House, owned by the biologist and physician Eric Acharius, 1810–19.

18 Linköping, Onkel Adam's House; C A Wetterberg (1808–89) (Onkel Adam) lived here.

19 Övralid, home of the writer Verner von Heidenstam, 1923–40.

20 Strand, home of the writer Ellen Key, 1911–26.

21 Råshult, rector's house, birthplace of Linnaeus (1707).

22 Snugge, the birthplace of the singer Christina Nilsson (1843).

23 Borgholm: Lilla Nyborg, the artist Vera Nilsson's studio around 1910–20.

24 Ebbestorp, manor house, built 1799–1800 by the artist and travel-writer J C Linnerhielm.

25 Visby, Villa Muramaris, built 1915–16 by Prof. Johnny Roosval and his sculptress wife, Ellen.

26 Skärva, manor house, built by Admiral F H af Chapman, who owned it 1785–1806.

27 Lund: Karl XII's House; the king lived here 1716–18.
Zettervall's Villa, built in 1871 by Helgo Zettervall

28 Svaneholm Castle, given in 1782 to Rutger Maclean, whose reforms led to the redistribution of land in 1803.

29 Göteborg: Gathenhielm's House, built in 1740 on land granted to the privateer Lars Gathenhielm.
Chalmers' House, built in 1805–07 for William Chalmers, Director of the East India Company.

30 Kungälv, "Thorild's House", where the poet Thomas Thorild went to school, 1767–72.

31 Lysekil, villas built in 1873 and 1878 by Carl Curman, doctor at the spa.

32 Alingsås, Alströmer's Storehouse, built in 1731 by Jonas Alströmer.

33 Dagsnäs, manor house built in the 1770s by the amateur archeologist Per Tham.

34 Karlstad, Freemason's Lodge, built in 1869. The Union with Norway was dissolved here in 1905.

35 Östervik, chapel built in 1869–71 with a farm dairy built in 1892, the studio of the sculptor E Rafael-Rådberg, 1922–60.

36 Mårbacka, manor house built in 1796, birthplace of Selma Lagerlöf, rebuilt 1921–23.

37 Ransäter, mill-owner's mansion built in 1750. Erik Gustaf Geijer was born here in 1763.

38 Långban, mill-owner's mansion built in 1783. Nils and John Ericsson were born here in 1802 and 1803.

39 Holmedal, guest house where Karl XII is said to have spent the night before invading Norway.

40 Alster, manor house built in 1772. Gustaf Fröding was born here in 1860.

41 Säffle, Karl XII's storehouse, said to have been used by the army in 1718.

42 Ljung, castle built in 1774 by Axel von Fersen the Elder.

43 Göksholm, castle from the late Middle Ages; Engelbrekt was murdered here in 1436.

44 Karlbo, Tolvmansgården, late 18th century. Erik Axel Karlfeldt was born here in 1864.

45 Åkerö, castle built by Carl Gustaf Tessin in the 1750s.

46 Sjurberg, Tånggården, from 1908 owned by the architect Isak Gustaf Clason and rebuilt in the national romantic style.

47 Brunnsvik, Storgården, bought in 1897 by Karl-Erik Forsslund, who made it a cultural centre.

48 Sveden, two-room cottage from about 1730. Linnaeus married Sara Moraea here in 1739.

49 Sundborn, Carl Larsson's home. He lived here from 1901.

50 Fröson, Sommarhagen, built in 1914 by the composer Wilhelm Peterson-Berger as a summer villa, later his home.

51 Karesuando, "Laestadii Pörte", log cabin used by the revivalist preacher Lars Levi Laestadius (1800–1861).

HISTORIC BUILDINGS CONNECTED WITH WELL-KNOWN PERSONS OR EVENTS

1:10 000 000

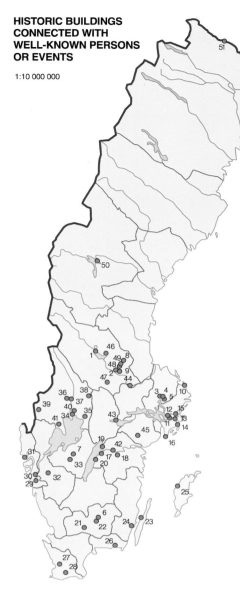

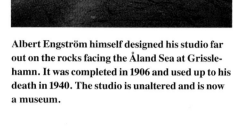

Albert Engström himself designed his studio far out on the rocks facing the Åland Sea at Grisslehamn. It was completed in 1906 and used up to his death in 1940. The studio is unaltered and is now a museum.

All historic buildings have associations with historic persons, of course. We have presented some 60 objects which are connected with people who were famous in various, mainly cultural, fields. (L121)

The present Culture Heritage Act dated 1988 regulates the terms of protection for the most valuable buildings owned privately or by municipalities. At the same time the 1920 directives for state-owned historic buildings were replaced by a new regulation, and both statutes prescribed the same terms.

APPLICATION

For a building to be listed it has to be "particularly noteworthy on account of its cultural-historical value" or be part of "a particularly noteworthy architectural area". Thus the term "particularly noteworthy" has been taken over from the previous law, but has been much debated. Parks, gardens, bridges and other such structures can be listed. Decisions concerning historic buildings owned privately or by municipalities are made by the county administrative boards, and any private person can suggest to a county board that a certain building should be listed. Decisions concerning state-owned historic buildings are made by the government on the recommendations of the Central Board of National Antiquities.

For each historic building special protective rules are drawn up in consultation with the owner and the administrative authority (for state buildings) respectively. These can apply to individual buildings or groups of buildings. Listing can also apply to a whole building or parts of a building, such as the exterior, the ground plan and the permanent fixtures. Surrounding land can also be included.

Historic buildings should reflect the living and working conditions of various periods, social systems and social conditions, architecture, esthetic standards and so on, and the selection should be based both on regional features and on the country as a whole.

By the end of 1991 some 1,100 buildings and the like owned privately or by municipalities had been listed as historic buildings. They comprise a wide range of buildings: castles and manor houses; villages, farms and crofts; vicarages and "church towns"; merchant, trade and craft premises: ironworks, smelting works, mills and other industrial buildings, including workers' dwellings; fishing villages and a lot of other buildings.

The number of state-owned historic buildings is about 400, but many of them include several buildings. Among them are the royal palaces and the Vasa castles, former noblemen's palaces, fortresses, royal demesnes, official residences, courthouses, university buildings and other types of buildings.

- ● Closed village or hamlet
- ● Single farm
- ● Croft or cottage
- ● Farm building
- ● Mill

Norrboda in Ore, Da-
larna, consists of two
farms but looks like
a hamlet. Twenty-sev-
en of 39 timber houses
have been preserved.
The oldest ones are
from the first half of
the 17th century.

HISTORIC BUILDINGS IN AGRARIAN SETTINGS

About 180 historic buildings are farm buildings or at least
stand in the countryside. About two thirds of them consist
of isolated farms, about ten of them are whole or almost
whole hamlets, another ten or so are crofts or the like,
23 consist of isolated barns or the like and 21 are mills.

The distinction between villages, hamlets and farms is
not very clear. Some isolated old farms with multi-build-
ings system look somewhat like hamlets, for example Hö-
gen in Lillhärdal, Härjedalen. Some hamlets probably
arose from farms that were divided, for example Äskhult
in Halland. Several single farms form part of partly-pre-
served village environments, for example in Dalarna and
Småland, which increases the value of the whole village,
of course. Many farms represent regional variants of high
quality, for example the farms on Gotland built of limestone and the southern and northern Swedish farms with
enclosed courtyards.

Both farm labourers' crofts and soldiers' crofts are represented, as well as a labourers' barracks. Half of the farm
buildings are not primarily of an agrarian nature, since
they are parish or Crown storehouses or the like. Fifteen
of the mills are windmills, most of them in Skåne and adjacent provinces; the remainder are watermills.

Gaustäde Farm in Bunge on Gotland, which is built completely in stone,
grew up up from the Middle Ages until 1865. The farmhouse is an 18th-
century double cottage. The picture shows the long barn, whose oldest
part is medieval.

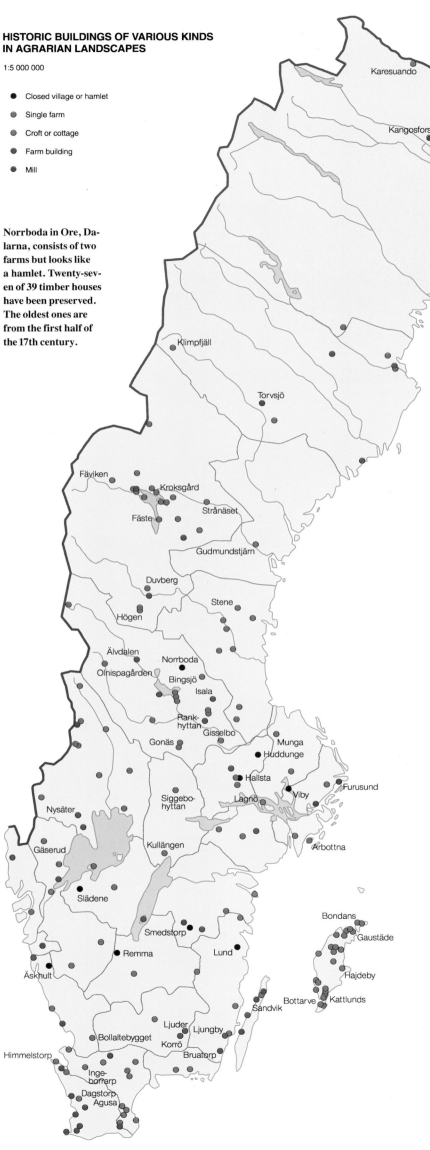

The former Svea Cinema in Sundsvall was built to the design
of Ragnar Östberg in 1911; it is now used as a billiard hall.

About the year 1900 public baths were built in many Swedish towns. The heated baths in Karlskrona,
which were built in 1903–04 to the design of Wilhelm Klemming, are typical; here, the first-class pool.

1 Stockholm:
  The Royal Opera House
  The Royal Dramatic Theatre
  The South Theatre and
  Bowling Alley
  The Circus
  Oscar's Theatre
  The Sture Baths
  Bern's Saloons
  The C Hall at the Tennis
  Stadium
  The Stadium
2 Drottningholm:
  Drottningholm Theatre
  The bathing house at the
  palace
3 Växjö Old Theatre
4 Kalmar Theatre
5 The Great Theatre, Göteborg
6 Karlstad Theatre
7 Örebro Old Theatre
8 Gävle Theatre
9 Sundsvall:
  Sundsvall Theatre
  The former Svea cinema
  Hotel Knaust
10 Norrköping:
  Norrköping Theatre
  The Ling Hall
11 Östersund Old Theatre
12 The Theatre Barn, Hedemora
13 Dalarö:
  The Club House
  Villa Jungfruberget
14 The Club House, Varberg
15 The Club House, Marstrand
16 Uppsala, the Health Spa
17 Karlskrona, the Bathing House
  at the Naval Harbour
18 Medevi Spa
19 Flistad's Spa
20 Himmelstadlund's Spa
21 Gustafsberg, the bathing resort
22 Ramlösa Spa
23 Gustaf's Well, Kallebäck
24 Mösseberg's Sanatorium
25 Sala, the former public baths
26 Vilan:
  The Club House at Hvilan's
  Hydro
  The Gymnastics Hall at Hvilan's Folk High School
27 Karlsborg's Garrison Hotel

28 Rönnebo, a former boarding-
  house in Trosa
29 Åmål Town Hotel
30 Hotel Billingen, Skövde
31 Kristinehamn Town Hotel
32 Västerås Town Hotel
33 Falun:
  Grand Hotel
  Hammar's Coffee House
34 The Doctor's House at Åre,
  previously a boarding-house
35 The Railway Hotel, Storuman
36 Marholmen's Holiday Home
37 The restaurant Stallmästargår-
  den, Solna
38 The former inn at Söderfors
  Ironworks
39 Ekolsund's Inn
40 Bötterum's former inn
41 Hede Inn, Tanum
42 Klev's Inn, Mårdaklev
43 The inn at Överhörnäs
44 The King's Hunting Lodge,
  Ottenby
45 Villa Gustafshäll, Boo
46 Villa Gransäter, Gustavsberg
47 Lidingö:
  Apelsinvillan
  Villa Finedal
  Villa Högudden
48 Lunda Villa, Lovö
49 Villa Finntorp, Nacka
50 Beehive Villa, Saltsjöbaden
51 Abborreberg House, Lindö
52 Borgholm:
  Wollin's Villa
  Gerlofsson's Villa
  Per Ekström's Villa
53 Villa Muramaris outside Visby
54 Oretorp Hunting Lodge, Maltesholm
55 Petersson-Berger's Sommarhagen on Frösön
56 English Hunting Lodge, Bod-
  sjöedet
57 Old Gymnastics Hall, Strängnäs
58 The High School Gymnastics
  Hall, Linköping
59 The Gymnastics Hall at Karl
  XII's House, Lund
60 Norrbyskär's Bowling Alley

The historic buildings that are now used as local
museums and folklore museums might well be
included in the category of buildings in the entertainment and leisure sector. Since they were built
for other purposes, however, they are not
included here. (L123)

Interior of Siggebohyttan, a foundry-owner's
home in Linde, Västmanland, which is now used
as a local museum. It was built in 1780–1800 —
a long, timbered, two-storeyed building with an
outside gallery and a turfed roof.

**HISTORIC BUILDINGS
USED FOR RECREATION,
ENTERTAINMENT,
LEISURE, TOURISM**

1:10 000 000

- Theatre, cinema
- Seaside resort, spa,
  baths, club-house
- Hotel, holiday
  home, restaurant,
  coffee-house
- Summer
  residence,
  hunting lodge
- Sports
  ground,
  gymnasium,
  tennis hall

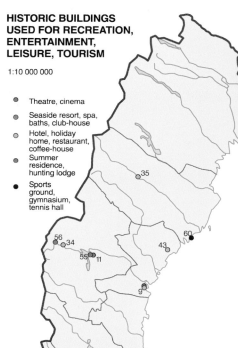

Historic buildings not owned by the state are distributed fairly evenly among the various categories of buildings. If a comparison were made with
the total number of buildings, however, the distribution would be considerably less even; agrarian
buildings and town dwellings in particular would
be under-represented.

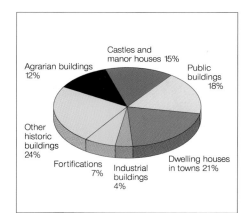

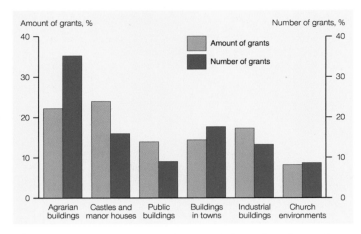

Amount of grants, %   Number of grants, %

- Amount of grants
- Number of grants

Agrarian buildings | Castles and manor houses | Public buildings | Buildings in towns | Industrial buildings | Church environments

The way in which the total amount of grants and the number of grants for building conservation are distributed among the various categories differs in some cases. During the period 1981/82–1991/92 a total of SEK 204.5 million was allocated at an average cost of almost SEK 59,000 per object. Public buildings have the highest average cost per object (c. 90,000) and agrarian buildings the lowest (c. 37,000). The former group consists of 316 objects and the latter of 1,225 objects.

The distribution of grants among counties during the same period is fairly uneven, both in total amount and number. The number of grants is larger than the number of objects, since some objects have received grants for several years. Two counties have considerably higher average figures per grant than the rest: Göteborg och Bohus county with about 108,000 and Västmanland county with about 86,000, and two have considerably lower average figures: Kronoberg and Halland counties with 21–22,000 each.

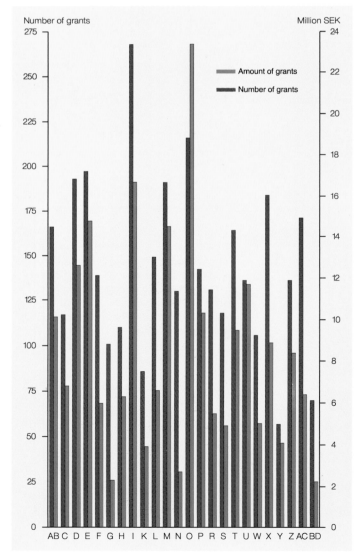

Number of grants   Million SEK

- Amount of grants
- Number of grants

A B C D E F G H I K L M N O P R S T U W X Y Z AC BD

Grants for Building Conservation

State grants for the conservation and maintenance of buildings of cultural-historical value are a relatively recent innovation. Small grants could be made in the late 19th century after special resolutions by the Riksdag. Since 1880 the national budget has included a permanent grant for "the conservation and maintenance of the ruins of Visby". As a result of the 1942 law on historic buildings this grant was changed in the mid–1940s, so that it applied to conservation throughout the country. At that time it amounted to SEK 30,000. Grants from donations were also important.

Even though the state allocation was increased to compensate for the decline in the value of money, a special commission pointed out in 1979 that it was totally inadequate and proposed a large increase to deal with the

most urgent problems. The allocation has thereafter increased successively and in the 1991/1992 budget year a little more than SEK 31 million was allocated for conservation and maintenance.

Grants can be applied for to cover the extra cost of construction work for cultural-historical purposes, and the cost of commissioning experts for surveying, planning and executing the work. Applications are made to the county administrative boards, which from the 1993/94 budget year also make the decisions. The need for grants is, however, far greater than the amount of money available. The changes in business life and public administration which are at present in progress can be expected to increase the need even more.

Owners of apartment houses of cultural-historical value can also receive financial assistance for reconstruction, for example, or for reinforcing foundations, in the form of cultural grants, which have replaced a previous system of favourable loans. The 1993/94 budget allocated SEK 160 million for such purposes.

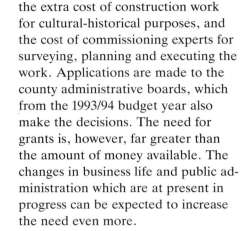

Bollaltebygget in Knäred in the forest district of Halland is an enclosed four-sided farm built of timber and post and planking, with its oldest parts dating back to the 18th century. The thatched farmhouse is of the south-Geatish type with a ridged cottage and two storehouses. The roof was re-thatched in stages with the help of building preservation grants between 1982 and 1987. The last farmer-occupant (left) left it in 1935, but was still able to take part in the work.

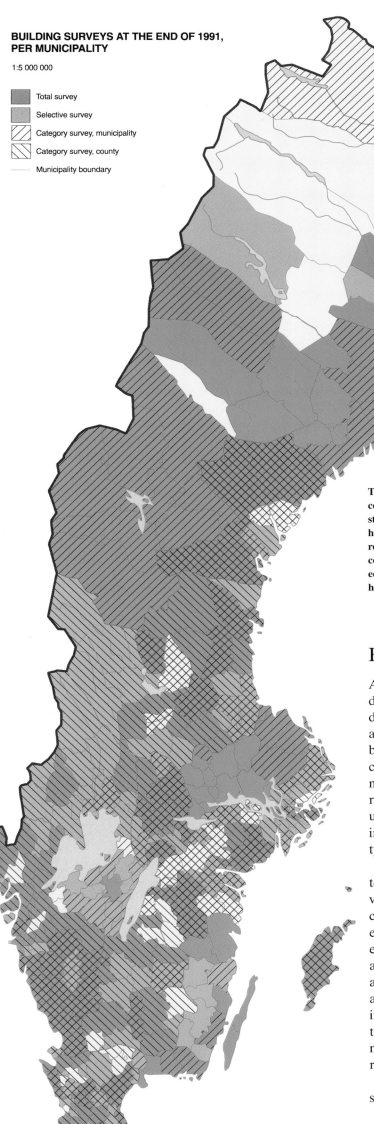

- ▨ Total survey
- ▧ Selective survey
- ▨ Category survey, municipality
- ▨ Category survey, county
- — Municipality boundary

Total surveying means that all the properties and buildings in one area, for example a parish, a town district or a municipality are documented. This method is relatively expensive but has been used in some counties and municipalities.

Selective surveying means that within a given area only properties and buildings deemed to be of cultural-historical interest are documented. It is important that the criteria for these decisions are reported. Surveys of this kind have been carried out in many parts of the country.

Category surveying means that all the buildings in a certain category, usually throughout the country, are documented. Such surveys have become more common and have embraced old pharmacies, public baths, cinemas, breweries, prisons, tanneries, mines, railway stations and power stations. Local category surveys also exist.

The Lion Chemist's in Malmö has its ornamented premises from 1898 still very well preserved.

The standard of surveys varies from county to county and within counties. If a municipality is stated to have both total and selective surveys, it has been interpreted to mean that the former has replaced the latter. As far as category surveys are concerned, only their existence has been recorded. National category surveys are not included here. (L124)

Building Surveys

Art and architecture historians have devoted great care for many years to documenting castles, manor houses and church buildings. This has often been in the form of documenting as carefully as possible selected monumental buildings. This work has often resulted in a monograph. It was not until recent years that more general inventories of, for example, different types of churches, were made.

After 1910 the newly-awakened interest in old peasant culture led to investigations of buildings in the countryside. This interest was directed in the first place at relict areas with especially old building constructions and buildings from the 18th century and earlier. This documentation was also fairly detailed, but more general inventories of, for example, various types of timbered buildings were also made. In towns, too, some inventories were made of old buildings.

It was not until the 1960s that more systematic and general inventories of profane buildings were made. Work on national physical planning in the early 1970s revealed a large pent-up need in this field. Inventories of buildings were therefore a necessary instrument in the subsequent municipal and regional culture heritage preservation programs. The municipalities were also directly interested in getting information about buildings, both general for overall planning and more detailed for dealing with building permits and detailed development plans. The early inventories often had a primary scientific purpose, whereas most of those made today are related to town planning in one way or another.

Most inventories of buildings are nowadays financed by municipalities. Many of them are commissioned by municipalities and carried out by regional and municipal museums. National inventories of more unusual types of buildings have usually been financed by the Central Board of National Antiquities. Inventories are often published as a report with accompanying maps and photographs.

Planning with Knowledge

Until late in the 20th century it was reasonable to see Sweden as an agrarian society involved in a slow process of change. In this fairly stable setting the interests of cultural heritage preservation were centred on individual objects whose value could be related to a long, legitimate tradition or were based on dominant evaluations of a social or esthetic nature.

When the transition to an urbanised society after the middle of the century became a reality for an increasingly large majority of people, it became obvious that the physical environment is not a stable background to developments but a dynamic part of them. Against this background attitudes towards culture monument preservation broadened in several ways. The objects that were worthy of preservation were seen to be parts of the cultural environment where in fact they had always belonged, and people could also see that these valuable cultural environments existed even where individual objects in the traditional sense were not particularly noteworthy. Furthermore, people gradually became aware of the fact that the whole landscape has to be seen as a cultural heritage which we all hold in trust.

Our efforts to protect our cultural heritage have thus acquired two new dimensions: culture environment preservation as concern for the organically developed *totalities in the cultural environment*, and culture environment preservation as an overall term for the *ideology of trusteeship* which ought to characterise our management of the cultural heritage and which comprises all activities directed towards this goal. In this context the more specific first aspect has been more in focus, but the second will be decisive for the way in which cultural protection can interact with social development in general.

PLANNING AS A TOOL

Concern for the cultural values of the environment has to play a part in all decisions that involve changes to the physical environment. Culture environment preservation has therefore been integrated with physical planning. This is a system for preparing decisions on land and buildings that concern many different parties and which therefore need to be coordinated. Planning should utilise knowledge of the external environment and of needs and interests in changing it, so that coordination and balancing of different interests can take place in open, democratic forms. The cultural values of the environment are a resource that needs to be utilised as actively as changes and additions to the environment are dealt with.

Knowledge of the cultural values of the environment must be effectively included in the material used for municipal planning if cultural environmental interests are to be taken into account there. This need has encouraged the development of *culture heritage preservation programmes.*

These programmes summarise for a municipality or a county the knowledge of cultural environments that has been collected by new inventories, local research, investigations and the like. They usually begin with a chronological overview of cultural history and traces of it in the landscape, and then report on each individual area where these traces characterise the landscape and buildings in the municipality.

Beside their importance for physical planning, cultural-heritage programmes also play an important role for one of the main aims of cultural-environmental protection: to make the cultural heritage a living and accessible resource for everyone.

LAWS

The Planning and Building Act (PBL), which was passed in 1987, places the main responsibility for planning and the external environment with the municipalities.

The Natural Resources Act (NRL) of the same year ties together twelve different land and environmental laws with planning and states that this should safeguard the resources which the existing environment contains, including their cultural values: "Areas that are of importance in a general way because of their cultural values should as far as possible be protected from any action that may noticeably affect the cultural environment."

A map accompanying a description of a cultural environment in a municipal culture heritage preservation programme may look like the one for Kungsåra church village in Västerås. The values inside the environment boundary lines are specified in the text, but places worthy of protection outside the boundary may also be marked on the map.

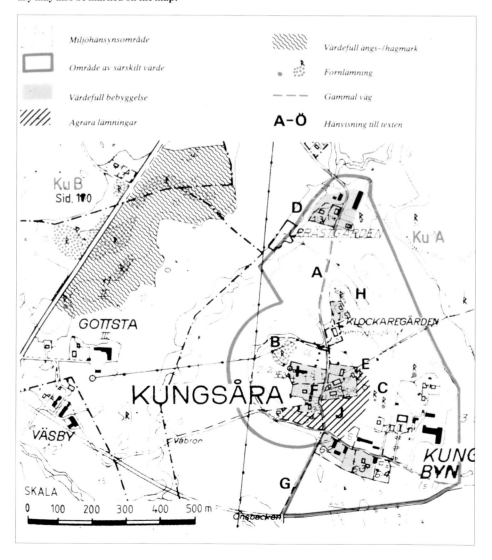

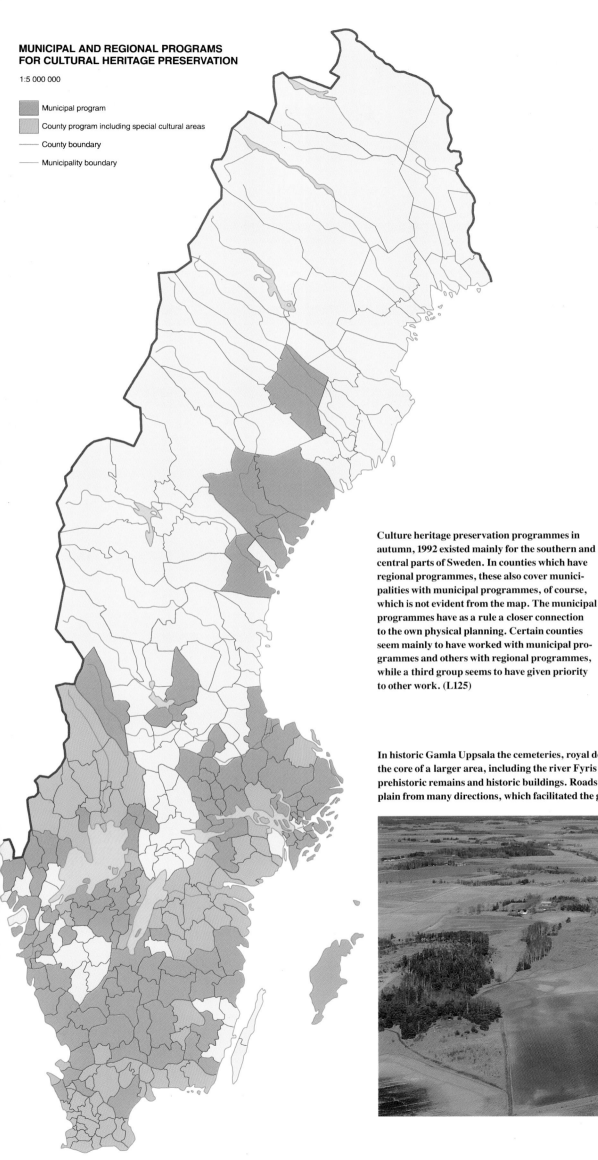

MUNICIPAL AND REGIONAL PROGRAMS FOR CULTURAL HERITAGE PRESERVATION

1:5 000 000

- Municipal program
- County program including special cultural areas
- County boundary
- Municipality boundary

Areas of national interest are included in an absolute requirement that they are protected from such action.

Thus the NRL does not protect areas from changes in general but prevents any action that might noticeably damage cultural-environmental values. If this law is to be effective, it is essential to clarify what values are involved. This is where culture heritage preservation programmes can play a part.

AREAS OF NATIONAL INTEREST

The NRL speaks of areas of national interest to indicate that certain interests in the use of land are not merely local (municipal), but are of general importance for everybody. Here the state still has some influence left on municipal planning.

The 1974 bill on culture and politics establishes that cultural-environmental preservation should throw light on the ways in which the history of Sweden is expressed in environments that depict the life and conditions of previous generations. Special emphasis is placed on the whole country and all its people being included. Areas which are of importance from a national point of view are listed as areas of national interest for cultural-environmental preservation.

The Central Board of National Antiquities (RAÄ) should specify what is of national interest for cultural-environmental preservation according to the NRL. A catalogue containing brief descriptions of the 1,702 areas of national interest was published by RAÄ in 1990.

Culture heritage preservation programmes in autumn, 1992 existed mainly for the southern and central parts of Sweden. In counties which have regional programmes, these also cover municipalities with municipal programmes, of course, which is not evident from the map. The municipal programmes have as a rule a closer connection to the own physical planning. Certain counties seem mainly to have worked with municipal programmes and others with regional programmes, while a third group seems to have given priority to other work. (L125)

In historic Gamla Uppsala the cemeteries, royal demesne, church village and archbishop's church are the core of a larger area, including the river Fyris and the open cultural landscape of the plain, rich in prehistoric remains and historic buildings. Roads and fairways by land and water led to this central plain from many directions, which facilitated the growth of a central power.

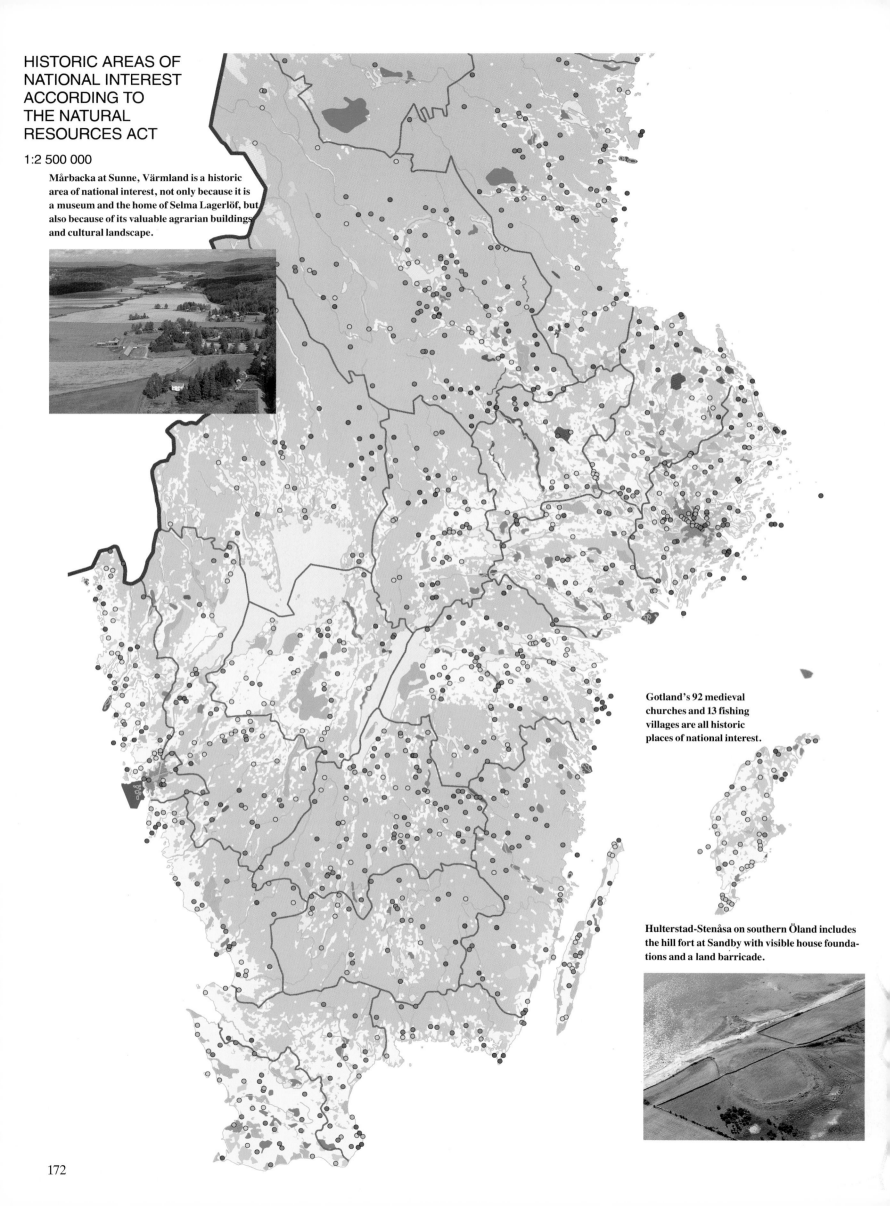

HISTORIC AREAS OF NATIONAL INTEREST ACCORDING TO THE NATURAL RESOURCES ACT

1:2 500 000

Mårbacka at Sunne, Värmland is a historic area of national interest, not only because it is a museum and the home of Selma Lagerlöf, but also because of its valuable agrarian buildings and cultural landscape.

Gotland's 92 medieval churches and 13 fishing villages are all historic places of national interest.

Hulterstad-Stenåsa on southern Öland includes the hill fort at Sandby with visible house foundations and a land barricade.

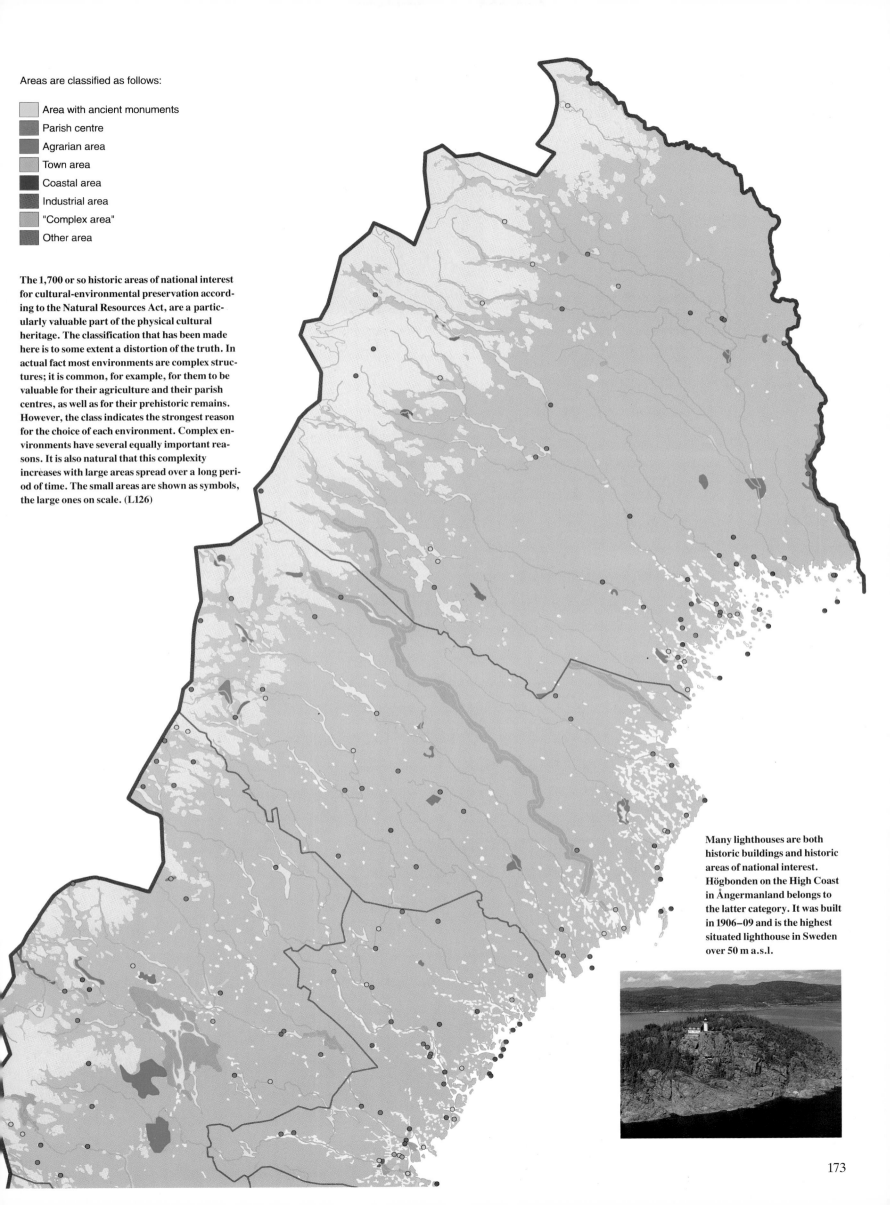

Areas are classified as follows:

- Area with ancient monuments
- Parish centre
- Agrarian area
- Town area
- Coastal area
- Industrial area
- "Complex area"
- Other area

The 1,700 or so historic areas of national interest for cultural-environmental preservation according to the Natural Resources Act, are a particularly valuable part of the physical cultural heritage. The classification that has been made here is to some extent a distortion of the truth. In actual fact most environments are complex structures; it is common, for example, for them to be valuable for their agriculture and their parish centres, as well as for their prehistoric remains. However, the class indicates the strongest reason for the choice of each environment. Complex environments have several equally important reasons. It is also natural that this complexity increases with large areas spread over a long period of time. The small areas are shown as symbols, the large ones on scale. (L126)

Many lighthouses are both historic buildings and historic areas of national interest. Högbonden on the High Coast in Ångermanland belongs to the latter category. It was built in 1906–09 and is the highest situated lighthouse in Sweden over 50 m a.s.l.

Culture-Environment Preservation in Physical Planning

Our environment carries with it our cultural heritage and should be safe-guarded so that its manifestations last for as long as possible. At the same time the environment has to function in a changing society and give something in return to those who look after it—property owners and society. This conflict between preservation and change is solved by planning legislation which lays down that the owner of property is obliged to take care of the environment in a way that corresponds to its cultural values. However, if this means that "existing land use is severely affected", that is, it leads to financial burdens on the property, he is entitled to compensation.

These requirements apply in principle to all properties, but are only to be enforced where they are justified by cultural values. The purpose of planning is to find solutions which combine concern for cultural values with a reasonably profitable use of the property involved. In this respect the PBL states that "both private and public interests should be considered". Thus the authorities and property owners must cooperate to find mutually acceptable solutions.

Ancient monuments, churches and historic buildings are protected by the Culture Heritage Act regardless of what planning according to the PBL results in and regardless of whether the object lies within or outside a listed environment.

PLANNING

Since 1990 all municipalities must have a comprehensive plan showing the municipalities' intentions with regard to land use and buildings. This plan should also indicate how national interests of various kinds are to be provided for.

Comprehensive plans are approved by the municipal councils and should guide the municipalities in their decisions concerning land use and buildings. Comprehensive plans should also guide decisions relating to the twelve land and environment laws which the NRL connects with physical planning. As a result the municipalities can also influence decisions made in accordance with these laws, which in most cases are made by state authorities.

Nämforsen in the river Ångermanälven, with its nearly 2,000 rock carvings on the islands, was the first touchstone of environmental policy towards ancient monuments. The planned dam right across the rapids was never built, so it is still possible to see the carvings and the rushing water.

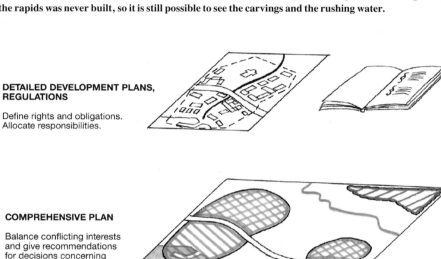

DETAILED DEVELOPMENT PLANS, REGULATIONS

Define rights and obligations. Allocate responsibilities.

COMPREHENSIVE PLAN

Balance conflicting interests and give recommendations for decisions concerning land (water) and buildings.

CULTURE HERITAGE PRESERVATION PROGRAM

Provide information on areas of cultural value, define areas needing protection, may form part of a comprehensive plan.

SURVEYS

A municipality documents the history contents and value of an environment.

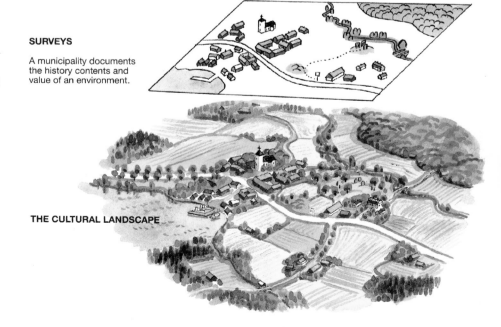

THE CULTURAL LANDSCAPE

The 1950s Stockholm suburb of Vällingby has become a historic area of national interest as an international reference for what is called its ABC structure (ABC = Work, Housing, Centre) round the centrally located underground railway. In the outlying parks there are also a few hidden remains of the old agrarian landscape.

AREAS OF NATIONAL INTEREST IN THE COUNTY OF VÄRMLAND REGISTERED IN DETAILED DEVELOPMENT PLAN OR AREA REGULATIONS

1: 2 500 000

● Area of National Interest registered in detailed development plan

▲ Area of National Interest registered in area regulations

▢ Other area of National Interest

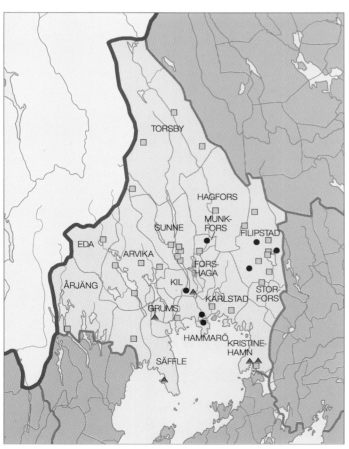

Area regulations and detailed development plans have, up to now, been used to protect relatively few historic areas of national interest. The historic areas of national interest in Värmland are also mostly rather small in area. (L127)

EXECUTION

A comprehensive plan which covers the whole of a municipality is of necessity rather a clumsy instrument. In order to specify the intentions in an area of special cultural interest, a municipality may draw up a more detailed plan, in principle as detailed as necessary. However, it is still only society's intentions that are expressed, and they must then be coordinated with the intentions of the property owners in the relevant areas.

The most important point, of course, is the property owners' involvement in concern for cultural values in the environment they administer. The opportunities given by legislation for culture environment preservation must be seen as complementary to this involvement. In order to achieve coordination and shared responsibility for mutual interests in a fair way, the laws support three approaches: information, dialogue and regulations.

Information. Many land and environment laws, like the Culture Heritage Act, contain "paragraphs of concern" which support cultural values in the environment. Even though they are not backed up by requirements for permission, they give each property owner responsibility for paying concern to cultural values in their property. The way in which they live up to this responsibility is, of course,

dependent on their being able to understand these values and the demands they make. Thus pure information is an important way of seeing that the law is applied.

Regulation. When many interests conflict, or where claims for the protection of the environment are very far-reaching, the community is responsible for coordinating them in an organised form. This can be achieved in detailed development plans and in area regulations in accordance with the PBL, or in nature reserves, for example, in accordance with the Nature Conservation Act. The general requirements of the law are then given a legally binding interpretation in the areas that are to be regulated. If the claims are so far-reaching that "existing land use is severely affected", regulations of this kind are necessary.

Dialogue. An intermediate form between information and regulation is an application for permission to undertake certain action. These applications may be made in all the twelve laws that the NRL ties up with physical planning. They make it possible for both public and private interests to be satisfied with regard to the action that the applicant requests permission for. The advantage is that society can influence the decision in a more flexible way than through regulation with its binding rules.

This model has been developed furthest in the PBL, which allows requirements for permission to vary according to the need for influence in each individual case. Thus external alterations to buildings outside the detailed development plan do not require permission, unless the municipality has specified this in area regulations because of an environment's special value. By requiring permission, a municipality can indicate what actions require special attention from a cultural-historical point of view.

The technique of varying the need for permission is an interesting one, but it has been expressed in a way that makes culture enviroment preservation difficult to handle, and after five years the method has not been generally adopted. The map of the county of Värmland illustrates the fact that culture environment preservation in town and country planning is being developed but still has some way to go before it finds satisfactory forms of expression.

Culture Environment Preservation in a European Future

The period since the Second World War has been characterised by great social changes, which have radically affected the physical and social environment. These changes have been accompanied by increased public awareness of the importance of the environment for the individual, but also for the identity of the local community and society in general. The size of the changes has also underlined the need of development from cultural monument protection, aimed at individual objects, to culture environment preservation, which will work actively for careful conservation and historical continuity in the whole of society.

National physical planning in the 1970s introduced new criteria for as-

sessing cultural values. Previously, qualitative concepts such as "particularly noteworthy" or "of cultural-historical value" had been used. Now we have a clearer awareness of spatial values and a clearer hierarchy for assessment and conservation. Behind this lies a clearer realisation of the need for quantitative data and consideration for representative factors for large and small areas and regions.

Today we need to raise our sights even more in order to see the cultural heritage within Sweden in a wider Scandinavian and European, or even for certain purposes, a global perspective. There are several reasons for this.

One is, of course, the increase in European and international cooperation and the increased international orientation that individuals and organisations have today. Another is the necessity of using sparingly the resources that can be set aside for preservation and care of cultural values.

The main reason, however, is that Sweden has a special responsibility for protecting and caring for those parts of our cultural heritage that are of international importance, such as structures or settings that are common here but less frequent on the continent. This is the result of Sweden being a late-developing, sparsely-populated peripheral country in a global context. For these very reasons we have a great deal preserved here that may already have vanished from other parts of the world.

The international perspective feels strange both for those working professionally in culture environment preservation and for people in general. One reason is that in the past it has been above all the great monuments around the world that have been the focus of often esthetically-based interests. Now that attention is being directed more and more towards the cultural heritage as an expresssion of the special features of different periods and areas, we see that there are in Sweden a number of features that are of international value both from a cultural and from a scientific point of view.

This is true of the *Norrland hunting culture*, which we can follow through the whole of prehistoric time and

The offices of the Central Board of National Antiquities are quite rightly in a historic building, a regimental barracks very close to the previous military exercise grounds at Ladugårdsgärde. It was built in the early 19th century for the Horse Guards to the design of Fredrik Blom. On Culture Houses' Day in 1993 it was natural to remind people of the building's military background.

whose basis, hunting and fishing, has been continued in historic times as important parts of the economic life of Norrland. There are numerous relics of this culture all over the Norrland region, which provides unusually favourable conditions for studying and experiencing variations in hunting culture in time and space.

One particular expression of a period in our earliest history is our *Bronze Age rock carvings*, most of which are found in a few areas only. Thanks to the large number of sites which have been preserved, the richness of the images and their relationship with other traces of Bronze Age society, the rock carvings of Sweden are of great international interest.

We have in *Mälardalen* a clear and, from an international point of view, unusual example of a large cultivated landscape which has been under continuous cultivation for a long time and where remains of various eras lie well preserved side by side. Cemeteries, dwelling sites, rune stones and ancient roads from the Iron Age, medieval churches and farm sites, villages and manor houses from historic times, as well as place names, all present more than 2,000 years of history.

We can follow the development of *iron manufacturing* in Sweden from prehistoric times through the Middle Ages and into our own time. Thanks to the fact that the relics of old technology, equipment and buildings have been preserved to such a large extent, we have unique opportunities to study development processes from the Iron Age up to the present.

In our buildings, too, there are special features that are worth studying, for example, our well-preserved *medieval country churches* whose architectural history and rich store of treasures reflect the lives and cultural links of various districts. Not least the richness of such jewels as these should arouse great interest abroad.

Swedish *manor-house culture* sets its special mark on many districts. These manor houses are not all alike, yet it is quite justifiable to speak of "the Swedish manor house" as a concept, both by the role manor houses played in country life and by their architectonic value. Individual buildings as well as the total environment clearly demonstrate how a native building tradition has absorbed outside influences to create a style of its own.

The large stock of *timbered and wooden buildings* from various periods are a dominant feature of the agrarian landscape and must be looked upon as an international responsibility. Despite great destruction still retains homogenous and well-preserved environments of great significance for our understanding of the building techniques and societies of bygone days. Among them are the villages of Dalarna and Öland, the "church towns" and shealings of Norrland, a few old town centres and the farm buildings in post and plank technology in southern Sweden.

Finally, we have a special responsibility for the monuments and environments of *Saami culture*. Here is a truly great cultural heritage which is not restricted by national boundaries but has to be studied in a broader perspective. Saami monuments and environments also bear a particularly clear mark of mankind's dependence on and interaction with nature.

What is common to many of these cultural settings is their high degree of preservation and the long continuity of their settlement patterns and use of land, which can be studied in these monuments and environments. It is perhaps precisely these qualities that make the Swedish cultural heritage particularly important from an international point of view.

Thus a task of ever-increasing importance for culture environment preservation will be to create understanding for the need to preserve the great quantity of our relatively modest ancient monuments, buildings or environments, which in turn requires knowledge that gives perspective and a broad view of the problem. If we have better information and a broader and deeper insight into the characteristic features of the cultural heritage—local, regional, national and international—it will be easier to evaluate and get support for special efforts.

Thus we have every reason to speak of the national and international responsibilities of culture environment preservation to protect and conserve our cultural heritage in the future.

Yet the cultural heritage and culture environment preservation are first and foremost a matter of personal responsibility, which concerns each and every one of us in our everyday environments. All round us we have memories: memories of people who have cultivated the land we now cultivate, memories of people who have lived and worked in the place or town where we now live, memories of people who have decorated the church we ourselves belong to, memories of people who built the popular movement centres which now are ours.

Cultural monuments are monuments to people. They help us to understand and preserve a time perspective—for forefathers we know by name or for anonymous generations of predecessors across hundreds and thousands of years. Cultural monuments and cultural environments give an identity to Sweden and its districts. It is the responsiblity of each and every one of us to cherish and preserve that identity for the sake of future generations.

Literature and references

Acking, C.-A., Olsson, C. and Sjögren, U, 1977, *Hur står det till i Teckomatorp?* Kollegiet människa miljö. Lund.

Alla tiders landskap Dalarna. Riksintressen för kulturmiljövården i Kopparbergs län (ed. A. Liepe). 1990. Dalarnas hembygdsbok. Falun.

Ambrosiani, B., 1964, *Fornlämningar och bebyggelse.* Studier i Attundalands och Södertörns förhistoria. Uppsala.

Andersson, H., 1990, *Sjuttiosex medeltidsstäder—*aspekter på stadsarkeologi och medeltida urbaniseringsprocess i Sverige och Finland. Medeltidsstaden 73.

Andersson, H. O. and Bedoire, F., 1980, *Bankbyggande i Sverige.* Stockholm.

Arkeologi på väg. Undersökningar för E18 Enköping-Bålsta (ed. A. Modig). 1989. RAÄ. Stockholm.

Arkeologi i Sverige 1980–1987 and *new series 1–2.* RAÄ 1983-. Stockholm.

Arnell, N., 1979, *Fjällägenheternas tillkomst och utveckling.* Umeå. (App. to Ds Jo 1980:2).

Arwidsson, G., 1965, Källa. Källkult. *Kulturhistoriskt lexikon för nordisk medeltid 10.*

Atlas över svensk folkkultur. 1. Materiell och social kultur (ed. S. Erixon), 1957. Uddevalla.

Attman, A., 1986, *Svenskt järn och stål 1800–1914.* Jernkontoret, Stockholm.

Bartholin, Th. S., 1990, Dendrokronologi—ang. metodens anvendelsesmuligheter indenfor bebyggelsehistorisk forskning. *Bebyggelsehistorisk tidskrift 19.*

Baudou, E., 1968, *Forntida bebyggelse i Ångermanlands kustland.* Arkiv för norrländsk hembygdsforskning. Härnösand.

Baudou, E., 1989, Hög—gård—helgedom i Mellannorrland under den äldre järnåldern. *Arkeologi i norr 2.*

Baudou, E., 1992, *Norrlands forntid—ett historiskt perspektiv.* Viken.

Baudou, E. and Selinge, K-G., 1977, *Västernorrlands förhistoria.* Härnösand.

Bergling, R., 1964, *Kyrkstaden i övre Norrland.* Kyrkliga, merkantila och judiciella funktioner under 1600- och 1700-talen. Umeå.

Bertilsson, U., 1987, *The Rock Carvings of Northern Bohuslän.* Spatial Structures and Social Symbols. Stockholm.

Björkenstam, N., 1990, *Västeuropeisk järnframställning under medeltiden.* Jernkontoret, Stockholm.

Bonnier, A. C., 1987, *Kyrkorna berättar.* Upplands kyrkor 1250–1350. Upplands fornminnesförenings tidskrift.

Brink, S., 1983, *Ortnamnen och kulturlandskapet.* Ortnamnens vittnesbörd om kulturlandskapets utveckling och dess utnyttjande i södra Norrland. Uppsala.

Brink, S., 1990, *Sockenbildning och sockennamn.* Studier i äldre territoriell indelning i Norden. Uppsala.

Byggnadsminnen 1961–1978 (ed. A. Unnerbäck), 1981. RAÄ. Stockholm.

Byggnadsminnen 1978–1988 (eds. B. Almqvist and M. Bergman), 1989. RAÄ. Stockholm.

Carlsson, D., 1979, *Kulturlandskapets utveckling på Gotland.* Stockholm.

Carlsson, H., 1942, *Fyrväsendets utveckling och de svenska insatserna för fyrteknikens förbättrande.* Föreningen Sveriges Sjöfartsmuseum i Stockholm, Årsbok.

Collinder, B., 1964, *Ordbok till Sveriges lapska ortnamn.* Uppsala.

Cullberg, C., 1970, Gånggrifternas landskap. *Svenska Turistföreningens årsskrift.*

Ekman, S., 1983, *Norrlands jakt och fiske.* Reprint. Umeå.

Ekonomi och näringsformer i nordisk bronsålder (eds. L. Forsberg and T. B. Larsson), 1993. Umeå.

Enequist, G., 1935, Övre Norrlands storbyar i äldre tid. *Ymer.*

Eriksson, E., 1990, *Den moderna stadens födelse.* Svensk arkitektur 1890–1920. Stockholm.

Erixon, S., (1947) 1982, *Svensk byggnadskultur.* Lund.

Fornlämningar och bebyggelsehistoria (ed. K-G. Selinge), 1986. *Bebyggelsehistorisk tidskrift 11.*

Forntidsminnen—om arkeologien och hembygdsrörelsen, 1984. Riksförbundet för hembygdsvård. Stockholm.

Forsberg, L., 1985, *Site Variability and Settlement Patterns.* An analysis of the Hunter-Gatherer Settlement System in the Lule River Valley. Umeå.

Forsberg, L., 1989, Economic and Social Change in the Interior of Northern Sweden 6000 B.C. – 1000 A.D. *Approaches to Swedish Prehistory.* Oxford.

Furingsten, A., Jonsäter, M. and Weiler, E., 1984, *Från flintverkstad till processindustri.* De första 9000 åren i Västsverige, speglade av UV Västs undersökningar. RAÄ. Stockholm.

Furuland, L., 1975, *Statare.* Nordiska museet/Sveriges Radio. Stockholm.

Fångstfolk för 8000 år sedan—om en grupp stenåldersboplatser i Västsverige (eds. S. Andersson, J. Wigforss and S. Nancke-Krogh). 1988. Göteborg.

Förteckning över byggnadsminnesmärken (ed. G. Sillén), 1976 RAÄ. Stockholm.

Granberg, G., 1934, Den kalendärt fixerade källdrickningen. *Folkminnen och folktankar 21.*

Gravfältsundersökningar och gravarkeologi (ed. A. Lagerlöf), 1991. RAÄ. Stockholm.

Gren, L., 1991, *Fossil åkermark.* RAÄ. Stockholm.

Gustafsson, E., 1973, Tankar i Teckomatorp. *Bygd och natur.*

Hagberg, U. E., 1957, *Skedemosse—studier i ett öländskt offerfynd.* Stockholm.

Hahr, A., 1930, *Nordiska borgar från medeltid och renässans.*

Hellberg, L., 1967, *Kumlabygdens ortnamn och äldre bebyggelse.* Kumla.

Hellspong, M. and Löfgren, O., 1989, *Land och stad.* S Sandby.

Hildebrand, K.-G., 1987, *Svenskt järn. 1600-tal och 1700-tal.* Jernkontoret, Stockholm.

Hofrén, M., 1946, *Pataholm.* Stockholm.

Holmgren, P. and Tronde, B., 1990, Fornminnesinventeringen i Skåne 1985–87. *Arkeologi i Sverige 1987.*

Hyenstrand, Å., 1974, *Centralbygd—Randbygd.* Strukturella, ekonomiska och administrativa huvudlinjer i mellansvensk yngre järnålder. Stockholm.

Hyenstrand, Å., 1977, *Hyttor och järnframställningsplatser.* Några sammanfattningar kring inventerat material. Jernkontoret, Stockholm.

Hyenstrand, Å., 1984, *Fasta fornlämningar och arkeologiska regioner.* RAÄ, Stockholm.

Hällristningar och hällmålningar i Sverige (eds. S. Janson, E. B. Lundberg and U. Bertilsson), 3rd edition. 1989. Stockholm.

Industrilandskapet vid Strömmen i Norrköping, östra och västra delen. 1984, 1980. Norrköping.

Industriminnen. En bok om industri- och teknikhistoriska bebyggelsemiljöer (ed. M. Nisser). 1979. Stockholm.

Janson, S., 1974, *Kulturvård och samhällsbildning.* Nordiska museet. Stockholm.

Jansson, S. B. F., 1984, *Runinskrifter i Sverige.* 3rd edition. Stockholm.

Jennbert, K., 1984, *Den produktiva gåvan.* Tradition och innovation i Sydskandinavien för omkring 5 300 år sedan. Lund.

Johansen, B., 1991, Fornminnesinventeringen i Dalsland 1987–88. *Arkeologi i Sverige,* new series 1.

Järnfeldt-Carlsson, M., 1988, *Landskap, Jaktvillor & kurhotell.* Arkitektur och turism i Västjämtland 1880–1915. Umeå.

Jönsson, T., 1976, *Jordstugor i Sydsverige.* Lund.

Kjellén, E. and Hyenstrand, Å., 1977, *Hällristningar och bronsålderssamhälle i sydvästra Uppland.* Upplands fornminnesförenings tidskrift.

Klang, L., 1989, Det förhistoriska kulturlandskapet i östra Norrbotten. *Arkeologi i Sverige 1986.*

Kraft, J., 1977, Labyrint och ryttarlek. *Fornvännen 72.*

Kulturarvet i antikvarisk teori och praktik. (ed. G. Friberg). 1993. RAÄ. Stockholm.

Kulturhistoriskt lexikon för nordisk medeltid från vikingatid till reformationstid (Swedish ed. J. Granlund), 22 volumes, 2nd edition. 1980–82. Malmö.

Kulturmiljön i planeringen. 1992. Boverket and RAÄ. Karlskrona.

Kulturmiljövård, magazine (1976–88 named Kulturminnesvård), RAÄ, Stockholm. Often theme issues on special topics as cultural monuments and environments.

Kulturmiljövården. Compilation of existing laws and acts (ed. Th. Adlercreutz). RAÄ, Stockholm.

Kyrkobyggnader 1760–1860, 1–3 (eds. M. Ullén and B. Flodin), 1989–93. Sveriges kyrkor, Stockholm.

Lagerlöf, E. and Svahnström, G., 1991, *Gotlands kyrkor.* Stockholm.

Lagerqvist, L. O., 1978, *Medevi Brunn 300 år, 1678–1978.* Motala.

Larsson, L-O., 1986, *Småländsk medeltid.* Malmö.

Larsson, L., 1978, *Stenåldersjägare i mellersta Skåne.* Lund.

Larsson, L., 1988, *Ett fångstsamhälle för 7000 år sedan.* Boplatser och gravar i Skateholm. Kristianstad.

Larsson, L., 1994, De äldsta boplatslämningarna i Sydsverige. Fynd och boplatser kring Finjasjön, norra Skåne. *Ale,* Historisk tidskrift för Skåneland.

Larsson, M., 1984, *Tidigneolitikum i Sydvästskåne.* Kronologi och bosättningsmönster. Lund.

Larsson, T. B., 1986, *The Bronze Age Metal Work in Southern Sweden.* Aspects of Social and Spatial Organisation 1800–500 B.C. Umeå.

Levander, L., 1976, *Landsväg, krog och marknad.* Reprint. Lund.

Liedgren, L., 1992, *Hus och gård i Hälsingland.* En studie av agrar bebyggelse och bebyggelseutveckling i norra Hälsingland Kr.f.–600 e.Kr. Umeå.

Lindgren, M., Lyberg, L., Sandström, B. and Wahlberg, A-G., 1986, *Svensk konsthistoria.* Stockholm.

Lindström, C. and Rentzhog, S., 1987, *Byggnadstradition på den svenska landsbygden.* RAÄ. Stockholm.

Lundahl, I., 1961, *Det medeltida Västergötland.* Uppsala.

Länkar till vår forntid—en introduktion i Sveriges arkeologi (eds. G. Burenhult, E. Baudou and M. P. Malmer), 1988. Höganäs.

Magnusson, G., 1986, *Lågteknisk järnhantering i Jämtlands län.* Jernkontoret, Stockholm.

Malmer, M. P., 1975, *Stridsyxkulturen i Sverige och Norge.* Lund.

Manker, E., 1953, *The Nomadism of the Swedish Mountain Lapps.* The Siidas and their Migratory Routes in 1945. Nordiska museet. Stockholm.

Manker, E., 1957, *Lapparnas heliga ställen.* Nordiska museet. Stockholm.

Manker, E., 1961, *Lappmarksgravar.* Dödsföreställningar och gravskick i lappmarkerna. Nordiska museet. Stockholm.

Med arkeologen Sverige runt (eds. S. Janson and E. B. Lundberg), 3rd edition 1987. Stockholm.

Medeltida träkyrkor 1–2 (eds. M. Ullén and E. Lagerlöf), 1983–85. Sveriges kyrkor, Stockholm.

Medeltidsstaden. Den tidiga urbaniseringsprocessens konsekvenser för nutida planering (manager H. Andersson) 1976-. RAÄ och SHMM, Stockholm. (Ca. 70 monographs edited).

Modeer, I., 1936, *Färdvägar och sjömärken vid Nordens kuster.* Uppsala.

Montelius, S., Utterström, G. and Söderlund, E., 1959, *Fagerstabrukens historia.* Arbetare och arbetarförhållanden.

di Nescemi, M., 1988, *Kungaslott och herrskapshus.* Stockholm.

Nilsson, S., 1980, *Apotek i Sverige.* En kulturhistorisk inventering. RAÄ. Stockholm.

Nilsson, S., 1983, *Bryggerier i Sverige.* En kulturhistorisk inventering. RAÄ. Stockholm.

Nisbeth, Å., 1986, *Bildernas predikan.* Medeltida kalkmålningar i Sverige. Stockholm.

Noreen, S. E., 1988, Medevi Brunn källa till vederkvickelse. *Friskvård för hus, hem, kropp och själ.* Vadstena.

Norman, P., 1993, *Medeltida utskärsfiske.* En studie av fornlämningar i kustmiljö. Nordiska museet. Stockholm.

Nyman, Å., 1980, Olofskult och Olofstraditioner. *Jämten.*

Nyman, Å., 1982, Fäbodforskning i Skandinavien. *Svenska landsmål* 105.

Olsson, I., 1979, *Gotländsk natur och historia, speglade i ortnamnen.* Visby.

Olsson, L.-E., 1987, *Tegelbruk i Sverige.* En branschinventering. RAÄ. Stockholm.

Ortnamn i . . . 1982–1990 (AWE/Geber's series of provinces concerning place names comprise volumes of Blekinge, Bohuslän, Dalarna, Dalsland, Gotland, Hälsingland, Jämtland, Skåne, Småland, Uppland, Värmland, Västergötland, Västmanland, Öland, Östergötland and Stockholm archipelago).

Pamp, B., 1988, *Ortnamnen i Sverige.* 5th edition. Lund.

Paulsson, G., 1950–53, *Svensk stad.* Stockholm.

Planning and Urban Growth in the Nordic Countries (red. Th. Hall), 1991, London.

Rentzhog, S., 1986, *Stad i trä.* Panelarkitekturen, ett skede i den svenska småstadens byggnadshistoria. 2nd edition. Uddevalla.

Resa i Sverige, 1978. *Fataburen.*

Riksintressanta kulturmiljöer i Sverige (ed. B. OH Johansson). List. RAÄ. Stockholm.

Rosengren, A., 1979, *När resan var ett äventyr.* Örebro.

Rudberg, S., 1957, *Ödemarkerna och den perifera bebyggelsen i inre Nordsverige.* Uppsala.

Råberg, M., 1987, *Visioner och verklighet* 1–2. En studie kring Stockholms 1600-talsplan. Stockholm.

Sahlgren, J., 1964, *Valda ortnamnsstudier.* Uppsala.

Salvesen, H., 1979, *Jord i Jemtland.* Östersund.

Samer och germaner i det förhistoriska Norrland (ed. P. H. Ramqvist), 1987. *Bebyggelsehistorisk tidskrift 14.*

Selinge, K-G., 1974, *Fångstgropar.* Jämtlands vanligaste fornlämningar. Fornvårdaren 12.

Selinge, K-G., 1986, Stensättningar med variationer. *Arkeologi i Sverige 1984.* RAÄ, Stockholm.

Selinge, K-G., 1989, Det närvarande förflutna. 50 år med fornminnesinventeringen. *RAÄ and SHMM årsbok* 1987–88. Stockholm.

7000 år på 20 år. Arkeologiska undersökningar i Mellansverige (eds. T. Andrae, M. Hasselmo and K. Lamm). 1987. RAÄ. Stockholm.

Slott och herresäten i Sverige, 17 volumes, 1966–71. Malmö.

Sporrong, U., 1990, By. *Nationalencyklopedin* 3. Höganäs.

Spång, L-G., 1981, Fångstgropar—lämningar efter forntida älgfångst. *Västerbotten* 4.

Stackell, L., 1975, *Badortsmiljöns liv och bebyggelse under 1800-talet.* Östervåla.

Stadsförnyelse, kontinuitet, gemenskap, inflytande. SOU 1981:100. Stockholm.

Stahre, N.-G., 1986, *Ortnamnen i Stockholms skärgård.* Stockholm.

Strid, J. P., 1993, *Kulturlandskapets språkliga dimension.* Ortnamnen. RAÄ, Stockholm.

Ström, F., 1961, *Nordisk hedendom.* Tro och sed i förkristen tid.

Strömberg, M., 1971, *Die Megalithgräber von Hagestad.* Zur Problematik von Grabbauten und Grabriten. Lund.

Ståhl, H., 1976, *Ortnamn och ortnamnsforskning.* 2nd edition. Uppsala.

Ståhle, C. I., 1946, *Studier över de svenska ortnamnen på -inge.* Lund.

Städer i utveckling. Tolv studier kring stadsförändringar (ed. T. Hall). 1984. Stockholm.

Sveriges Industri. Survey edited by Industriförbundet, 1935-.

Sveriges Kyrkor, konsthistoriskt inventarium, 1912-. Ed. RAÄ and Kungl Vitterhets Historie och Antikvitetsakademien. (The series of monographs in 1993 comprise 213 volumes incl descriptions of about 600 church buildings).

Sveriges runinskrifter. Kungl. Vitterhets Historie och Antikvitets Akademien. 1900-. Stockholm. (All provinces except parts of Gotland and Norrland).

Söderberg, B.G., 1975, *Herresäten och kungaslott i Sverige.* Malmö.

Södermanlandsbygden 1–2. Känner du landet . . . Kulturhistoriska miljöer i Södermanlands län (ed. R. Ryberg). 1988. Nyköping.

Technology and Industry a Nordic Heritage (eds. J. Hult and B. Nyström). 1992. Stockholm.

Textilindustrins miljöer (ed. F. Bedoire), 1987. *Bebyggelsehistorisk tidskrift* 15.

Trästäder i Norden. 2nd revised edition, 1973, Oslo-Stockholm.

Vikström, E., 1991, *Platsen, bruket och samhället.* Tätortsbildning och arkitektur 1860–1970. Stockholm.

Vägar, dåtid, nutid, framtid (ed. B. Heddelin), 1991. Vägverket, Stockholm and Borlänge.

Västergötlands äldre historia (ed. E. Wegraeus), 1985. Vänersborg.

Västsvenska stenåldersstudier (eds. H. Brovall, P. Persson and K-G. Sjögren). 1991. Göteborg.

Welinder, S., 1977, Ekonomiska processer i förhistorisk expansion. Lund.

Westerlind, A. M., 1982, *Kustorter i Göteborgs och Bohus län, Orust.* Göteborg.

Widgren, M., 1983, *Settlement and farming systems in the early iron age.* Stockholm.

Zachrisson, I., 1984, *De samiska metalldepåerna år 1000–1350 i ljuset av fyndet från Mörtträsket, Lappland.* Umeå.

Åkerhielm, E., 1930, *Svenska gods och gårdar,* 2nd edition, vol. 1–2.

Åman, A., 1976, *Den offentliga vården.* Uddevalla.

Åström, K., 1993, *Stadsplanering i Sverige.* Trelleborg.

Övre Norrlands kyrkor (eds. A. Åman and M. Järnfeldt-Carlsson), 1991. *Bebyggelsehistorisk tidskrift 22.*

Acknowledgements for Illustrations

Permission for distribution of maps approved by the Security Officer. The National Land Survey 1993–11–16. Permission 93.0518.

AMR = Ancient Monument Register, RA
ATA = Antiquarian-Topographical Archives, RAÄ
GS = GreatShots
JG = Jill Gustavsson
JN = Jan Norrman
KGS = Klas-Göran Selinge
LMV = The National Land Survey
LUHM = Lund University, Historical Museum
N = Naturfotograferna
RAÄ = The Central Board of National Antiquities
RIK = Conservation Institute, RAÄ
SHM = Museum of National Antiquities
SHMM = Museums of National Antiquities

archeol. museum
30 L28, L29 SNA, data
Lena Olsson
Photos KGS
Drawing JG from
Nils Gillgren
31 L30 SNA, data
AMR, Lena Olsson
Photo upper KGS
Photo bottom Leif
Gren
Drawing JG from
Rolf Rydén
32 L31 SNA, data AMR
Photo top JN
Photo bottom KGS
33 L32 SNA, data AMR
Photos KGS
34 L33 SNA, data
AMR, Lena Olsson
Photo JN
35 Photo left Bengt A
Lundberg
Photo right JN
Topographical Map
Sheets 11ISV, 11ISO,
LMV, drawing JG,
data AMR
36 Photo upper JN
Photo bottom Tore
Artelius
Gröna kartan Stock-
holm 10I SV, L MV,
drawing JG, data
AMR
37 Economical Map
Sheet 6H0e Enerum,
LMV, top
Economical Map
Sheet 8G6b Gistad,
LMV
Map SNA
Drawing Nils Forshed
38 Map top SNA and JG
from Lars Liedgren
L34, L35 SNA, data
AMR
39 L36 SNA, data AMR
Photo P-N. Nilsson/
Tio
Map SNA and JG
from AMR
40 Map top SNA and JG
from B Windelhed
Map bottom SNA
and JG from B Win-
berg et al.
Photo top P. Manneke
Photo bottom Birgit
Brånvall/Nordiska
museet
41 Map top Mats Widgren
Map bottom SNA
and JG from AMR
Photo Sten Gauffin
42 L37 SNA, data
AMR, Lena Olsson
Photo JN
43 L38 SNA, data
AMR, KGS
Photo left Leif Gren
Photo right JN
44 Drawing JG
45 L39 SNA, data RAÄ
Photo bottom KGS
Other photos Bengt
A Lundberg
46 L40 SNA, data
RAÄ, H Christiansson
Photo Bengt A
Lundberg
47 Photo Bengt A
Lundberg
Drawing N. Forshed
48 Photo top Leif Gren
Photo centre JN
Photo bottom Leif

Gren
49 L41 SNA, data
enquiry to county
museums
50–51 L42 SNA, data Eliz
Lundin
50 Photos Leif Gren
51 Photos Stefan Nordin
52 L43 SNA, data
Carlsson 1942 and
AMR
Photo KGS
Drawing Forshed
from H Carlsson
53 L44 SNA, data from
Stahre 1986
L45 SNA, data AMR
L46 SNA, data
Nat. Mar. Museum
Photo left Kalmar
county museum
Photo right L. Klang
54 L47 SNA, data AMR
Diagram JG
55 L48 SNA, data Per
Hallinder et al.
Photo top left Gert
Magnusson
Photos top right and
bottom Birgit Jans-
son/Jämtland county
museum
56 L49 SNA, data AMR,
Å Hyenstrand et al.
57 Map SNA and JG from
Ing-M. Pettersson
Drawing N. Forshed
58 L50 SNA, data
Bergskollegii register,
R Åkerman Map 1878
Photo RIK from
drawing by S. Rinman
Photo KGS
59 Photo top Gert Mag-
nusson
Photo bottom Göran
Hansson/N
60 SNA, data AMR
61 Economical Map
Sheet 19E5i Sladder-
forsen, LMV, draw-
ing JG, data AMR
Photo KGS
Drawing top from
Erik Modin
Drawing bottom
Gunnar Brusewitz
62 Photo Bertil Gardell
63 L52 SNA
Drawings Animagica
Film & Video AB
Photo P. Hanneberg/
Tio
64 L53 SNA, data
National Board of
Planning
Photo left Gert Mag-
nusson
Photo right Claes
Grundsten/N
65 L54 SNA, data
AMR, RAÄ Luleå
Map SNA and JG
from Ingela Bergman
Photo upper Jämt-
land county museum
Photo bottom Claes
Grundsten/N
66 L55 SNA, data E Ire-
gren and I Zachrisson
Photo JN
67 Kartor SNA and JG,
data E Manker
Photos RIK of draw-
ings by E Manker
Photo JN
68 Photo top left SHM

Photo top right Sören
Hallgren
Photo bottom Ulf
Erik Hagberg/ATA
69 L56, L57 SNA, data
AMR
Photo left R. Jensen
Photo right Pål-Nils
Nilsson/Tio
70 L58 SNA, data AMR
Photo RIK, from
Erik Dahlbergh
71 Photo top Hans Hemlin
Photo centre M Elg
Photo bottom Gert
Magnusson
72 L59 SNA
Photo top H. Cinthio
Photo bottom Ragnar
Andersson/Tio
73 L60 SNA, data Kul-
turhist. lexikon,
Skånes Hembygds-
förbund
Photo upper Carl Filip
Mannerstråhle/ATA
Photo bottom JN
74 L61 SNA, data Sve-
riges Kyrkor, I Lun-
dahl, AMR
Photos top left and
top right Lennart
Karlsson/SHM
Photo bottom right
Gabriel Hildebrand
Drawings K. Palmgren
75 L62 SNA, data E La-
gerlöf and G Svahn-
ström
Drawings J. Nômmik
Photo top Bengt
A Lundberg
Photos bottom Ray-
mond Hejdström
76 Photo top B J Sjöblom
Photo centre Gabriel
Hildebrand
Photo bottom left Vå-
ga Lindell-Andersson
Photo bottom right
Sören Hallgren
77 L63 SNA, data
A Nilsén
L64 SNA, data
K Banning et al.
Photo G. Hildebrand
78 L65 SNA, data M Ul-
lén and E Lagerlöf
Drawing top Sveriges
kyrkor, photo Emil
Ekhoff
Photo top S. Hallgren
Photo bottom Gabriel
Hildebrand
Drawing bottom from
L. Karlsson
79 L66 SNA, data Kul-
turhist. lexikon and
I Swartling
Photo top G. Hilde-
brand
Photo centre Pål-Nils
Nilsson/Tio
Photo bottom left
Sören Hallgren
Photo bottom right
Gabriel Hildebrand
80 L67 SNA and plans
JG, data E Nordin
Photo top Chad
Ehlers/Tio
Photo centre Lars
Daniel Cnattingius
Photo bottom JN
81 L68 SNA, data
M Nodermann and
P Hörberg

Photo top Riksarkivet
Photo bottom Albin
Dahlström
82 L69 SNA, data L Uhlin
Photo Sune Jonsson
Drawings Sveriges
Kyrkor
83 Drawing S. Ljungstedt
Photo top Åsa
Klintberg
Photo centre and bot-
tom left Göran Sand-
stedt
Photo bottom right
Mikael Ullén
84–85 L70 SNA, data Sve-
riges Kyrkor
84 Photos from top Lars
Dahlström/Tio, Ann
Cathrine Bonnier,
Sören Hallgren,
Mikael Ullén
85 Photo Mikael Ullén
86 Photo top RIK from
Atlas över svensk
folkkultur 1
Photo bottom left
R. Andersson/Tio
Photo right KGS
Photo RIK. from
Sigurd Erixon
87 L71 SNA, data auth.
Drawings JG from
G Gustafsson and
N-A Bringeus
Photos Skånes hem-
bygdsförbund, Lund
88 L72 and diagram
SNA, data among
others Sigurd Erixon
Photo top Staffan
Brundell/GS
Photo bottom Jan
Rietz/Tio
89 L73 SNA, data field
surveys
Photo JN
90 L74 SNA, data RAÄ
National Interests
Photo left and top JN
Photo bottom right
K G Svensson
91 L75 SNA, data
R Broberg
Photo upper JN
Photo bottom Pål-
Nils Nilsson/Tio
92 Photo Sture Karlsson/
Tio
Topographical Map
Sheets 7ENO, 8ESO,
LMV, symbols SNA,
data K Bäck
93 L76 SNA, data public
statistics
Photo Nordiska mu-
seet
94 L77 SNA, data
among others Nor-
diska museet
Photo left JN
Photo right Jan Rietz/
Tio
Fjällkatan Z8, Helags
-Funäsdalen-Rogen,
LMV
95 L78 SNA, data auth.,
AMR
Photo left JN
Photo right Göran
Hansson/N
96 L79 SNA, data auth.
Photo JN
97 L80 SNA, data auth.
Photo top Ulf Sjö-
stedt/Tio
Photo centre Tore

Hagman/N
Photo bottom Klas
Rune/N
98 Photos from top Mag-
nus Josephsson,
Göran Hansson/N,
Tommy Arvidson,
KGS
99 L81 SNA, data auth.
Photo Bengt A
Lundberg of original,
Konstakademien
100 Photo top left Ulf
Sjöstedt/Tio
Photo centre ATA
Photo bottom left JN
Photo bottom right
Ralph Edenheim
101 L82 SNA, data auth.
Photo top Bertil K
Johanson/N
Photo bottom M Elg
102 L83 SNA, data listed
public historic build-
ings, Post Office lists
Photo JN
103 L84 SNA, data listed
historic buildings
Photos Nils-Johan
Norenlind/Tio
104 Photo top Bo Sundin
Photo centre JN
Photo bottom left
Torleif Svensson/Tio
Photo bottom right
Göran H Fredriksson
105 L85 SNA, data
among others AMR

Photo upper Anders
Borlin
Photo bottom Manne
Hofrén, 1933
106 L86 SNA, data
RAÄ, county mu-
seums
Photo top left Göran
H Fredriksson
Photo top right Jan
Rietz/Tio
Photo bottom Anders
Hillgren
107 L87 SNA, data Ös-
tergötland, investiga-
tion of vicarages and
culture environment
program
Photo upper Calle
von Essen
Photos bottom Ös-
tergötland county
museum
108 L88 and diagram
SNA, data RAÄ
category survey
Photo top Ragnar
Andersson/Tio
Photo bottom Kim
Naylor/Tio
109 L89 SNA, data RAÄ
category survey, list-
ed historic buildings
Photo upper Bengt-
Göran Carlsson/Tio
Photo bottom left
Västerbotten museum
Photo bottom right
Lars Guvå
110–111 L90 and diagram
SNA, data Medeltids-
staden et al.
111 Photo JN
112 Photo top Jan Rietz/
Tio
Photo bottom Lars
Dahlström/Tio
113 Diagram data Lars

Authors

Ahlberg, Nils, 1953, 1st Antiquarian, RAÄ, Stockholm

Berg, Kristian, 1959, Investigator, Boverket, Karlskrona

Bertilsson, Ulf, 1948, Princ. Adm. Off., RAÄ, Stockholm

Biörnstad, Margareta, 1928, former Director-
General, RAÄ, Stockholm

Blomkvist, Nils, 1943, Princ. Adm. Off., RAÄ,
Stockholm

Bonnier, Ann Catherine, 1942, 1st Antiquarian,
RAÄ, Stockholm

Brink, Stefan, 1952, Reader in Scandinavian Languages, Uppsala University

Damell, David, 1940, County Custodian of Antiquities, Örebro

Edenheim, Ralph, 1948, Curator, Stiftelsen Skansen,
Stockholm

Eklöf, Ivar, 1940, Princ. Adm. Off.,
RAÄ, Stockholm

Forsberg, Lars, 1954, Reader in Archeology, Umeå University

Furuhagen, Hans, 1930, Ph. Dr., Danderyd

Gren, Leif, 1956, Princ. Adm. Off.,
RAÄ, Karlskrona

Gyllenhammar, Ulf, 1942, 1st Antiquarian, RAÄ, Stockholm

Hoberg, Birgitta, 1942, Princ. Adm. Off.,
RAÄ, Stockholm

Hyenstrand, Åke, 1939, Professor in
Archeology, Stockholm University

Jensen, Ronnie, 1948, 1st Antiquarian,
RAÄ, Stockholm

Kjellström, Rolf, 1936, Curator, Nordiska
museet, Stockholm

Korhonen, Olavi, 1938, Professor in Fin-
no-Ugric Languages, Umeå universitet

Kyhlberg, Ola, 1945, Head of Division,
RAÄ, Stockholm

Larsson, Lars, 1947, Professor in Archeology, Lund University

Larsson, Mats, 1951, 1st Antiquarian,
RAÄ, Linköping

Larsson, Thomas B, 1953, Reader in
Archeology, Umeå University

Löthman, Lars, 1935, 1st Antiquarian,
RAÄ, Stockholm

Magnusson, Gert, 1948, Reader in Archeology, Stockholm University

Meschke, Christian, 1935, Princ. Adm.
Off., RAÄ, Stockholm

Morger, Kersti, 1938, 1st Antiquarian,
RAÄ, Stockholm

Norman, Peter, 1952, 1st Antiquarian,
RAÄ, Stockholm

Nyström Kronberg, Elisabeth, 1947, 1st
Antiquarian, RAÄ, Stockholm

Redin, Lars, 1940, Princ. Adm. Off.,
SHM, Stockholm

von Reis, Johan, 1943, Ass. Inspector of
Antiquities, Blekinge County Board

Riessen, Kerstin, 1938, 1st Antiquarian,
RAÄ, Stockholm

Rittsel-Ullén, Marian, 1934, 1st Antiquarian, RAÄ, Stockholm

Rosander, Göran, 1933, 1st Antiquarian,
Department of Ethnology, Oslo University

Schön, Ebbe, 1929, Head of Department,
Nordiska museet, Stockholm

Selinge, Klas-Göran, 1929, Expert, RAÄ,
Stockholm

Trotzig, Gustaf, 1937, Head of Department, RAÄ, Stockholm

Unnerbäck, Axel, 1938, Princ. Adm. Off.,
RAÄ, Stockholm

Wahlberg, Mats, 1948, Senior Archivist,
Place-names Archives in Uppsala

Winberg, Björn, 1950, 1st Antiquarian,
RAÄ, Stockholm

Zachrisson, Inger, 1936, 1st Antiquarian,
Mus. of National Antiquities, Stockholm

Åhlén, Marit, 1951, 1st Antiquarian,
RAÄ, Stockholm

Index

National Atlas of Sweden

A geographical description of the landscape, society and culture of Sweden in 17 volumes

NATIONAL ATLAS OF SWEDEN

MAPS AND MAPPING

From historic maps of great cultural significance to modern mapping methods using the latest advanced technology. What you didn't already know about maps you can learn here. A unique place-name map (1:700,000) gives a bird's-eye view of Sweden. Editors: **Professor Ulf Sporrong, geographer, Stockholm University, and Hans-Fredrik Wennström, economist, National Land Survey, Gävle.**

THE FORESTS

Sweden has more forestland than almost any other country in Europe. This volume describes how the forests have developed and how forestry works: ecological cycles, climatic influences, its importance for the economy etc. One of many maps shows, on the scale of 1:1.25 million, the distribution of the forests today. Editor: **Professor Nils-Erik Nilsson, forester, National Board of Forestry, Jönköping.**

THE POPULATION

Will migration to the towns continue, or shall we see a new "green wave"? This volume highlights most sides of Swedish life: how Swedes live, education, health, family life, private economy etc. Political life, the population pyramid and immigration are given special attention. Editor: **Professor Sture Öberg, geographer, Uppsala University, and Senior Administrative Officer Peter Springfeldt, geographer, Statistics Sweden, Stockholm.**

THE ENVIRONMENT

More and more people are concerning themselves with environmental issues and nature conservancy. This book shows how Sweden is being affected by pollution, and what remedies are being applied. Maps of protected areas, future perspectives and international comparisons. Editors: **Dr Claes Bernes and Claes Grundsten, geographer, National Environment Protection Board, Stockholm.**

AGRICULTURE

From horse-drawn plough to the highly-mechanized production of foodstuffs. A volume devoted to the development of Swedish agriculture and its position today. Facts about the parameters of farming, what is cultivated where, the workforce, financial aspects etc. Editor: **Birger Granström, state agronomist, and Åke Clason, managing director of Research Information Centre, Swedish University of Agricultural Sciences, Uppsala.**

THE INFRASTRUCTURE

Sweden's welfare is dependent on an efficient infrastructure, everything from roads and railways to energy production and public administration. If you are professionally involved, this book will provide you with a coherent survey of Sweden's infrastructure. Other readers will find a broad explanation of how Swedish society is built up and how it functions. Editor: **Dr Reinhold Castensson, geographer, Linköping University.**

SEA AND COAST

The Swedes have a deep-rooted love for the sea and the coast. This volume describes the waters which surround Sweden and how they have changed with the evolution of the Baltic. Facts about types of coastline, oceanography, marine geology and ecology, including comparisons with the oceans of the world. Editor: **Björn Sjöberg, oceanographer, Swedish Meteorological and Hydrological Institute, Göteborg.**

CULTURAL LIFE, RECREATION AND TOURISM

An amateur drama production in Hässleholm or a new play at the Royal Dramatic Theatre in Stockholm? Both fill an important function. This volume describes the wide variety of culture activities available in Sweden (museums, cinemas, libraries etc), sports and the various tourist areas in Sweden. Editor: **Dr Hans Aldskogius, geographer, Uppsala University.**

SWEDEN IN THE WORLD

Sweden is the home of many successful export companies. But Sweden has many other relations with the rest of the world. Cultural and scientific interchange, foreign investment, aid to the Third World, tourism etc. are described in a historical perspective. Editor: **Professor Gunnar Törnqvist, geographer, Lund University.**

WORK AND LEISURE

Describes how Swedes divide their time between work and play, with regional, social and age-group variations. The authors show who does what, the role of income, etc, and make some predictions about the future. Editor: **Dr Kurt V Abrahamsson, geographer, Umeå University.**

CULTURAL HERITAGE AND PRESERVATION

Sweden is rich in prehistoric monuments and historical buildings, which are presented here on maps. What is being done to preserve our cultural heritage? This volume reviews modern cultural heritage policies. Editor: **Reader Klas-Göran Selinge, archeologist, Central Board of National Antiquities, Stockholm.** Ass. Editor: **1st Antiquarian Marit Åhlén, runologist, Central Board of National Antiquities, Stockholm.**

GEOLOGY

Maps are used to present Sweden's geology — the bedrock, soils, land forms, ground water. How and where are Sweden's natural geological resources utilised? Editor: **Curt Fredén, state geologist, Geological Survey of Sweden, Uppsala.**

LANDSCAPE AND SETTLEMENTS

How has the Swedish landscape evolved over the centuries? What traces of old landscapes can still be seen? What regional differences are there? This volume also treats the present landscape, settlements, towns and cities, as well as urban and regional planning. Editor: **Professor Staffan Helmfrid, geographer, Stockholm University.**

CLIMATE, LAKES AND RIVERS

What causes the climate to change? Why does Sweden have fewer natural disasters than other countries? This volume deals with the natural cycle of water and with Sweden's many lakes and rivers. Climatic variations are also presented in map form. Editors: **Birgitta Raab, state hydrologist, and Haldo Vedin, state meteorologist, Swedish Meteorological and Hydrological Institute, Norrköping.**

MANUFACTURING, SERVICES AND TRADE

Heavy industry is traditionally located in certain parts of Sweden, while other types of industry are spread all over the country. This volume contains a geographical description of Swedish manufacturing and service industries and foreign trade. Editor: **Dr Claes Göran Alvstam, geographer, Göteborg University.**

GEOGRAPHY OF PLANTS AND ANIMALS

Climatic and geographical variations in Sweden create great geographical differences in plant and animal life. This volume presents the geographical distribution of Sweden's fauna and explains how and why they have changed over the years. There is a special section on game hunting. Editors: **Professor Ingemar Ahlén and Dr Lena Gustafsson, Swedish University of Agricultural Sciences, Uppsala.**

THE GEOGRAPHY OF SWEDEN

A comprehensive picture of the geography of Sweden, containing excerpts from other volumes but also completely new, summarizing articles. The most important maps in the whole series are included. Indispensable for educational purposes. Editors: **The editorial board of the National Atlas of Sweden, Stockholm.**

The work of producing the National Atlas of Sweden is spread throughout the country.